APPEAL TO ARMS

AN APPEAL TO ARMS, AND TO THE GOD OF HOSTS,
IS ALL THAT IS LEFT US!

> *—from Patrick Henry's address to*
> *the Virginia House of Delegates,*
> *March 23, 1775*

APPEAL to ARMS

A Military History of the
AMERICAN REVOLUTION

by

Willard M. Wallace

HARPER & BROTHERS PUBLISHERS

New York

To my wife

ELIZABETH MUELLER WALLACE

Contents

	Preface	vii
I	The Military Background of the Revolution	1
II	The Guns of Lexington and Concord	12
III	The Costly Victory at Bunker Hill	27
IV	The Trials of Organizing an Army	48
V	The Siege and Evacuation of Boston	57
VI	The Canadian Magnet	67
VII	Death, Defeat, and Disaster in the North	76
VIII	The Awakening of the South	88
IX	The Gathering of the Armies before New York	97
X	Long Island: the Battle and the Retreat	106
XI	The Loss of New York and the Retreat across Jersey	115
XII	The American Counterattack at Trenton and Princeton	124
XIII	Howe's Invasion of Pennsylvania	134
XIV	Burgoyne's Invasion of the North	146
XV	The Failure of Burgoyne's Campaign	158
XVI	Valley Forge and the New American Army	169
XVII	The British Withdrawal to New York	180
XVIII	The Expansion of the War	192
XIX	The British Offensive in the South	204
XX	The Critical Year, 1780-1781	216
XXI	American Retaliation in the South	228
XXII	The Yorktown Campaign	246
XXIII	The End of the War	263
	Notes	275
	Index	301

Maps

Action Area, April 19, 1775	19
Battle of Bunker Hill	31
American Invasion of Canada	79
New York Campaign, 1776	109

Battle of Trenton 128
Washington's Route through Princeton to Morristown 129
Howe's Invasion of Pennsylvania, 1777 137
Campaigns in New York State, 1777 and 1779 149
Freeman's Farm 160
Bemis Heights 161
Battle of Monmouth 183
The Carolinas and Georgia, 1779-1781 207
Battle of Guilford Courthouse 231
The Campaign in Virginia, 1781 249
Siege of Yorktown 257

Illustrations

Sketch: From Beacon Hill, 1775, No. 1
    (Looking toward Dorchester Heights) 63
Sketch: From Beacon Hill, 1775, No. 2
    (Looking toward Roxbury) 63
Excerpt from Arnold's letter to Washington, November 13,
    1775 83
Circular of Philadelphia Council of Safety 101
Caricature of Burgoyne 153
Cartoon: The Allies-Par Nobile Fratrum 155
Facsimile of the oath of allegiance required by Congress to be
    administered to the officers of the army before leaving Valley
    Forge 173
Instructions for the Captain from Steuben's *Regulations for the
    Order and Discipline of the Troops of the United States* 175
Caricature of Lord North (as Boreas) studying the Americans 186
André's sketch of himself the day before his execution 217
Sketch of Rochambeau, probably by Count Ferson, friend of
    Marie Antoinette 253

Preface

Virgil sang gloriously of arms and men to the delight of the true lover of poetry, and, one must add, to the despair of countless generations of schoolboys. The American Revolution also has been celebrated in song and story. If it has had no Virgil, it has had many gifted prose historians, but, generally speaking, the teaching of the Revolution in the classroom has scarcely been of a quality to encourage an abiding interest in the conflict. This is particularly true of the military history of the Revolution.

Interpretation of the Revolution by historians has been a subject of considerable diversity. It has varied from the conception of those early historians who saw in the Revolution a divinely ordained event to the view of those who consider any such occurrence as a matter chiefly of dollars and cents. All aspects of the Revolution have been given scrupulous attention, the point of view tending to reflect the historian's own interests and the climate of the age in which he has lived. I have chosen to consider the military aspect. It is by no means a neglected field, but not for a number of years has the military history of the Revolution as a whole received separate treatment.

In developing a subject from other than a rounded approach, whether the emphasis be on politics, economics, social classes, or military events, there is, of course, the danger of throwing a subject out of focus because of the emphasis. I have accepted such a hazard for two reasons. In the first place, such an abundance of manuscript material—notably the Clinton, Gage, and Germain Papers—has been made available to scholars within the past generation and so many monographs have appeared correcting, amending, or confirming former conclusions on military developments that there is need for a new study which should embody these findings, and which should redefine and reinterpret the problems and results of the military history of the Revolution. In the second place, military history, within recent decades, has been sacrificed to other considerations. As Allen French wrote in *The Day of Concord and Lexington,* "In place of the old descriptions of battles, of the prominence once given to kings, statesmen, and civilian or military heroes, history now occupies itself with economic and social conditions, and sometimes seems to

vii

regard happenings as mere accidents, to be allowed as little space as possible." To the extent that this change of emphasis establishes a balance with the old preoccupation with political and military developments it is a healthy corrective. But when any one aspect is shouldered aside, there is need to redress the balance, and it is with the hope of accomplishing that very objective that this study has been written.

I am indebted to many individuals and institutions for aid in the preparation of this manuscript, the bibliography of which is contained in the footnotes. I wish especially to express my appreciation to my former commanding officer, Colonel Matthew C. Pugsley, MC, for originally suggesting this study and for permitting me to have special time after VJ-Day both to organize it and to utilize the facilities of the excellent library of the Medical Field Service School, then at Carlisle Barracks; to Dr. Randolph G. Adams, Mr. Colton Storm, and staff members of the W. L. Clements Library in Ann Arbor for their generous assistance with the papers of General Gage, Lord George Germain, Sir Henry Clinton, and Nathanael Greene; to Mr. Arthur Pierce Middleton for permission to examine the Carleton Papers in Colonial Williamsburg and to Miss Fanona Knox, the librarian, for her kindness in placing them at my disposal; to the Wesleyan University Library, particularly to Miss Gertrude McKenna for her unstinting co-operation; to the Research Committee and the Trustees of Wesleyan University for travel expenses; to Mr. Bernhard Knollenberg for making a number of valuable suggestions on a pleasant spring day in 1948; to my colleague, Professor Eugene O. Golob, for his enthusiasm and practical assistance; to Mr. John Fischer of Harper & Brothers, whose interest and encouragement have been truly heartwarming; and to my wife, who accompanied me on numerous Revolutionary battlefields, risking fatigue, sunstroke, and snakebite, who copied unwearyingly many an execrable scrawl on days that were better passed in the bright outdoors than in a musty scriptorium, and who read and assayed this manuscript with rare judgment yet with a sense of humor that both assuaged and delighted the writer. My thanks to all.

WILLARD M. WALLACE

Wesleyan University
Middletown, Connecticut
February 14, 1950

APPEAL TO ARMS

I

The Military Background of the Revolution

Early in the nineteenth century, the great Prussian authority on war, Carl von Clausewitz, wrote, "A war both arises and derives its nature from the ideas, feelings, and political relations which obtain at the moment when it breaks out." The American Revolution was no exception. The prevailing conceptions of individual liberty and popular sovereignty were explosive issues which deeply engaged the passions of men on both sides of the Atlantic, but particularly in America, where they were being tested specifically in the drives toward political and economic equality. The Revolution, even at its inception, revealed the profound bitterness between the American Whigs, or Patriot party, a militant minority agitating against the taxing policy of the Tory ministry as an infringement of constitutional principles, and the American Tories, or Loyalists, who sought a solution of governmental difficulties without resort to force or tearing the fabric of empire. At the same time, the Revolution threw into prominent relief party differences in England, and state and regional differences in America. It revealed the exasperation and perplexity of the British government and its persistent hope that, through a policy of alternating force and peaceful persuasion, a reconciliation might still be effected. Evident, also, were the generally slow acceptance, even by Patriots, of the idea of a complete separation from Britain and, as the war dragged along, the irresoluteness or apathy of a considerable section of the population. Although the war started with a burst of enthusiasm among the Patriots, the American military effort so nearly succumbed to financial exhaustion that, but for the intervention of France,

1

coupled with the almost incredible mistakes of British commanders, the independence of the United States might well have been forfeited.

The agrarian type of society, not far removed literally or figuratively from the frontier, also helped to determine the nature of the conflict. The demands of the seasons were an important factor in keeping the war on a fluctuating basis. If winter fighting was not an eighteenth-century custom even for regular troops, neither was the planting or harvest season an appropriate time for the American farmer to join the army. The controversy with George III and Lord North's ministry might keenly whet his interest as he listened to the harangues at town meetings, the discussions by village store pundits, and the fulminations of the pulpit. Even so, the corn to be planted or the potatoes to be dug constituted an argument more concretely and immediately persuasive; the war simply had to wait. Eventually the farmer might sign up as militiaman or Continental, but he tended to look upon his service as temporary, and he was reluctant to assist outside his own region. Within his own region, where his loyalties and interests were most deeply affected and his knowledge of the countryside greater, he was likely to perform well. New England farmers turned out in large numbers to halt Burgoyne, while southern farmers and backwoodsmen ruined Cornwallis' Carolina campaign by their crushing victory at King's Mountain. At the same time, the farmer's individualism, his experience against the Indians, his localism, and his addiction to short-term enlistment were the despair of general officers who sought to enforce discipline within their commands, fight the British in the open, or wage sustained campaigns far away from the farmer's home.

On the other hand, the acrid, choking smell of burnt powder in the air at the Lexington green on April 19, 1775, at the bridge in Concord, and along the dusty road back to Boston was blown from muskets held in part by New England farmers who were by no means unprepared for a clash of arms. Preparation in the organization of units, in the training of men, in the procurement of munitions and equipment had been going on for months, even years. Consequently our colonial forebears had at least a vague idea of where they belonged when the bell in the village church rang wildly on that cool, sunny April morning. They whipped the old but well-oiled musket off the pegs above the fireplace and rushed to join their companies. Though the organization of these units might be crude, the training a joke so far as close-order drill was concerned, and discipline a sorry farce from the British, or any, point of view, beginnings had been made. Without those early attempts the subsequent siege of Boston, perhaps indeed the whole American cause, might have ended in tragedy. The war was tragic enough in any case.

In colonial days a knowledge of firearms was far more common than now. People were dependent on muskets as a means of procuring much of their meat, as protection against Indians at many times and against the French and Indians when the wars were on. Muskets were also brought to the muster on training days, which formed a bright feature of colonial life. The whole family would turn out to watch the menfolk, young and old, march and countermarch and fire their muskets. Rum played no small part in enlivening the occasion, and the presence of numerous of the opposite sex furnished the incentive not only to excel but also to indulge boisterous spirits.

A future quartermaster general of the American army, Timothy Pickering, wrote a vivid description of a muster in Massachusetts.[1] The men took their time falling into ranks and argued with each other for the favored places. When the column marched onto the field, several of the more exuberant members fell out, dashed over to the crowd of onlookers, surrounded one fluttering young female, and shot off their muskets. At her cries of fright they nearly split their sides alaughing. At length, when a laggard sense of duty, or some exasperated officer, called them back, they returned to the column. The day then proceeded with a little drilling, special entertainment for the commissioned officers, practice in musketry, and a sham battle as a climax.

As relations with the mother country grew tense, the colonial authorities stiffened the training of their militia.[2] In Virginia, Maryland, Rhode Island, and particularly Massachusetts, volunteers trained vigorously at parade-ground tactics and musketry. Rhode Island, in 1774, authorized company drill once a month, regimental drill twice a year, and brigade drill once every two years. In 1771, New Hampshire took steps to form its militia into a powerful and respectable body, while, in 1772, New York also organized several companies against the day when they might be needed. Connecticut was one of the best organized colonies, boasting, in 1774, twenty thousand men of military age formed into eighteen regiments with at least one troop of horse to each; regimental musters, however, occurred only once every four years.

The most significant development took place in Massachusetts. Meeting in Cambridge on October 26, 1774, barely more than seven weeks after the Continental Congress assembled in Philadelphia, the Provincial Congress faced the realities of the situation. The Port of Boston was closed and a strong British garrison occupied Boston itself. Punitive measures against other colonies were hypothetical; against the Bay Colony they were a stern reality. If the Bay, particularly Boston, had behaved lawlessly, even childishly, in provoking the British government and British soldiers beyond the point of endurance, it could not be said that Massachusetts was willing to cringe before the show of British disapproval. Nor, for that matter, was either the Bay or the London government disposed to air the whole disagreement and find some basis of compromise. Massachusetts, under the prompting of Samuel Adams, James Otis, and others, was too deeply committed and Lord North's government too thoroughly offended.

The Provincial Congress prepared for future contingencies. It created a committee of safety and authorized the committee to call out the militia if the situation should so warrant and to gather munitions and equipment. Concord and Worcester were designated as the principal depots for supplies. The Congress also appointed Artemas Ward and Seth Pomeroy officers of general grade. Officers of field grade were directed to recruit one quarter of all the militia into emergency companies of fifty men each. These companies should have the power to elect their own company officers but were to be under the over-all direction of the committee of safety. Referred to as minutemen because they were expected to be ready to answer the call of the committee of safety at a minute's notice, and composed in part of veterans of the French and Indian War, these organizations and the term applied to them soon became popular. They were not altogether a new conception in the Bay Colony. Alarm-list companies had been formed for service against the Indians twenty years before. For that matter, these last had as antecedents those units which had been organized during the ferocious struggle known as King Philip's War, in 1675-1676, and which were prepared to take the field at the moment of alert. Even as early as 1645, the thirty crack men of each militia company of one hundred were ordered to be ready to march at a half hour's warning. The minutemen of 1774 had a long New England tradition behind them.[3]

With the minutemen organizing, military preparations went on in earnest. The Provincial Congress, meeting again in winter and early spring of 1775, appointed William Heath and John Thomas as general officers and organized a committee of supplies. Early in April, it undertook to form an army and invited the co-operation of Rhode Island, New Hampshire, and Connecticut; then, on April 15, it declared itself adjourned until May 10. Meanwhile, thanks in good part to the energy of the Provincial Congress, militia and minute companies worked hard. Even before the organization of the minutemen, the militia companies had begun to take their training so seriously that Lord Percy, who originally regarded Americans as "sly, artful, hypocritical rascals, cruel, and cowards," could write home on September 12 that the Americans now "did not make a despicable appearance as soldiers," no mean compliment from an English soldier-aristocrat.[4] Large stores of military supplies and provisions were collected and stored in what were presumed to be safe places. Through most of March and the first half of April, 1775, Concord became the depot for so many stores that wind of the location and the contents reached the ears of the military authorities in Boston. It was to capture or destroy these supplies that Lieutenant Colonel Francis Smith marched in considerable force out of Boston on the night of April 18 and down the quiet country road toward Concord. That road led through Lexington and eight years of war.

British preparations were by no means inconsiderable, though scarcely adequate when the testing time arrived. The very fact, however, that the British intended to maintain a military establishment in America after 1763 roused antagonism. Years before Lexington and Concord, Governor Pitkin of Connecticut and Benjamin Franklin mentioned the dangers and the lack of wisdom in such a policy.[5] The Boston Massacre fanned popular fury to such an extent that the five hundred troops then stationed in the town were withdrawn, and the Whigs regretted that their bones had not been piled up on the Common as a monument to the bravery of Massachusetts.[6] The Continental Congress in its first meeting contended that the authority of the British commander in chief had been rendered independent of, and superior to, the civil government. Throughout the colonies a growing body of opinion resented and feared the existence in America of the scarlet-clad soldiers, known to the Boston street gangs as "Lobsterbacks."

There was some ground for such fears, too. The particularism of the colonies had made it impossible for many years either to administer effectively the trade and navigation acts or to provide adequately for any sort of common defense. Not until 1754, when the horrors of the French and Indian menace stalked the frontiers again, did the Board of Trade in London reach some sort of definite agreement, though, as early as 1748, Governor Shirley of Massachusetts had mentioned the desirability of a regular garrison in New York maintained by parliamentary taxation.[7] Stout Major General Edward Braddock, who subsequently left his bones under a wagon road in the Pennsylvania wilds after his terrible defeat, was appointed with power to work with colonial governors in securing men and supplies, to supervise Indian affairs, and to assume command of all forces. A succession of commanders after him proceeded on the same basis, though with some curtailment of power after 1758, thanks to Pitt, who was loath to antagonize both the colonial officials and the people themselves. On the other hand, the idea and, to a certain extent, the actual pattern of a unity of the colonies through military command were retained and given real substance by the Grenville ministry in 1763 with the announcement of its intention to station ten thousand troops in America, with headquarters in New York, and to provide in part for their maintenance by colonial assistance.[8]

The supreme commander in America after 1763 was Major General Thomas Gage.[9] A heavy, patient, rather kindly man, occasionally given to impulsiveness, he encountered grave problems, not only those of an essentially military nature and those dealing with the Indians, but also problems concerned with the civil authorities, with whom he was to co-operate in maintaining order. If his discharge of this latter aspect of his duties angered certain of the populace, Gage's patience was tried by the aid given to British deserters, particularly in New York and New England. An examination of his correspondence reveals the multitude and complexity of problems which the man was called upon to face, from scotching an Indian uprising in the West or recovering a deserter from the Florida swamps to refusing tactfully but firmly Governor Penn's request to oust Connecticut settlers from a highly controversial part of Pennsylvania.[10]

Not until the arrival of troops in Boston in 1768 did people there and elsewhere begin to understand the significance of a British military command in America. As colonial opposition to the commercial and financial policy of the British government grew, so, likewise, angry sentiment sprouted against the presence of regular troops, the strong arm of the crown. The Boston Massacre was an unpleasant incident, but only one of several clashes with the British authorities throughout the colonies. Finally, after the celebrated tea party took place in Boston, and Parliament enacted its repressive measures against the town, with Gage himself displacing Hutchinson as governor, realization spread quickly that a unity in British command in the colonies might work as effectively against recalcitrant colonies as for the colonies against the French and Indians. Though combating the regular establishment of Great Britain seemed no small task, the Provincial Congresses had to consider ways and means of doing that very thing.

But, in any war with its colonies, Britain faced a formidable undertaking. Though its population of nine million exceeded that of America by over three times, and though its industrial and financial resources were immensely superior, its professional army was small, expensive, and trained to operate on the cleared fields and flat terrain of Western Europe rather than in America with its tangled woods, its rugged hills, its stone-walled or fenced pastures, and its swamps. Furthermore, the widely scattered farms and the paucity of towns and villages made living off the country so uncertain that supplies for the army were brought from overseas in ships which often arrived with their cargoes spoiled. As an additional handicap, the absence of good roads outside the towns, or any roads at all in certain regions, created a transport problem of the first magnitude. The road conditions, few towns, and a vast hinterland made it difficult to eliminate specific centers of opposition.

The most vulnerable area in America was the seaboard, though to close off effectively over fifteen hundred miles of coast line was virtually out of the question. On the other hand, with its command of the sea, Britain could seize the ports considered so vital to America's existence. Such limited operations, which were probably the most

effective means of reducing the revolt, required a high degree of
co-operation between the armed services, and few British generals
and admirals evinced the necessary understanding of the contribution
which each service would have to make. Without the support of sea
power, however, the British army had scant chance of re-establishing
the authority of the crown.

In 1775, before Lexington, British land forces, exclusive of militia,
included fewer than forty-nine thousand officers and men.[11] Slightly
more than thirty-nine thousand of this total were infantry. While
garrisons were stationed through the world-wide British possessions,
the bulk of the army was distributed in England, Ireland, and America. Forces in America amounted to eighty-five hundred, most of
them mustered in eighteen regiments of infantry.

The British infantry regiment varied in size, sometimes running as
high as a thousand. Usually the infantry regiment in England numbered four hundred and seventy-seven officers and men divided into
ten companies, each company consisting of thirty-eight privates. Two
of the ten companies were picked troops. One was composed of the
tallest and strongest men in the regiment; these were the Grenadiers,
though the throwing of hand grenades had disappeared from the
army. The other company consisted of lean, agile, aggressive men
carrying lightweight muskets, just the type of men for skirmishers;
these were the Light Infantry, and they owed their existence mainly
to the efforts of Sir William Howe just before the Revolution. Their
usual place in battle, and also that of the Grenadiers, was on the
flanks.

The three famous Foot Guards regiments—the Grenadiers, the
Coldstream, and the Scots—and the three Horse Guards regiments
took no part as such in the Revolution. From these crack household
troops, however, fifteen men from each of their sixty-four companies
were formed into a special brigade of Guards and sent to America.
All the Guards regiments were picked men, and the nine hundred
and sixty chosen for American service formed the very flower of
those elite units.

Officers of a regiment of the line were distributed much the same
as today. Field and staff officers usually included one colonel, one
lieutenant colonel or major, one chaplain (who led a happier life if
he could hold his liquor with the colonel), one surgeon and one

surgeon's mate (neither being regarded as wholly acceptable socially). With a company about the size of a platoon in one of the present armies, there was a liberal complement of commissioned and non-commissioned officers. Normally a captain commanded a company of thirty-eight privates, and he received assistance from two lieutenants, two sergeants, three corporals, and one drummer. Grenadier companies had also two fifers.

The organization of the cavalry and the artillery was less uniform. Usually a cavalry regiment consisted of six troops of two hundred and thirty-one men each, and it was Gage's misfortune not to have any cavalry available on April 19, 1775; otherwise, the course of the day might have been decidedly different. The artillery in 1775 was organized into four battalions, eight companies to a battalion, one hundred and sixteen officers and men to a company. The drivers were not soldiers but civilians, normally in the employ of the contractors who supplied the army with horses. Most guns, even 3-pounders, required at least three horses, and by custom two guns were assigned to each infantry regiment. Known as battalion guns, their allotment to infantry regiments was lamented by many artillery officers since it forfeited the effective results obtained from massed fire-power.

There were, of course, other departments of the army. While military artificers (sappers, we should call them today) and engineers existed, their numbers were small. The commissariat and the transport service were headed, the first by a commissary general who was under orders of the Treasury, the other by a wagonmaster general who was an officer. Medical service was of the crudest. Though there were a physician general, a surgeon general, and inspectors of hospitals, field medical service was rendered by the surgeon and the surgeon's mate attached to each regiment. The surgeon, who was likely to be a Scot from one of the universities at Glasgow or Edinburgh, received his appointment from the colonel and a mere stipend for his services. In an emergency he might call for assistance from the wives who accompanied enlisted men to battle in that day. Often these women, who might be mistresses rather than wives, brought their children along for the campaigns. Howe allowed six wives per company for his campaigns in the Middle Colonies, Burgoyne three wives per company for his invasion of northern New York. Regardless of the morals of some of these women, they rendered valiant aid in times of extreme peril. They were indeed of far more comfort to the troops than most of the chaplains of the day, a sorry lot in general, more spiritually lax than many of their military flock. In an age when bishops rode to hounds and tippled right along with the ruggedest fox-hunting squire, little spirituality could be expected of an under-paid army chaplain. Fortunately there were a few chaplains who upheld the Word. These did not hesitate to contend mightily with colonels who would rather see their men in barracks on a Sunday than using the church service as an excuse to get drunk, though the colonels themselves might be notorious winebibbers and pot-tossers.

This small army was, for all its deficiencies, an effective force for the eighteenth century. Commissions might be bought (a lieutenant-colonelcy in the line sold for £4,500) and officers might spend the largest part of their time drinking and gambling, but most of them, especially the younger officers, had a fair knowledge of their profession and plenty of bulldog courage in battle. As professional soldiers, they displayed the utmost contempt for the American militiaman and the Continental, while, as Englishmen, they despised the American as both a rebel and a colonial. Even Loyalists felt the sting in their attitude toward people born on this side of the Atlantic.

The heart of the British training system was the noncommissioned officer, who usually manifested toward Americans a contempt as profound as that evinced by his superior. If noncoms were often brutal, it was a rough age, and a mild manner and a gentle voice in a sergeant were hardly regarded as suited to whip into shape the rank and file, who were, for the most part, criminals given their choice of jail or the army, the sweepings of gin houses and stews, and the unruly clansmen of the Scottish highlands. The lot of these en-listed men was not one of the easiest. They had to forfeit a goodly proportion of their eight pence a day for clothing accessories and odds and ends of maintenance, wear a tight, cumbersome uniform, carry muskets three feet and eight inches in the barrel surmounted by a 14-inch bayonet (the weight of the entire weapon being fifteen pounds), expose themselves to a discipline so harsh that punishments of a thousand strokes were by no means uncommon, and submit to being classed as a cut below sailors and on a level with dogs. Never-theless, they generally remained loyal and obedient, with no incident on record such as that of one French regiment in the Seven Years' War which hated its officers so fiercely that it shot them rather than the enemy.

For all its bumbling, bungling generals, this army did not do so badly when it was given a chance. It suffered terribly from poor leadership but worse from maladministration in London, where Lord George Germain presided in charge of military affairs as secretary of state for the colonies from late 1775 to 1782. This was the same officer who, disobeying orders at the Battle of Minden in the Seven Years' War, had later been court-martialed and prohibited from holding any subsequent military office. The friendship of George III, however, meant much, and Germain was presently enjoying his position of high authority. The British should have won the Revolution handily. The fact remains that they did not, thanks to their own blunders, the valor of their adversaries, the arrival of French military and financial assistance for the Americans, and the indomitable will and gradually acquired skill of Washington. As a fighting machine the British army was at first infinitely superior to anything the Americans had to offer. But the longer the war went on, the marvel became not so much one of how the Americans did so well as how the British could do so poorly. The explanation lay in the higher echelons of command and administration. With all due credit to the Americans and their French allies, it is not too much to say that the British government and the British generals lost the Revolution for England.

II

The Guns of Lexington and Concord

Although in the revaluation of our early history there is a tendency, often warranted, to play down the so-called heroism of the Patriots' part in the American Revolution, the initial encounters of the Revolution were quite remarkable. If one tires of hearing and reading allusions through the years to the valor of the trusty farmers who dared stand up to the British at Lexington and repelled them at Concord, the naked fact remains that irregular troops soundly trounced regular troops. What does it matter that the conditions favored the former and that, had the Americans been as accurate shots as legend would have one believe, few redcoats would have survived the terrible retreat to Boston? History is influenced as strongly by myth as by fact, but, in the events of April 19, 1775, the cold reality of a British defeat, at once unexpected and severe, as well as profound in its effects, persisted for decades as a reasonable excuse for giving the eagle screaming room. Fortunately the passing of time and of animosities has now rendered the 19th of April, especially in Boston, as less to be celebrated for the ride of Paul Revere and the fight at Lexington and Concord than for the annual running of the Boston Marathon.

For the ride of Paul Revere there was more than sufficient reason. After long deliberation, General Gage had decided to send troops into the country to destroy the military stores at Concord. Contrary to general belief, Gage did not order out the troops entirely on his own initiative.[1] He waited for reinforcements and for the fateful instructions from London which should, as he anticipated, require him to take offensive measures.[2] Through Dr. Benjamin Church, a man deeply trusted by the Patriots, he obtained extensive intelligence concerning the work of the Provincial Congress and the collection of

military supplies, while from scouts who reconnoitered the countryside he learned information that confirmed certain of Church's
reports. Finally, on April 14, a man-of-war that had left Plymouth,
England, on March 13 arrived in Boston bearing a duplicate copy
of a letter of January 27 from the Earl of Dartmouth, secretary of
state for the colonies. The authority of the kingdom, Dartmouth insisted,[3] had to be supported and its laws enforced. However pressing
Gage's need of reinforcements might be, "a smaller force now, if put
to the test, would be able to encounter [the Americans] with greater
probability of success than might be expected from a greater army,
if the people would be suffered to form themselves upon a more
regular plan, to acquire confidence from discipline, and to prepare
those resources without which every thing must be put to the issue
of a single action."[4] On receipt of this message, Gage relieved the
Grenadiers and Light Infantry from their regular duties. Forty-eight
hours later, April 16, HMS *Falcon* entered Boston with the original
of Dartmouth's dispatch, and on the 18th Lieutenant Colonel Smith
received his marching orders.

The expedition consisted of about seven hundred men, burly
Grenadiers and agile Light Infantry under fat, slow-minded Lieutenant Colonel Francis Smith of the 10th Infantry and Major John
Pitcairn of the Marines, a bluff, choleric, warmhearted man friendly
to Americans. The British marched in the evening of April 18 to the
foot of the Common and were rowed across the Charles River to
Phips' farm, Lechmere Point. After wading ashore through water
over their knees, the men were kept waiting on the road until at least
one o'clock while provisions were brought from the boats and distributed. Finally, the long-awaited order rang out, and the troops,
tired and chilled, their feet sloshing in their shoes, moved toward the
road (now Massachusetts Avenue) in North Cambridge which led
from Boston through Menotomy (now Arlington) and Lexington to
Concord.[5]

The Americans had long suspected that the British would march to
Concord. Gage failed to realize that the Americans were even better
informed of British activities and intentions than he was of theirs. The
large number of men thrown out of work by the closing of the Port
of Boston were more than agreeable to keeping the provincial authori-
ities alert to any suspicious movements along the waterfront or near

the British barracks. Moreover, a skilled mechanic like Paul Revere, one of the dispatch riders for the Patriot party, had a coterie of associates who watched the British with tireless eyes.

Aware that the launching of the boats from the transports at midnight on Saturday, April 15, portended something significant and that the Grenadiers and the Light Infantry had been removed from their routine duties, Revere conferred secretly with Dr. Joseph Warren. Warren sent him on Sunday to warn Adams and Hancock, then visiting in Lexington with the Reverend Jonas Clark, whose wife was Hancock's cousin. It is possible that Revere rode on to Concord, too, for it is reported that the town received warning that day that the British might soon be there. His duty done for the time being, Revere returned to Boston by way of Charlestown, where he and Colonel William Conant agreed that, if the British marched by land, one lantern should be shown from the spire of Christ Church; if they started by water, the signal should be two lanterns.[6]

Monday passed without event, but on Tuesday afternoon Gage dispatched groups of mounted officers to cover the roads after dark and intercept any messenger from the town. If their departure attracted little attention from the townsfolk, the change of position by HMS *Somerset* to the mouth of the Charles must have evoked some interesting speculation; it was clear that any hostile craft thereafter crossing to Charlestown would do so at great hazard. Yet Gage continued to believe in the secrecy of his expedition. Sending for Lord Percy after sundown, he informed him that the expedition was bound for Concord but that even Colonel Smith, while aware of his command responsibilities, had not been apprised of the objective.

As Percy returned to his own quarters, he overheard street-corner gossip which convinced him the secret was out. He therefore wasted little time in getting back to Gage, who, greatly disturbed, insisted that he had confided his design to only one person besides Percy. It has often been conjectured that the one person was Margaret Kemble, the general's wife and an American, the implication being that she betrayed the plan to her husband's opponents. Of this, however, there is no proof.[7] Furthermore, such betrayal, besides being unlikely, was scarcely necessary, for the townspeople must surely have heard the march of the troops or, at any rate, have seen the large number of soldiers at the foot of the Common. Everyone knew, too, that the

Patriots' supplies were at Concord. It is also possible that the officers who left in the afternoon might have talked excitedly among themselves and one of them in an unguarded moment let slip˙ what they were going to do.

However the information got out, Revere was summoned by Warren about ten o'clock and instructed to go to Lexington and inform Adams and Hancock that the troops were on their way. Warren added that he had just sent William Dawes, also an express rider for the Whigs, by the land route with the message. Revere, Warren said, must use the route across the Charles River. After leaving Warren's house, Revere arranged with his old friend, Captain John Pulling, or, more probably, Robert Newman, sexton of Christ Church, to display the proper signal to Colonel Conant in Charlestown. Despite the presence of troops in North Square, he managed to slip past them to the north part of the town. Two friends, Joshua Bentley and Thomas Richardson, accompanied him to where he had a boat hidden. Afterward, with oars muffled (so legend has it) by the still warm flannel petticoat of a girl friendly to the Patriot cause, Bentley and Richardson rowed Revere across the Charles east of the *Somerset.* Farther up the river the troops were being ferried to the Cambridge shore. It was now young flood, the man-of-war winding, and the moon on the rise. The watch aboard the *Somerset* must have been extraordinarily lax, for the boat was not hailed. Soon the three men reached the Charlestown shore. While his companions returned to Boston, Revere went on to Colonel Conant's and was presently astride the finest horse belonging to wealthy John Larkin. In the meantime, the shrewd, humorous Dawes, with the help of a friendly British soldier, had slipped through the gates on the land side and, like Revere, was soon riding the night wind spreading the alarm. Both riders had two to three hours' start on the British. Gage's elaborate precautions for secrecy had thus been all for naught.

Although two mounted officers on patrol tried hard to prevent Revere from warning the countryside, he was in Lexington by midnight. He went directly to the Clark house, where Adams and Hancock were staying, and was stopped by a militia sergeant who told him that the family had just gone to bed and had requested not to be disturbed by any noise.

"Noise!" shouted Revere. "You'll have enough noise before long. The regulars are coming out!"

Revere was admitted at once. Curtly he described what had happened. Hancock, in a curious blend of sincerity and vainglory, was all for joining the minutemen, but Adams finally convinced him that, as recently elected delegates to the Second Continental Congress, they had a higher duty. Then Dawes arrived, a scant half hour behind Revere, and after both riders gulped a hasty lunch, they pushed on to Concord. On this leg of their journey they were accompanied by a Concord man, Dr. Samuel Prescott, who had been courting a Lexington girl for the evening. He offered to help the two messengers since he knew many of the people along the road.

It was well that Prescott went along. Halfway to Concord, while Dawes and Prescott stopped to warn a family, Revere rode on toward the next house. Suddenly he saw two mounted British officers blocking the highway. As he shouted to his companions to come up, two other officers appeared, and the four Englishmen compelled Revere, as well as Prescott, when he galloped up ahead of Dawes, to enter a pasture, the bars of which were down. Instantly Prescott swung sharply in one direction, Revere in another. The physician took his horse over a low stone wall, and it was he, rather than Revere or Dawes, who carried the alarm to Concord. Revere made for the woods near by, but, as he reached them, six officers spurred out from the trees, seized the bridle of his horse, and forced him to dismount. Though rough words passed, one officer finally questioned him courteously. Learning that he was Paul Revere, the Englishman told him they were out after deserters. Revere assured the officers that he knew better and that five hundred men would soon be on hand to oppose the troops. Even when a Major Mitchel held a pistol at his head and threatened to blow out his brains if he did not tell the truth, Revere gave the same answers. Presently a distant volley was heard, whereupon the officers let the American go and galloped back toward Cambridge.

Meanwhile Captain John Parker, commander of the Lexington minutemen, had not been inactive. Hearing the news that Revere had brought, Parker summoned his one hundred and thirty men to the green. After about an hour of waiting in the cold, clear night for the British to come, he sent his men away until the drums should beat assembly. It may have been when they were dismissed that they fired the volley that startled Major Mitchel.[8]

As the men of Lexington waited, the British were pushing more rapidly through the darkness. During a rest halt, Colonel Smith instructed his officers that the troops were not to fire unless fired upon. He also detached Pitcairn with six companies of Light Infantry to take possession of the two bridges on the other side of Concord. Presently, between three and four o'clock, Major Mitchel and his fellow officers galloped through to Smith and told him of the encounter with Revere and that the country was aroused, a report confirmed by the sound of alarm guns and the tolling of the church bells in neighboring villages. Very likely it was on Mitchel's advice that Smith shook off his sluggishness long enough to make the decision that saved his command that day; he dispatched a messenger to Gage requesting reinforcements. It is quite likely, too, that he then sent forward Mitchel with his companions to act as guides for Pitcairn.

Pitcairn, whose advance guard had nearly captured the mounted Lexington scout, Thaddeus Bowman, became uneasy when the patrolling officers, on their way to Smith, mentioned that five hundred armed men were waiting in Lexington. The major resolved to take no chances. Halting his troops until Colonel Smith should come up, he had the men load their muskets. When this was done, he ordered them on no account to fire without orders.[9] Then, with the main column by this time close behind, Pitcairn moved his troops into Lexington.

Word of the approaching ribbon of scarlet and steel was brought into the town by Bowman between daylight and sunrise. Instantly Captain Parker ordered guns fired and the drums beaten. As the men caught up their muskets and tumbled out of the inn or ran from their homes near by, Sergeant Monroe, recently released from his guard over Adams and Hancock, who were now on their way to safety, formed the men in two ranks on the green. There were about seventy in the formation. With this handful Parker prepared to face the column of regulars now swinging toward him. Though there is no record of his having uttered the famous words attributed to him, "Don't fire unless fired on, but if they mean to have a war let it begin here," the thought could not have been entirely absent from his mind; else he must surely have hesitated to present his command to the overwhelming force drawing near. He may have had no intention of opposing the British unless insult should be offered, but surely he must have realized that the British could hardly regard an armed force on the green as other than a challenge to their right to pass.

At any rate, instead of swinging on to Concord and thereby exposing his flank to possible attack, Pitcairn marched his troops to the right past the meetinghouse, with its belfry at one side, and directly toward Parker. Accompanied by fellow officers, one of whom was probably Major Mitchel, Pitcairn galloped around the other side of the meetinghouse toward the minutemen. When he pulled up his horse near them, he ordered them to lay down their arms and disperse. Parker now saw that keeping his men in formation was utter folly, that assembling them in the manner and the place at that time had probably been a mistake, too. He had, therefore, no choice save to order his men to disperse and not to fire.[10]

But Pitcairn had no intention that the Lexington company should withdraw with its arms. As he swung toward his troops to order them to disarm the minutemen, he thought he saw a flintlock from behind a stone wall flash in its powder pan. Several shots then followed and, an instant later, a smashing volley from each platoon. Pitcairn did his utmost to get the troops to cease firing, but there was no restraining them. Dashing forward, they completely scattered the already retiring farmers. Only a few of the latter returned the fire of the British. One man, however, stouthearted Jonas Parker, not only returned the fire but refused to budge from the line. Wounded by the British, he was in the act of reloading his musket when he died by a bayonet thrust. Altogether, eight Americans lost their lives and ten were wounded before Pitcairn and the company officers finally could get their excited men under control again and march them off, still huzzaing, toward Concord.[11]

The question of who fired the first shot became at once a subject of bitter controversy. It has been variously ascribed, now to a Provincial firing from behind a stone wall or from a window in Buckman's Tavern, now to Pitcairn or to another Englishman, perhaps some nervous young officer whose pistol went off accidentally or whose finger became "trigger-happy" at the sight of Provincials defying king's troops. Pitcairn himself believed that he saw an American's gun off to one side flash without going off, followed by a number of shots, one ball wounding his own horse and a man near him. Yet one

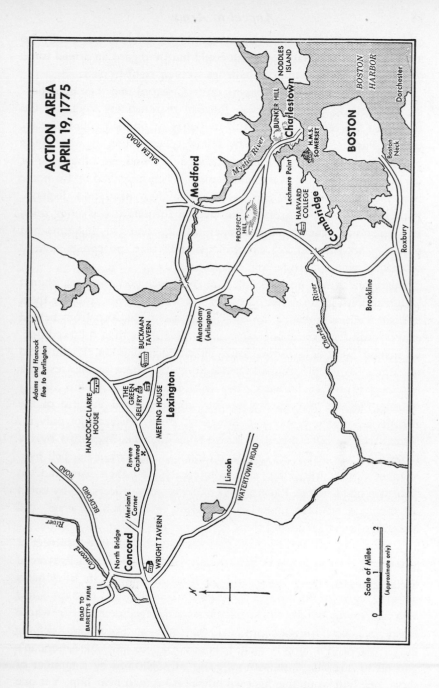

ACTION AREA
APRIL 19, 1775

thing is quite certain from the mass of testimony analyzed so carefully by historians:[12] Pitcairn did not give the order to fire; in fact, once the mischief was done, he tried to prevent even worse occurring. But regardless of who fired the first shot, men had died on the Lexington green by the action of British troops. Civil war had begun, and agitator Samuel Adams, hearing the fateful guns of Lexington from a distance of two miles, could lift his voice in full awareness of the significance of what was happening and say, "O! What a glorious morning is this!"

It is doubtful if the brush at Lexington, from the time the British troops appeared at sunrise until they resumed their march to Concord, had taken longer than fifteen or twenty minutes. The five miles of the subsequent march passed swiftly and without significant opposition, though a number of Provincials were sighted in the woods. Not until the troops were within about two miles of Concord did they sight any considerable body of Americans. These consisted of something over a hundred men, Lincoln militia and two Concord minute companies less a number who were absent with Colonel Barrett securing the vital stores of munitions. If the British expected a fight with this force, they reckoned without a certain common sense in the Americans that impelled the latter, in the face of such superior numbers, to about-face and march back into town, their drums and fifes going merrily. The British took this in good part and began to play, too. One American remarked, years afterward, "we had grand musick."[13]

The return of the Concord reconnaissance force with news of the British close behind caused a general withdrawal; and, by eight o'clock, the troops had entered the town without resistance. After his force was fully assembled, Smith detached one company of Light Infantry to seize the South Bridge and six companies to secure the North Bridge and the stores at Colonel Barrett's. With the bridge soon in his possession, Captain Laurie of the 43d remained at the structure with three companies of Light Infantry, while Captain Parsons of the 10th set out with the other three companies to take Colonel Barrett's farm.

In the meantime, Concord under British control was undergoing an experience which was to furnish material for many a blast of fervid oratory in the succeeding century. Actually the British behaved extraordinarily well, paying for their food and drink and, on the whole, not molesting the inhabitants. Women were treated with scrupulous courtesy, and private property was respected. This was even true at the Barrett farm. Captain Parsons uncovered a certain number of gun carriages and had them thrown into a pile to burn, but when Mrs. Barrett protested that the pile was so near the barn the building might catch on fire, Parsons obligingly had the carriages transferred to the road.[14]

The good people of Concord, however, held certain grievances against the British. The troops cut away a flag flying from a liberty pole and chopped down the pole. On the green they burned a number of entrenching tools and the carriages of two 24-pounders. They were responsible for a fire breaking out in the town hall, though they extinguished the blaze. They destroyed a considerable amount of flour which they suspected was being stored for military reasons. It is said that a number of soldiers also entered the church, but, thanks to one thoughtful woman, the communion silver had been removed to a place of safety. A few threats were made to men who were believed to be hiding munitions or supplies, though, once the sought-for items were discovered, particularly the 24-pounders, no injury was offered. The profanity of the troops also excited anger among a number of the populace. Anglo-Saxon troops have ever possessed a reputation for being profane, at least as far back as the Hundred Years' War, when Frenchmen referred to the English bowmen and men-at-arms as the "goddams." Yet, incredible as it may seem to any American veteran of one of the two World Wars, an oath in the minute companies merited a fine!

Major Pitcairn, in particular, came in for a heavy share of abuse for being profane, blustery, and bellicose. It is alleged that at Wright's Tavern, after the skirmish at the North Bridge, he "called for a glass of brandy, and stirred it up with his bloody finger, remarking, 'He hoped he should stir the Yankee blood so before night.' " This sentiment seems quite unlike Pitcairn and may well have been expressed by another officer who was confused with the major.[15]

During the British occupation, the Americans began to gather on the other side of the North Bridge and finally marched in a column of twos toward it. Not to be caught shorthanded, Laurie sent back to Smith for help. As the three to four hundred Provincials approached, he retreated across the span and fired two or three warning shots into the water, but these failed to halt the movement. Then the British lashed out with a volley at a range of seventy-five yards, killing two men. Leaping into the air, Major Buttrick, the American commander, excitedly ordered his men to return the fire. In the exchange of musketry that followed, one redcoat fell dead, two were mortally wounded, and four officers and five enlisted men were hit. Laurie now ordered a retreat. The Americans had thus won the North Bridge and pushed cautiously across it. The "battle" had lasted probably less than five minutes.

Presently, as the Americans sat down to breakfast off whatever snacks they had brought along, a youth crossed North Bridge with an ax in his hand. As he passed two wounded redcoats lying in the dust, one of them stirred and possibly tried to sit up. Frightened, the boy hit the soldier with his ax and left him with his face and head covered with blood. Shortly afterward, the three companies under Captain Parsons arrived from Colonel Barrett's, and the Americans let them cross unmolested. Suddenly the British came upon the mutilated soldier, who was still alive. The sight so startled them that they did not even stop to succor him but fled at top speed for Concord. The news they bore of the atrocity lost nothing in the telling. Gage, in his account to London, reported that the soldier had been "scalped, his head much mangled, and his ears cut off, tho not quite dead."

Despite the storm gathering about him, Smith kept his tired men marching hither and yon about Concord and failed to leave the town until noon. Then, bedding down the wounded in wagons, he placed his Grenadiers in column in the road, and ordered his Light Infantry to the ridge as flankers. In that formation the British retreated without incident as far as Meriam's Corner, where the ridge ended; the flankers now joined the main body. As the rearguard of the British was traversing a small bridge over a brook, the Americans, now strengthened by men from surrounding towns, fired on the mass of redcoats. Staggered, the rearguard returned the fire weakly. From that moment the British retreat to Lexington became a terrible experience for them. At one point under a rocky ledge the British leaders tried to get their column into order again, but, in the attempt, Pitcairn's horse threw him and fled, while Smith was painfully though not seriously wounded. The situation of the British grew desperate, for they were indeed, as Gage later conceded, "a good deal pressed."[16] Their flankers began to tire, their wounded lagged, and their ammunition was almost gone. A mile from Lexington their retreat turned into an anguished run.

Fortunately for Smith and his despairing men, Gage had ordered the 1st Brigade out in support, and it was scarcely his fault that a foolish delay before the orders were received postponed the start of the relief force for several costly hours. The 1st Brigade, consisting of the 4th, 23d, and 47th Regiments and the 1st Marine Battalion, was under the command of Brigadier General Hugh Earl Percy. The earl, thirty-three years old, left Boston with his musicians playing "Yankee Doodle," and not until Lexington did he have positive indication of the work ahead of him. Some time before two o'clock, a chaise bearing a wounded officer reached Percy. The latter then learned for the first time of the desperate condition of Smith's troops.[17] Fifteen minutes later, shots were heard and, presently, a steady rattle of musketry. By half past two, the brigade had pushed into Lexington and deployed in a hollow square, its flanks anchored on two low hills and its two 6-pounders placed to cover the road from Concord.

Great must have been the joy of the footsore, harassed Grenadiers and Light Infantry when they sighted Percy's long lines of scarlet and white. Tired as they were, they set up a vigorous shouting; and the firing died away for a time. Percy and Smith, both with their advance guards, met, and one can well imagine Smith's relief as the fat colonel, wounded and sweating, shook hands with the slim, young brigadier. Both Smith and Pitcairn were now spared the humiliation of having to consider surrendering to the Provincials. By a quarter before three, all the exhausted troops had reached safety and fell to the ground, literally gasping for breath. Though the rearguard was hotly pursued, a few well-placed cannon shot scattered the Americans. When a number of the latter took refuge behind the meetinghouse, a cannon ball crashing through the structure sent them to the protection of a swamp, from which they exchanged shots with British marksmen during the rest given Smith's men.

After something over a half hour, the troops formed in column for the march to Boston. The Grenadiers and Light Infantry were posted in the van of the brigade. Flankers took position, and the 23d, the Welsh Fusiliers, acted as rearguard, though each unit of the brigade took its turn at this post before the march was over. From the time the order to march was given, the troops were exposed to the same harassing, nerve-racking fire as before, not only from stone walls and trees but also from the empty houses along the road. Under this constant potshotting, Percy kept his head, maintaining his flankers and shrewdly employing his fieldpieces, which demoralized even if they did not destroy. The earl, moreover, did not hesitate to send his men into any house from which his troops were fired on. With the scalping atrocity leaping from tongue to tongue and undoubtedly growing in horror, the soldiers showed little mercy to any marksmen within.

But the Americans continued to come on. Though they possessed no unified command, General Heath and Dr. Warren eventually assumed such general direction as they could. Both Heath and Warren were hampered throughout by the fact that as each American's supply of powder and bullets gave out, he dropped out of the pursuit. Even so, Heath kept Percy hotly engaged and, with the arrival of militia from Roxbury, Brookline, Dorchester, and Danvers, stopped the earl's retreat momentarily at the Foot of the Rocks in Menotomy. For several minutes the firing was brisk on both sides. Only when the 6-pounders were used could the British move on again.

It is possible that had not Percy decided to swing into Charlestown and cross over to Boston under cover of the guns of the fleet, he might have lost his command. At any rate, he would have suffered much more heavily. As it was, he was halted in the shadow of Prospect Hill and had to rely on the cannon to disperse the growing body of Americans. Moreover, in the distance between Prospect Hill and Charlestown Neck, his troops might have been caught in the flank by the well-drilled Salem detachment of three hundred men if the British had not been aided both by the leisurely turn of mind on the part of the Salem commander, Timothy Pickering, and by the timorous caution of General Heath, whose overdeveloped respect for the two cannons led him to throw away in the dusk his one last chance of dealing a smashing blow at the British column. Fortunately, too, so far as the British were concerned, they were close to Charlestown and safety. In Charlestown, where the firing ceased, fresh troops took over the defense as Percy's tired men rested for a half hour on Bunker Hill. Then the earl marched the Grenadiers and Light Infantry and finally the brigade down to Charlestown for embarkation to Boston.

But it was not until after midnight that many of the troops reached the Boston shore; the Grenadiers and Light Infantry had been on their feet for over twenty-four hours.

Quite apart from the element of physical exhaustion, the day had been a bitter experience for the British. Out of a total of from fifteen hundred to eighteen hundred men engaged, they lost seventy-three killed, one hundred and seventy-four wounded, and twenty-six missing. If the musket had been a more effective weapon and the farmers better shots even with such a clumsy firearm, the British casualty list might have been forbidding indeed. But what, if anything, was more astonishing to the British was the manner in which the Provincials remained unimpressed by the fact that they were opposing regular troops. Even Percy, whose own courage and leadership were commended by Gage, admired their perseverance and resolution. Still, if the Americans elicited a certain amount of praise, British criticism of their own expedition to Concord was sharp, whether the critic was the fussy naval commander, Admiral Samuel Graves, who believed that if he had not covered Charlestown with the *Somerset* Percy would have been taken, or Lieutenant John Barker of the King's Own Regiment, who considered the expedition poorly planned and as badly executed. On the other hand, as the historian of the British army has remarked, "To blame Gage for attempting the enterprise and Smith for not abandoning it when he found that the alarm was given, is mere wisdom after the event."[18] Similarly, criticism would have been infinitely more pointed had the officers and men been able to foresee the result, two months later, of Gage's decision, the day after Lexington and Concord, to abandon a redoubt being thrown up on Bunker Hill to command Charlestown Neck.

For the gathering host of Americans, whose numbers had probably impelled Gage to demolish his works on Bunker Hill and withdraw to Boston,[19] the day had been one of shock, sorrow, and exaltation. From their total of practically four thousand involved at one time or another in the fighting, the casualties in dead, wounded, and missing reached ninety-three. Though small, the losses were magnified in the people's minds as they considered the circumstances of the day, particularly the opening blast at Lexington. But if their sensibilities were roused in this respect, their enthusiasm at their own military prowess knew no limits. Thus bound with the threads of anger and excited confidence, the package of news was carried by fast couriers to all the colonies. The information was explosive. Not only did it quicken the emotions of men of that day, but, even now, the significance of Lexington and Concord awakens a response in Americans that goes far beyond the details of the day or the identity of the foe. An unmilitary people, at first overrun by trained might, had eventually risen in their wrath and won a hard but splendid triumph. We have seen parallels or near-parallels too many times in subsequent history to let the significance remain but an epitaph in stone on the Lexington green.

III

The Costly Victory at Bunker Hill

The events of April 19 were decisive in altering relationships between the colonies and the mother country. If news of the day appalled Tories in London and touched off a good deal of Whig sympathy for the Americans, it electrified the colonies. The Middle and Southern Colonies appropriated arms and munitions and organized militia companies, while the Second Continental Congress, which convened on May 10, provided for the purchase of munitions and weapons. The Provincial Congress of Massachusetts, faced with the immediate situation, met on April 22, estimated that thirty thousand men would be required for defense, and authorized the raising of thirteen thousand six hundred troops within the Bay Colony itself. Artemas Ward, old, sick, and indecisive, but impressive in service experience during the French and Indian War, was made general. He was assisted by a capable second-in-command, John Thomas, and by Colonel Richard Gridley, the engineer who had demonstrated such remarkable ability at the siege of Louisburg.

Massachusetts, however, was not left to fight alone. On the 25th, Rhode Island agreed to send to Boston fifteen hundred men under Nathanael Greene, a young Quaker with a penchant for reading military history. The very next day, Connecticut set its quota at six thousand, with the judicious Brigadier General Joseph Spencer as leader of its contingent and the grizzled, old Indian fighter and West Indian veteran, Brigadier General Israel Putnam, as its outstanding personality. Finally, on May 20, New Hampshire decided on a force of two thousand under the stubborn, tough-minded farmer, John Stark.

The New England army gathering around Boston had its work cut out for it. Regimental organization was crude, and men were appointed to command positions whose ability might be nil but whose family or local influence was important. Luckily the Americans had in Dr. Warren the dynamo of their cause. Living at Ward's headquarters in Cambridge, Warren proved the moving spirit in both the Provincial Congress and the committee of safety. Ward also helped in holding together the miscellaneous assortment of colonial forces. Each colony maintained its own establishment, enlisting its personnel, appointing and commissioning its officers, setting its own pay scale, and providing the necessary supplies.[1] Enlistments were generally for the duration of the year, but it was not easy to hold all the raw troops in the routine of camp life as the farming season advanced. Nor were there enough troops or cannon to secure the network of defenses which, in May, Colonel Gridley started to construct from the Mystic to Dorchester. Though hope, not unfounded, persisted that a sufficient number of troops might eventually be available, the cannon posed a graver problem.

Plans were not lacking to obtain ordnance. The greatest park of artillery in the colonies was at Fort Ticonderoga. Though it was now garrisoned by only forty-two officers and men under a Captain Delaplace of the 26th Regiment, Gage, on April 19, had requested Sir Guy Carleton in Canada to send the 7th Regiment to Crown Point or Ticonderoga without delay.[2] The idea of capturing the fort before reinforcements could arrive seemed to have occurred more or less simultaneously to several individuals, including Ethan Allen, Benedict Arnold, and Major John Brown of Pittsfield, who may have suggested the venture to Silas Deane, Samuel Parsons, and Samuel Wyllys of Connecticut. After Arnold arrived at Cambridge with a well-trained, well-equipped militia company from New Haven, he submitted a detailed report of the condition of Ticonderoga to the committee of safety and set forth a plan to take the fort and Crown Point. The committee duly commissioned him and authorized him to raise an expeditionary force of four hundred men in western Massachusetts. Scarcely had he arrived in Stockbridge on May 6 when he heard of another expedition under Ethan Allen assembling for the same purpose at Castleton, Vermont. Leaving the recruiting to subordinates, Arnold dashed for Castleton.

His expectations of taking command of Allen's force were disappointed. Though Arnold claimed the command by virtue of his commission from the Massachusetts committee of safety, Allen rested his case on a commission from the Connecticut Assembly and declined to give up his "Green Mountain Boys," some two hundred men from Vermont, Massachusetts, and Connecticut. The Boys, moreover, favored Allen. After hot argument, a kind of joint-command was agreed on, though the Boys tended to regard Arnold as just another volunteer rather than as their co-commander.

The expedition now wasted little time in starting. Converging on Hand's Cove on the east side of Lake Champlain, about two miles north of Ticonderoga, the raiders, numbering between three and four hundred by the night of May 9, combed the vicinity for boats. Though not enough were found to transport all the raiders across the lake, Allen and Arnold managed to get eighty-three men onto the west shore by just before daylight. Allen harangued the men and led them over a cart path skirting the lake side of the fort and through the wicket gate onto the parade ground. When a sentry sought to interpose, Allen wounded him slightly with his sword and ordered the bewildered soldier to show the way to Delaplace's quarters. The man pointed to a stairs leading to the officers' quarters in the second story.

Leaping up the stairs, Allen shouted for Delaplace, the "damned old rat," to come out or the garrison would be put to death. Holding his breeches in his hand, and possibly followed by his wife, the sleepy commander opened the door. Allen at once demanded the surrender of the fort. When asked by what authority, Allen allegedly replied, "In the name of the great Jehovah and the Continental Congress."[3] With Allen's sword literally held over his head, Delaplace might be pardoned for deciding, however reluctantly, that he had no choice but to comply. Allen was a rough character.

Congress, of course, had given Allen no such authority, but the claim was not out of keeping with the man's flair for exaggeration. For example, according to him, his men displayed such resistless fury that the garrison was terrified into not firing. At any rate, when the sun rose with "a superior lustre" that morning, said Allen, the "conquerors . . . tossed about the flowing bowl"; and this last exploit we may well believe. Surely it had been a thrilling victory, a bloodless triumph over Delaplace's detachment, which included, apart from commissioned personnel, thirty-seven enlisted men, with twenty-four women and children. On the other hand, despite the contemporary and subsequent hyperbole attributed to the venture in terms of its hardships and derring-do, the capture of the fort proved of inestimable value. It was the heavy guns of Ticonderoga that eventually drove the British out of Boston, while lighter calibers, presently sent on after Arnold's inventory, helped hem the British in until the weightier ordnance could be sledged eastward the following winter.

But more victories were still to come. Two days after the fall of Ticonderoga, one of Allen's detachments under Seth Warner seized Crown Point, which the English had hastily demolished and evacuated before the Americans arrived. Another band captured Skenesborough and a schooner belonging to the prominent Loyalist, Major Philip Skene, a British army veteran. Arnold at once took command of this craft, armed it, and sailed north to capture Fort St. John on the Sorel. He succeeded in taking the fort, its garrison, and a sloop, and then sailed back down the lake, only to meet Allen and a force rowing northward in bateaux bound for the same objective. It is not difficult to imagine the fiery Arnold's satisfaction at having finally beaten his blustering rival to the punch. His enjoyment, however, was brief. When he proceeded to garrison Crown Point and to assume command of such craft as might pass for a little navy on the lake, Connecticut claimed a usurpation of its rightful authority and conquests, an assertion to which Massachusetts reluctantly assented. Disgusted, Arnold discharged his recruits and returned to Cambridge in June.

Meanwhile the siege of Boston had begun to tighten. New Hampshire minutemen arrived by sunrise of April 21, about the same time that Israel Putnam, after having rounded up many of the militia near his Connecticut farm, galloped into camp. As volunteers from neighboring colonies reported for duty, the total number of Americans around Boston swelled to considerably over ten thousand. Detachments of these troops now busied themselves in driving the livestock from the islands in and around Boston harbor. Several small actions resulted which were generally favorable to the Americans. Actually the British navy should have secured the livestock as soon as the investment of the town commenced, but Admiral Graves appears to have believed that, until orders should arrive from the Admiralty explicitly directing him to assist Gage, the navy was not yet at war;

despite Bunker Hill, this state of mind persisted through a large portion of the summer.[4]

On the other hand, it is probable that Graves, like many of the British, regarded the siege as merely a temporary inconvenience which would be abruptly terminated with the arrival of reinforcements from England. Though reinforcements did appear, doubling the size

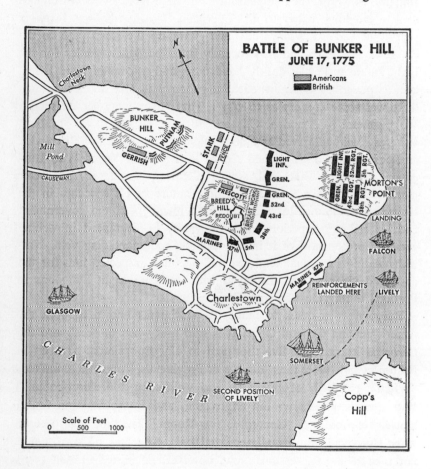

of the garrison, the total force available fell far short of the twenty thousand men Gage had asked for in late 1774. More significant was the distinguished cargo brought in by the 36-gun frigate *Cerberus* on May 25: Major Generals William Howe, Henry Clinton, and John Burgoyne.

The arrival of this "triumvirate of reputation," as Burgoyne described it,[5] was hailed by a London wit with a bit of derisive verse:

> Behold the Cerberus the Atlantic plough.
> Her precious cargo, Burgoyne, Clinton, Howe.
> Bow, wow, wow!

Initially, however, their appearance on the American scene did not seem a laughing matter to all Americans. Howe, who was forty-six years old, had led Wolfe's advance guard up the steep path to the Plains of Abraham and had recently introduced new tactics for the Light Infantry. Portly, darkly handsome, and a lover of good living, he was nevertheless renowned as a gallant and able soldier, though there was some mystery as to why a Tory government should send a Whig general to America. Clinton, thirty-seven years old, stubborn and irascible, had served as aide-de-camp to the Prince of Brunswick and possessed a distinguished record in the Seven Years' War. Burgoyne, fifty-three years old, was a picturesque and racy character more widely known for the histrionic nature of his speeches in the House of Commons, his intimacy with members of the government and his military superiors, and the vanity he evidenced in writing verse or prose, most of it in a pompous, rodomontading vein. Notwithstanding such qualifications, military men respected him for the dash and vigor he had displayed with the 16th Light Dragoons in Portugal during the war with France.

Burgoyne was quick to make his sentiments known to both the Americans and General Gage. It is said that when those aboard the *Cerberus* learned that five thousand regular troops were shut up in Boston by only twice their number of Provincials, Burgoyne remarked, "What! . . . Well, let *us* get in, and we'll soon find elbow-room."[6] Wits quickly picked up the expression, and Burgoyne soon found himself referred to as "General Elbow-Room." The time was to come when Burgoyne, who usually enjoyed jests, especially his own, could not tolerate the expression. Now, however, he busied himself complaining about Gage to his superiors in London and helping the governor compose a proclamation issued June 12. The proclamation imposed martial law, declaring those in arms against the king and those abetting them to be rebels and traitors. Nevertheless, pardon was offered to all in arms except the "parricides," Samuel Adams and

John Hancock, whose "flagitious" offenses were deserving only of "condign punishment."[7]

The American reply to the haughty, unbending, ferocious nature of the proclamation was not long in coming. Meeting on June 15, the committee of safety agreed to recommend to the council of war that Bunker Hill be fortified. As early as May 12, a joint committee from the committee of safety and the council had urged that works be constructed on, among other places, Winter Hill, Prospect Hill, and Bunker Hill. Though agreement existed on the first two, strong differences of opinion prevailed about Bunker. Ward and Warren thought its occupation might bring on a general engagement which the Americans, for lack of munitions and proper training, would not be able to sustain. On the other hand, Putnam and Colonel William Prescott welcomed the chance to combat the growing dissatisfaction at the inactivity of the army, and felt that on Bunker the British could be met on equal terms. As Putnam pointed out, the Americans would have the distinct advantage of fighting from entrenchments. "Americans," said the old veteran with shrewd insight, "were not afraid of their heads, though very much afraid of their legs; if you cover these, they will fight forever."[8] But more cautious counsel obtained at the time. Bunker Hill and Dorchester Heights would be occupied only when the army was sufficiently organized, trained, and equipped to defend them.

Though Gage's proclamation helped change the minds of the American command, its effect was more in the character of completing a change already in process. That change had originally been initiated by intelligence reaching headquarters on June 13 that Gage had made up his mind to seize Dorchester Heights on the night of June 18. On the 15th, the committee of safety, professing to know little about the Dorchester situation, left to the council's discretion the fortification of Dorchester but urged the occupation of Bunker Hill.[9] The military complied at once with the recommendation concerning Bunker and ignored the Heights.

The isthmus on which lay Charlestown, at that time a community of between three and four hundred houses, contained three principal elevations: Bunker Hill, Breed's Hill, and Morton's Hill. Dunker, round, smooth, and one hundred and ten feet high, lay nearest the neck connecting Charlestown with the mainland, the Neck itself

being so low that occasionally the tides swept across it. South of
Bunker a ridge of land joined Breed's Hill, seventy-five feet high, an
elevation steep on the east and west; the upper east slope was used
for hayfields and pastures, while at the foot of the east slope were
clay pits and brick kilns. Morton's Hill, thirty-five feet high, lay to
the southeast and sloped to Morton's Point. A road extended from
the Point directly over Bunker and across the Neck. Another road,
connecting with the one first mentioned, as well as with Charlestown
and the main road from Charlestown to the Neck, encircled Breed's
Hill.

The British were aware of the advantages of having the entire
isthmus under their control. Even so lethargic an officer as Admiral
Graves had recommended, shortly after Lexington and Concord, that
Charlestown be burned, Bunker Hill occupied, Roxbury destroyed
and its elevation seized. Gage had protested that the Americans were
too strong and that his own army was too weak. In mid-June, however, he felt more secure. His force augmented to approximately
ten thousand and his will strengthened by the major generals and
their eagerness to find "elbow-room," he determined to seize Dorchester Heights on the 18th, the one position where heavy cannon
could sweep his lines on Boston Neck, drop shells into Castle William, and make the fleet anchorage untenable.[10] Unfortunately for
Gage, within hours of the execution of his plan, he found himself
compelled to face the other way, toward Charlestown and its neighboring hills.

The American occupation of the isthmus was swiftly and efficiently
carried out. Parts of the regiments of Colonels Frye, Bridges, and
Prescott, Captain Samuel Gridley's two-piece battery, and a fatigue
party of two hundred Connecticut troops under Captain Thomas
Knowlton assembled on Cambridge Common at six o'clock in the
late afternoon of June 16. Altogether, they totaled about twelve hundred. Orders stipulated that they come equipped with packs, blankets,
and one day's rations. A tall, broad-shouldered, energetic officer,
Prescott had displayed such coolness and skill at Louisburg, years
before, that he had been offered a commission in the British regular
establishment. On the Common, President Langdon of Harvard
prayed that the Almighty would bless the enterprise, and later, at
nine o'clock, the column moved quietly toward Charlestown under

cover of darkness. Upon arrival, the leaders decided to make the chief stand on Breed's, nearer to Boston and the shipping, and to construct covering works on Bunker as well.[11] Presently dirt began to fly as hundreds of strong hands plied pickaxe and spade in nervous haste.

There was reason enough for both haste and silence. Colonel Gridley, the engineer in charge, planned a redoubt, roughly square, with about forty yards on each side. Aware that, against the British, the militiamen would need as much protection as possible, he arranged for a 6-foot parapet with firing platforms of earth and wood. He also directed the construction of a 6-foot breastwork, one hundred yards in length, from the northeast angle of the redoubt. He hoped to have the major portion of the fortifications ready before the daylight, which began about four o'clock, revealed the position to the British; it was now midnight.

But if Gridley had hopes, Prescott, on whom the command responsibility devolved, had worries. He was constantly harassed by the likely possibility that such extensive works would require more time to complete than the British would allow him. As soon as ground was broken, he sent a guard detachment to the lower part of Charlestown and the shore line southeast of the redoubt. At least twice during the night he joined the patrols to keep an anxious eye on the Boston shore and especially on the men-of-war. Off Morton's Point lay the *Falcon*; some two hundred yards southwest of her, the *Lively*; opposite Charlestown, the big *Somerset*; considerable distance to the northwest of her, the *Glasgow*; while the *Cerberus* and a number of floating batteries swung at their moorings within cannon-shot range. In the stillness of a clear, starlit night the American patrols could hear from the watch aboard ship and even from the sentries in Boston the cry "All's well!" Although no challenge came from ship or shore until darkness began to fade, Clinton's keen ears heard the activity in the course of the night and recommended, with Howe's approval, an attack at daybreak; but Gage considered the uncertainty of the new development hardly worth losing a night's sleep.

It was about four o'clock, perhaps as the watch was changing, that sailors aboard the *Lively* spotted the entrenchments. Without waiting for instructions from Admiral Graves, Captain Bishop ordered his boatswain to pipe to quarters and bent a line from his ship's quarter to her cable so that by hauling in or slacking it he could bring her into the most effective firing position. Presently the crash of the *Lively*'s broadside guns shattered the morning stillness. The rolling echoes had scarcely subsided before a battery on Copp's Hill joined in the uproar. One can imagine the shock to British complacency as the Boston garrison sprang from their beds to view through the high, drifting smoke from the *Lively* and the Copp's Hill battery the fresh earthen walls on Breed's Hill. At first Graves ordered the firing to cease; then he issued a "commence firing" order to the entire fleet.

While the fleet was thus testing the Provincials, the British held a council of war. All the officers present were agreed that the works must be carried, but the method of attack opened up an area of discussion in which differences of rank counted. Clinton was strongly of the opinion that the Americans should be attacked at once, not frontally but in the rear after he himself had landed with troops on Charlestown Neck.[12] His idea was entirely sound. Though a dam would prohibit a landing from the Charles, British command of the sea could easily have made possible a landing from the Mystic. In their criticisms of the battle, writers from the time of the contemporary historian, Stedman, have not failed to point out that a shallow-draft transport like the *Symmetry,* armed with eighteen 9-pounders and supported by the floating batteries, could have cut off an American retreat and prevented the arrival of reinforcements; this done, the Americans could then have been attacked in the rear where the redoubt was unfinished so early in the day, or could have been overcome simply by being starved out. As a British officer, writing on July 5, 1775, remarked, "Had we intended to have taken the whole rebel army prisoners, we need only have landed in their rear," a move which would have "shut them up in the Peninsula as in a bag. . . ."[13]

Gage, however, felt differently. It may well be, as has been alleged,[14] that he thought it a violation of military practice to interpose a part of his army between two divisions of the Americans. Certainly, so far as time was concerned, it was adjudged unwise to attempt a landing before early afternoon when the tide would be high.[15] Hence the whole venture must wait until the Americans completed their work and then the British would deliver a powerful frontal attack. This was the military thing to do! Once impress the rebels with a real show of force and their entire army might melt away in terror and impotence. Provincials, even behind entrenchments, could not stand against British bayonets in the hands of troops led by General Howe. Howe's assault force was to consist of the 5th, 38th, 43d, and 52d Regiments and a detachment from the 4th Artillery Battalion. The 47th Regiment and the 1st Marine Battalion were to be held in reserve.

Meanwhile, despite the cannonade, the Americans stood fast. Though shot from the ships did little harm, the noise was terrifying to many of the men. Presently, moreover, a cannon ball killed a soldier, and there was a moment of panic as Prescott himself was spattered with the brains of the victim. Quickly brushing off the blood and wiping his hands with a handful of clay, Prescott leaped to the parapet and unconcernedly strode along its length, encouraging the militia and joking with them. Other officers soon followed his example. This display of calmness and self-possession broke the tension to such a degree that the men actually began to cheer each ball that came near them.

As the forenoon slipped along, signs of activity in Boston disturbed Prescott. His men were hungry and exhausted. After consulting with his officers about nine o'clock, he sent Major (later Governor) Brooks to General Ward for reinforcements and supplies. Though Putnam had previously tried to induce Ward to hurry reinforcements, Ward was reluctant because of his fear that Gage might make his main attack on the American headquarters at Cambridge. Even after Brooks's representations, Ward remained unpersuaded except for dispatching one-third of John Stark's regiment. Not until the committee of safety, acting on advice from Richard Devens, supported Prescott's request did the general give in. Accordingly, at eleven o'clock, Ward ordered Stark's entire regiment, and Reed's as well, to Charlestown.

A half hour after the two New Hampshire regiments started, the British paraded on Boston Common in full fighting equipment, including packs and rations for three days, and marched in two columns, one to Long Wharf, the other to the North Battery. Their movement to the boats and barges was the cue for the ships, the floating batteries, and the guns on Copp's Hill to increase their fire. The ground in front of Breed's Hill was covered by the *Falcon* and *Lively*, that above the ferry landing by the *Somerset* and two floating batteries; the Neck

by the *Glasgow* and the *Symmetry*; and the works on Breed's by the
Copp's Hill battery, which was presently directed by Burgoyne. With
this massed fire in front of them, the troops were rowed to the Charlestown shore. Landing at Morton's Point at one o'clock, they fell into
three lines, munched their rations, and watched their commander as
he studied the American entrenchments. What Howe saw prompted
him, at two o'clock, to send the boats back to pick up his reserve,
the 47th Foot and the 1st Marines, both landing nearer Charlestown
and something over two hundred yards southwest of the initial
landing.[16]

The scarlet tide flooding the base of Breed's and overlapping the
shore along the Mystic was proof enough to the American leaders
that the test would not be long deferred. No reinforcements had as
yet arrived. In fact, the men ordered by Putnam, who had put in an
appearance, to carry the entrenching tools back to Bunker Hill had
not returned. Soon, however, General Warren strode into the redoubt
with the welcome word that reinforcements were on the way. When
Warren approached him, Prescott offered to give him the command,
but the physician declined; though suffering from a headache, he was
determined to fight as a private soldier in the place where the hottest
fighting was likely to occur.

The area now occupied by the British led Prescott to weaken his
center to protect his left flank. Detaching Captain Knowlton with the
Connecticut troops and two cannons, the colonel, perhaps acting on
Putnam's advice, sent them to a position behind a stone-and-rail fence
about two hundred yards to the rear of the redoubt and covering the
slope of Bunker Hill. Knowlton quickly constructed a zigzag rail
fence in front of this and filled the space between with hay curing
in the field. Before three o'clock, he was joined by Colonel Stark,
who had steadfastly refused to hurry his regiment across the Neck
despite the British fire since, in his opinion, "One fresh man in action
is worth ten fatigued ones."[17] Though Putnam had kept part of Stark's
command to strengthen the entrenchments being dug on Bunker Hill,
Stark led the rest to Knowlton's position, where they helped extend
the fence by building a stone wall on the beach to the water's edge.
Presently other reinforcements belatedly arrived from Cambridge,
most of them Massachusetts troops. With six cannons and between
fourteen hundred and seventeen hundred men and boys, Prescott

faced Howe and the British general's assault force of between twenty-two and twenty-five hundred well-trained troops.

About three o'clock, Howe deployed his troops into assault positions. The Light Infantry were to push along the beach, hit the extreme left, and roll up the entire American left flank, while the Grenadiers, with the 5th and 52d in support, engaged the rail-fence position frontally. The British left wing under Brigadier General Pigot was more extended, the 43d and 38th aiming for the breastwork, the 47th and Major Pitcairn's Marines concentrating on the redoubt. The main thrust was to be made by the British right against the rail fence, and Howe led these troops in person. It was anticipated that, once the Americans were dislodged from this position, the British right could bear to the left and completely encircle the entrenchments on Breed's.

Meanwhile, to cover the deployment and advance, the eight British fieldpieces and howitzers opened a sharp but generally ineffectual fire on the breastwork. Presently this fire died away, and Howe learned to his annoyance that the 6-pounders had been supplied with a number of 12-pound balls. Though he requested that grapeshot be used at once, the guns sank in the marshy ground at the foot of the hill near the brick kilns. The distance from that point was so great for grape that the guns were useless. It was alleged by one British combatant that the artillery blunder was directly attributable to an officer of high rank who, instead of attending to his duties, spent his whole time "dallying" with the daughters of a Boston schoolmaster.[18]

Though Pigot's attack was considered of secondary importance to Howe's, its conspicuous position made it the center of attention. Pigot's orderly ranks covered the green fields, and the scene on this cloudless day must indeed have been brilliant for the spectators in Boston who crowded the rooftops and even huddled against the steep slopes of church spires. Gage himself studied the panorama through a glass from Christ's. Through the mounting smoke from the guns of the fleet and on Copp's Hill the lines of scarlet and white were plainly visible. If the sight of such splendor and might gave Gage cause for satisfaction, evidence indeed that the rebels would soon appreciate the real consequences of their challenge to the British crown, the troops themselves could not have felt so pleased or comfortable. Their equipment—musket, ammunition, cartridge box, rations, and pack—was estimated by a contemporary to weigh one hundred and twenty-five pounds. If the estimate was correct, the remarkable fact, as one historian has pointed out, was that the troops were ever able to get up the hill.[19] Very likely the equipment weighed only about half that estimated, but, even so, it was heavy enough for troops engaged in such desperate work. Yet as they pushed through the high grass and climbed the numerous fences, their confidence appeared in no wise affected by the obstructions, the scorching heat, or the enemy awaiting them. On the other hand, not all the British were so unperturbed at this early stage, for American skirmishers posted in Charlestown were making conditions rather disagreeable for Pigot's left flank.

In the meantime, the Americans restrained their emotions as best they could. Though Prescott bade the men hold their fire until he gave the order, the practice of the British in firing by volley as they came on proved too much for a number of the Americans; in their impatience or their nervousness, they fired at the redcoats. Prescott and his subordinates had to work quickly to get the men in hand. Some officers even ran along the parapet kicking up the hastily leveled muskets. When Prescott finally gave the order, and a blast of fire slashed from the bristling mass of muskets, the British line staggered. Though halted, the troops tried stoutly to return the fire of the defenders. Within a few minutes, however, the storm of shot proved so deadly that Pigot's wing fell back. Moving ahead was like walking into a furnace.

Over on the right Howe was meeting no better fortune than Pigot. Though the latter's advance extended over a wider front, it was more in the nature of a demonstration, and, even as that, fell short of expectations because of the distracting fire from the American marksmen posted in the houses of Charlestown. On Howe, however, rested the main British hopes, and with him were the choicest troops, the Grenadiers and Light Infantry, many of whom were probably burning to avenge their frustration on April 19. They ignored the gaps made in their ranks by the American cannon and pushed proudly on. When about one hundred yards from the rail fence, Howe deployed from column into line. This movement drew the fire of a few of the Americans, much to Putnam's anger; he threatened to shoot the next man who fired without orders. The scattered shots brought on several volleys from the British, but the shower of missiles was too high to do any real damage. Meanwhile the Americans waited, as had Prescott's men at the breastwork and the redoubt. Their attention was called to the point where the pipe-clay shoulder belts of the British soldiers crossed near the waistband; if such a mark proved too small, they could hardly miss the scarlet coats. As for the British officers, these could be distinguished by their more splendid attire and their gorgets glittering in the sun. Possibly it was now that Putnam made the famous statement attributed to him, "Men, you are all marksmen —don't one of you fire until you see the white of their eyes."[20]

When the mass of scarlet advanced to within fifty yards, a range at which the eighteenth-century musket was highly effective, Putnam gave the order to fire. At once the rail fence seemed almost to break into flame, and the wind of death blew harshly over the field. Many an American had crammed not only a bullet but also several buckshot down the barrel of his musket, while, if he lacked buckshot, he had decided that rusty nails and bits of glass would suffice.[21] Though horribly decimated, the officers suffering with particular severity, the British tried to return the fire. But the carnage was so dreadful that the troops were forced to withdraw, and only with the greatest difficulty were the American leaders able to restrain their men from jumping the fence and pursuing the retreating redcoats.

Neither Howe nor Pigot would think of letting the battle go by default at this stage. With the American cheers ringing in their ears, the British regrouped, the 52d, 43d, 38th, and 5th forming respectively to the left of the Grenadiers, and the 47th and the 1st Marines still on the extreme left. Howe made up his mind that this time the troublesome fire on Pigot's flank should be eliminated. Presently, after his messenger reached Boston, shells from Burgoyne's battery on Copp's Hill set Charlestown ablaze and smoked out most, though not all, of the marksmen there. Now, once again, Howe and Pigot led their troops toward the entrenchments.

Burgoyne, watching the battle through a glass from Copp's Hill, described the scene in lively if somewhat florid language:

And now ensued one of the greatest scenes of war that can be conceived, if we looked to the height, Howe's corps ascending the hill in the face of entrenchments and in the face of a very disadvantageous ground, was much engaged; to the left the enemy pouring in fresh troops by thousands, over the land, and in the arm of the sea our ships and floating batteries cannonading them; straight before us a large and noble town in one great blaze; the church steeples being of timber, were great pyramids of fire above the rest; behind us the church steeples and heights of our own camp, covered with spectators of the rest of our army who were (not) engaged; the hills round the country covered with spectators, the enemy all in anxious suspense; the roar of cannon, mortars, and musketry, the crush of churches, ships upon the stocks, and whole streets falling together in ruin to fill the ear; the storm of the redoubts with the objects above described to fill the eye, and the reflection that perhaps a defeat was the final loss to the British Empire in America, to fill the mind, made the whole a picture and a complication of horror and importance beyond anything that ever came to my lot to be witness to. . . ."[22]

This second ascent was much more difficult for the British than the first. The ground was liberally sprinkled with the bodies of their dead and wounded comrades. Yet the men stepped over these as if they were so many logs of wood. In places, too, the grassy slope was now mucky with clay and blood. Notwithstanding such horror, the scarlet lines pushed coolly on. Then the American muskets crashed, and the front rank went down. The American aim was simply too deadly, particularly for the 52d owing to its especially exposed position near some brick kilns. Suddenly a number of the attackers could stand the continuous stream of fire no longer and broke for the protection of the beaches. Soon Pigot's entire line was retreating in disorder.

The sight was too much for General Clinton. Having been ordered by Gage to send the 1st Marines and the 47th Regiment to Howe if the occasion seemed necessary, he had long ago dispatched them at Howe's request; now he ordered the 2d Marines and the 63d Regiment readied. He also threw himself into a boat, hastened across the Charles, and landed to the north of Charlestown under so deadly a fire from sharpshooters still hiding in the town that two men in his boat were hit before he left it. Once ashore he discovered that officers could not control their men. "I never saw so great a want of order," he said.[23] But Clinton was equal to the occasion. Hurriedly he gathered together a number of the bewildered troops, encouraged some of the ambulatory wounded to join them, and formed all in line for one last try. It was a spirited act for which Howe hardly gave Clinton sufficient credit.[24]

As for Howe on the right, his troops were in as bad a plight as

Pigot's. "Our light-infantry," wrote one Englishman, "were served up in companies against the grass fence, without being able to penetrate . . . Most of our grenadiers and light-infantry . . . lost three fourths, and many nine tenths of their men. Some had only eight or nine men a company left; some only three, four, and five."[25] Desperately the British officers sought to get their men forward, but at thirty yards from the murderous muskets the scarlet ranks toppled as if blown down. Noncoms took over when the officers fell, and when the sergeants and corporals likewise crumpled, the senior privates stepped into their places. Howe himself seemed to bear a charmed life. Every member of his personal staff was shot down. But, alive though he remained, his exhortations proved of little avail. His men had had enough of looking death in the face and now fell back swiftly to the beaches. Though they did not actually break, Howe admitted that "there was *a moment that I never felt before.*"[26] In view of his appalling losses and the imminence of defeat and disgrace, it is understandable if, as so many writers have since asserted, and not without reason, Howe's nerve was never quite the same after Bunker Hill.

The crisis of the battle was now approaching. The burning question in both forces was whether Howe would try it again. His left had clearly been staggered, while his right had incurred heavy losses. He had early committed his reserve, the 47th and the 1st Marines, and had received as reinforcements only a small number of Marines; neither the 63d nor the 2d Marines had yet arrived.[27] A number of Howe's officers implored him not to return to the hill, but others could not hide their humiliation at the treatment they had received and were hot to venture the slope again. His splendid scarlet coat and white knee breeches stained with his own sweat and with blood that had spatted from comrades' wounds, Howe made the fateful decision: he would try the hill once more.

Now Howe was more realistic. He ordered his men to drop their packs and depend on the bayonet. This time, moreover, the attack would be concentrated on the breastwork and the redoubt. The Light Infantry were simply to demonstrate at the rail fence, while all other units were deployed farther to the left than the last time. The Grenadiers were to converge on the breastwork with the 43d and the 52d. The 38th and 5th swung into new positions, the 38th forming on the 43d's left flank and aiming for the extreme right of the breastwork, the 5th deploying to the left of the 38th with the redoubt as its objective. The 47th and the 1st Marines, in the order named, were to fan out to the left of the 38th and close in on the long southwest face of the redoubt. Howe also ordered the artillery, swampy ground or not, into a position where it could enfilade the breastwork with grape. Howe was all crisp decision; he felt that his personal honor and the honor of the army were at stake. He purposed to lead the right again in person, while Pigot and Clinton took care of the left.

With this regrouping taking place, the Americans made ready as best they could. Sensing the British disposition to concentrate on the breastwork and the redoubt and that this would be the climactic assault, Prescott resolved to hold the hill to the last. He had little real hope, however, unless reinforcements arrived from Bunker Hill, where Putnam was vainly trying to straighten out the tangle of regiments and get at least a few companies onto Breed's. It was actually not the fresh troops themselves that Prescott most desired so much as the powder in their possession. His own troops had expended fully thirty rounds per man, and there was barely one round left for each; only by breaking open a brace of cannon cartridges remaining were some of the troops able to secure a couple of rounds apiece. Unfortunately such reinforcements as did arrive were too few to strengthen the defense appreciably, except at the rail fence, before the British columns moved grimly to the assault.

If there had been hesitancy on the part of the British while near the shore at renewing the battle, there was none now. Though, as Stark said, their fallen lay as thick as sheep in a fold, they pressed forward relentlessly. The Americans obeyed Prescott's order strictly and waited until the British were within twenty yards. Once again, redcoats went down at the burst of flame, but not enough powder remained in American possession to hold off the British. Their bayonets came bristling over the breastwork and redoubt from three sides. In the van, at the head of the 1st Marines, was Major Pitcairn. Wounded twice previously in the afternoon, and now shot down with four bullets in his body, he died in the arms of his son after urging his men to show what the Marines could do. Likewise Lieutenant Colonel Abercrombie, commander of the Grenadiers, was taken to the boats with a mortal wound; yet he begged that his old friend, Israel Putnam, be saved from the hangman's noose.

But if distinguished Britons fell in the moment of victory, the suffering was not confined to their side. Though reduced to throwing stones or parrying bayonets with musket butts, many Americans stoutly opposed the onrush as hundreds of their comrades hurried for the exit of the redoubt. The dust, however, rose so thickly that it obscured the exit. Panic-stricken, numbers of Provincials climbed to the top of the wall and dropped over, fighting their way through the enemy to the open field beyond. Prescott himself turned away several bayonet thrusts with his sword and escaped with difficulty, his clothes tattered. The entrenchments now theirs, the British cheered lustily, formed ranks, and opened on the retreating Americans with a heavy fire. General Warren was killed, his body being left where it fell. Colonels Bridges and Gridley were hit, while Colonel Gardner was mortally wounded as he was leading troops of his regiment toward Breed's to cover the retreat to Bunker Hill. His second-in-command, Major Jackson, took over and, with companies from regiments belonging to Gardner, Ward, and Gerrish, carried out the covering action with notable skill. But most of the troops on Breed's might still have been cut off had not the men at the rail fence held their ground and covered the retreat from their position. Only when the hill was evacuated did the rail-fence units withdraw.

Once on Bunker, and on the way across the Neck, the retirement became less orderly, though even Burgoyne conceded that "The retreat was no flight; was covered with bravery and even military skill."[28] Great slaughter occurred on the crest of Bunker as Putnam, sweating and swearing, rode up and down entreating the troops to defend the unfinished works. "In God's name," he begged, "form, and give them one shot more!"[29] His efforts and those of General Pomeroy to rally the men were largely in vain. The troops pushed rapidly down the slope and streamed across the Neck, where shot from the *Glasgow,* the *Symmetry,* and the floating batteries killed numbers more.

With the British in possession of the peninsula, and the time being only five o'clock on a bright summer's afternoon, the pressing question now on each side was what the other army intended to do. Clinton entreated Howe to go on. Cambridge was but two miles away and inadequately defended, while the organization of the entire American army was in a state of vast confusion and ammunition was low.

Fortunately for the Americans, Howe exhibited at this stage a caution which he had not shown on the battlefield. Possibly he expected the Americans to try to recover the peninsula. Certainly his own troops had lost heavily, and, as he stated in his report to Gage, they were "too much harassed and fatigued to give much attention to the pursuit of the rebels. . . ."[30] Yet had he ventured on, taking half the chance he did in storming Breed's, he might have smashed the entire American army and scotched the military aspect of the rebellion then and there. Such, however, was not the disposition of William Howe that dreadful afternoon.

It is true that some inclination existed among the Americans to go back. Prescott stormed into Ward's headquarters at Cambridge, complained bitterly of the lack of support, and offered to retake the lost ground that night if Ward would give him fifteen hundred well-equipped troops. Tactfully Ward declined the offer. He felt that too much was at stake to risk such a dubious venture. Besides, he was in great anxiety lest Howe drive on to Cambridge. In addition, he was well aware that his army's losses had been considerable.

The complete tally of losses made the Battle of Bunker Hill, or the Battle of Charlestown, as it was alluded to by contemporaries, the bloodiest conflict on the continent until the Battle of New Orleans in 1815. Of the twenty-five hundred British troops engaged, one thousand and fifty-four were killed or wounded, or a total of forty-two per cent of the effective force. American casualties amounted to one hundred killed, two hundred and seventy-one wounded, and thirty taken prisoner. Five of the six American fieldpieces were abandoned.[31]

Whatever can be said of the steadfastness, determination, and raw, red courage amply displayed by both combatants, one must agree with Charles Francis Adams that "a more singular exhibition of apparently unconscious temerity on one side, and professional military incapacity on the other, it would be difficult to imagine."[32] The American occupation of the peninsula was a monumental blunder exceeded in its stupidity only by the British failure to nip off Prescott's entire force by seizing the Neck. Actually Fortune smiled on the Americans in at least three respects.[33] It was American good luck that the British chose to make a frontal attack instead of landing at the Neck. It was American good luck that Prescott was defeated on the third drive; had the Americans won, the British would have had no recourse but to follow Clinton's advice. Finally, it was American good luck that Prescott's offer to lead a force back over the Neck was declined; he would have been trounced and perhaps his entire force captured.

On another score the American luck was rather less than good. Certainly the battle appeared to be the great confirmation of the myth starting with the day of Concord and Lexington that amateur, half-disciplined militia were fully the equal of trained troops under any circumstances provided they possessed the ability to shoot. This myth, combined with the persistent, traditional, seventeenth-century English distrust of a standing army, has jeopardized the security of this country on not a few occasions. But as for the immediate situation, Gage had won his hill; and although the moral victory belonged to the Americans, they felt initially a greater sense of frustration and depression than of triumph.

IV

The Trials of Organizing an Army

While the siege of Boston was moving toward the bloody test at Bunker Hill, the Continental Congress considered the selection of a commander in chief for the army, whose regulation and direction the Massachusetts Congress had urged the Continental Congress to assume.[1] Colonel Washington of Virginia appeared the obvious choice. In the first place, the reputation he had acquired in the French and Indian War, especially his work in extricating the survivors of Braddock's expedition from the Pennsylvania woods, counted heavily, despite the fact that there were others with greater military experience. His presence, silent, forceful, commanding, was always impressive, an impressiveness deepened now by his attending Congress in the blue-and-buff uniform of the Virginia militia. Perhaps of even greater weight, however, was that such an eligible candidate came from Virginia. John Adams deemed it so necessary to swing Virginia and the other Southern Colonies to the side of New England that he could pass over the military aspirations of his fellow townsman, John Hancock, and, by allying with the Lees, bring about the election of Washington.[2] Though reluctant to leave his family and his beloved Mount Vernon, Washington accepted the position of general, for which Congress voted five hundred dollars per month as salary and expenses. Graciously Washington declined any salary but agreed to keep an accurate account of his expenses. Truly, as he wrote to an acquaintance, he had now "Imbarked on a tempestuous Ocean."[3]

But Congress did more than select a leader. It voted to raise fifteen thousand troops as a Continental army and ordered two million dollars struck for payment of the troops. It also proceeded to choose Washington's lieutenants. Four major generals were picked: Artemas

Ward, Charles Lee, Philip Schuyler, and Israel Putnam. Ward was virtually an inevitable choice because of his command of the troops around Boston. Described rather testily by Charles Lee as "a fat old gentleman, who had been a popular *church-warden*,"[4] Ward continued to serve until the British evacuated Boston. Lee was made the second major general. Possessed of a sharp tongue and a mercurial, unpredictable disposition, this odd, gangling person sold himself to the Americans. He had had an adventurous career, fighting in Central Europe and the Balkans and seeing service in America under Braddock and Sir William Johnson, whose Mohawks adopted him and aptly christened him "Boiling Water." Though retired on half pay in the British establishment, and living on his estate in Virginia, Lee threw in his lot with the Americans. Never lacking in self-esteem, he felt quite put out that Ward had been appointed over him. The third major general, Philip Schuyler, was a haughty, wealthy, well-intentioned New York landowner, prominent in the activities of the colony and of considerable experience as a soldier in the French and Indian War. The fourth major general, Israel Putnam, though deficient in a number of the larger abilities required, and most of the graces expected, of a general officer, was long on energy and courage, and possessed a rough but warm personality that endeared him to the troops. Putnam, incidentally, was the only one of the four on whose choice Congress was unanimous.

Eight brigadiers also were selected. Massachusetts topped the list with three, Seth Pomeroy, William Heath, and John Thomas. Connecticut followed with two, David Wooster and Joseph Spencer; New York with one, Richard Montgomery; New Hampshire with one, John Sullivan; and Rhode Island with one, Nathanael Greene. If a majority of these brigadiers were New Englanders, it was only natural, for most of the troops then in arms were from New England, but if political and geographical considerations prompted the selection, not all the brigadiers were lacking in military qualifications.[5] Pomeroy, Wooster, Spencer, and Thomas had served in earlier wars, though the first three were over sixty years of age and of doubtful physical stamina. Montgomery, an Irishman and one of Wolfe's veterans, had settled in the colonies in 1772. Along with Sullivan and Heath, he was under forty; neither Sullivan nor Heath, however, had had any battle experience prior to the outbreak of hostilities. Nathanael

Greene, thirty-three years old, also was innocent of battle until the siege of Boston. Of all the appointees, major generals as well as brigadiers, Greene was to become the most distinguished, though had Montgomery lived he might have rivaled the Rhode Island Quaker.

Congress presently made three other appointments of significance. Horatio Gates was designated as adjutant general with the rank of brigadier; Thomas Mifflin, on Washington's recommendation, was established as quartermaster general; and Colonel Joseph Trumbull of Connecticut was made commissary general. Gates, a friend of Washington, had been a major in the British army, was a veteran of Braddock's expedition, and had settled in Virginia in 1773. Mifflin was a young man of thirty-one, eminently successful as a Philadelphia merchant and politician. He was to discover, however, that supplying an army was far less simple than either he or his friends had anticipated; and before the war was over, he was to become a bitter enemy of Washington. Trumbull was the son of the vigorous, capable war governor of Connecticut, Jonathan Trumbull, and possessed much of the same energy and organizing ability as his father. He, too, was to find his work no sinecure.

Fully aware that he himself had been chosen by "the partiality of the Congress, joined to a political motive," Washington felt that should the worst happen, notwithstanding the use of his best judgment, he would have the consolation of knowing "the blame ought to lodge upon his appointers."[6] On the other hand, he was prepared to employ all his resources in carrying out the instructions of Congress. Briefly, he was to hold together the existing army, increase it if necessary to twice the size of the enemy's, and make it, through discipline and training, an effective fighting force.[7] He left Philadelphia on June 23, arrived in Cambridge on July 2, and assumed actual command the following day.

Washington found the condition of the army of which he now took direction "very healthy," but that was about all that pleased him. He was disturbed that only fourteen thousand five hundred men were fit for duty and that there existed a dearth of artillery, an insufficient number of trained engineers, and an inadequate war chest.[8] He found this a curious sort of army, curious by European or almost any standards. Except for the Rhode Island contingent, which alone was equipped with tents, the troops were quartered in the Harvard dormitories, in private homes, and in shelters of their own devising. Chaplain William Emerson, grandfather of Ralph Waldo, thought the variety of huts, shanties, and lean-tos "rather a beauty than a blemish in the army."[9] Washington, however, had an eye only for the blemish; without adequate tentage, the army could not take the field, and the lack of similar cover for all was not conducive to discipline.

The clothing deficiency, particularly among the Massachusetts troops, was another serious problem. To remedy the lack, and also to provide a sort of uniform, Washington hit upon the idea of a hunting shirt. A few units had their own uniforms, particularly those from Rhode Island and Connecticut. Generally the Americans fought in whatever clothes they could acquire, and the hunting shirt proved about as acceptable a uniform as any. Washington wrote Congress that ten thousand such shirts could be used at once. Congress, however, decided in November to provide adequate uniforms of brown cloth with facings in the regimental colors.[10] Eventually eleven of the thirteen states chose a dark blue as the most suitable shade for a uniform.

The problem of discipline was one of the most troublesome factors in the New England army. Most officers were elected, and the lamentable system persisted in lending itself to all manner of military evil for many years after the Revolution, the test of a militia officer being not military capacity but popularity. A number of officers even pooled their pay in a common stock, in the returns of which officers and privates shared equally, while other officers did not hesitate to cheat the government by drawing more pay and provisions than they had men in their companies.[11] Troublesome, too, was the refusal of many privates to recognize distinctions of rank, frequently, it would seem, with good reason, considering the character of a number of their superiors. But certain officers went out of their way to prove how democratic they were; despite vigorous measures adopted to enforce observance of distinctions of rank, a Connecticut cavalry captain, as late as October, 1776, was caught shaving one of his men (possibly an old customer!).[12]

Washington would have none of this "leveling" tendency, which may have been created, at least in part, by small-farm ownership and the peculiarities of the New England political and religious organization. Washington was accustomed to the use and observance of authority, as were so many Southerners, perhaps because of the nature of the plantation system.[13] Whatever the reasons for the existence of familiarity between officer and enlisted man, the Virginian sought to eliminate this free-and-easy attitude. One way, apart from punishment, was by enforcing the wearing of special insignia from the light-blue riband across the chest of the commander in chief to the stripe of green cloth on the left shoulder of a corporal.[14]

Both officers and men were strongly impressed with the need for discipline, and where moral suasion failed, the court-martial and the whip usually succeeded. Washington was especially anxious to rid the army of cowardly officers, and several who had shown the white feather at Bunker Hill were court-martialed. Attempts were also made to enforce a reasonably high level of camp sanitation. Old latrines were filled up and new ones dug each week. All offal and carrion were to be burned immediately. Barracks and company streets were ordered swept every morning. Company officers were directed to make daily inspections of camp kitchens and to see that the men prepared their food in a clean and proper manner. Remissness in guard duty was severely punished, while indiscriminate applications for furloughs were discouraged, loose women run out of camp, and drunken soldiers, of whom there were not a few, flogged. Washington relied heavily on flogging and, before the war ended, urged Congress to increase the Biblical maximum of thirty-nine strokes to five hundred; Congress, more conservative in this matter, rejected the request.[15] One way or another, however, Washington created an army at Boston. That was an achievement the luster of which no amount of criticism could dim. It was almost a miracle.

Still it was his good fortune, and that of the American cause as well, that the inactivity of the British made it possible for him to build one army and recruit another from the summer of 1775 into the winter of 1776. Though the New England army was reinforced as a result of a resolution of Congress on June 14 authorizing the enlistment of six companies of riflemen in Pennsylvania, two in Virginia, and two in Maryland, the terms of all the troops before Boston ran out by the end of the year. Washington, therefore, initiated his recruitment campaign for a Continental establishment in the third week of October. Assurance of a furlough and continuance of the pay scale then obtaining were offered as inducements. Sergeants were promised forty-eight shillings per month; corporals, forty-four; and privates, forty. Since the company officers felt slighted that they received so little more, representations to Congress secured the necessary raises so that a captain might henceforth draw twenty-six and two-thirds dollars per month; first and second lieutenants, eighteen dollars; and ensigns, thirteen and one-third dollars. Both officers and men were expected to furnish their own firearms. New clothing was to be issued to every noncom and soldier, for which a stoppage of ten shillings per month was to be made from each man's pay until the whole was cleared up, a provision which proved exceedingly unpopular. Such was the shortage of blankets that two dollars were allowed every noncom and soldier who brought his own blanket, and he was even permitted to take it away with him at the end of the campaign. The regiments into which the newly enlisted men were to be formed were to consist of eight companies, with each company having one captain, two lieutenants, one ensign, four sergeants, four corporals, two "Drums and Fifes," and seventy-six privates. All personnel were to be physically able, the stipulation being plainly expressed that "Neither Negroes, Boys unable to bare [sic] Arms, nor old men unfit to endure the fatigues of the campaign are to be inlisted."[16]

The military service of Negroes has been a recurrent problem in the history of this country. One factor which has invariably complicated the situation has been the Negro's patriotism. In the Revolution, whether freeman or slave, he was anxious to serve. Free Negroes fought at Bunker Hill, one of them, Salem Poor, winning the commendation of Colonel Prescott. Though, in July, the Provincial Congress came out against the enlistment of Negroes, and though, on October 23, the generals took a similar stand, the punitive activities of Lord Dunmore in Virginia may have forced Washington's hand; one of Dunmore's acts was a proclamation in November freeing slaves and servants to persuade them to serve with the British. At any rate, on December 30, Washington granted permission to recruiting officers to enlist free Negroes and promised to lay the matter before the Continental Congress, which he believed would approve. Congress did approve but with the reservation that only those free Negroes who had served faithfully in the army at Cambridge might re-enlist.[17] Notwithstanding continued attempts to prevent the use of Negroes, large numbers of them persisted in serving in the army, especially in the campaigns north of the Mason-Dixon Line. Southern slaveowners as a group were generally opposed to employing colored troops, and a suggestion that Negroes be organized into regiments under white officers, with a sprinkling of white soldiers in the ranks, was not happily received. It was pointed out that the enemy might make a practice of arming slaves, an act which might well bring about military and economic ruin for the South.[18]

Trouble over the enlistment of Negroes was only one of Washington's problems in connection with the entire process of recruitment. Sectional rivalry raised its head, with no colony wanting in its military establishment anyone but its own citizens. Earlier Washington had had trouble with the generals, Spencer's disgust at Putnam's promotion being so great that he left the army without signifying his intention to Washington or even visiting him. Thomas, who ranked Pomeroy and Heath in the Massachusetts forces, found himself below both in the Continental establishment and made up his mind to resign despite the entreaty of Washington who wrote to him personally. Fortunately Pomeroy resigned instead, leaving a vacancy to which the Continental Congress elevated Thomas.

At times the Virginian's celebrated temper broke under the trying conditions in Massachusetts. Writing testily to his cousin, Lund Washington, he said, "The People of this government have obtained a Character which they by no means deserved; their officers generally speaking are the most indifferent kind of People I ever saw . . . I dare say the Men would fight very well (if properly Officered) although they are an exceeding dirty and nasty people. . . ."[19] But the richest expression of his wrath was reserved for the Connecticut troops, most of whom, despite the pleas of their own officers, refused to re-enlist unless given a bounty. They were requested to remain until December 10, while, to offset their going, plans were made to call up three thousand minutemen and militia from Massachusetts and two thousand from New Hampshire. Notwithstanding the request, many of the Connecticut contingent left on December 1. Washington was thoroughly exasperated at the "dirty, mercenary spirit" of men "upon whom I reckoned" and who "basely deserted the Cause of their Country."[20] Not even the hisses and groans of the remaining troops, the showers of stones they hurled, or the insults and even the blandishments of the few female camp followers could induce the Connecticut men to remain.

Certainly Washington had good cause to be put out. Until the 1st of December, barely thirty-five hundred men had come forward to re-enlist, and to secure even this number it had been necessary to allow as many as fifty furloughs a regiment. Powder was alarmingly short, and hard money difficult to procure. He likewise deplored to Joseph Reed "that those who are employed to sign the Continental bills should not be able, or inclined, to do it as fast as they are wanted. They will prove the destruction of the army, if they are not more attentive and diligent." Exploding with wrath and despair, he continued, "Such a dearth of public spirit, and want of virtue, such stock-jobbing, and fertility in all the low arts to obtain advantages of one kind or another, in this great change of military arrangement, I never saw before, and pray God I may never be witness to again . . . Could I have foreseen what I have, and am likely to experience, no consideration upon earth should have induced me to accept this command."[21]

Though his feelings in the matter are quite understandable, Washington assumed a rather extreme view, owing, no doubt, to the heavy responsibilities of command. A wealthy man himself, he had difficulty at first in realizing that service in the army meant for most of the officers and practically all the enlisted men a great sacrifice. Farms were left untended save for such labor as wives and children could give. Army pay was small and uncertain; hence a bounty seemed eminently desirable, certainly something worth bargaining for. Stockjobbing and the like might flourish, but it was nothing new, and after his experience in the French and Indian War, Washington must surely have been aware of this. Furthermore, it is doubtful that the army was quite so mercenary or thoughtless as he may have considered; contemporary soldiers' diaries reveal loyalty and a religious earnestness that must surely be indicative of some moral purpose.[22]

With the approach of winter, the fortunes of the army began to improve in certain respects. Captain Manly, a privateersman both able and lucky, captured a royal ordnance brig, the *Nancy*, in late November. Among other items, the *Nancy* contained two thousand muskets, one hundred thousand flints, over thirty tons of musket shot, thirty thousand round shot, eleven mortar beds, and a brass mortar. When the stores reached Cambridge from Cape Ann, the troops shouted their exultation. Amid roars of laughter, "Old Put" climbed the 13-inch mortar with a bottle of rum in his hand and, at Mifflin's suggestion, christened the piece, "Congress."[23] The recruit situation also improved temporarily. Though the withdrawal of the Connecticut troops resulted in a flood of comparatively undisciplined militia from Massachusetts and New Hampshire, Washington was pleased with the response. True, firewood and hay were lacking, but energetic measures were undertaken by the army and the provincial authorities to remedy the matter. Powder, of course, was as scarce as ever. On the other hand, food was fairly plentiful, though prices were inclined to be dear, the bread was often sour, and, until Greene held a board of inquiry consisting of butchers, the "beef" was usually horse meat. But complaints were not overly numerous or serious. If a soldier's stomach is kept full, he can stand privation in other respects with a reasonable degree of cheerfulness. There were so few really hungry soldiers in the siege lines around Boston that winter that one might say it was with food rather than with troops and arms that Washington kept the British locked up in the city.[24]

V

The Siege and Evacuation of Boston

Meanwhile, if the Americans were having their troubles holding the siege, the British were not exactly enjoying their confinement. Bunker Hill had been a shocking experience, and the criticisms that broke out within the garrison did not hesitate to blame Gage. Burgoyne's complaint was less one of criticism of the strategy of Bunker Hill than of exasperation at Gage's amiable incompetence as a governor who should have seen that adequate provision had been made for food, forage, money, intelligence, and the like. The sharp commentary on Gage became rather general in England as well, with the result that presently he was recalled and Howe given command, Gage sailing for England on October 10. Wits recommended that he be elevated as Lord Lexington, Baron of Bunker Hill.[1]

But if the British expected the change of commanders would bring about a vigorous attempt to break the siege, they were disappointed. Though decidedly more popular than his predecessor, and militarily more capable, Howe proved quite as lethargic. Howe and Graves, moreover, pulled together no more effectively than had Gage and Graves. The admiral, who had a certain affinity for graft, and who had risen through the patronage of the corrupt Earl of Sandwich, head of the Admiralty, continued as procrastinating and incompetent as ever, permitting the New Englanders to slip privateers into the English shipping lanes and quarreling with the military and the commissioner of customs. Burgoyne was quick to assess, and bitter in his comments on, the admiral's feelings, though his was but one of many voices whose growing volume of criticism eventually induced the king to withdraw Graves.[2] Still Admiral Shuldham, who arrived the last of December, proved about as inactive a successor to Graves as Howe was to Gage.

While they were cooped up in Boston, the great problem facing the British was that of supply. Virtually every bit of food had to be brought in by sea, a situation which generally obtained for the British throughout the war. Cork, in Ireland, was the main food and troop depot. Though the West Indies supplied the vast quantities of beer and rum consumed, Cork shipped to America most of the meat, vegetables, and cereals. Unfortunately for the British, bad weather and privateers played hob with the sailings, while such supplies as did arrive were as often as not scarcely fit to eat, the bread moldy, the biscuit asquirm with weevils, the butter rancid, the flour sour and augmented with sand, the peas worm-eaten, and the beef crawling with maggots. Corrupt contractors were in good part responsible for the condition of the supplies, but though the commissary general rejected much of the food as unfit for consumption, this act hardly allayed the hunger of the men. At times, the latter were given ship biscuit several years old and so hard that cannon balls were used to break it. The saving grace for the private soldier was the daily ration of rum and the occasional allotment of claret, spruce beer, or porter.[3]

But liquids, however pleasing to the tongue and warming to the stomach and brain, were scarcely sufficient as nourishment for the army, which was forced to live from hand to mouth. Hundreds of men were prostrated with famine and scurvy, not to mention those still suffering from the wounds of Bunker Hill, and the number of daily deaths steadily increased. There were few fresh provisions and an almost total lack of vegetables except for the sick. Lord Rawdon, stationed on Bunker Hill, evidently counted it a luxury to have "a red herring, some onions, and some porter."[4] To make matters worse, smallpox raged, and fuel became scarce. Though inoculation saved many lives from smallpox, the disease was so widespread that the British considered its mere prevalence in the town a deterrent to American attack.[5] As for fuel, fence posts, doors, trees, some two hundred houses, and even Old North Church helped feed the fires of the freezing garrison until a coal ship arrived after the first of the new year.

In the midst of this distress Howe did his utmost to preserve discipline and order. Deserters were hanged, as were any poor devils caught making away with so much as a fence post for fuel,[6] while housebreakers were not infrequently given between four hundred and one thousand lashes with the cat-o'-nine-tails. Those who received stolen goods were also held guilty. Moreover, for striking a commissioned officer in the infantry, a Marine was sentenced, on November 24, 1775, to receive eight hundred lashes. Company officers and noncoms were urged to see that gambling was suppressed and that no deviation be tolerated in the standard of soldierly appearance; enlisted men offended in these respects on pain of the lash.

Though flogging was an integral part of the entire penalty system, far more prevalent, indeed, than in the American establishment, Burgoyne hated to see the lash applied. In fact, with his eye on the Prussian system, he deplored the whole idea of training men by a rod as if they were dogs. He contended that if officers took pains to understand their men and treated them sympathetically, there would be little need for harsh measures. He insisted that the English soldier should be treated as a thinking being and that officers should strive to discern the character of each man and apportion encouragement and punishment accordingly. Unlike Howe and most general officers, Burgoyne sought to devise adequate substitutes for the lash. Small wonder that, indifferent general as he was in certain respects, his men loved him. His departure for England on December 5 must have been viewed with deep regret by many an enlisted man.[7]

Despite these dismal conditions, diversion was not lacking. Thanks to Burgoyne, Faneuil Hall was used for amateur theatricals which entertained the garrison through the winter, the proceeds going to the soldiers' families. Old South Church was converted into a riding school for cavalry recruits, a desecration also allegedly effected by Burgoyne. Gambling and cockfighting flourished among the officers. Howe, in particular, his strictures on gambling solely for the enlisted men, loved to while away the hours with cards and fine liquors. If the table could be spiced with the company of pretty women, so much the better. And it was in Boston that he met Betsy Lloyd Loring, wife of Joshua Loring, who, in October, 1775, was appointed by Gage "sole vendue-master and auctioneer" of Boston; subsequently Howe made him commissary of prisoners. Her complacent husband thus taken care of, blonde Betsy captivated the dark, handsome Howe with her good looks and her vivacity, her skill at cards and her readiness to gamble. Judge Jones, an embittered New York Tory, said that, because of this "illustrious courtesan," Howe forfeited "the honor, the laurels, and the glory of putting an end to one of the most obstinate rebellions that ever existed." Though Jones attributed far too much power to her, she held Howe's attention throughout most of his stay in America. His officers referred to her as "the Sultana" and sought her favor as a way of winning recognition from Howe. Whether in Boston, Halifax, New York, or Philadelphia, she became, as Howe's mistress, the dazzling center of army society. In her company Howe could not have found the siege of Boston by any means so unpleasant as did many of his officers and most of his men.[8]

But the British had no intention of remaining indefinitely inactive. On August 7, 1775, Clinton had indicated to Gage that New York was a better base of operations than Boston, being a more central location. It was also an island the approaches of which could be covered by the navy, a center of American Loyalists, and a place where provision was plentiful.[9] Ten days later, Burgoyne, in a memorandum to Gage, also advised evacuating Boston and concentrating at New York for almost the identical reasons.[10] The decision of the British government, furthermore, to send troops from Britain to restore crown authority in the Carolinas, and to detach Clinton from Boston in January to take command of those troops, made it seem increasingly senseless to maintain the army in Boston. Yet, as a matter of fact, Howe had been authorized to leave when he considered the situation warranted, but until sufficient shipping should arrive to effect an orderly and complete evacuation, he felt that all he could do was to wait. At the same time, he was doubtful that the Southern expedition would achieve any success, and he deplored such a weakening of his main army, which was to be concentrated at New York.[11]

Howe was to leave Boston sooner, and in much greater haste, than he anticipated, thanks to a strengthening of the American army. The outlook at the start of the year had not been so promising, and Washington wrote in early January that "The same desire of retiring into a chimney-corner seized the troops of New Hampshire, Rhode Island, and Massachusetts, (so soon as their time expired,) as had worked upon those of Connecticut."[12] Echoing a sentiment of Washington, Greene doubted if there had ever been another instance of one army disbanding and a new one being organized in the face of an enemy.[13] The scarcity of powder, moreover, continued serious, and one American colonel wrote, "Old Put . . . is still as hard as ever, crying out for powder—powder, ye gods, give us powder!"[14] Fortunately, in certain respects, a turn for the better was at hand.

The improvement in the situation started in the latter part of January when Colonel Henry Knox, former bookseller turned artillerist, arrived with a large number of heavy cannons from Ticonderoga. After inconceivable labor, facing difficulties with ice that cracked under the weight of the guns, sledges that broke down, oxen that gave out in the up-and-down haul over the steep New England hills, Knox finally brought his transportation into Cambridge on January 24. With the arrival of the guns, Washington proceeded to strengthen his fortifications, particularly on Lechmere Point, and he longed to throw his troops at the British. His patience was so sorely tried by the intolerable embarrassment of trying to keep the semblance of an army about Boston that he had proposed an assault on the town on three occasions, September 11, October 18, and January 16. Each time he was strongly urged not to attempt the project, the council of war opposing his idea originally consisting of Ward, Lee, Putnam, Thomas, Spencer, Heath, Sullivan, Greene, and Gates. On February 16, he again made the proposal, stressing that he had nearly nine thousand fit for duty and fifteen hundred additional troops who could join at once, that the British could muster not over five thousand fit for duty, and that this was about the last time an attack could be launched over the ice before a thaw set in. To his bitter disappointment, even with ten regiments of militia being called up, the council cautioned him not to attack. Ward believed that seizing Dorchester Heights was a much safer, more economical, and equally effective way of either bringing on the general engagement that Washington desired or driving the British from the town. Agreeing with Ward, the generals then resolved to begin preparations to obtain the Heights.[15]

The Americans now worked with something of the energy and enthusiasm that had characterized their activities from Lexington to Bunker Hill. Ward's Roxbury troops were especially industrious making wicker cylinders filled with earth or sand called gabions, bundles of sticks bound together known as fascines, and chandeliers, which were frames of wood in which the fascines could be set, picketed down, and heaped over with earth;[16] all these objects were to be placed on the two main hills comprising the Heights. This activity, together with Ward's closing all channels of intercourse between his

lines and those of the British, excited the men. They had little difficulty guessing that the Heights were the objective, and they were
eager for a showdown with the enemy after the long months of siege.
No doubt the burning of Falmouth (Portland) by British Captain
Mowat's ships in the late fall, the destruction of Norfolk by Lord
Dunmore on New Year's Day, and the publication of Tom Paine's
pamphlet, *Common Sense*, would not, as Washington himself remarked, "leave numbers at a loss to decide upon the propriety of a
separation" from Britain.[17] To a part of the army, therefore, the
struggle may well have started to assume the proportions of more
than a mere contention for their rights as Englishmen.

A wild rumor on February 27 that the British were landing in
force on Dorchester Neck impressed Washington with the necessity
of prompt action. Why Howe had not tried to seize the Heights himself before this is not too clear. Possibly overconfidence was responsible, or apprehension at further dividing his forces, or failure to
evaluate the importance of the position, or sheer procrastination, or
(as of late winter) a conviction that such action was unnecessary in
view of his impending evacuation; at any rate, he appeared in no
fear that the Americans would attack him.[18] Washington, who had
hitherto been a little dubious himself about the Heights, called a
council of war on March 2 and decided to wait no longer but to seize
them on the night of March 4. Thomas was to take two thousand
men and fortify them. The council also resolved, with Washington's
approval, that, should the British attempt to storm the Heights, Putnam was to move four thousand troops in two brigades under Sullivan
and Greene by rowboat to Boston, one brigade heading for Beacon
Hill, the other for Copp's Hill, then both joining in a drive toward
Boston Neck. Given the reduced number of troops that would be
available to Howe for a defense of the city, the plan was feasible,
notwithstanding the hazards of an amphibious operation and the
strength of the Boston forts.

The grand design started on the nights of March 2 and 3 with a
fierce artillery preparation from the guns at Cobble Hill, Lechmere
Point, and Roxbury; on the night of the 4th, the batteries intensified
their fire to the terror of the inhabitants of Boston. To this bombardment the British replied vigorously, returning three shots for every
one fired at them. They seem not to have had the slightest inkling

that the American cannonade was only a feint for more decisive action elsewhere, and, under the protection of such darkness as existed on a bright moonlight night, Thomas moved into position. Eight hundred of the men allotted to him comprised a covering party, half of them deploying on Nook Hill, the rest on the point opposite Castle William.

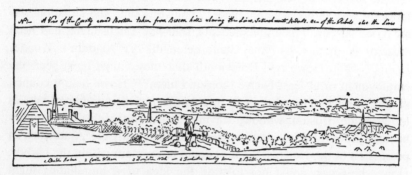

Sketch: From Beacon Hill, 1775, No. 1 (Looking toward Dorchester Heights)

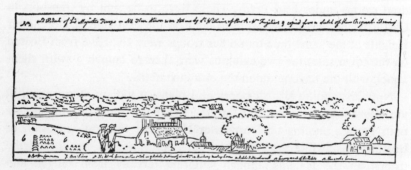

Sketch: From Beacon Hill, 1775, No. 2 (Looking toward Roxbury)

The fatigue detail consisted of twelve hundred men who were accompanied by three hundred and sixty carts loaded with fascines, gabions, chandeliers, and great bundles of twisted hay weighing up to eight hundred pounds. As the carts moved along, the bundles of hay were dropped along the Neck to serve as a screen, behind which the carts toiled back and forth during the night and artillery was brought up. Meanwhile two forts rose on the Heights under the supervision of Colonel Gridley and Colonel Rufus Putnam of Massachusetts, an outstanding engineer. A relief party arrived by four o'clock, while five companies of riflemen slipped into ambush near the water side. Apple trees near by were cut down and made into abattis, and barrels filled with rocks and sand were placed in position for being rolled downhill toward an assault force.

The surprise of the British when they viewed the works in the morning was as great as on June 17, but this time the situation was far more serious. The entrenchments, said one Englishman, had been created as though by "the Genii belonging to Aladdin's Wonder Lamp," while Howe told Dartmouth that they "must have been the employment of at least twelve thousand men."[19] Howe held a council of war at once. Though he still had an insufficient number of vessels to evacuate Boston without leaving untold quantities of supplies behind, Admiral Shuldham assured him that, with the Americans in possession of the Heights, the fleet could not remain within the harbor. Howe, however, could not tolerate the idea of a humiliating flight from the original seat of the uprising before a half-trained body of American rebels. He decided to fight, and readied twenty-four hundred troops under Earl Percy. These were to be sent by transport to Castle Island and thence were to land on the east side of Dorchester Heights at the same time that other troops were to arrive from Boston on the town side; the two columns were then to launch a swift, silent attack with the bayonet upon the entrenchments.[20]

Notwithstanding British hopes and plans, a violent storm arose in the afternoon and continued through the night, rendering impossible both Percy's landing on Dorchester Neck and Putnam's invasion of Boston. Meanwhile the American guns continued to cough, and the troops on the Heights, though suffering terribly from fatigue and exposure, extended and strengthened their entrenchments. Finally, to the disappointment of many in the American lines, including Washington himself, Howe gave up the proposed attack. He decided on the 7th to evacuate the town and proceed with the army and the Loyalists to Halifax. And presently there was the greatest "uproar and confusion; carts, trucks, wheel-barrows, coaches, chaises . . . driving as if the devil was after them."[21]

Howe would undoubtedly have preferred moving on to New York rather than Halifax, but certain factors militated against New York. To Howe, Halifax appeared the only place where the army could safely remain until supplies arrived from Europe, while "the present condition of the troops—crowded in transports, without regard to conveniences, the inevitable dissortment of stores, and all the encumbrances with which I am clogged—effectually disable me from the exertion of this force in any offensive operations. . . ."[22] One might infer that Halifax had not been decided on as the destination until the troops had embarked, which was not so at all.

Washington himself believed that Howe was bound for New York. To prepare for such a contingency, he and his council resolved on March 13 to dispatch to New York the very next day a rifle regiment and, the following day, five other regiments. He also wrote Governor Trumbull, requesting that two thousand troops move into New York from Connecticut, while Brigadier General William Alexander (Lord Stirling), now commander of New York since Lee had been ordered southward on March 7 in view of Clinton's expedition to the Carolinas, was urged to solicit the New Jersey authorities for one thousand more men.

Though Washington never officially recognized it, an informal agreement existed whereby if the Americans permitted the British to carry out their evacuation of Boston without molestation, Howe would not burn the town. Despite a heavy cannonade from both sides on the night of the 10th as a result of an American attempt to extend their hold to Nook Hill on the Dorchester peninsula, the agreement was generally adhered to. Washington became increasingly anxious to speed the British on their way; hence, on the 16th, he seized Nook Hill in force and fortified it. Though the British shelled the works, the Americans did not reply. Yet the American seizure of so vital an eminence had the hastening effect the Virginian desired, for on Sunday, the 17th, Howe completed embarking his troops and about one thousand Loyalists, whose mournful lot was not appreciated even by the troops of the king they served. The fleet then dropped down to Nantasket Roads, where it remained for ten days. Abigail Adams counted one hundred and seventy sail, and so massive an armada created much uneasiness among the Americans before it finally sailed for Halifax.

The victory was a splendid one for the Americans, as in the following days, spearheaded by troops who had already had smallpox, they entered the battered town. Though Howe had thrown most of his powder away and spiked such cannons as were left behind, the Americans found a tremendous quantity of abandoned supplies and military stores.[23] Welcome as these supplies were, the most heartening fact was what American possession of them signified: the "Ministerial Army" was gone. The news caused great rejoicing in the colonies, and Congress passed a vote of thanks to the army and its leader.

Washington was chiefly responsible for maintaining the siege of Boston and for bringing it to such a happy conclusion. The man possessed an extraordinary singleness of purpose and a dogged determination to carry out his design notwithstanding the obstacles created by nature, the enemy, or his own army. Not that he was perfect. Patience was not his long suit, criticism came easily to his pen, his judgments of military situations and of men sometimes lacked soundness, a sense of class consciousness existed in his mind, and a certain hauteur and coldness colored his relationships with both his officers and men. Although intelligent, he could scarcely be considered truly intellectual, while such sense of humor as he may have possessed was usually of an ironical turn, if not actually grim. But he persisted in his unenviable and immensely difficult job with exceeding tenacity and courage and a profound sense of responsibility. Perhaps he realized in the end, regardless of his disappointment at the time, that his generals, in advising against his four proposed attacks upon Boston, had given him wise counsel; certainly he had bowed to their caution, which was to his credit. Perhaps, too, he even felt more kindly disposed toward the general run of New Englanders, of whom he had occasionally been so contemptuous (not without reason!), but whom he had molded into an army from which much of the dross had been eliminated.[24] One may hope so. Though colonies outside New England had sent men to Cambridge who served well, it was mainly the New Englanders, particularly the men from Massachusetts, whose efforts could evoke from the Duke of Manchester the following stinging words, uttered in the House of Lords, words which summed up rather well the situation in Boston as of March 17:

The mode of the retreat may, to the general [Howe], do infinite honor, but it does dishonor to the British nation. Let this transaction be dressed in what garb you please, the fact remains, that the army which was sent to reduce the province of Massachusetts Bay has been driven from the capital, and that the standard of the provincial army now waves in triumph over the walls of Boston.[25]

The Canadian Magnet

While the siege of Boston was in progress, the United Colonies launched their most ambitious enterprise of the war, the invasion of Canada. The invasion grew out of the American desire to make Canada a fourteenth colony, to present a truly continental political front to the British, and to preserve the English-speaking colonies from military attack. Memories were yet fresh of the bloody use which the French had made of the famous lake-and-river chain from the St. Lawrence to the Hudson, and there was every reason to suspect that the British might eventually employ the same route and thereby sever New England from the Middle Colonies; subsequent events proved this fear fully justified. At first, Congress viewed with certain misgivings the initial drive by Allen and Arnold up through the lakes since invasion seemed hardly consistent with the colonial fight for freedom. Presently, however, reports that the British were dickering with the Iroquois to attack the American forts on Lake Champlain furnished substance to American fears, and Congress hastened to make Philip Schuyler commander of the Northern army, put him in charge of Ticonderoga, and authorized him to push into Canada.[1]

Before Arnold had left the lakes, he proposed to Congress, on June 13, 1775, a plan of campaign to take Montreal and Quebec with two thousand men, cutting off St. Johns and Chambly with seven hundred, guarding the boats and the line of retreat with three hundred, sending one thousand on to Montreal, which, with the help of friends within, would fall like ripe fruit, and then moving on to Quebec.[2] Arnold's offer to lead such an expedition was ignored, but his plan in its essentials was the one generally followed. On the other hand, little attention was paid to his insistence that the success of such a venture hinged on the speed with which it was executed. The tall, dark-eyed, now cheery, now petulant Schuyler was the last man to have been given command of an offensive, however capable he later showed himself to be as a defensive leader. A thoroughly loyal, generous, kindhearted man, a great landowner who was as honest with his tenants as he was prompt in collecting their rents and in demanding their courtesy, he appeared unable to get work accomplished with the dispatch which he himself acknowledged was necessary. True, he was faced with disagreeable realities in his need for troops, equipment, and supplies, but the man was almost too courteous, too tolerant of complaints, too inclined to believe that others, whether soldiers or politicians, were as conscientious as himself.[3]

Fortunately he had in Richard Montgomery an unusually able lieutenant, and one on whom the actual command of the expedition eventually devolved. When Schuyler took over, there were in the Ticonderoga area fewer than fourteen hundred men under Colonel Benjamin Hinman, whose troops were mostly from Connecticut. Schuyler at once called for more men. New Hampshire's efforts to comply bogged down in a struggle between Ethan Allen and Seth Warner over the command of the Green Mountain Boys. The attempts of New York to defend its own territory were almost equally futile, though officers abounded and several companies of poorly clothed and equipped troops finally arrived in August. Hence it was Connecticut which again supplied the lack. Of the troops dispatched to the defense of New York under old Major General David Wooster, the ranking officer in Connecticut's forces though only a brigadier in the Continental establishment, one thousand under Colonel Waterbury were detached for service with the Northern army. Though Montgomery had scant respect for the New Yorkers and less for the New Englanders, whom he described as the "worst stuff imaginable for soldiers" and in whose units, he thought, every private considered himself a general, he and Schuyler whipped these forces into something resembling an army.[4]

In vain, however, did Montgomery seek to convince Schuyler of the urgency of driving northward with such forces as were available. Finally, while Schuyler was absent at an Indian council in Saratoga, Montgomery, who had become increasingly anxious over General Guy Carleton's measures to defend Canada, set September 2 as the day for starting the campaign, a date which he subsequently moved up to August 28. It was as if this were what Schuyler had needed, someone to make the decision for him, for as soon as he received the information, he concurred with Montgomery's decision and rushed northward to join the army.

Meanwhile Carleton hastened his own preparations to meet the Americans moving down the Sorel (or Richelieu) River in their rude bateaux. Carleton, later Lord Dorchester, was a thoroughgoing aristocrat and an officer who held the Americans in contempt as rebels and poor soldiers. He was also an administrator whose colonial policy was largely embodied in the Quebec Act of 1774, a settlement which, if it appeased many of the French Canadians, deeply antagonized the English colonies and the Whig minority in Parliament.[5] In midsummer of 1775, Carleton had fewer than one thousand regular troops at his disposal. Though this number could be augmented by about three hundred volunteers from Englishmen living in Montreal and Quebec and by possibly fifteen hundred French, the latter could scarcely be relied upon except for the small number of seigneurs and bourgeois. In fact, while both sides in this civil contest received some assistance from French Canadians, most of the latter refused to render satisfactory aid to either combatant.

Carleton chose to make his main stand at St. Johns. He stationed more than half of his regulars there with over a hundred Canadian volunteers, threw eighty regulars and some volunteers into Fort Chambly between St. Johns and Montreal, and set up temporary headquarters at Montreal, where he could remain in touch with the frontier forts by the Sorel and with Quebec by the St. Lawrence. It was Carleton's construction of two armed vessels at St. Johns to secure the Sorel against invasion that impelled Montgomery to advance the date of his drive down the river; an armed sloop or schooner could play havoc with his open bateaux loaded with troops.

Montgomery's siege of St. Johns, which he sighted on September 1, proceeded laggardly at first. The long delay at Ticonderoga had sapped enthusiasm, the sick list was formidable, fear of surprise made cowards of the raw troops, and Schuyler soon fell ill of a fever and was evacuated to Ticonderoga. Montgomery, however, was able to slip a force around St. Johns which, joining with a Canadian contingent under Colonel James Livingston, who was related to Montgomery's wife, succeeded in cutting off the British supply line to

Montreal and brought the fort under fire from the north. Presently, too, Montgomery was reinforced by several hundred troops from New York and New Hampshire.

While the siege of St. Johns went on, the American cause suffered a setback at Montreal. Colonel Ethan Allen, that aggressive, loose-lipped Paul Bunyan from the Green Mountains, burned to distinguish himself as he had in the spring. Detached to raise volunteers among the Canadians, he enlisted about one hundred, then went to the vicinity of Longueuil and had a talk with Major John Brown, who commanded a small force at Laprairie. Allen and Brown went into a huddle and came out determined to capture Montreal. Allen was to take his men to the south of the town and Brown his two hundred to the north. To Allen's wrath and chagrin, Brown and his men failed to appear at the appointed time, and, on September 15, after a sharp skirmish, the British, who were supported by a thousand Canadians terrified by Allen's reputation, took Allen prisoner along with forty of his men. After being assured by Colonel Prescott, the British commander, that he would "grace a halter at Tyburn, God damn ye," Allen was placed in chains, subsequently conveyed to England where his badman reputation earned him a notoriety not altogether displeasing to him, and exchanged after three years. Had Brown supported him, Allen would likely have taken Montreal.

The removal of Allen from the arena of war appeared to relieve rather than dismay the generals, particularly Washington and Montgomery, who thought Allen imprudent and overly ambitious.[6] Certainly Allen's capture failed to daunt Montgomery, who now pressed the siege with such vigor as his ill-disciplined, apathetic troops could muster. Luckily Livingston had the bright idea of besieging Chambly with three hundred of his Canadians and fifty of Brown's men provided Montgomery could spare a few cannons. Montgomery readily agreed, and Livingston succeeded in floating the guns past the St. Johns batteries at night. The fire of the American 9-pounders finally intimidated the Chambly commander, "The Honourable Major Stopford," into surrendering, on October 8, his garrison, his large stores of war materials, and abundant supplies of food.[7] Stopford was scarcely the man to command such an important post; he possessed far more elegance in manner and dress than competence in the field.

Stopford's surrender came just in time to help Montgomery. Despite the reinforcements fed it by Schuyler, the army was melting away. The September rains and the October frosts, along with despondency, sent the men in droves to the hospital, thence—many, at any rate—to be discharged. But now, with cannon, a large supply of powder, and additional hundreds from Ticonderoga, Montgomery put such increased pressure on St. Johns that Major Preston, his own supplies running out, decided to surrender the battered town. And, on November 3, more than five hundred British regulars and volunteers marched out of Fort St. Johns as prisoners of war. Among them was a young lieutenant of fateful future, one John André.

Montgomery pressed on overland toward Montreal, which was thrown into a panic at his approach. This time there was no thought of defense. A wild man like Allen with one hundred and fifty men, most of them Canadians, was one thing; a victorious, resourceful general like Montgomery with over twelve hundred American rebels at his back was quite another. Carleton himself had barely one hundred and fifty regulars under Prescott, and these he sadly embarked aboard eleven small craft on the 11th for an escape downriver to the more defensible area around Quebec. Two days later, November 13, a citizens' committee surrendered Montreal to Montgomery.[8]

But the end of American successes was not yet. On the 12th, one of Carleton's vessels ran aground. While the fleet delayed to float her clear, the wind failed, and for two days the ships tugged at their anchors just above Sorel where the river runs narrow and deep. On the morning of the 15th, Carleton was startled by the roar of heavy cannons from a row-galley working upstream. Soon a flagboat appeared. It bore Ira Allen, Ethan's brother, who presented a note from Colonel James Easton, requesting Carleton's surrender in view of strong American batteries stationed at Sorel. The request was refused, and the fleet quickly weighed anchor. But when it withdrew up the river to try for a landing at Lavaltrie, a Canadian contingent, encouraged by the knowledge that on land and water Montgomery was hurrying reinforcements to them, repulsed the British landing attempts.

Major Brown, that canny New Englander who would have made a grand poker player, now entered the situation again. He suggested that the fleet send an officer the following morning to see for himself what little chance the squadron had to escape. The British accepted the offer, whereupon Brown performed a startling bit of mental legerdemain. It is not clear what Brown showed the officer, possibly a small battery, but he assured the man that, if the British chanced to escape the battery, he had a grand battery at the mouth of the Sorel which would infallibly sink all their vessels. Actually, according to Congressman Charles Carroll of Carrollton, who visited the location several months afterward, Brown's "grand battery was as badly provided with cannon as his little battery, for not a single gun was mounted on either."[9]

But the officer had heard enough; Brown's smooth, confident speech and manner had been utterly convincing. The report of the officer must also have been equally convincing, because the fleet surrendered on Sunday evening, November 19, hauling down the flag, so the Americans scornfully remarked, to "a single gondola."[10] And when the British troops reached Montreal on the 22d, "Savage Prescott," as the Americans referred to the redcoat commander, was received with jeers. Montgomery remarked, "I blush for His Majesty's troops!"[11]

In spite of such successes, the most important prize of all slipped through the American net. Early resolving not to be caught in any surrender, and indignant at the faintheartedness of his officers, Carleton persuaded a Canadian captain, one Bouchette, to row him past the American batteries on the night of November 16-17. Dressed as a farmer, Carleton, who was joined by another Canadian officer and a sergeant, dropped quietly over his ship's side into a boat and floated downriver. At Berthier, where a number of Americans were bivouacked, the men lay down in the boat and, stretching their arms over the gunwales, paddled with their hands. From their position they could hear the routine calls of the American sentries. When they reached Three Rivers, Carleton sought rest in a gentleman's house, rest which was interrupted a few hours afterward when the Americans swarmed into the area and a detail entered the house. Tradition has it that Carleton escaped by nonchalantly walking out the door in his peasant's guise. Finding his boat, he continued a little way farther until picked up by the *Fell,* a British brig, which bore him to Quebec. He arrived at the fortress town on the 19th only to discover that he scarcely had time to catch his breath; Quebec now needed the redoubtable 51-year-old governor as sorely as had Montreal.[12]

The tense situation at Quebec had been created by the arrival of an American force that had pushed through the wilderness of Maine and emerged before Quebec on November 5. When Benedict Arnold returned in midsummer from the lakes, his ambition to invade Canada from that quarter thwarted and his reputation for pecuniary honesty in his accounts assailed, he was a thoroughly frustrated, angry man. But Washington, who appreciated the enterprise and dash of Arnold, had work for him. The drive by Schuyler's army into Canada was to become merely one arm of a pincers movement; the other was to consist of an expedition up the Kennebec, over the Height of Land, and down the Chaudière River to the St. Lawrence and Quebec, which was to be taken by surprise while Carleton's attention was being held by Schuyler's army. Proposing such a route was by no means a novel conception, since both the French and the English had thought of using it in their colonial wars, while Colonel Jonathan Brewer of Massachusetts had presented to the Provincial Congress in the spring of 1775 a plan to conduct five hundred troops to Quebec by the route. Washington, who undoubtedly knew of Brewer's suggestion, may well have first considered it seriously when Gates, as adjutant general and a man friendly to Arnold at the time, laid before the commander in chief a similar plan by Arnold.[13]

Such an expedition required careful planning and prompt decision, for the way was long and the time short. Anxious for Schuyler's opinion, Washington wrote the New Yorker on August 20, pointing out the military advantages of the move and requesting a swift reply.[14] Meanwhile Arnold conferred with a Kennebec shipbuilder from Gardiner, Reuben Colburn, as to the amount and cost of food supplies along the Kennebec and the time and materials necessary to construct two hundred bateaux, each capable of bearing a half dozen men with their provisions and baggage. As a result of a meeting between Washington and Arnold, it is reasonably clear that the Virginian saw in Arnold the courageous, aggressive sort of leader essential to the success of the venture and that Arnold viewed the enterprise as the very type of move that would suit his daring, restless spirit; a move, furthermore, that would vindicate him to his foes. After Schuyler's favorable response,[15] Colburn was soon sent off to Gardiner to build the bateaux, to organize a small, efficient maintenance force for the expedition, and to round up supplies, strenuous duties indeed, with barely three weeks to fulfill them.

The expedition captured the imagination of the troops before Boston, many of whom were bored to death by the inactivity of the siege. There was no lack of volunteers. Altogether, ten companies of musketeers, formed into two battalions, were enlisted, and three companies of riflemen, one from Virginia and two from Pennsylvania. The battalions were commanded by Lieutenant Colonel Roger Enos, a Vermonter who had served in the British army, and Lieutenant Colonel Christopher Greene, the son of a justice of the supreme court of Rhode Island. Outstanding among the riflemen was the giant officer, Captain Daniel Morgan, a born leader of men who had once served as a teamster with Braddock's army, and whose back still showed the scars from a British whip. Among the other officers, of whom a number later acquired military or political fame, was the 19-year-old son of the president of Princeton College, Aaron Burr. The total number enlisted for the expedition amounted to approximately one thousand and fifty.[16]

Reaching Gardiner took several days. When the troops paraded in Cambridge on September 11, a considerable proportion of them, with their families in mind, simply would not leave until they received a month's pay in advance.[17] Nevertheless, certain units started for Newburyport that day, and the rest followed on the 13th. By Saturday, the 16th, the troops were bivouacked in Newbury, near Newburyport, which Arnold had reached the night before. Wind and weather combined to prevent the expedition from embarking until Monday, the 18th. Then, one of the three patrol vessels having returned with news that no British man-of-war was on the coast, the little fleet of eleven sloops and schooners set sail on Tuesday from Newburyport. Aboard the "dirty coasters and fish boats," as one landsman described them, many of the troops probably shared the sentiments of Simon Fobes, whom the heavy sea made so sick that he did not care whether he lived or died,[18] a not uncommon feeling beyond the shelter of breakwaters and headlands. Even so, the fleet made a quick run to the mouth of the Kennebec, raising Wood's Island in ten hours. In working up the river the ships went astray, taking different courses, even running aground. Notwithstanding such difficulties, the entire fleet arrived at Gardiner on the 22d.

Near Gardiner lay Reuben Colburn's shipyard. Arnold inspected the bateaux, and what he saw in no way pleased him. Colburn had completed the two hundred bateaux, but Arnold found many of them smaller than specifications and most of them poorly constructed.[19] On the other hand, Colburn had been given a tremendous job to accomplish in short time, and the surprising feature is that the construction, such as it was, had been completed. It is possible, too, as Justin Smith suggests, that, so seldom had anyone attempted the waters of the upper Kennebec, neither Colburn nor his chief carpenter, Agry, appreciated what was required.[20]

As if his disappointment over the bateaux were not sufficient, Arnold received unpleasant news from a scouting party that had been sent out by Colburn. Members of the party reported that, on reaching an Indian camp thirty miles up Dead River, Natanis, the prominent Indian in those parts, informed them that he was employed by Carleton to keep an eye on an army expected from New England, that there were more spies at the head of the Chaudière, and that farther down the river a British officer and six soldiers were encamped. Natanis said he would notify Carleton if the party continued, a threat which he did not carry out.[21] After one day more, however, the party gave up and returned. Though this was distressing information, Arnold refused to let it disturb him overmuch. He diligently studied such surveyors' records as existed, particularly the map and journals of Lieutenant John Montressor, who, in 1761, had made a reconnaissance through the Kennebec region from Quebec. Arnold also received some encouragement from the arrival of several St. Francis Indians who were reputed to know the forest trails.

Presently Arnold pushed on to Fort Western, opposite what is now Augusta. Less fort than barrack in 1775, it served more as a stepping-off place for the real advance than as the main supply depot which Arnold would have desired. After dispatching two scouting parties on his own on Sunday, the 24th, Arnold, who had divided his little army into four parts, ordered the first division forward the very next day; these were the riflemen under Morgan, who was directed to clear roads over the carrying places. Greene was to follow on Tuesday with three companies, Major Meigs of Connecticut on Wednesday with four companies, and Enos on Thursday with the three companies of the fourth division. Actually, such were the last-minute details to be taken care of that Enos's division did not leave Fort Western until Saturday. Notwithstanding disappointment, delay, and the fast-approaching autumn, the daring push through the wilderness had begun at last, and the second arm of the pincers had started to close on Quebec.

VII

Death, Defeat, and Disaster in the North

The entire Canadian venture, which reached its climax in storm and battle in Quebec, was a campaign of desperate daring. Yet difficult as was Montgomery's task, strenuous and futile as were the Americans' sacrifices in the conflict at Quebec and in the ensuing siege and retreat, the most remarkable part of the venture in many respects was the struggle that Arnold's Kennebec troops waged against the wilderness and starvation. In fact, the course and hardships of the wilderness army leave one wondering how any considerable number ever got to Quebec.

Their difficulties started almost at once. At Ticonic Falls, above Fort Halifax, the men had their introduction to the work of carrying the 400-pound bateaux made of green pine planks. Then followed the Five-Mile Falls and the gorge at Skowhegan, after which the men fell exhausted to the ground and awoke to discover their drenched clothes frozen to them. But on they pushed to the triple-tiered Norridgewock Falls, where white water abounded and the river dropped ninety feet in the course of a mile.[1] Handspikes were again pressed under the bateaux, and, with two men on each side, the awkward craft, splintered, battered, and leaking, were borne around to safer water above.

Great was the wrath against the builders when the dangerous condition of the bateaux became clear. Seams had parted, and so much water had been shipped that much of the salt fish, salt pork, salt beef, dried peas, and biscuit had spoiled. The men repacked the food, and presently Colburn and his maintenance crew arrived to repair the bateaux. Afterward came Carritunk Falls and soon the Great Carrying Place, where four portages of eight miles through rain and over soggy ground were needed to reach Dead River. Then on and on for days, with supplies getting alarmingly short, through a "Prodigious fall of rain" which lifted the river level to a flood that overturned bateaux and washed away stores.[2] So serious had the situation become that, on October 23, Arnold held a council of war with the leading divisions, now the first and the third. Though the army was haggard and half starving, wills were still strong. Only a few of the invalids were sent back. A strong company plunged ahead to secure supplies along the Chaudière, while Arnold himself took the lead.

Equally portentous in its way was the result of the council of war held by the second and fourth divisions on the 25th. Greene decided to press on with the second, but Enos, overcautious and fearful of starvation, took the fourth division home. By so doing, he may have saved the lives of many of his own division, but his action probably forfeited what chances the expedition had for success.[3] Washington at once placed him under arrest when he returned to Cambridge. Though the subsequent court-martial acquitted him with honor, the verdict, delivered on the basis of testimony from witnesses who were Enos's own officers, was unconvincing to many of his contemporaries, especially to the men who remained with Arnold.[4] Young Henry Dearborn, who later became Jefferson's secretary of war, wrote, "Our men, made a General Prayer, that Colo: Enos and all his men, might die by the way, or meet with some disaster, Equal to the Cowardly dastardly and unfriendly Spirit they discover'd in returning Back without orders, in such a manner as they had done, And then we proceeded forward."[5]

The hardships of the seven hundred faithful persisted and even increased. Worn out with portaging, the troops had little or no food to revive them. Hides intended for moccasins were chopped into fine pieces and boiled for whatever nourishment they might render. The skinless jawbone of a pig was considered sumptuous fare. Yet the men stumbled across the Height of Land—the great spine of the Appalachians—and, with some walking and others rowing, they pressed on through the chain of ponds to Lake Megantic. Montressor, who in 1775 was General Howe's chief engineer in Boston, had unwittingly done the crown a signal service by neglecting to enter on his map of 1761 several important bodies of water,[6] with the result

that part of the American army went astray and nearly perished of
cold and exhaustion. Eventually, however, the expedition worked its
painful way along the Chaudière, most of the boats abandoned because of the rapids. Supplies were so far gone that the men gnawed
at their cartridge boxes, shoes, and shaving soap, and even made
gruel from barber's powder. Now, when soldiers fell to the ground,
utterly fatigued, there were few others strong enough to lift them to
their feet. Crawling over fallen trees, gasping up the hills, the troops
resembled a long file of straggling skeletons rather than an army of
the living.

In the meantime, Arnold had dashed ahead down the roaring,
swollen Chaudière; then, after nearly drowning, he landed and
marched as fast as possible to the nearest Canadian settlements. The
Canadians were assured that the Americans would do them no harm,
and were shown Washington's pledge for the safety of their lives and
property. Indians near by also were persuaded that the Americans
came as friends. Thus placated, Canadians and Indians brought back
supplies to the starving army, "to the inexpressible joy" of the soldiers.[7] Men fell upon bullocks and devoured the flesh raw, while the
stronger, helped by the Canadians, carried back food to revive their
less fortunate fellows lying unconscious in the snow. Though numbers
of the army suffered dearly from overeating, the experience must
almost have been welcome after the recent ordeal, which still stands
as one of the ruggedest marches in our military history.

Urged on by Arnold, the army soon plunged through the snow to
the St. Lawrence, reaching Point Levis on November 8. Across the
river lay the high, frowning mass of Quebec. Arnold had no thousands
of well-equipped troops backed by a powerful fleet as had Wolfe in
the French and Indian War. Neither, for that matter, had Quebec a
Montcalm with his battalions of whitecoats. Its commander, Cramahé,
had only a weak body of militia and a small force of Marines and
regulars at his disposal. In the river, however, rode the sloop-of-war
Hunter and the frigate *Lizard,* just arrived, while a number of small
armed craft hung off the shores. Arnold collected canoes and dugouts
and decided to chance a night crossing. To his bitter disappointment
the wind blew so strongly on Friday and Saturday, November 10 and
11, that he had to postpone the plan. The delay was fatal. The High-
lander, Allan Maclean, whom Major Brown had driven from Sorel

when Montgomery was sweeping on to Montreal, had started for Quebec in a leisurely fashion until he intercepted two Indians in a canoe, one of whom, a messenger from Arnold, mistakenly handed him a letter from Arnold to Montgomery. Grasping the situation at once, Maclean drove on at top speed with two hundred men and

reached Quebec over the weekend while Arnold was anxiously waiting for wind and water to subside.

Finally, on Monday night, Arnold decided to wait no longer. Under cover of darkness his canoes and dugouts slipped across the river unseen, landing troops at the very spot where Wolfe himself had stepped ashore. Back and forth the craft plied, ferrying five hundred of the six hundred and fifty men until the moon broke through and made it dangerous to transport the balance. Up to the Plains of Abraham the troops climbed, thence to the city wall, where by taunts they sought to provoke Maclean into venturing forth to do battle as Montcalm had done. But the canny Scot sat tight, and Arnold was forced to threaten the city. Round shot, however, greeted the white flag of his envoy. Then learning that Maclean had received reinforcements, and that Carleton himself was near, and well aware that his own men had scarcely five rounds each, Arnold stifled his impatience and marched his troops away to Pointe aux Trembles, there to wait for Montgomery.

Meanwhile the latter was having serious trouble with his command. The enlistment terms of most of his men were about up and the troops anxious to go home rather than endure the bitter Canadian winter. Montgomery's promise that those who remained until the middle of April would receive an issue of winter clothing at government expense and a dollar in bounty money roused little enthusiasm. "An unhappy homesickness prevails," wrote Schuyler to John Hancock.[8] So many troops set out for the south that Montgomery was left with only eight hundred. Leaving garrisons at St. Johns and Montreal, he sailed downriver with three hundred men and a considerable supply of food, military stores, and warm clothing to join Arnold's shivering units.

The two leaders met on December 3 and got along famously, while the little army, barely a thousand in number, proceeded back to Quebec and laid siege to it. Carleton would not receive Montgomery's order to surrender or hold any kind of parley with rebels. Thus rebuffed, the American leaders wrestled with their problem. To add to their difficulties, winter set in early and hard, snow piling up to the second story of many houses in the city. The frozen ground proved so resistant that the Americans had to construct their entrenchments of snow and ice. Smallpox broke out, and food began to run short. Nor was the leaders' peace of mind facilitated by information that Carleton, whose arrival had electrified the defenders, had succeeded in mobilizing eighteen hundred men, eight hundred of them soldiers and sailors. But most distressing of all to Montgomery and Arnold was the knowledge that the terms of service of many of their men expired with the old year.

In their desperation the two young officers put their heads together and resolved to storm the city on the first snowy night. Several diversionary attacks were to be made, chief of which was a push by Livingston's Canadians against the upper town. The main assaults, however, were to be thrown against the lower town. Montgomery was to move along the Wolfe's Cove-Cape Diamond road, while Arnold was to smash along the St. Roque road almost directly opposite Montgomery. Once the two columns met in the lower town, they were to push, provided Carleton still held out, up Mountain Street into the upper town. The plan was well devised and might have succeeded if Enos's troops and Montgomery's fireside seekers had remained with their comrades. As it was, the Americans were simply too few. Furthermore, the number of those who had been under fire before was so limited that both commanders felt impelled to lead their respective columns in person; the decision was an unlucky one for both. Finally their plan to attack on the first stormy night was betrayed by deserters.[9]

It was now a race between a stormy night and the expiration of the men's service. At length, with barely hours remaining to the latter, snow began to fall late Saturday afternoon, December 30. The men pinned a piece of white paper to their caps for identification; at two in the morning, they assembled and moved out. Arnold with his men slipped silently from St. Roque toward the Palace Gate, while Montgomery's column picked its way from Wolfe's Cove to the stockade under Cape Diamond, his troops now plowing along the two-mile, drift-strewn road and now stumbling over the ice cakes thrown up by the river.

Just before five o'clock, soaring rockets signaled the attack. At once American mortars crashed from St. Roque, and Livingston's Canadians before the upper town and Captain Jacob Brown's small force above Cape Diamond opened a sharp diversionary fire. The surprise element, however, was virtually lacking, because the rockets had scarcely gone off before Captain Malcolm Fraser, commander of the main guard, spied men creeping toward the walls and turned out his troops. Church bells clanged wildly, and alarm guns went off with a roar that hurried the garrison to quarters. The battle for Quebec was on.[10]

Montgomery's attack was brief. With his carpenters working frantically to clear an opening through two palisades, Montgomery became so disturbed by the way his New Yorkers straggled that he dispatched runners to hurry the men along and personally took the lead of his column. Once inside the second palisade, Montgomery gathered a party of fifty or sixty men about him and swept toward a house blocking their path. Four cannons were mounted in the structure, which was garrisoned by sailors and Canadians. Loaded with grape, the guns blasted a deadly swath through the storm and the Americans, cutting down Montgomery, his aid McPherson, Captain Cheeseman, and ten others. Panic at once seized the Americans, and though young Burr tried to rally the men, his efforts were useless. Cautious Colonel Campbell, who took command, lacked the fortitude to continue, and ordered a retreat. With this official encouragement the men broke and ran for their lives. Montgomery's body was later found in a snowdrift, one hand upraised as if in protest at his troops' behavior; Carleton gave the corpse a decent burial.

Arnold's attack from the other side of the town took longer but was even more tragic. The flight of Livingston's Canadians from before the upper town, together with the rout of Montgomery's troops, revealed to the British that the musketry from Captain Brown's troops was merely diversionary and that the only serious threat remaining was from Arnold. They were therefore free to concentrate on the latter's attack. When the signal rockets arched up through the stormy sky near Cape Diamond, Arnold led an advance body of about thirty, followed by Captain Lamb's company, and then by the main column. With Arnold in front, the men dashed forward Indian-file, covering their rifles with their coats as best they could to prevent the powder and the locks from being wet by the snow. The troops were past the Palace Gate and the Hotel Dieu before being discovered. Approaching the defense barrier at the Sault au Matelot, the men had to pass through a narrow street. This passage was covered by cannons in front and by muskets in the hands of troops and sailors lining the windows of houses along the way. Arnold, with a shout of encouragement to his men, rushed forward. Suddenly he toppled into the snow, his leg pierced by a bullet. Undaunted, he got to his feet and, with the help of two men, stumbled along for a few steps until the pain became too excruciating to move farther. Even then, he would not retire until the main column, with Morgan now in complete charge of the assault by agreement of the officers, trooped past.

Thanks largely to Morgan's magnificent leadership, the barrier was carried, though Morgan himself sustained a bruised knee and powder burns on the face and was the target of a score of muskets. Another barrier brought the advance troops to a pause. They had more prisoners than they could handle; the main body of their own column was slow in coming up because of the storm, the darkness, and the unfamiliar streets; and, besides, Morgan's orders were to await Montgomery here. Morgan held a council of war, and reluctantly complied when the officers cautioned against a further advance. The decision proved costly. Had the Americans driven on, as they most

Excerpt from Arnold's letter to Washington, November 13, 1775

assuredly would if Arnold had been there, they might have taken the entire lower town; the door to the barrier was open and panic gripped the British. The opportunity soon passed, however, for Carleton quickly re-established control, manned the barrier, and threw troops into houses around the Americans.

The battle now turned sharply against the latter, who found themselves the target of converging fire. Vainly they fired at windows with such weapons as still had dry priming. Vainly they attempted to storm the barrier. Vainly they tried at last to retreat. Carleton had effectually surrounded them, and the troops, floundering through the snow in the tortuous streets, encountered musketry and grapeshot wherever they turned. Morgan was everywhere, leading this charge and that, endlessly cheering on the weary men, and offering to cut a way in person through the redcoats blocking escape, an offer which the other officers refused to accept. Finally the leaders, on assurance of good conduct and tender usage from Carleton, agreed in the early forenoon to surrender. Morgan would have none of this for himself. Weeping with rage, the gigantic rifleman placed his back against a wall and, sword in hand, defied all comers. When the British threatened to shoot him, he told them to go ahead and shoot. He even ignored the pleas of his own men for him to give up. In the end, he handed his sword to a priest, remarking in bitter anger that "not a scoundrel of these cowards shall take it out of my hand."[11] Quebec was thus lost forever to the Americans.

The battle had indeed been utterly dismal to American hopes. Montgomery was dead, Arnold sorely wounded, and the bulk of the Kennebec column in British hands. Figures from different sources fail to agree, but, as approximate totals, the Americans lost one hundred killed and wounded and nearly four hundred prisoners, while the British lost barely a score in all categories.[12] But Arnold refused to despair. From his hospital bed he issued the orders that kept Quebec under a kind of siege throughout the winter. It was ridiculous in one sense, and magnificent in another, a few hundred half-starved, freezing wretches keeping twice their number shut up in the fortress town. Carleton was probably content to have it so. He had supplies which could be stretched, if thinly, through the winter, and reinforcements were almost certain to arrive by sea in the spring. Let the Americans fight the elements. Let Arnold, a "Horse Jockey,"[13] eat his heart out in despair at his own impotence. Meanwhile Carleton treated his prisoners surprisingly well as misguided men, and awaited the thaw.[14]

Somehow the Americans hung on. In the meantime, Schuyler's frantic appeals for help to Washington and Congress resulted in the immediate raising of one regiment each by Massachusetts, Connecticut, and New Hampshire for the Canadian venture and authorization by Congress for the dispatch of troops and supplies to Canada, especially units from Pennsylvania and New Jersey.[15] Reinforcements, however, did not arrive in force until April 1, when General Wooster took command of the army. Arnold, whose wounded leg was injured by the fall of his horse on the 2d, and who considered that Wooster had not consulted him sufficiently, asked to be relieved and went to Montreal to take command there.

With Arnold's departure all likelihood of another attack on Quebec vanished. Wooster lacked aggressiveness, and Thomas, who succeeded him on May 1, decided, four days later, that the means available for the reduction of the town were so insignificant as to warrant raising the siege.[16] Preparations for departure were begun before the sun went down. The day following Thomas's decision, three British men-of-war with troops aboard bucked through the river ice to Quebec, and the town went wild with joy. Carleton at once organized a field force of nine hundred men from the garrison and the new arrivals, threw them across the Plains of Abraham, and drove the Americans, already frightened by the appearance of the warships, into headlong flight. Cannons, clothing, carts, food, papers, even the sick—everything was recklessly abandoned. Though Thomas eventually restored something approaching order, he continued the retreat to the Sorel and up to Chambly. To make matters more uncomfortable for the Americans, a British force west of Montreal, backed by a small number of Canadians and a host of Indians under the great Mohawk chief, Thayendanegea, or Joseph Brant, stormed an American outpost at The Cedars and slaughtered large numbers of a rescuing party.

These defeats deeply dismayed the invaders, especially, perhaps, the commission which Congress had sent to Canada, the 70-year-old Benjamin Franklin, Samuel Chase, Charles Carroll of Carrollton, and his brother, John Carroll, a Catholic priest. The commissioners had already discovered the Canadians lukewarm to hostile. Now they saw the American army on the verge of starvation, dispirited, and rotten with smallpox. Sick himself, Franklin, attended by John Carroll, left for home on May 11; the hardships of the journey and his illness nearly killed the old man. The other two commissioners, after embarrassing Thomas by their interference, though their authority was partially military and their intention good, finally gave up and went home the last of May. Even before they departed, poor Thomas came down with smallpox and died. He was succeeded in the first week of June by General John Sullivan.

Sullivan was inclined to rashness. Though heavy reinforcements, both British and Hessian, were arriving in Quebec, he threw General Thompson against Three Rivers on June 7. Carleton had anticipated the attack, possessed stronger forces and an able lieutenant in Burgoyne, who had returned to the wars, and utilized his command of the river effectively in making his dispositions. To add to the Americans' difficulties, their Canadian guide led them astray. Though the troops, chiefly Pennsylvanians, fought skillfully and bravely, they were compelled to withdraw, losing twenty-five killed and two hundred prisoners; among these last was Thompson himself. The British loss was negligible.

The battle decided Sullivan. Arnold wrote him on June 13, "The junction of the Canadas with the Colonies . . . is now at an End let us quit them & Secure our own Country before it is too late."[17] Of the same mind, Sullivan evacuated Sorel on the 14th just before the British came up, and destroyed fortifications, boats, and stores at Chambly two days later. On the 17th, when Sullivan reached St. Johns with his wreck of an army, he met Arnold, who had made an overland dash from Montreal with its garrison of three hundred. From St. Johns the army pushed on to Isle-aux-Noix. The British, having no boats, now left them alone, though Indians cut off American scouting parties. On the low, steaming island the men died like flies from smallpox, malaria, and dysentery, their bodies being thrown into huge pits in the center of each regimental camp. It became clear to the leaders that they must leave this pesthole. The sick were taken off first. Unfortunately many of them were placed on rafts that sometimes became awash, with the result that numbers of the victims grew more ill while others floated overboard and drowned. On June 26, the rest of the army commenced its evacuation and started for Crown Point. Soon this post also was abandoned except for the 6th Pennsylvania, left there as an advance guard. The bulk of the fewer than three thousand effectives of the Northern army then went into quarters at Ticonderoga in early July.

The expedition was a tragic failure. Canada was irretrievably lost, a vast amount of money had been spent, and casualties from death, disease, desertion, and capture numbered probably five thousand. A heavy pall of discouragement spread over the colonies which even the evacuation of Boston and the British repulse in the Carolinas did not succeed in lifting. The colonies, after an initial shilly-shallying, had set their hearts on making Canada one of them. Nor was the disaster made more bearable by the knowledge that Carleton was gathering an army and building ships to transport it southward. He was almost certain to strike before the summer ended.

Tragic as was the failure of the venture, it might have succeeded, and the "ifs" are interesting to contemplate: if Arnold had reached the St. Lawrence a few days earlier, if Arnold's messenger had not been intercepted, if Enos and the bulk of Montgomery's men had remained, if there had been no short-term enlistments to impel Montgomery and Arnold to attack when they did, if Montgomery had survived and Arnold not been wounded, if Arnold had been given command of the spring reinforcements. These are only a few of the "ifs" that rose to haunt the military and the politicians in the months that followed. In the last analysis, capable as was Carleton, atrocious as was their lack of good luck, it was mainly their deficiencies in enlistment, organization, and training that defeated the Americans. Even so, they came extraordinarily close to winning this most daring and spectacular thrust of the entire war. Had they won Quebec, the British might have retaken the city in the spring or the French might have asked for it in return for their assistance in the war. On the other hand, it is not at all improbable that the United States might now extend in an unbroken mass from the Rio Grande to the Arctic Ocean.

VIII

The Awakening of the South

While action flared in the North, the South was by no means idle. In March, 1775, Governor Martin of North Carolina informed London that troops were being organized against the crown. After citizens in Mecklenburg County issued a spirited declaration of independence in May, the governor found it expedient to move his quarters aboard a man-of-war. In South Carolina provision was made for the training of troops and the procurement of munitions. Powder from a captured British ship was sent to Boston, while South Carolina militia occupied British military installations, forcing Governor Campbell to take refuge aboard a man-of-war in September, 1775. In Georgia, British powder was seized, a ship commissioned for naval service, and the governor captured, though he subsequently escaped. Throughout 1775, resistance elements were likewise alive in Virginia, where Governor Dunmore depended heavily for support upon the strongly loyal mercantile town of Norfolk and the activities of his agent, Dr. John Connolly, in the Fort Pitt area, which was claimed by Virginia as well as Pennsylvania. When the burgesses, following Jefferson's lead, rejected, in June of 1775, a scheme of conciliation proposed by Lord North, and riflemen presently began to converge on Williamsburg to their assistance, Dunmore also fled to a British warship. Thus there appeared throughout most of the South a kind of gubernatorial flight to the sea, with a consequent weakening of crown authority.

At the same time the governors were quite certain that, with help from England, the authority of the crown could be re-established. With a few redcoats to show the flag, they thought, a host of Loyalists would rise from the back-country districts and from the thousands of Scottish Highlanders who had recently settled in both North and

South Carolina.[1] Accordingly, the government in London worked out a plan in the summer and fall of 1775 to send an expedition to the South. Regiments were to be mustered at Cork and were to sail in early December, escorted by a squadron under Sir Peter Parker. Lord Cornwallis's request to accompany the expedition was granted, but Clinton was to be given command when he joined it at Cape Fear after sailing from Boston. The government expected that the provincial governors, particularly Martin and Dunmore, would synchronize their Loyalist risings with the appearance of Clinton's expedition.

But the affair did not come off quite as anticipated. In the first place, the Earl of Dartmouth was succeeded as secretary of state for the colonies during the late fall by Lord George Germain. If Dartmouth was naïve, Germain was close to being morally bankrupt, besides showing consistently poor judgment in the management of his office and letting his decisions be continually colored by his personal tastes. He had little liking for Clinton, distrusted Howe, and hated Carleton. At the same time, he was eager to crush the rebellion and willing to continue with the expedition to the South. Unfortunately for the British, disputes with the Irish executive, contrary winds, and winter storms held the bulk of the expedition in home waters until April. By the time it had gathered off the American coast, events had occurred in the South which altered the original plan of operations.

The initial frustration to the British effort took place in Virginia. Dunmore encountered opposition from most sources except the citizens of Norfolk, who felt their interests so strongly jeopardized by the Patriot assembly in Williamsburg that, in October, 1775, they invited Dunmore to take possession of Norfolk.[2] When the Patriots mustered three hundred militia from Princess Anne and Norfolk Counties, Dunmore, with a few regulars, Scottish clerks, and Negroes, marched toward Kempsville and easily dispersed the rebels. Thereafter Dunmore received oaths of allegiance from several thousands, harassed the shores with marauding expeditions, pledged slaves their freedom on November 17 if they deserted their masters, and raised two regiments, one of them colored.

Dunmore had thus thrown down the gage to Williamsburg. Even the most conservative members of the tidewater aristocracy could not tolerate Dunmore's pandering to the slaves. The assembly dispatched two regiments to Norfolk, while Dunmore, with about five hundred regulars and auxiliaries, took up a defensive position at Great Bridge commanding the route to Norfolk. On December 11, Colonel William Woodford attacked him with seven hundred Virginians and, with a reinforcement of two hundred North Carolinians, drove him headlong into Norfolk, which he soon evacuated. After receiving additional men and munitions from Boston and St. Augustine, Dunmore exchanged fire with Patriot forces ashore on New Year's Day, 1776, destroying numerous warehouses and about fifty residences. This was all the encouragement the militia needed. Eager to wipe out the nest of Loyalism, the Patriots went on a wild spree of incendiarism that consumed nearly nine hundred houses; in February, they finished off the four hundred remaining structures to make Norfolk useless henceforth to Dunmore.[3] Thus war came to Virginia. Not only did Dunmore receive the onus for destroying Norfolk, but his precipitating hostilities seriously impaired the efforts of the government in London to secure the aid of known Loyalists in Virginia and to split the Patriot party.

Virginia was not alone in creating difficulties for the British. In North Carolina, Martin issued orders in January to the Highlanders to rally around the king's standard under Brigadier General Donald McDonald. The Loyalists were to assemble as secretly as possible and march to the coast to join the governor and the expected regiments from Ireland. Presently, McDonald and his field commander, Captain McLeod, reached the bridge crossing Moore's Creek seventeen miles from Wilmington with upward of sixteen hundred men. Gathered to oppose them under Colonel Richard Caswell were a battalion of minutemen from New Bern and militia companies from Craven, Johnston, Dobbs, and Wake, and, under Colonel Lillington, a second battalion of minutemen from Wilmington. When the Loyalists, other bridges demolished, converged on Moore's Bridge, the Patriots halted their advance on February 27, 1776. Making a frontal attack upon Patriot entrenchments, the Loyalists encountered a fierce fire from muskets and artillery, losing thirty men killed or wounded, and eight hundred and fifty captured. The survivors scurried for the back country, pursued and harassed by angry and rather merciless bands of Patriots, who suffered only two men slightly wounded in the fracas.[4]

Although Governor Martin made light of the defeat, General Clinton took a contrary view when he arrived at the Cape Fear River six weeks afterward. Cornwallis and the Irish expedition had not arrived; in fact, they did not put in an appearance in full force until May. By that time, as Martin mournfully wrote to Germain, Clinton considered an invasion of North Carolina unfeasible since the Patriots now dominated the province, the army lacked the necessary land transportation on which it had been counting, and time was running short for Clinton's rejoining Howe at New York.[5] Clinton had little sympathy for Martin or other colonial governors. In his opinion governors were "too sanguine and the malady is catching, ministers are soon infected."[6]

Putting aside the North Carolina venture, Clinton decided on a quick thrust at Charleston. His instructions, which explicitly provided for his return to New York within specified time limits, made a sudden heavy smash at Charleston the only alternative to leaving for the North without further delay. With him he had Cornwallis with three full regiments and seven companies from three other regiments, the whole supported by Sir Peter Parker's squadron of two 50-gun ships and six frigates. A combined attack by land and sea, if executed before the South Carolinians had time to construct proper defenses, would carry the city, make possible its use as a British base in the South, and encourage the Loyalists to rise. Hence Clinton left the Cape Fear in early June for Charleston.

As early as January 1, 1776, Congress was aware of a possible attack on the Carolina port. It had already provided for the addition of twelve Southern battalions to the Continental establishment and now authorized South Carolina to increase its allotment by two more battalions. Congress also detached Charles Lee from New York for command of the forces at Charleston. Congress considered Lee the ablest field commander it had and wanted him where action was most imminent and the stakes were highest. He appeared to have the dash and vigor needed for high-pressure situations. It was said of him that once when an individual mentioned the propriety of appointing a day of fasting and prayer for the assistance of the Almighty, Lee replied, "Give me ten thousand more good fighting Fellows; and God Almighty may take which side he pleases." By thus making provision for troops and by sending its most distinguished officer to the scene of action

Congress may well have thought that it had nicely taken care of any contingency.[7]

But South Carolina was leaving nothing to chance or Congress. For months her men had been throwing up earthworks, mounting cannons, and raising troops.[8] It may have been her good fortune, too, that Colonel William Moultrie had nearly finished his fort on Sullivan's Island before Lee arrived to take command three weeks before the British assault. The defenses of Charleston were by no means inconsiderable. To the north of the harbor entrance the city was covered by Sullivan's Island, on which lay the fort soon to be named after its defender, Colonel Moultrie. Palmetto logs enclosed a fill of soil to the thickness of sixteen feet. There were four bastions, a ditch in front of the outside wall, and thirty guns available. The small garrison consisted of the three hundred and forty-four officers and men of Moultrie's 2d South Carolina Regiment, plus a small artillery company. But Moultrie was not the only fortified point. Between Sullivan's Island and Long Island to the north ran a strip of water known as "The Breach." Since the Americans anticipated a possible British landing on Long Island, they stationed the 3d Regiment under Colonel Thomson at the eastern end of Sullivan's Island to cover any amphibious attempt across "The Breach." To the right of the harbor lay James Island with Fort Johnson garrisoned by the 1st Regiment under Colonel Gadsden. Nearer the city were batteries at Haddrell's Point and on the wharves. Altogether, approximately one hundred guns were in place, and the numbers of the Americans grew steadily with the arrival of Continentals from Virginia and North Carolina on June 11 and an additional regiment from Virginia on the 24th. Over six thousand troops were now in position. Lee himself appeared on June 4, and, in Moultrie's opinion, his presence was worth a thousand men.

Meanwhile, Parker's fleet hove in sight of the city on the first day of June. The American fortifications probably concerned Parker far less than the problem of getting his ships across the bar and avoiding shoal water on his way to the city. Information, acquired from sounding operations in the next few days, indicated that his fleet must pass close to the fort on Sullivan's Island to gain the harbor reaches. He landed Clinton's troops on Long Island on June 9 and succeeded, on the following day, in crossing the bar. On the 12th, and again on the

25th, he made as if to move up toward the harbor, but contrary winds forced him back.

Clinton was likewise having his troubles. His troops were to cross to Sullivan's Island at the same time that the ships engaged the fort, the men-of-war doing their best, as Parker said, "to cause a Diversion."[9] To Clinton's "unspeakable mortification," the ford, which had been reported to have been only eighteen inches deep at low tide, was now found to be seven feet.[10] Clinton expressed his willingness to co-operate with Parker, but informed the commodore that, unless the latter provided more boats, the troops would be unable to effect a successful crossing. Though Parker replied to the letter, he appears to have done little toward helping Clinton out of his predicament. Instead, he evidently resolved now to depend largely upon the fleet. Thus, even as co-operation between the services broke down in Boston, so now did it fail in Charleston.[11]

The plan of action was well conceived, though circumstances of nature and the resistance of the Americans made its execution difficult. The *Solebay,* 28 guns, was to lead the heavy division under topsails off Moultrie; following her were the *Experiment,* 50, the *Bristol,* 50, which was Sir Peter Parker's flagship, and the *Active,* 28. Another division, consisting of the *Sphynx,* 20, the *Actaeon,* 28, and the *Syren,* 28, was to move south of the first division and take a station west of the fort where the ships could enfilade the unfinished face of Moultrie with their starboard broadsides and hammer the batteries at Haddrell's Point from the other side. The mortarship *Thunder Bomb* and the frigate *Friendship,* 22, were to shell Moultrie from the southeast. Meanwhile an armed schooner and a sloop were to aid the boats in ferrying Clinton's troops across the Breach to assault Moultrie from the landward side.

Lee regarded the fort as a slaughter pen and urged Moultrie either to abandon it or to finish quickly the construction of a second bridge between the island and the mainland north of Haddrell's Point. Moultrie, however, had such confidence in the strength of his fort that he would not consider evacuating it, nor did he hurry the construction of an auxiliary bridge. Since Moultrie's view was supported by the energetic President Rutledge of South Carolina, Lee sent additional troops to Colonel Thomson at the Breach and busied himself strengthening the defenses on the mainland.

On the morning of June 28 came the favoring breeze that Parker needed. Attack signals flew from his flagship, and the vessels took places in their respective divisions. The men stood at their battle stations, tense but probably relieved that the ensuing action would bring a victory that would soon send them northward where their bare feet would no longer burn on the hot decks, and where they would not have to fight the hordes of mosquitoes that clustered about the low-lying shores. This crude fort of logs and earth certainly did not look as if it could withstand the broadsides of the king's ships at a range of half a musket shot. At eleven o'clock in the morning, the heavy division let go its anchors off the fort, and the order to fire rang along the stifling gundecks.

Ashore the cannonade—the most furious fire, Charles Lee said, that he ever heard or saw[12]—had an effect quite unlike what either Lee had feared or the British obviously hoped for. Moultrie, on horseback, was inspecting the defenses at the north of the island when the movements of the redcoats across the Breach and the activity in the fleet sent him galloping back to the fort. He arrived none too soon, for the men-of-war were already drawing abreast of the fort. Moultrie was an old Indian fighter, as was one of his chief subordinates, Francis Marion, who was later to employ so successfully against the British the fighting tactics he had learned against the Cherokees. Moultrie ordered his men to take their time and make every shot tell. A naval bombardment has a special horror all its own in volume and weight of fire. When delivered at short range as against Fort Moultrie, it was no wonder that at first the gun crews in the fort returned the fire with a nervous rapidity that made alarming inroads on the supply of powder. But presently they steadied and, at Moultrie's explicit direction, concentrated on the 50-gun ships with a deadliness that became appalling as the bombardment stretched into the early hours of the evening.

Everything seemed to go wrong for the British. The crew of the *Thunder Bomb* overcharged their mortar so that it sprang loose from its bed and became inoperative. The division of light frigates passed the heavy division but went aground for several hours on the sand bars, the "middle ground shoal," where Fort Sumter was later constructed. One of them, the *Actaeon*, never did float clear, so its crew set it afire early the next morning and blew it up rather than let it fall into the hands of the Americans.

But the worst destruction occurred in the heavy division. Both the *Experiment* and the *Bristol* suffered severely in loss of life and the number of wounded, while the damage was so extensive that fears were expressed among the crews that they might never get the ships over the bar again. At one time, the *Bristol*, her cable cut by a round-shot, swung helplessly stern-to, whereupon the Americans raked her so effectively that they cleared her quarterdeck of every man save the commodore. Even he had his breeches blown off and suffered painful wounds in his knee and thigh. Had not the fort run short of powder, the losses on the *Bristol* might have been larger. But by the time Rutledge and Lee succeeded in getting an additional supply of five hundred pounds to Moultrie, the ship had swung into a safer position. Finally, at nine o'clock, Parker ordered his fleet to retire. All vessels were damaged, his flagship alone had been hit seventy times, and his losses totaled sixty-four dead and one hundred and sixty-one wounded, a number of whom died after the battle.[13]

The garrison of the fort won high praise from both American and British combatants. Even Lee professed himself "astonished" by the behavior of the garrison, both men and officers. He had "no idea that so much coolness and intrepidity could be displayed by a collection of raw recruits."[14] The behavior of Sergeant William Jasper must have been quite incomprehensible to him, for when the flag was shot away in the midst of the battle and fell outside the fort, the gallant Jasper, reported Moultrie, jumped through an embrasure, climbed back with the banner, and, fixing it to a sponge staff, planted it solidly upon the ramparts. Moultrie lost, according to Lee's report, only ten killed on the spot and twenty-two wounded.[15]

While the ships were pounding the fort, the army failed in its assault mission. Clinton admitted that he doubted the result of the fleet action as soon as he noticed the misfortunes Parker was experiencing, but he did what he could. Notwithstanding the difficulties presented by the ford and the opposition, Clinton said that he "made every demonstration, every Diversion by Cannonade while the Sands were uncovered, I ordered small Arm'd Vessels to proceed towards the Shore, but they all got aground." Eventually, he even disposed ordnance and troops for one attack which he considered as dictated by necessity, although contrary to military principle.[16] Perhaps it was his good fortune that the fleet retired when he was ready. Though Clinton was bitterly criticized for not supporting his end of the contest, the fault was as much Parker's as Clinton's for not making more boats available. Yet surely the troops had been encamped long enough on Long Island to have constructed the necessary number of craft for the amphibious operation contemplated. On the other hand, according to Lord Rawdon, the troop-laden boats would have had to proceed through a channel "so narrow as only to admit one boat abreast, exposed to the fire of a three gun battery which directly confronted them."[17] Notwithstanding the oversights and breakdown of co-ordination between the services, the king subsequently approved Clinton's decision not to commit his troops to "so desperate and hopeless an undertaking."[18]

The whole affair was a sharp reverse for the British, particularly for the ambitious Clinton, who, after keeping his troops exposed for three weeks longer to the mosquitoes, heat, short rations, and brackish water, sailed for New York on the *Solebay*. Any hope of immediately regaining the South for the crown by the combined efforts of the British armed services and the Southern Loyalists was utterly smashed. The wave of elation that swept over the South made it hazardous in the extreme for any man to speak out for the king; for the forces that had driven off the British and crushed the power of the Cherokees, whose rising had been timed to coincide with the attack upon Charleston, could now be turned with dreadful effect against the Loyalists. Most of the latter, therefore, bided their time until the crown should once again focus its attention on the South. They had to wait three years.

The Gathering of the Armies before New York

The score of the war by early summer of 1776 was slightly in the Patriots' favor. To balance the enforced British evacuation of Boston, the Americans had been driven out of Canada. On the other hand, the sturdy defense of Charleston had decisively checked, for the time being, the British attempt to invade the South. But it was clear to the Americans that the great British thrust was yet to come and that New York was the likely objective.

Washington had sent Lee to organize the New York defenses as soon as the intelligence reached him of Clinton's visit there en route to Charleston. Lee had little time to do more than plan certain defenses and organize militia from New York, New Jersey, and Connecticut before Congress hurried him southward to take over the new Southern Department.[1] Fortunately Howe's departure from Nantasket Roads permitted Washington himself to move south to New York and assume personal command of the defense of the port. By land to Norwich, Connecticut, and thence by the Sound to New York, Washington soon placed his troops in the strategic city and its environs.

Plans for the defense required a far larger force than Washington had available. As of the middle of May, he had only about ten thousand troops on hand. Finally, on the third day of June, Congress decided to support the army with thirteen thousand five hundred militiamen from Pennsylvania, Maryland, and Delaware.[2] Yet even when British topsails rose in clouds over the horizon off Sandy Hook on June 29 the American army was hardly adequate for its task.

When Lee came down in the winter, he had been puzzled by the difficulty of defending New York, surrounded as it was by navigable waters which would permit the British complete command of its approaches. He planned, however, to control the East River from the Battery to Hell Gate by forts on both banks; to invite an attack to the west and south and make such a landing costly; to fortify numerous places north of the town; and to hold Brooklyn, whatever happened, since it commanded the town itself. Washington further developed this plan, attempting indeed to keep the enemy out of the North River. Though Lee's early judgment that the North River could not be closed was later borne out, Washington, confirming Putnam's estimate of the importance of securing certain key points, placed seven guns on Governor's Island and five on Red Hook. To guard the Jersey shore, Paulus Hook, an island at the time, was fortified with eight guns.

Washington made an additional change to Lee's plans. He extended Lee's lines on Brooklyn Heights to a position approximately one mile back of the Heights and running from Gowanus Creek to Wallabout Bay. From his park of assorted artillery gathered from Boston, Ticonderoga, and the Bahamas, he made over a score of guns available to secure the line. Possession of this area on such a scale would appear to indicate an early conviction by Washington that the place could be held. It is interesting to note that it was not until after the Battle of Long Island that Charles Lee declared he would have had nothing to do with the islands near New York.

The final step in fortifying the New York position was taken during the summer. Works were constructed to secure a possible retreat by way of Kingsbridge and at the same time close the Hudson. Predominant on the island was Fort Washington, enclosing an area of great natural strength consisting of steep ground, rocks, and woodland. Fort Lee over on the Jersey bank also provided some protection. With these last fortifications being rushed to completion, Washington might well feel some confidence in his position. He had at least done everything he could to strengthen his defenses, even to sinking hulks in the channel of the East and North Rivers, constructing fireships, and helping make preparations for the construction of a great chain, over two thousand feet long, which was to be stretched across the Hudson in the vicinity of Fort Montgomery.[3]

Such forces as the Americans could muster were in no way sufficient to cope with the massive British armament destined for New

York. Much of the British force was Hessian. Though Parliament had voted to raise an army of fifty-five thousand men, recruiting became such a slow business that the government went into the German market and negotiated with the Landgrave of Hesse, the Duke of Brunswick, and various minor princelings for the loan of troops on a cash basis.[4] The government undertook to pay all expenses of all soldiers obtained, as well as $35 for every soldier killed, $12 for each one wounded, and over a half million annually to the landgrave himself. Three-fifths of the thirty thousand troops thus obtained were from Hesse.[5]

For the first great drive, which the government hoped would scotch the rebellion, the British planned to send seventeen thousand Hessians, as the Germans were collectively labeled. These, added to the British forces either already in or being dispatched to America, would raise the army to about forty-two thousand men. This number was considered sufficient to dispose of whatever masses of Continentals and of half-trained militiamen the Americans might throw against them.

The British were counting heavily on their expedition to New York, for New York was the key to what was evidently a strategic plan which aimed to split New England from the Middle Colonies. Though the outline of this plan did not become clear to all until 1777, it was clear enough to Washington when he wrote, the very day the Declaration of Independence was signed in Philadelphia, that it seemed beyond question the British would attempt to unite their two armies, Carleton's and Howe's.[6] The connecting link was the Hudson and the waterways to the north, a route only too well known to Sullivan's "small-pox army" in its tragic retreat. Sea power would give the British control of the Hudson, which was navigable as far as Albany. A junction of forces at that point would sever the hotly rebellious colonies of New England, which supposedly could be subjected at once or kept isolated until the revolt was suppressed elsewhere and then be reduced at will. Evidently the British were now aware, as Adjutant General Harvey had been in 1775, that a settled plan of operations was absolutely necessary, because, in the words of that realistic bulldog, the revolt in America was "an ugly job . . . a damned affair indeed."[7]

Howe embarked close to ten thousand troops at Halifax on June 7 and, four days later, weighed anchor for New York with nearly one hundred and fifty sail, including transports, warships, and miscellaneous craft. He himself flew on ahead in the fast frigate *Greyhound* to hold secret conversations with Governor Tryon of New York. Raising Sandy Hook on July 25, he talked with Tryon and important New York Loyalists and formed the opinion that he could safely land his troops at Gravesend. Subsequent intelligence, however, gleaned largely from Loyalists who indicated where Washington had placed his batteries and disposed his troops,[8] convinced him that the American position was too strong to be taken before the arrival of the main body of British and Hessian forces.

Meanwhile the British convoys began to make the offing. Sight of the gathering mass of sail within the Hook prompted Washington to issue evening orders on July 2 that his men keep their firearms by them during the night and be ready to turn out at a moment's warning.[9] With fifty ships plowing up the bay that evening and anchoring on the Staten Island side, his apprehensions appeared justified. The next day he ventured his opinion to Congress that the British might be intending to cut off Long Island and secure the livestock on it.[10]

As a matter of fact, Howe felt himself in no condition to open hostilities. Scarcely half his troops had arrived, he was woefully short of camp equipage, and, as Washington had judged, he lacked adequate food supplies. Learning that the Americans were working to prevent passage of the North and East Rivers by batteries and sunken ships, he made up his mind to take up a position of watchful waiting on Staten Island until he held all the high cards. More cautious since Bunker Hill, he was henceforth a general who would leave nothing to chance. But when Howe was ready, he could hit hard.

In the course of the next few weeks, he obtained what he wanted. His brother, Admiral Lord Howe, appeared on July 12 with one hundred and fifty loaded transports convoyed by a powerful squadron, consisting of numerous frigates and several ships of the line. On August 1 came the transports bearing the troops of Clinton and Cornwallis from the abortive Southern campaign. The main reinforcements, however, along with the camp equipage, arrived on August 12, when Commodore Hotham brought in twenty-six hundred British troops and eighty-four hundred Hessians literally sick from the endless sea voyage, the wormy biscuit, the maggoty peas porridge, and the

In COUNCIL of SAFETY,

Philadelphia, *December* 8, 1776.

SIR,

THERE is certain intelligence of General Howes army being yesterday on its march from Brunswick to Princetown, which puts it beyond a doubt that he intends for this city —This glorious opportunity of signalizing himself in defence of our country, and securing the Rights of America forever, will be seized by every man who has a spark of patriotic fire·in his bosom. We entreat you to march the Militia under your command with all possible expedition to this city, and bring with you as many waggons as you can possibly procure, which you are hereby authorized to impress, if they cannot be had otherwise—Delay not a moment, it may be fatal and subject you and all you hold most dear to the ruffian hands of the enemy, whose cruelties are without distinction and unequalled.

By Order of the Council,

DAVID RITTENHOUSE, Vice-President.

To the COLONELS or COMMANDING
OFFICERS *of the respective* Battalions *of*
this STATE.

TWO·O'CLOCK, P.M.

THE Enemy are at Trenton, and all the City Militia are marched to meet them.

Circular of Philadelphia Council of Safety

rotten, stinking pork. The Hessians were relieved indeed at the prospect of being out of quarters so cramped that the men had had to lie spoon-fashion. (When they grew weary of lying on one side, one man would call "About face!" and the whole file would turn over.[11]) Finally, three days later, Sir Peter Parker limped in with his fleet battered by the guns of Moultrie. A formidable assemblage of military and sea power at their command, the Howes could dispose of thirty-two thousand troops, over four hundred transports, ten ships of the line, and twenty frigates. The naval force alone could muster ten thousand seamen and twelve hundred guns, many of them of the heaviest caliber of the day.[12] The enthusiasm of the British, moreover, was high. "This morning, as soon as it was light, we were gladdened with the sight of the grand fleet in the offing," wrote Ambrose Serle, Lord Howe's secretary, on Hotham's arrival. "The joy of the navy and army was almost like that of a victory. . . . So large a fleet made a fine appearance upon entering the harbor, with the sails crowded, colors flying, guns saluting, and the soldiers . . . continually shouting."[13] But to the anxious watchers in the city who lined the housetops and the wharves there appeared little to rejoice about in this great display of British might.

Powerful as their forces were, the Howes showed considerable reluctance to touch off the fireworks. They had demonstrated to Washington on July 12 that his defenses could be breached by sending the *Phoenix*, 40, and the *Rose*, 20, up the North River despite the hot challenge from the American batteries. The ships remained unmolested in the upper river until a fireship attack on August 16. Their passage, however, had proved that the British could cut at will the water communications with Albany and the American forces in the north. Washington was distressed not only by this fact but also by the effect that the women and children, running helter-skelter and shrieking their fright of the cannonade, might have on his half-trained troops. While he himself was not averse to a trial of strength, the Howes chose to temporize.

There is little doubt that the Howes disliked fighting Americans. They could not forget that Americans had placed a statue of their brother in Westminster Abbey after he fell during General Abercrombie's blundering campaign to take Ticonderoga in the late war with France. Neither could they forget that they were Whigs and that a Tory government sat in London. Richard Howe particularly abhorred the whole situation. Unlike the pleasure-loving William, "Black Dick" was a serious, earnest man. He was also a superb sailor and a rugged fighter. His seamen used to say that when Black Dick smiled, a fight was brewing. Though in opposition to Lord North's government, he was nevertheless an Englishman and the Americans were undeniably rebels. Yet he had high hopes of inducing them to see the folly of their ways without bloodshed. Hence he brought to America a commission to make peace, if possible, and instructions to make war if peace was out of the question.[14]

Lord Howe arrived after the Declaration of Independence was signed. Word of the signing had reached New York only two days before Black Dick appeared on July 12, and a howling mob had signalized their joy by pulling down the 4,000-pound lead statue of George III on Bowling Green, which the patriotic ladies of Litchfield, Connecticut, ran into bullets. Word of the Declaration did not deter Admiral Howe. He sent forward a letter of introduction to Adjutant General Reed from Reed's wife's brother, who expressed a hope that Reed would be hospitable. Distinctly embarrassed, Reed sent the letter on to Congress.[15]

Admiral Howe's next step was to dispatch a flag of truce with a request for a conference with Washington. Reed was sent down to meet the naval officer who arrived with the request. When the Englishman said he had a letter from Lord Howe to "Mr. Washington," Reed replied that he knew of no such person. The officer then produced a letter addressed to "George Washington, Esquire," and offered it to Reed. When the latter said that he could not receive a letter addressed in such a manner, the officer expressed concern and disappointment, since Lord Howe had come with great powers. Upon hearing from Reed that the general's station in the army was well known, he returned to Admiral Howe.[16] As Washington wrote Congress, more was at stake than a point of punctilio. He considered it a duty to his country and to his position to insist upon a respect which, in other than a public view, he would willingly have waived. At the same time, he was sure that, in view of the supposed nature of the mission, the Howes would repeat their attempt.[17]

Washington had guessed shrewdly. The second attempt was made on July 19, this time by William Howe, who sent in a flag, asking if his adjutant general might hold an interview with "General Washington." But when Colonel Patterson, the adjutant general, arrived, he took from his pocket a letter addressed to "George Washington, Esq., etc. etc." Again Washington refused to receive it, whereupon Patterson delivered a verbal report of its contents. Actually it had to do only with the British general captured at Montreal, "Savage" Prescott, who was alleged to be suffering from his treatment by the Americans. When Washington replied that Ethan Allen and other American officers were as badly treated by the British, Patterson remarked that they were beyond General Howe's jurisdiction. He proceeded to express the hope held by Admiral Howe that a reconciliation was still possible, and announced that both the Howes had been specially nominated as peace commissioners by the king. Washington retorted that, from what had transpired, they had only the power to grant pardons, and that those who had committed no fault needed no pardon. Furthermore, he pointed out, it was Congress with whom the commissioners should negotiate. Patterson then expressed his appreciation for not having been blindfolded, declined Washington's offer of lunch, and returned to deliver his report.[18]

It became clear to the Howes at this juncture that the Americans were not now of a mind to listen to the sweet reason of a British point of view. The Declaration, of which Lord Howe's secretary said that "a more impudent, false and atrocious Proclamation was never fabricated by the Hands of Man," had stiffened wills and given a new and inspiring direction to the opposition to the crown. "The Faction," continued Serle, "have thrown aside all Appearances at length, and declare openly for Independence & War."[19] Perhaps they would be more amenable after they had sampled British power in action. Accordingly, staff meetings were held and plans developed for the transfer of large numbers of troops from Staten Island to Long Island under the protecting guns of the men-of-war.

With the British readying for an attack, and Long Island their obvious objective, Washington may well have been relieved at the prospect of coming to grips with them at last. Peace rumors were playing such hob with his army that he actually issued an order against rumormongers.[20] It is unlikely that he was greatly discouraged by the presence of such large enemy forces. His orders to his troops indicate a strong conviction of his ability to withstand the assault when it should come. At the same time he pointed out their responsibility when he told them that the fate of unborn millions depended on their courage and conduct.

And yet Washington, for all his seeming confidence, must have had a few qualms, for he was a practical man and experienced at least in frontier warfare. Desperate efforts by his subordinates and Congress that hot, anxious summer had raised his troops to barely twenty thousand effectives, most of them without field training, poorly equipped, inadequately clothed, and on short-term enlistments.[21] Against the British in the open many of them would run at the first volley. Their forte was fighting behind entrenchments or cover of some sort, and Washington labored to produce another Bunker Hill on Brooklyn Heights, but on an extended scale. He had disposed his army in five divisions under Putnam, Heath, Spencer, Sullivan, and Greene, with one division on northern Manhattan, three at the southern end, and Greene over on Long Island. Greene did his best to strengthen his position. The Long Island mosquitoes, however, showed no favorites, and Greene came down with malaria along with hundreds of his men. By the third week in August, he was critically ill, and was removed to Manhattan. His place was taken by Sullivan.

Thus it was the garrulous Sullivan, a soldier whom ill luck dogged consistently, whose division faced Howe when, on August 22, the British commander with twenty thousand crack troops landed on Long Island.

X

Long Island: the Battle and the Retreat

The British landing operations took place after a night of fierce lightning which killed American soldiers in both New York and Brooklyn. This was at least the third time Howe had crossed water in the face of an opponent: to lead Wolfe's column up the cliffs of the St. Lawrence to the Plains of Abraham, over the Charles to the slaughter at Bunker Hill, and now from Staten Island to the beaches of Gravesend. As in the Boston operation, so now he had superior forces. He had organized the British troops into seven brigades, an advance corps of four battalions of Light Infantry with the 16th and 17th Dragoons, and a reserve of four battalions of Grenadiers with the 33d and 42d Foot.[1] The Hessians he had divided between Colonel Carl von Donop, with the Chasseurs and the Grenadiers, and General Philip de Heister, with two brigades of infantry. All told, Howe had available on Long Island about twenty thousand troops and forty pieces of artillery.

Howe planned well the drive up the beaches, while, to aid him, he had in his brother one of England's greatest admirals. Organized into ten squadrons, landing craft met the transports as the heavily loaded vessels came up in turn. As quickly as possible the troops climbed down into the bobbing craft, which pushed off without delay for the beaches. It was a stirring scene, the bay a scarlet flood of uniforms, the oar blades like silver wings flashing in the sun, the towering white sails of the transports and the men-of-war, the bands aboard the ships playing lively marches to spur on Admiral Howe's bluejackets who manned the flatboats, bateaux, and galleys. So precisely and swiftly did the whole affair go off that, two hours after it began, four thousand troops had landed; by noon, Howe had fifteen thousand men with cannons and equipment ashore. Three days later, the 25th, Heister's Hessians were put ashore with similar dispatch, Donop's men having landed on the 22d with the British. Howe could thus dispose of a force more than double that of the Americans facing him from the defenses of Brooklyn.

The British spread over the beaches unopposed. Perhaps the presence of the men-of-war near shore, with their broadside guns run out and the gunners standing by with lighted matches, had a deterring effect on any American resistance. Colonel Edward Hand had one American regiment in position, but he withdrew it when he learned that Howe had landed in force and contented himself mainly with burning wheatfields as he retreated. Meanwhile the British and Hessians in the reserve under Cornwallis drove on through Gravesend to reach Flatbush by evening of the 22d. Thereafter, for the succeeding three days, the Americans persisted in harassing the invaders with roundshot and grape, while their snipers kept the British in a constant state of uneasiness until the green-clad Hessian Chasseurs and Jägers armed with rifles finally dispersed them.[2]

In the face of the enemy landings, Washington now gave the over-all command in Brooklyn to Putnam, the ranking major general. Washington also reinforced his Brooklyn troops with about ten regiments. Still not content, he personally inspected the defenses with Putnam on the 25th and sharply criticized what he described as "loose, disorderly and unsoldier-like firing."[3] Putnam was in a bad spot, unfamiliar with the ground and the troops. With time running out, he continued Sullivan's dispositions. Between the British and the Americans lay the thickly wooded Guana Heights, which were intersected by four possible troop arteries. Putnam posted regiments to watch the Narrows road, the Flatbush-Brooklyn road, and the Flatbush-Bedford road, but he did nothing to secure the road running from Jamaica to Bedford, particularly where it was bisected by the Flatlands-Flushing road. Yet there is reason to doubt that, even if he had had a regiment covering the vital Jamaica Pass, now at Atlantic and Vesta Avenues, he could have maintained his position for long. His troops were too few and the ground was too extensive. Perhaps the best he could have done would have been to keep from being surprised, to make a rugged defense, and to effect an orderly withdrawal while protecting his flanks.

Meanwhile Howe drew up his plan of battle. His conception was masterly, though his estimate of the American forces exceeded their actual strength.[4] Major General Grant, with two brigades, was to push along the Narrows road and engage Lord Stirling, a New Jersey man who claimed the title from a lapsed and currently unrecognized Scottish peerage. The American left under Sullivan was to be pressed by Lieutenant General de Heister with a total of three brigades. Both Stirling and Sullivan were to be contained until the main British force of five brigades, with Clinton, Percy, and Cornwallis in command, pushed along the Flatlands-Flushing road, swung left at Jamaica Pass and came down the Jamaica road toward Bedford and Brooklyn in the rear of the American forces along the ridge. Howe knew how to conceive a turning movement and had the strength to execute it.

The British started about nine o'clock in the evening of the 26th. Clinton, with Loyalist guides, led off from Flatlands with the advance guard, accompanied by the reserve under Cornwallis. Behind him marched Percy with the main body, which consisted of the Guards and the 2d, 3d, and 5th Brigades. Two hours before daybreak, Clinton halted and ordered out patrols to reconnoiter the pass. Presently one patrol returned with five American mounted officers, all young and, with one exception, lacking in experience.[5] They had been the only Americans near the pass. Had they been alert, one or two at least might have escaped to spread the alarm. As it was, they had been taken in the rear by a British patrol. Still cautious, Clinton waited until dawn before moving forward again, only to find the pass undefended. With Howe himself now in personal command,[6] the troops swung down the Jamaica road toward Bedford. The jaws of the trap were closing upon the Americans, and they knew nothing of their situation.

Meanwhile the British left wing carried out its task. Soon after midnight, Grant's patrols clashed with an American picket under Major Burd of Pennsylvania. Presently the major himself was taken prisoner, but the British advance slowed as Stirling arrived before dawn with orders to hold the line. Stirling sent forward Colonel Atlee and his Pennsylvania rifle battalion to a point in the rear of Red Lion. Atlee quickly moved into high, wooded ground between Grant and Stirling.

Grant had a Scotsman's tenacity. Furthermore, he felt a deep contempt for Americans which dated back to the French and Indian War.

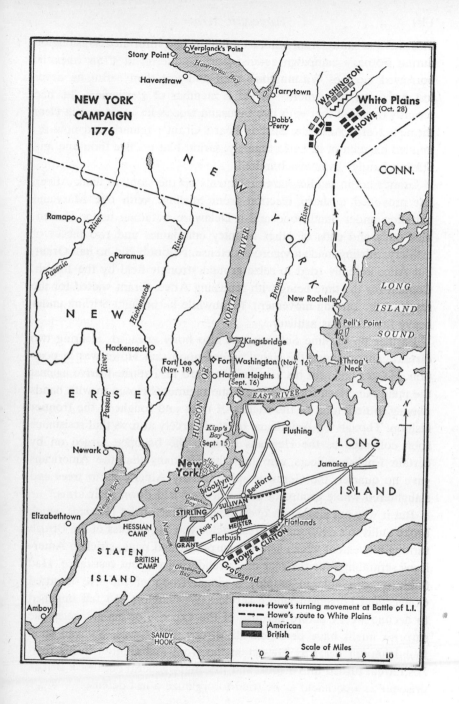

NEW YORK
CAMPAIGN
1776

Stony Point
Verplanck's Point
Haverstraw
Haverstraw Bay
Tarrytown
WASHINGTON
White Plains
(Oct. 28)
HOWE
Dobb's Ferry
CONN.
Ramapo
Paramus
NEW YORK
LONG ISLAND SOUND
New Rochelle
Hackensack
Pell's Point
Kingsbridge
NEW
JERSEY
Fort Lee (Nov. 18)
Fort Washington (Nov. 16)
Throg's Neck
Harlem Heights (Sept. 16)
EAST RIVER
Newark
Kipp's Bay (Sept. 15)
Flushing
New York
LONG
Jamaica
Brooklyn
Bedford
ISLAND
SULLIVAN
STIRLING
(Aug. 27)
Elizabethtown
HESSIAN CAMP
HEISTER
Flatlands
Flatbush
HOWE & CLINTON
GRANT
STATEN
BRITISH CAMP
Gravesend
ISLAND
Gravesend Bay
Amboy
SANDY HOOK

•••••• Howe's turning movement at Battle of L.I.
– – – Howe's route to White Plains
American
British
Scale of Miles
0 2 4 6 8 10

N

This was the same Grant who, as a major, had infuriated Washington during Forbes's campaign against Fort Duquesne in 1758 when he borrowed most of Washington's men and lost them.[7] But he never lost his scorn for Americans. As a member of Parliament, he had recently declared that with five thousand troops he could march clear through North America. Stirling heard Grant's remark and now reminded his men of it. Unfortunately, Grant had his five thousand and Stirling barely seventeen hundred.

Grant's act in sending three regiments up the slope to flank Atlee's left provoked a sharp reaction from Stirling. With one Maryland battalion under Smallwood and a Delaware battalion under Haslett, plus odds and ends of other infantry companies and two pieces of artillery, Stirling made a vigorous defense. Not only did he halt Grant, but Atlee actually tried to seize ground strongly held by the British. Content for the time being with repulsing Atlee, Grant waited for the result of the turning movement. Meanwhile he brought Stirling under heavy fire from his artillery.

Farther up the line Sullivan was also hotly engaged. Hearing two distant cannon shots, the signal agreed upon that Howe was in position, Heister had sent his Hessians forward in a spirited drive against the main American force. While some regiments closed in with bands playing, others took to the shelter of trees and fought in the frontier fashion. Though the Americans resisted fiercely at first, that resistance soon collapsed as the Hessians took to the bayonet. Urged on by certain English officers who told the Hessians that the Americans gave no quarter, the Germans spitted many Americans to trees and slaughtered whole groups of men who had laid down their arms.[8]

But it was not simply an overwhelming fear of the Hessians which broke Sullivan's defense. The real factor was the success of the British turning movement which sent the surprised and panic-stricken Americans scrambling for the rear or surrendering without resistance. Had Sullivan been able to employ a single troop of the five hundred Connecticut horsemen whose services Washington had felt impelled to decline weeks before because of the expense of maintenance, the surprise might have been less disastrous. As it was, Sullivan soon found himself beset by Heister in the front and Clinton in his rear. His retreat turned into a rout, and the angry general became a British prisoner in a cornfield as he tried to organize a last defense.[9]

The pressure on Stirling was now intolerable. American fugitives from Sullivan's force were disrupting both his lines and the morale of his troops with their tales of British and Hessian atrocities. His outposts confirmed the heavy pressure by Clinton and Heister, while Grant had again closed in. He was now surrounded on three sides by the British, Cornwallis having come up into his rear and seized the Cortelyou House which controlled the road to South Brooklyn, while on the left lay the Gowanus marshes with the tide flowing in. At eleven o'clock Stirling belatedly ordered a retreat. Numbers of his troops struggled across the marshes, several drowning in the attempt. Others scattered through the woods toward Hell Gate. Though Atlee surrendered to the Highlanders, Stirling with the Maryland and Delaware troops fought brilliantly. Foiled by Cornwallis in an effort to smash through to the American lines, and feeling the strength of Grant, Stirling moved up a hill only to run into Heister's men pouring over the brow. The American general then deliberately surrendered to the Germans rather than to the hated Grant.[10]

The Americans had been defeated all along the line. The turning movement had been so successful and Sullivan's collapse so complete that it was said even the women camp followers of the British army took prisoners.[11] The only bright spot in an otherwise dismal day had been Stirling's stout defense, tardy though his order of retreat. American casualties in killed, wounded, captured, and missing totaled about fifteen hundred, while the British and Hessians lost sixty-three killed, two hundred and eighty-three wounded, and thirty-one missing.[12]

The British victory, brilliantly conceived and as skillfully executed, might have been even more overwhelming had Howe brought the American entrenchments before Brooklyn under immediate attack. He had several hours of daylight left, and a number of his subordinates stormed with rage when their troops, moving eagerly forward for the kill, were ordered to retire. Howe himself admitted in his report that it required repeated orders to dissuade them from charging the principal redoubt, but, following "the dictates of prudence rather than those of vigor,"[13] he explained, "as it was apparent the lines must have been ours at a very cheap rate, by regular approaches, I would not risk the loss that might have been sustained in the assault. . . ."[14] Perhaps he remembered Bunker Hill, and, like a burnt child dreading fire, refused to be drawn into another ghastly frontal attack. It might also have been that the same reasons, perhaps political, which persuaded him not to crush Washington in subsequent battles were operating now.[15] Whatever the real reasons, they cost him the chance of destroying the American army in Brooklyn and possibly taking Washington himself.

The American commander had earlier arrived at Cobble Hill, site of one of the Brooklyn forts, and viewed the sturdy defense and agonizing retreat of Stirling's men. To strengthen his forces against the expected British assault on the entrenchments, Washington sent to the mainland for additional regiments. One of these was the well-drilled, well-uniformed, and thoroughly equipped Marblehead regiment under the able Colonel John Glover. Glover's command consisted almost entirely of fishermen, and they were shortly to prove their worth on the waters of the bay and later on the ice-strewn Delaware during the surprise attack on Trenton.

There was no time to be lost. Late on the 28th, the British broke ground six hundred yards from Fort Putnam, thus starting the network of approaches so typical of eighteenth-century sieges. As if to add to American difficulties, rain started to fall that afternoon, spoiling a great part of the American ammunition. Moreover, it was only too likely that, when the storm subsided, the British fleet would cut Washington off from the mainland. Accordingly, a council of war in the late afternoon of the 29th decided to evacuate Long Island.

Washington had actually started to organize a withdrawal before the council met. Orders were sent off to General Heath at Kingsbridge and to Hughes, the assistant quartermaster, to collect any boats that would float, equipped with oars, sails, or both, and have them in the East River by dark.[16] To keep up morale, the army was told that since the sick were an encumbrance, and since reinforcements were expected from New Jersey, the sick would be evacuated along with a proportionate number of regiments. Regimental commanders were accordingly directed to assemble their men at seven o'clock, fully equipped, at the head of their encampments and await further orders.[17]

With darkness the evacuation began. Scores of small craft crowded close to Brooklyn waiting to take aboard their cargo. An unfavorable tide and gusts of air from the northeast threatened to pile them onto the shore, but, about half past eleven, the breeze shifted to the southerly and died down.[18] Meanwhile Mifflin with six picked regiments of Continentals remained in the entrenchments to cover the disengagement operation. On the whole, that operation went off very well, but, about two o'clock, with the retreating troops continuing to crowd the boats manned by Glover's Marbleheaders and a number of Gloucestermen from Colonel Hutchinson's regiment, a cannon accidentally went off with a tremendous roar that momentarily made the troops frantic lest the British discover the withdrawal.[19]

Worse still was the error committed by Washington's aide, Alexander Scammel, who gave orders for all the regiments to march to the ferry as he reached them riding from left to right. Mifflin, who was on the left facing Clinton's troops, protested that his covering troops should remain, but, since Scammel insisted that the order was correct, Mifflin withdrew his men. On the way down, Washington, astride his gray horse, halted the column. When Mifflin rushed up to see what was the matter, Washington exclaimed, "Good God! General Mifflin, I am afraid you have ruined us by unseasonably withdrawing the troops from the lines." Mifflin replied with some warmth that he had done so by Washington's order. When the latter declared this to be untrue, Mifflin's edgy temper broke out of bounds. "By God, I did," he roared. "Did Scammel act as an aide-de-camp for the day, or did he not?" Upon Washington's admitting that he did, Mifflin snapped, "Then I had orders through him."

Washington told him it was a dreadful mistake. He also informed him that matters were in such confusion at the ferry that, unless the troops resumed their posts before the enemy discovered they had left them, the most disagreeable consequences would probably follow. Mifflin then ordered his command at once to march back to their former stations, which they reached without the enemy perceiving what was going on.[20] As a matter of fact, however, a Loyalist woman who lived near the ferry had sent her Negro slave to warn the British of what was happening, but the first officer encountered was a Hessian who did not understand him and placed him under arrest.[21]

Despite mishaps, the water operation proceeded without interruption from the British. In the early hours of the morning a fog set in. Although its providential character was probably overrated, since it arrived when the evacuation was well on its way to completion, it helped to mask the withdrawal of the covering party and of Washington himself, who left in one of the last boats.[22] Then the astonished British rushed down the hill, opened a brisk fire, captured a few stragglers, and forced one boat to return.

Thus ended the Battle of Long Island and the famous retreat. From a military point of view, the battle should never have been fought; the Americans should not have been posted in Brooklyn, given the British command of the sea. Washington was still learning at painful sacrifice the lessons of warfare. It is not surprising that Howe won. It is only surprising that he did not capture or destroy the entire American force in Brooklyn. Later, after Howe's cautious tactics became almost a standard order of procedure, nothing was surprising about the British general's behavior. On the other hand, the withdrawal to Manhattan was a remarkable feat, a real Dunkirk performance but executed by the side which did not have command of the sea. Here again, Lord Howe was as negligent on sea as his brother was on land; apparently not even a patrol boat was on hand to challenge the exodus.[23] Underestimating Washington was dangerous, but the British commanders never learned. Even so, the British had won, and Clinton could write, "We have obtained a little victory, it may be, I hope will be great in its consequences."[24] By taking Brooklyn, the British had uncovered New York, and this fact, in addition to their sea power, now made New York untenable for the Americans.

XI

The Loss of New York and the
Retreat across Jersey

The defeat on Long Island raised serious problems for the Americans, not the least being that of morale. "The merry tones of drums and fifes had ceased," wrote that stalwart Loyalist, Pastor Shewkirk.[1] The militia, thoroughly dispirited, quit the war as a bad thing, leaving, as Washington reported in alarm and disgust to Congress, "almost by whole Regiments, by half ones and by Companies at a Time."[2] With deep concern he confessed his "want of confidence, in the generality of the Troops." What to do about the city likewise distressed him, because, while he favored pulling out of what was an obvious trap, he knew the moral effect such a move would have on the fainthearted. Greene and John Jay, a property owner, urged him to evacuate New York at once and burn it to the ground. Congress, however, was adamant against destroying the city for the reason that it would be useful upon recovery, while the generals were at first deeply divided on evacuation. Eventually Washington, instead of withdrawing from the entire island, divided his forces between Manhattan and the mainland at Kingsbridge.

Meanwhile, the Howes, after holding futile discussions with a commission from Congress, prepared again for sterner measures. Men-of-war, transports, and flatboats pushed up into the East River. At the most favorable point troops were to be landed to nip off the island and thereby take the city and capture any American troops lingering in it. On the 12th of September, the American staff belatedly decided to evacuate, but there were troops still in the lower island when on Sunday morning, the 15th, the British unleashed a furious offensive at Kip's Bay, at about the present 34th Street and East River.

115

For some time Howe had readied at Newtown Creek units of British Light Infantry and Hessian Grenadiers and Chasseurs. These were rowed into the East River behind five frigates and sent shoreward when Hotham's frigates opened fire on the position held by the Connecticut brigade under Colonel William Douglas. Unable to stand the bombardment, the Americans broke. Thus the scarlet-laden boats, resembling, as an American remarked, "a large clover field in full bloom,"[3] reached land without mishap, and the troops scrambled ashore without encountering effective resistance. Clinton, who was in command, then formed ranks and drove toward the residence of the Quaker merchant, Robert Murray, on Inclenberg Heights.

Four miles away in Harlem when the men-of-war went into action, Washington spurred to the scene. The panic he observed infuriated him, for both the supporting brigades of Colonel Samuel Parsons of Connecticut and General John Fellows of Massachusetts were in wild retreat. Washington and Putnam used every means in their power to rally the troops but to no avail. The "disgraceful and dastardly conduct of the troops," as Washington described it, compelled him to withdraw toward Harlem, though not before he himself came perilously close to being captured.[4] It was indeed only Howe's supreme confidence, lethargy, caution, or design that kept him from gathering in the troops below the line occupied by Douglas's brigade. This held especially true for Colonel Gold S. Silliman's Connecticut brigade and the artillery under Henry Knox. Desperately Putnam, of whose division they were a part, sought to extricate them, for if the British extended their lines to the North River, these men were lost. There is a pretty story that Mrs. Murray graciously plied the British staff with cakes and wine and listened to the jesting remarks of Governor Tryon about her American friends while Putnam and his sweating, anxious men, led by young Aaron Burr, who knew a route farther to the west, slipped by the British outposts, which were soon extended from Bloomingdale, at the present 97th Street and Broadway, through McGowan's Pass, in Central Park at 107th Street and Fifth Avenue, to Horn's Hook, at 86th Street and East River.[5] Whether Mrs. Murray's hospitality was responsible or not, the British neglected to follow up their initial advantage, thus allowing Putnam's troops to enter the American lines at Harlem after darkness. Possibly some credit was also due a farmboy who, shortly after the last American of one unit had passed through McGowan's Pass on the main road to Harlem, deliberately gave wrong directions to a British mounted scout.

But if there was little commendable in the American conduct on the 15th, the following day witnessed the reverse. Before dawn on the 16th, Lieutenant Colonel Thomas Knowlton, who had fought so ably at Bunker Hill, led out his picked body of one hundred and twenty men, known as "Rangers." Instructed to reconnoiter the enemy's lines, Knowlton pushed down the west side of the island over Claremont Hill for well over a mile until, at about what is now 126th Street, he flushed pickets on the British left flank belonging to General Leslie's brigade. After a spirited half hour of firing, Knowlton retired in an orderly manner, followed by a force of three hundred of the British Light Infantry. When Adjutant General Reed, who had been with Knowlton, made his report, Washington, on Reed's urging, decided to nip off the British detachment. The latter, in high spirits, was now racing toward a little valley, the so-called "Hollow Way" below Riverside Drive at 130th Street, while its bugler tauntingly sounded the notes of the fox chase. Reed said, "I never felt such a sensation before, it seem'd to crown our Disgrace."[6]

Washington moved cautiously until he was sure that the British detachment was not supported; then he made his arrangements swiftly and shrewdly. Lieutenant Colonel Crary of Hitchcock's Rhode Island regiment advanced with one hundred and fifty volunteers to lure the British into the Hollow Way. The feint succeeded, and Nixon's brigade of nine hundred lay hidden in the woods as Crary's support. Meanwhile Knowlton's command, reinforced by three hundred riflemen under Major Andrew Leitch of the 3d Virginia, was sent around to the British rear. Unfortunately, the enemy had evidently discovered the nature of the American attack on their front and, feeling Nixon's pressure, dropped back only to run into Knowlton and Leitch on their flank. Both Knowlton and Leitch fell mortally wounded in the first minutes, but the Rangers and riflemen drove on so vigorously that after an hour of resistance the British withdrew to a buckwheat field on the crest of a hill, where Barnard College stands at 116th Street. There they were joined by two Light Infantry battalions and the 42d Highlanders, the famous "Black Watch" which had fought so heroically, if futilely, in 1758 during Abercrombie's stupid assault on Montcalm's entrenchments at Ticonderoga. Also driving up were the

British Grenadiers, the 33d, a Hessian Grenadier battalion, a company of Hessian Jägers, and a battery of fieldpieces.

Washington countered the British support by throwing in reinforcements, including Colonel Douglas's troops who had fled so ignominiously the day before. Altogether, fully eighteen hundred Americans under Putnam, Greene, and George Clinton challenged the British power in a two-hour give-and-take battle that finally sent the British tide rolling back through an orchard, across a valley, and over another hill to a position near their own main lines at what is now 105th Street. The Americans' blood was up, and it was with some difficulty that the men were halted before charging full tilt into heavy British and Hessian reinforcements pushing up under Cornwallis. Though a large-scale engagement might easily have resulted, Washington judged it prudent to withdraw. After all, he had achieved his purpose: by his little victory he had helped to restore the morale of the American army. The British and Hessians lost fourteen killed and one hundred and sixty-five wounded; the Americans, thirty killed and one hundred wounded.[7]

The strong works at Harlem kept William Howe bottled up for nearly a month, leaving the British commander only the satisfaction of occupying New York itself. The British were wildly received by the Loyalists, women as well as men carrying officers about on their shoulders, while one woman "pulled down the Rebel Standard upon the Ford, and . . . hoisted up in its Stead His Majesty's Flag, after trampling the other under Foot with the most contemptuous Indignation."[8] The joy of the Loyalists, however, and that of the British, who looked forward to using the full facilities of New York as a base of operations, was quickly tempered by the disastrous fire that broke out early on September 21. Nearly five hundred houses were destroyed, which made life very difficult for Loyalists and troops who were looking for adequate quarters. Though the fire was long believed to have been of American origin, the British themselves eventually doubted such rumor.[9] Meanwhile, the day following the fire, young Nathan Hale, a captain in Knowlton's Rangers, was hanged as a spy when caught in his voluntary effort to secure intelligence concerning British troop movements. The brief, immortal words he uttered still catch at the heart in their simplicity and selfless devotion.

The contemplated troop movements of which Hale might eventually have given a full report did not materialize until October 12. Until then, little action occurred apart from that on the 9th when British men-of-war and transports ran past the batteries at Fort Washington on Manhattan and Fort Lee on the Jersey side of the river; even the sunken hulks in the river and the network of chains and booms failed to stop the ships. If this success made Washington uneasy, Howe's subsequent moves were not calculated to quiet his apprehensions. Howe decided at last on what should have been his obvious procedure immediately after the battle on Long Island, or at least after the Battle of Harlem, namely to get onto the mainland, cut Washington's communications, and menace his entire rear.

Howe started this movement on October 12. Since his own works with their focal point at McGowan's Pass were strong enough to be held by a small force, he left Lord Percy there with three brigades, put the rest of his army afloat at 86th Street, threaded his way through Hell Gate, and landed the troops at Throg's Neck, site of the nineteenth-century Fort Schuyler, which now houses the New York State Maritime Academy. This peninsula was virtually an island linked to the mainland by a bridge which Washington promptly destroyed. Any attempt by Howe to cross by fords or to construct another bridge would have been bitterly contested by the Americans swarming in the rifle pits on the opposite shore. Hence, on the 18th, just one day after he had landed his last boatload at Throg's Neck, he re-embarked his army and put the men ashore at Pell's Point below New Rochelle. Why Howe had not landed here in the first place is not clear in spite of his explanation that it would have been an unnecessary hazard.[10] Notwithstanding a sharp skirmish, he easily dislodged the small force under Colonel Glover which attempted to hold up his operation. On the 21st, Howe pushed six miles toward New Rochelle, where he received heavy Hessian reinforcements, and, by the 25th, bivouacked his thirteen thousand men along the Bronx River, four miles from White Plains. With his bad maps Howe must have stared in astonishment at the winding Bronx River, no wider or deeper than a brook. It is said that British headquarters, with its eye on a map of the region, had ordered the navy to take its men-of-war up the Bronx and destroy all American shipping in the river![11] Regardless of this ludicrous proposal, unless Washington could interpose an effective opposition, Howe's flanking movement would soon pay off.

But Washington had anticipated Howe's movement and had taken advantage of the British general's leisurely advance to improve his own position. Spencer's division spread out along the hills back of the Bronx, while his scouts kept in contact with Howe's advance. With the exception of two thousand men left in Fort Washington and over four thousand under Greene at Fort Lee, Washington ordered the rest of his army into Westchester and built a camp at White Plains. The position near White Plains was especially strong, consisting of tiered entrenchments anchored on the left by a swamp and on the right by the Bronx. Farther to the right rose Chatterton's Hill, which was held by Colonel Haslett's Delaware regiment and two guns from Alexander Hamilton's battery, with McDougall's brigade in support.

Howe now moved to the attack on October 28, sending the 2d Brigade and two Hessian battalions directly against the front of Chatterton's Hill and Colonel Johann Rall with his Hessian battalion against the flank. If Chatterton could be taken, the entire American line could be rolled up. Presently four thousand men moved toward the sixteen hundred Americans on the hill; "A bright autumnal sun shed its full lustre on the polished arms, and the rich array of dress and military equipage gave an imposing grandeur to the scene."[12] But the British forded the river and delivered their frontal attack before Rall was in position. The result was that the Americans poured such a devastating fire upon the assault troops that the latter were forced to withdraw. Re-forming, they climbed the hill again; and now Rall swept around to the left, hitting Haslett on the right. The militia wavered, and McDougall wisely ordered a retreat by which he saved the guns and most of his command. It had been a very sharp action, the British and Hessians losing over three hundred killed and wounded, the Americans less than two hundred. Though the hill was now in British hands, such victories were costly, considering the results.[13] For some reason, an attack against the main American position, timed to synchronize with the assault against the hill, never came off. Howe, "for political reasons," refused to explain to the House of Commons why this attack was not delivered, and Cornwallis supported his silence.[14] Could Howe still have been hoping to end the rebellion by mild measures, was he trying to vindicate the Whigs, or was the main American position simply too strong to be carried in view of the probably indecisive results which would ensue?

Whatever his reasons, Howe could not postpone indefinitely his attack. He was reinforced three days after the battle by two brigades under Percy and by General Knyphausen's division of Hessians fresh off their transports. In overwhelming force Howe proposed to attack the American lines on October 31. A heavy rainstorm, however, caused a further postponement, and, on November 1, in the darkness, Washington marched out of his lines to a strong defensive position at North Castle behind the Croton River, five miles away. It would appear that Howe was again checkmated. Certainly he had failed either to cut Washington's communications or to fall upon his rear. On the other hand, Howe was in an admirable position in other ways. Retiring to Dobbs Ferry on November 5, he lay between the American general and Fort Washington, which was at about 183d Street, while with his command of the Hudson he could seriously threaten the troops over at Fort Lee, from which he might move toward Philadelphia.

Washington saw the danger in the division of his forces. Though he was now of a mind to evacuate both Forts Washington and Lee, particularly the former, and pointed this out to Greene on November 8, he left the evacuation of Fort Washington to Greene's discretion.[15] Congress had strongly urged that the fort not be given up, the generals had agreed in a council of war in mid-October, and Greene shared the opinion of Colonel Robert Magaw of Pennsylvania, the fort's commander, that the fort could be defended.[16] When Washington, leaving Lee with five thousand men at North Castle and Heath with three thousand at Peekskill, joined Greene on November 13, he could not make up his mind whether Greene was right in not withdrawing the garrison. Though he trusted Greene's judgment, he was now on the ground himself, and therefore responsible for the failure to evacuate the fort.[17] On the 16th, deciding to inspect the situation at first hand, he crossed the river with Greene, Putnam, and Mercer. They had scarcely set foot on land when the British guns opened on Fort Washington. After observing the battle, they left a bare half hour, or, as some said, but fifteen minutes before Magaw surrendered.

Howe had planned and executed his assault upon the fort with great skill. The fort occupied the crest of the western ridge and possessed five bastions. It was protected by steep, forested ridges studded with guns and entrenchments. Howe had thirteen thousand men available, and mounted batteries on the east side of Harlem Creek to support his attack. Four columns were to converge on the fort: Knyphausen's Hessians to the number of five thousand against the north side from Kingsbridge; Cornwallis with the Guards, the Grenadiers, the Light Infantry and the 33d against the east front from the creek at 196th Street; the 42d Highlanders to the south of Cornwallis in a feint at 165th Street; Percy with nine battalions and a Hessian brigade against the southern sector at 125th Street. On the 15th, Howe threatened to put the Americans to the sword if they did not surrender. When Magaw refused, the guns on Harlem Creek and from a man-of-war in the river burst into a roaring barrage, and the columns at once moved forward.

American resistance to the heavy onslaught was spotty. At first the militia stood so firm that, between the American small-arms fire and the rugged ascent, the British made little headway. Then, as their pressure increased, particularly as the 42d was reinforced and its feint converted into a real attack, the Americans began to give way and came stumbling up to the protection of the fort. The Maryland troops under Colonel Rawlings who faced Knyphausen and Rall, a stout fighter again that day, bore the brunt of the defense and coolly picked off the Germans. But heavy masses of the latter swarmed over the redoubts and up against the abattis and the felled trees, Knyphausen himself in the lead tearing aside the branches with his own hands. Finally, after two hours of furious combat, the Germans forced their way to the fort, which filled rapidly with beaten men. Convinced that further resistance would be useless and frightfully costly, Magaw complied with Knyphausen's demand for surrender. Even so, the Hessians, who had started to ply the bayonet on their prisoners, were restrained only with difficulty from carrying out Howe's threat of no quarter.[18] They had suffered two-thirds of the total attackers' casualties of four hundred and fifty-eight killed and wounded. The Americans lost fifty-nine killed, ninety-six wounded, and two thousand eight hundred and eighteen captured. Many of the victors thought that if Howe had slaughtered the garrison, an act of severity countenanced by the laws of war in that age, "it would have struck such a panic as would have prevented the Congress from ever being able to raise another Army."[19]

For a usually dilatory general Howe followed up this action with surprising rapidity. On the 18th, Cornwallis landed on the Jersey shore eight miles above Fort Lee and swept down on the fort with forty-five hundred men. Luckily a deserter warned Greene, who was forced to decamp so quickly that he left all his stores, guns, and standing tents behind. The British captured over a hundred prisoners, raising the tally from the two forts to three thousand men, one hundred and forty-six cannons, more than twelve thousand shot, nearly three thousand small arms, and four hundred thousand cartridges.[20] Greene now rushed to join Washington, who was gathering troops at Hackensack. Lee for his own devious purposes refused to comply with Washington's pleas to join him with the large body of troops at North Castle.[21] Hence, when Cornwallis, reinforced on the 24th by nine battalions, drove on, Washington retreated across Jersey with an army that was vanishing from desertion.

The loss of so many men and munitions in the forts was a body blow to Patriot hopes, and the retreat across Jersey a bitter experience. Cornwallis pushed Washington hard as far as New Brunswick, marching twenty miles in one day only to stop at the Raritan on orders from Howe, who felt apprehensive about Lee. Though Lee began at last to move on December 2, Howe knew Washington to be the important prey. He therefore continued a steady, if laggard, pursuit, joining Cornwallis at New Brunswick on December 6. Perhaps, in spite of Howe, the British advance elements stepped up their pace, for they entered Princeton barely an hour after Washington's rearguard had departed. If Howe had wanted to destroy Washington, he could have caught up with him at the Delaware. Instead, he dallied for inexcusable hours in Princeton while the Americans, reduced to about three thousand, rushed toward Trenton, gathered up all the available boats, and crossed over into Pennsylvania. The redcoats, finally on the march, poured into Trenton as the last of the Americans were on the river.

The outlook for the Americans was dark. Howe had only to construct boats or rafts from the plentiful lumber supplies in Trenton to get his army into Pennsylvania and on to Philadelphia. If the Americans made a stand, they were too small in numbers to succeed, for the Pennsylvanians had sent only two thousand men and, to Washington's bitter resentment, the Jersey militia had scarcely raised a helping hand.[22] He summed up the situation neatly when he wrote Lund Washington that, if the army were not speedily enlarged, "I think the game will be pretty well up. . . ."[23]

The American Counterattack at Trenton and Princeton

The entire prospect for the American cause appeared dismal. Congress fled Philadelphia to the doubtful security of Baltimore, blaming short-term enlistments for the American collapse and giving Washington virtually dictatorial powers. Putnam, appointed military commander of Philadelphia, had great difficulty raising troops. In view of the disasters, men were loath to enlist even for a few months, let alone for three years, notwithstanding the promise of Congress to pay a bounty of $10, provide a suit of clothes, and guarantee a certain amount of land. The list of British conquests was itself depressing: Long Island, New York as far as the Highlands, and New Jersey, while, when Cornwallis was harrying Washington, Howe had dispatched Clinton by sea to take Newport, Rhode Island, which was seized on December 8 without resistance. Ominously significant, too, as one thought of them, were the errors in military judgment made by Washington, the losses in American personnel and matériel, and the overwhelming superiority of the British and Hessians in numbers, equipment, and training. The situation had thus changed drastically since March 17, 1776, when Howe was ignominiously driven from Boston.

Notwithstanding the catalogue of disaster, there were a few rays of hope visible to the discerning eye. The first lay in the north, where the army under Sir Guy Carleton had not succeeded in slicing down the Hudson Valley and effecting a junction with Howe. Including Hessians, Canadians, and Indians, as well as British, Carleton had close to ten thousand men. Against this assemblage Schuyler and Gates eventually gathered nine thousand, most of them poorly equipped and wretchedly clothed, and many still suffering from smallpox. They were hardly an effective obstacle to the victorious British, who halted only until the construction of their fleet at St. Johns was finished. Then the scarlet wave would roll down Lake Champlain.

It was now that Benedict Arnold stepped forward and, with Gates's administrative assistance, performed, first, a prodigy of labor and, second, an epic of resistance. Two hundred shipwrights and carpenters, together with sailcloth and naval supplies, were hastily assembled from the coast towns of Connecticut, Massachusetts, and Maine. Axes rang in the woods of the virgin forest fringing Lake Champlain, and out of the green timber Arnold fashioned an oddly assorted fleet of two small schooners, two sloops, four galleys, and eight gondolas. They were sluggish, overgunned, and manned largely by men who had never been aboard ship. With this armada, and not enough powder to spare for target practice, Arnold sailed up the lake and formed a line of battle between Valcour Island and the western shore.

On October 11, Arnold was sharply attacked by the British squadron, which had been augmented in numbers since Carleton had learned of Arnold's activities. It consisted of one ship, two schooners, one floating battery, one large gondola, twenty gunboats, and four armed longboats. The main British ships were larger, built of seasoned timber, better gunned, and manned by officers and men of the royal navy. Notwithstanding the British superiority, the Americans fought a heroic, desperate battle that lasted seven hours, while the Indians tried to make the American decks untenable by firing from the treetops along the shore. At sunset the British withdrew to refit, Carleton realizing that, with the Americans having lost a schooner and a gondola, and their casualties numerous, he could take Arnold in the morning. Despite such calculations, Arnold escaped in a fog, fought the enemy on the 13th at Split Rock until his own galley was utterly shattered, then ran her and the remnant of the fleet ashore, set fire to the ships, and escaped to Crown Point, ten miles below. Though Carleton subsequently captured Crown Point, he considered Ticonderoga too strong to be taken except by a siege and the season too late for such operations. Hence, probably wisely, he withdrew to Canada, but his departure left Burgoyne no advance base for the next campaign and permitted Schuyler to release troops to Washington. It is the considered judgment of no less an authority than Admiral Mahan that the Revolution was saved that summer by the naval efforts of a soldier, Benedict Arnold.[1]

Another ray of hope, not very apparent at the time, lay in the fate of Charles Lee. The American Revolution turned up as singular a collection of characters as any war in our history, and "Boiling Water" Charles Lee proved one of the most extraordinary. He was an able, versatile man, though by no means the genius he thought himself to be. He suffered from a grossly inflated ego, and most people, including Washington, took him at face value. At North Castle he left his commander in chief to struggle with Cornwallis as best he could. He quarreled with Heath. He pointed out to the Massachusetts legislature that Howe really intended no drive into the Jerseys, but into New England. He sought to undermine Washington's position with the latter's own officers. He created the mischief of a divided command, and only at Washington's insistence did he finally set his troops in motion. Even then, he attached to his own command part of the troops released by Schuyler. Then, on December 12, Lee came a cropper. He decided not to bivouac with his troops but at a tavern in Basking Ridge. It was there on the 13th while breakfasting in his dressing gown and slippers, after having written to Gates the notorious letter concerning Washington in which he said, *"entre nous,* a certain great man is most damnably deficient,"[2] that Lieutenant Colonel Harcourt and a patrol of British dragoons from the regiment with which Lee had served in the Seven Years' War surprised him. The capture depressed the Americans and elated the British, particularly George III, who promised to take care of Harcourt's future; Harcourt eventually became a general. It would have been better for the Americans had the British held onto Lee instead of releasing him in a few months. But, through Lee's capture, Sullivan, who had been exchanged for Savage Prescott, assumed command of Lee's troops and joined Washington on December 20. At about the same time, Gates and Arnold arrived with the troops from the Northern army.

There were three other rays of hope. Thanks to the exhortations and promises of General Mifflin, Pennsylvania sent nearly two thousand men to Washington, though these were all too few. Secondly, the British blundered badly with the Jersey Loyalists. Thousands who were eager to take the oath of allegiance were turned into angry rebels by the depredations of the British and Hessian soldiers, particularly the latter. Rape was not uncommon, but the lust to plunder became such a menace to discipline that Howe issued many injunctions against it, blaming it, however, on the shortage of officers.[3] Finally, Howe decided to halt the campaign at the Delaware, a decision which enraged the Loyalists, exasperated his own officers, and gave the Americans time to regroup and plan anew. What motives prompted his decision are as obscure as those which had previously kept him from crushing the American army. Possibly he felt that American opposition might disappear during the winter after his own display of overwhelming superiority in the fall; then he might be able to resume the role of peace commissioner. On the other hand, he may have anticipated greater resistance, have made his plans accordingly, and, faced now with a rapidly changing situation, have been reluctant to alter materially those plans. Whatever the reasons, he was an indolent man addicted to comfort and, like most eighteenth-century soldiers, regarded a winter campaign as something to be avoided at all costs.[4]

It was necessary, however, to provide for the defense of the conquered province. Accordingly, Howe set up cantonments of troops at Perth Amboy, New Brunswick, Princeton, Trenton, and Bordentown. Howe had not wished to include Trenton and Bordentown, since they were so distant. At Cornwallis's insistence, he complied, though he admitted that the chain of cantonments was too extensive.[5] The troop dispositions finished, he granted Cornwallis leave to ship for England, while he himself went back to New York on December 13 to enjoy a pleasant winter with his wines, his comrades, and his mistress.

Washington saw the weakness in Howe's dispositions as early as December 14.[6] Through John Honeyman, a Patriot butcher and cattle dealer who was known in Trenton as a notorious Loyalist, he obtained accurate information concerning the brigade of Hessians there under Colonel Rall. The brigade consisted of Rall's own blue-coated regiment, the black-clad Knyphausen regiment, and the scarlet Lossbergs; in addition there were fifty Jägers, twenty British dragoons, and a detachment of artillery—in all about fourteen hundred men.[7] Rall was reported as being almost constantly drunk. A thoroughly capable officer on campaign, he believed in utterly relaxing when the fighting was over. He was quite contemptuous of the Americans, whom he alluded to as "country clowns," and he ignored the instructions to construct redoubts given by Colonel Carl von Donop, who lay at Bordentown with another brigade of Hessians and the 42d Highlanders. Rall scornfully ridiculed the anxieties of his second-in-command, Major von Dechow, and agreed with the sentiments of his

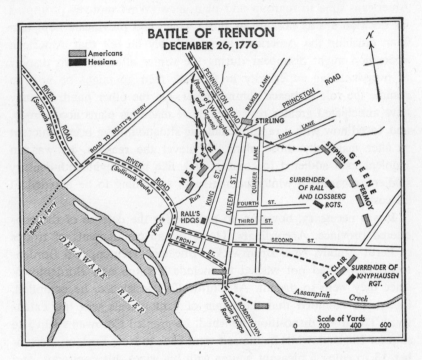

superior, Major General Grant, who, at New Brunswick, vowed that he would undertake "to keep the peace in New Jersey with a corporal's guard."[8] A stalwart fighter, a lover of strong liquor and stout women, a commander who thought nothing of keeping his shivering bandsmen standing in the snow serenading him while he leisurely dressed in the morning, Rall was the man whose downfall Washington contrived.

Washington acted quickly. Just before Christmas his troops numbered approximately six thousand effectives organized into two divisions, eight brigades, and thirty-seven small regiments.[9] They were extended along the fords for twenty miles above Bordentown, while below, at Bristol, lay Colonel John Cadwalader with a Pennsylvania militia regiment. The Pennsylvania navy of gondolas also patrolled the river from Philadelphia to Bordentown. Washington purposed to take the Hessians by surprise on the morning of December 26, one hour before dawn. Cadwalader, reinforced by a New England brigade, was to cross near Bordentown and divert the enemy in that area. General James Ewing was to lead a thousand militia from Pennsyl-

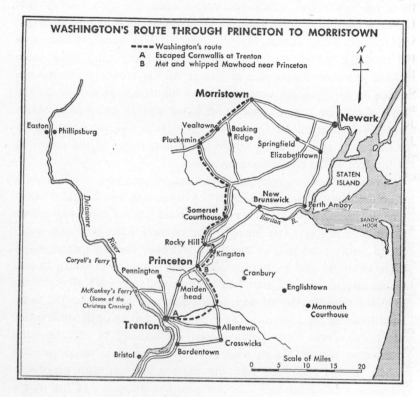

vania and New Jersey over the river from a point directly opposite Trenton and block an enemy retreat by way of the bridge across the Assanpink. Meanwhile the main force of twenty-four hundred men and eighteen guns was to land on the east bank nine miles above Trenton and march upon the town by two roads, Sullivan's division on the river road, Greene's division on a road two miles east. The main street of Trenton was formed by these roads converging from the southeast and northwest. A profound silence was enjoined and no man permitted to break ranks on pain of death.[10]

The whole venture was a hazardous operation, but the general situation demanded that something drastic be done; the Revolution had virtually collapsed. In keeping with the dangerous nature of the enterprise, the night and the river turned forbidding. The wind rose sharply, and, at eleven o'clock, snow mixed with sleet set in and wet the priming of the flintlocks. Thin, jagged cakes of ice floated down from the north and struck the troop-laden boats so heavily that Glover's Marbleheaders, again at the oars as they had been in the retreat from Long Island, had difficulty. It had been expected that the columns would march at midnight, but not until after three o'clock was Knox, who was in charge of the crossing, able to announce in his booming bass voice that all troops were now on the Jersey shore. By four o'clock the column was on the march. Major James Wilkinson later followed the route with ease by watching for the bloodstains in the snow where the frozen ridges of the road had cut the feet of the thinly shod men.

The movement went off like clockwork. A half hour after daylight the column arrived within a mile of the town, and, about eight o'clock, a sleepy Hessian advance guard on each road was surprised and driven in, while shouts of "The enemy! The enemy! Turn out, turn out!" echoed through the roar of the storm. At once the town burst into a welter of sound and wild confusion as the stupified Hessians rushed into the streets, many of them half clothed, and only the Rall regiment, the guard regiment for the day, fully equipped. Though he had to be called twice by his adjutant, Rall eventually tried to bring some order out of the chaos. Then Knox placed his artillery to enfilade King Street, now Warren Street, while the right wing of Greene's division pushed toward Sullivan's left; the cannon opened with grapeshot. American small arms now crackled sharply, and many of the troops of Greene and Sullivan raced in with the bayonet, shouting the immortal words of Tom Paine which had first appeared in Philadelphia on December 19 and had been read before the army on December 23: "This is the time to try men's souls!" Driven out of the north end of the town by the artillery fire, Rall attempted to escape to the east. When this exit was closed off, he ordered a charge but fell mortally wounded. Surrender soon followed.

By half past nine it was all over. While the Hessians threw down their muskets in anger and humiliation, the Americans waved their hats and cheered. They had lost only two men frozen to death on the march and two officers and one private wounded, the officers being Captain William Washington and young Lieutenant James Monroe, the future president. The Hessians had lost thirty killed and thirty-two officers and eight hundred and eighty-six men taken prisoner.[11] Owing to Ewing's inability to cross the river, over four hundred of the enemy escaped to Donop at Bordentown. Greatly disturbed, Donop retired to Perth Amboy at once, thus permitting Cadwalader to occupy Bordentown. Truly might Washington say, "This is a glorious day for our country, Major Wilkinson!"[12] Ironically, a note was found in the dying Rall's pocket from a Pennsylvania Loyalist farmer giving ample notice of the American expedition. When informed of the contents, Rall could also say with equal truth, "If I had read this . . . I would not be here now!" Or, as a young lieutenant of his own regiment wrote for a bitter epitaph:

> Hier liegt der Oberst Rall
> Mit ihm ist alles all![13]

What to do now was a compelling question. The failure of Ewing and Cadwalader immediately to cross the river because of the ice made any attempt to close in on Donop an impossibility. Though Washington would have liked to advance toward Princeton, he was burdened with prisoners, and his own troops were worn out; some of them, moreover, had found the Hessian rum supplies and were celebrating in their own way. Hence Washington retreated into Pennsylvania with his spoils. Once safe, he induced those troops whose enlistments ran out at the end of the year to re-enlist for six weeks longer on payment of a bounty of $10. He ordered Heath to march from Peekskill to Morristown and Cadwalader and Mifflin to join him east of Trenton behind Assanpink Creek. Then, raring to go on the offensive again, he recrossed the Delaware on December 30 and 31.

The British reaction to the disaster at Trenton and Washington's new move was swift and incisive. Cornwallis, about to sail for England to see his ill wife, was ordered back to the Jerseys. Grant, who growled that he never thought all the rebels in America could have captured the Hessian brigade, left six hundred men at New Brunswick and marched on New Year's Day to Princeton, where he was joined in the evening by Cornwallis with a heavy column of troops. Cornwallis was eager to end this winter uprising. He sent his baggage back to New Brunswick, left the 4th Brigade under Colonel Mawhood in Princeton as a rearguard with instructions to follow him on January 3, and marched toward Trenton on the 2d with nearly six thousand men. He drove in the American skirmishers and brought up his artillery. His quartermaster general advised an attack at once on Washington's force of fifty-two hundred, half of them militia, remarking, "My Lord, if you trust those people tonight, you will see nothing of them in the morning."[14] Cornwallis, however, pointed out that his troops had been marching and fighting since dawn, that the Americans could not retreat across the river because they had left their boats above Trenton, and that he could just as well "bag the fox" the next morning.[15]

The American council of war deliberated hard that night. Then someone came up with the idea of a night march by the road to Sand Town, and after that to the northwest on the new Quaker Bridge road. This way the army could get into Cornwallis' rear, march to Princeton, and possibly even seize the British war chest of £70,000 at New Brunswick. Mercer and St. Clair were said to have proposed the idea; even Arnold was credited with it, though that was absurd since Arnold had been ordered to New England a fortnight before. Reed probably knew of the road since he had lived in Trenton and had been a student at Princeton. Furthermore, a map furnished by a spy showed a way out of the impasse. At any rate, it is likely that Washington was prepared to make capital of his situation, and must have had some inkling beforehand of an escape route which he could use to excellent advantage, else he could scarcely have let Cornwallis pin him into such a vulnerable position.[16]

The army now moved swiftly but silently away, muffling the artillery wheels in heavy cloth and leaving the campfires burning brightly. The troops made eleven miles in the night, slower than hoped for, but the roads were wretched and the men tired; for Cadwalader and Mifflin's men it was the second consecutive night march. Sunrise on a frosty morning found the army still two miles from its objective. And there on the road to Princeton Mercer's brigade practically bumped into two regiments of the British brigade under Colonel Mawhood. The latter thought at first the Americans were Hessians; then, learning their identity, he believed them fleeing Cornwallis and sought to halt their retreat.[17] Ordering up the 40th Regiment from Princeton to support the 17th and 55th, he opened fire with his guns, and sent the 17th forward with the bayonet. The violent attack killed Mercer and several high American officers and caused the utmost confusion among Mercer's men. Washington dashed up, helped calm and re-form the fugitives, and brought up additional regiments of veteran New Englanders. Many of Mawhood's men now broke, and Washington joined in the pursuit with the exultant shout, "It's a fine fox chase, my boys"![18] A portion of the indomitable 44th escaped to Cornwallis, though it lost sixty-six killed and wounded and thirty-five captured. The other regiments were smashed back through the town and never stopped until they reached New Brunswick. The total British casualties amounted to two hundred and seventy-three. The Americans lost forty officers and men killed and about one hundred wounded.[19]

This had been a pretty little action, both Washington's evasion of Cornwallis and his rout of Mawhood's brigade, and he would have given much to race on to New Brunswick, capture the great war chest, and isolate the British in southern New Jersey. But those seventeen miles were too much for his exhausted men, who at this stage were simply putting one foot ahead of the other. Knox might well lament that, had a thousand fresh men been available, one of the most brilliant strokes in history could have been recorded. On the other hand, the Americans had already upset the British badly since Christmas Day, boxing them about in Jersey "as if we had no feelings," in the words of a British officer.[20] Hence Washington decided to march toward Morristown; and in the protection of its hills and woods he went into winter quarters on January 7. Into this fastness Cornwallis's cursing, breathless troops dared not push their way. Howe, shocked out of his lassitude, evacuated all Jersey save for the river line from New Brunswick to Perth Amboy. For six months he did nothing singular except to celebrate his new knighthood as a Companion of the Bath, the reward of his New York victories which had been expected to end the Revolution!

XIII

Howe's Invasion of Pennsylvania

How to finish the Revolution quickly was a question which the British attempted to answer in various ways in the course of the war. The strategic move that appealed to certain military minds was the one which Carleton had tried and, in the opinion of his enemies among his own people, bungled. Lamenting to Clinton that "a secondary station in a secondary army is at no time agreeable," Burgoyne sailed for England in the early winter to see what he could do about bettering his position and his country's prospects.[1] On February 28, he submitted to Germain his plan for a three-pronged attack: a main army of not less than eight thousand regulars to push southward from Canada down Lake Champlain, a much smaller force to operate from Oswego through the Mohawk Valley, and a large force under Howe to move up the Hudson. By meeting at Albany, these prongs would cut off New England, and the British could then crush the rebellious sections in detail.[2] Both Germain and the king endorsed the plan and appointed Burgoyne to command of the army from Canada.

Howe had his own ideas of a campaign. He suggested, on November 30, that an army of ten thousand should operate from Providence toward Boston, another one of equal force should move up the Hudson to Albany, and a third, slightly smaller, should cover New Jersey. Once Boston and Albany were taken, the armies should converge on Philadelphia and then march into Virginia and southward. He said he would require fifteen thousand additional troops. Three weeks later, he changed his mind: he would defer action against Albany and Boston and concentrate on Philadelphia since he believed popular opinion in Pennsylvania was receptive to the crown. By the time Germain approved the Philadelphia offensive, Howe reported on

April 1 that he intended to go by sea. Again Germain approved, though he expressed the hope that Howe would be finished in good season to assist Burgoyne. It has been contended on rather dubious evidence that, subsequently, Germain ordered Howe explicitly to move up the Hudson but that, since the instructions were not ready for Germain's signature at the time that Germain was prepared to sign, they were never sent.[3]

The whole situation was confusing. By trying to run the war strictly from London, and by failing to co-ordinate the operations, Germain, even more than Howe, was responsible for the ultimate defeat of Burgoyne. But Howe could not evade a large share of the responsibility, although he certainly never anticipated having to save Burgoyne. His duty was to open the Hudson as far as Albany, but he intended to complete his Pennsylvania campaign first.[4] Clinton deplored the move to the south. He hated the idea of being left in command of the New York garrison and, on July 8, spoke his mind freely on the war. Howe simply stared at him, though he later agreed that Clinton's own force, half of it Loyalist militia, made "a damned starved offensive."[5] Going by sea to Philadelphia had become an obsession with Howe; the objective appeared logical and the route logistically easier and militarily safer. He owed less than is generally supposed to the captured Charles Lee, who, perhaps fearing that Howe might hang him as a deserter from the British army, had proposed an expedition to the Chesapeake.[6]

Meanwhile Washington was having his hands full raising an army and watching Howe. Though, in the fall, Congress had authorized the raising of seventy-six thousand troops, Washington reported on March 14 that his total numbers in Jersey were under three thousand, of which more than two-thirds were militia.[7] While enlistments continued to lag, he possessed by the last of May slightly over eight thousand troops organized into ten brigades and five divisions under Sullivan, Greene, Stirling, Lincoln, and Stephen. Keeping his eye on Howe, he was powerless to check Governor Tryon's raid on Danbury, Connecticut, but had the satisfaction of learning that, after destroying a large store of military supplies, the British were driven back with heavy casualties by the militia under Arnold and Wooster, though Wooster lost his life. In late May, believing Howe intended to march to Philadelphia, Washington moved from Morristown into a strong position at Middlebrook. Howe then tried on two occasions in June to tempt him into a general engagement. The first time he failed; the second time, Washington left Middlebrook, nearly lost Stirling in a British trap, and withdrew thereafter as quickly as possible to Middlebrook. Howe then returned to New York. He embarked his fifteen thousand troops in the first days of July, kept them sweltering aboard ship until the 23d, and finally sailed out into the Atlantic, passing the Sandy Hook lighthouse, which Admiral Howe's secretary acidly described as "a stinking Edifice, by means of the oil and the Provincials stationed in it."[8]

Washington could scarcely believe that Howe had deserted Burgoyne. He did not realize that Howe believed the best way to aid Burgoyne was to draw Washington himself into Pennsylvania. Howe, finding an invasion by way of the Delaware inadvisable because of the river forts, and learning that Washington was already across the Delaware, sailed up Chesapeake Bay and landed at Head of Elk on August 25. Though Washington now quickly marched to meet him, and called upon all New England to turn out and crush Burgoyne, he had lost the opportunity of doing that very thing himself. Operating on interior lines, he might have moved up to assist Schuyler and Gates, and very likely have wrought the downfall of Burgoyne six to eight weeks before it actually occurred. Strengthened by large units from the Northern army, he could then have swung quickly south to meet Howe in Pennsylvania. True, he would have had to give up Philadelphia, but he was forced to do this in any event and suffered two severe defeats before facing the dreadful ordeal of Valley Forge. Furthermore, he weakened himself by sending three thousand troops to reinforce Gates.[9] Over in London, Germain was delighted. "I confess," he said, "I feared that Washington would have marched all his force towards Albany, and attempted to demolish the army from Canada, but the last accounts say that he has taken up his quarters at Morristown after detaching three thousand men to Albany. If this is all he does, he will not distress Burgoyne."[10]

Howe now pushed cautiously across country. Washington, who had marched through Philadelphia to the vicinity of Wilmington, met him along the Brandywine at Chad's Ford on the Philadelphia road. Greene held the center of the American line, his division reinforced by two brigades. To his left were the Pennsylvania militia under Armstrong,

while to his right for two miles upstream in wooded, hilly country lay
Sullivan with his own division and those of Stirling and Stephen.
Altogether, the Americans had eleven thousand men in the line when
the British attacked on September 11. Howe employed a plan that

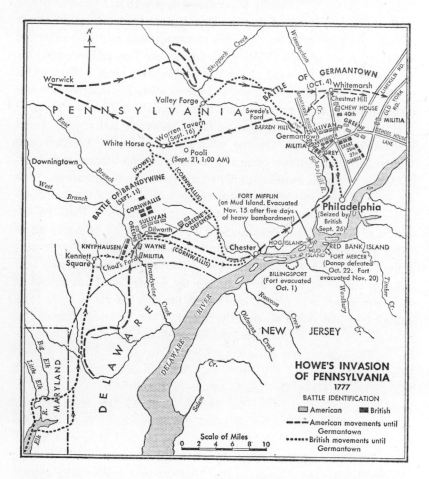

resembled the one used at Long Island: Knyphausen marching eastward to feint at Chad's Ford, while Cornwallis, whose column normally constituted the right wing, was to slip past Knyphausen's rear
twelve miles toward the forks of the Brandywine, ford the stream,
march inland, and come down on Sullivan's rear.

Howe's plan brought the American army very close to destruction.

Up at daybreak, Knyphausen was in position by ten o'clock and commenced a furious cannonade to which Greene replied. Meanwhile Cornwallis disappeared on his march, and American intelligence of this movement was, as Washington admitted to Congress, "uncertain and contradictory."[11] Finally Sullivan's scouts, who had been confused most of the day, reported that the British were readying for an attack in Sullivan's right rear. Sending this announcement on to Washington, Sullivan formed at right angles to his former position and extended his right wing across the road above the Birmingham church. Cornwallis hit him at four o'clock with such violence while his troops were still taking position that, presently, all three American divisions broke.[12]

Fortunately succor was close at hand. Sullivan's last report caused Washington to detach Greene with the brigades of Weedon and Muhlenberg, the fighting preacher, to Sullivan's assistance, thus leaving Wayne with his Pennsylvania brigade opposing Knyphausen. With the roar of cannon and musketry rising ominously as the battle increased in intensity, Greene's column set a fast pace. Even as the march of A. P. Hill's division saved Lee's right wing at Antietam in 1862, so the rush of Greene's division saved the American right wing at the Brandywine. His two brigades are said to have raced nearly four miles in forty-five minutes.[13] Coming up, he deployed his troops in such a manner as to let Sullivan's men through his ranks to re-form behind him and effect an orderly retreat. Then he swept forward to hold the vital escape road and the bisected wooded ridge commanding it. The deathly harvest grew on both sides as the British pressed Weedon's brigade on the ridge and the Hessians swarmed toward Muhlenberg's along the road. Much of the fighting was hand to hand with the bayonet, but the Americans stood firm until Weedon was slowly forced down by sheer weight of numbers. With darkness setting in, Greene brought off both brigades in good order to Chester, where Washington had retreated after Knyphausen, upon hearing Cornwallis engaged, had converted his feint to a real attack, crossed the ford, and smashed back the weak American center.

The action had been severe. In his report, Howe listed his casualties as ninety killed, four hundred and eighty wounded, and six missing; American casualties, never accurately totaled since the dead and wounded were left where they fell, were estimated at three hundred killed and twice that number wounded.[14] Notwithstanding the losses and the defeat, Washington reported the troops to be in good spirits. It was fortunate this was so, for he had clearly been outgeneraled by Howe, whose numbers engaged barely, if at all, exceeded those of Washington. Howe's mistake, as usual, was in not following through, but this time it was understandable in view of the growing darkness and the weary condition of Cornwallis' troops after their approach march and the battle. For men two weeks off transports they had done well.

But Washington was still smelling gunpowder. On September 16, he took the offensive at Warren Tavern, twenty miles west of Philadelphia. His arrival surprised the British, and he might have achieved a notable success if time had not been wasted in preparing the attack. Presently a hard two-day rain put an end to the fighting and Washington withdrew across the Schuylkill, leaving Wayne's troops as a rearguard to worry Howe's left flank. Howe dealt summarily with Wayne. On September 21, at one o'clock in the morning, Major General Grey, who had ordered his troops to remove the flints from their muskets, hurled three battalions with the bayonet upon Wayne's camp at Paoli, catching Wayne completely by surprise. Without firing a shot, and losing only eight of their own number, the British killed and wounded three hundred Americans and captured nearly one hundred more.[15] Wayne never forgot the effectiveness of "No-Flint" Grey's use of the bayonet in the so-called "Paoli Massacre."

Howe moved adroitly in the next three days. Thrusting at Washington's right, he caused the Virginian to withdraw farther up the Schuylkill. Howe then backtracked, crossed the river at Swede's Ford, and drove a wedge of troops between Washington and the capital. Warned by Alexander Hamilton that the city could not be defended, Congress fled to York, giving Washington dictatorial powers for a second time.[16] Not all congressmen shared the feelings of John Adams, who consoled himself by looking forward to seeing a new part of the country. Adams, however, had little liking for Philadelphia and possibly was not surprised to learn that, when the British entered the city on the 26th, thousands crowded the streets, the windows, and the housetops to observe them. Patriots were depressed and referred to the city as a nest of Tories. But Benjamin Franklin, over in Paris, had a different conception. When informed that Howe had captured Philadelphia, he shook his wise old head and remarked, "No, Philadelphia has captured Howe!"

Perhaps it was the ease with which he had taken Philadelphia that impelled Howe to relax. Because of his desire to impress the countryside with British power he refused to authorize entrenchments at Germantown for his main force of less than nine thousand, which extended along School House Lane three miles from the banks of the Schuylkill, its center in the market place where the lane crossed the Philadelphia-Chestnut Hill road. Other troops were stationed in Philadelphia itself and three thousand across the river in Jersey. Such a division of forces had its dangers, but Howe had little choice in view of the American possession of the lower Delaware.

The weakness in Howe's dispositions was not lost upon Washington at his bivouac along Skippack Creek, twenty miles from Germantown. He planned a surprise attack in the early morning of October 4. Hoping for another Trenton, he proposed to have columns march at night over different roads and arrive at a common goal simultaneously at daybreak. Sullivan, leading his own and Wayne's troops, was to move along the main road and engage Howe's center and left. Armstrong with the Pennsylvania milita was to proceed down the Manatawny road between the Schuylkill and the Wissahickon, ford the latter, and harass the rear of the British left. Greene was to take his own division, Stephen's division, and McDougall's brigade over the Limekiln road farther to the northeast and fall upon the British right. Still another mile to the northeast the Maryland and Jersey milita under Smallwood and Forman were to swing down the Old York road and get into the rear of the British right. Stirling's division, acting as the reserve, lay behind Sullivan. To carry out this intricate operation with eight thousand indifferently trained and disciplined Continentals and three thousand unsteady militia, Washington was placing his army's future somewhat recklessly upon the gaming table when his columns, seven miles separating their extremes, shouldered their muskets and footslogged into the night on the long march toward Germantown.[17]

On the 3d, the British had received some intimation that Washington intended to bring on a general engagement, and, although they did not believe it, the staff issued an order for increased vigilance on the part of the British sentries. The effect of the order was largely nullified by a dense ground fog which covered the entire area. The battle began at about four o'clock when Conway's brigade in Sullivan's column tangled with British patrols at Mount Airy. As these were driven in, they fell back on the Light Infantry and the 40th Regiment under Colonel Musgrave. Both units were hurled back as Sullivan developed his attack. Howe, hastening up, cried out in anger, "For shame, Light Infantry! I never saw you retreat before. Form! Form! It is only a scouting-party." Then a serried mass of American infantry shouldered through the fog, and cannon opened upon Howe and his mounted staff. The feelings of the Light Infantry were well expressed by an officer of the 52d who wrote, "I never saw people enjoy a discharge of grape before; but we all felt pleased to hear the grape rattle about the Commander-in-Chief's ears after he accused the battalion of having run away from a scouting party."[18]

Fortunately for the British, Justice Benjamin Chew's stone house, "Cliveden," stood in the path of retreat, and the resourceful Musgrave threw six companies of the 40th inside. Though part of Sullivan's column passed, the Cliveden defenders loosed such a volume of fire upon the balance of the column and the reserve under Stirling that Washington, on Knox's advice, decided not to leave this "hedgehog" in his rear. Accordingly, cannon as well as musketry were soon vainly trying to reduce the house. The stone walls were like a fortress, and the British, refusing to consider a surrender, wounded an officer coming up under a flag of truce to make the demand. At last Washington, leaving one battalion to cover the house, ordered Sullivan on.

Musgrave's defense and the fog, particularly the fog, upset the American plan. Greene's guide led him astray, and he had two miles farther to cover than Sullivan.[19] This made Greene over a half hour late in moving into action. His right soon ran into trouble. Because of Greene's delay, Sullivan, fearing the gap thus created, had deployed Wayne's division to the left of the main road leading from Chestnut Hill to Germantown. Wayne therefore occupied at least part of the sector which was to have been covered by Stephen, whose division comprised Greene's right. Adam Stephen was a brave officer, but he rarely let duty stand between him and the pleasures of good liquor, a weakness which the British judged to have been shared by a number of Americans that particular day.[20] Hearing the tremendous firing back at Cliveden, Stephen swung out of line without Greene's knowledge, extended his division so far to the right that it came up squarely in the rear of Wayne's troops, who were hotly engaged in front of them, and, without reconnoitering, ordered his division to open fire. Wayne's troops, caught between two fires, retreated. Presently they became entangled with Stephen's men, whereupon both divisions broke. Only with the utmost exertions could their officers restore something like order. For the time being, their flight left a gaping hole in the American line.

Meanwhile the attack was not progressing too badly despite Musgrave's defense, the fog, the refusal of Armstrong's militia to cross the Wissahickon, and the strange failure of the Maryland and Jersey militia even to get into the fight.[21] One regiment from Wayne's division and one from Sullivan's were thrown out to support Conway on the right in view of increased British pressure applied by No-Flint Grey because of the delinquency of the Pennsylvania militia. Then, on the American left, Greene struck like a piledriver, smashing the Guards, the 25th, and the 27th back into the town. Muhlenberg, Scott, and McDougall, particularly Muhlenberg, drove their brigades deep into the scarlet lines. As the British dashed into the houses and fired from the windows, the Americans swarmed in after them. Street fighting of a very bitter nature thus ensued, with the fog and smoke so thick that the only way one could identify a foe was by the flash of the muskets. Meanwhile, in the center, Wayne and Stephen restored order in most of their commands and started to bring them back into the melee.

But, all at once, everything went wrong. British General Grant threw the 5th and 55th into the gap which Wayne and Stephen had not yet succeeded in closing, while Grey hurried to support the hard-pressed British right with troops which had previously been deployed to check Armstrong's militia. In addition, Cornwallis was rushing up with reinforcements from Philadelphia. Notwithstanding these measures, the Americans might still have forced a general retreat had not panic struck them. Running out of ammunition, feeling Grant's pressure on their left where Wayne should have been, and blinded by the fog and smoke, Sullivan's men began to retreat rapidly. Wayne's men, coming up, quickly reversed their direction, while Stephen's troops scurried away in wild flight from a body of redcoats who were trying to surrender to them. As Washington said, "In the midst of the most promising appearances, when every thing gave the most flattering hopes of victory, the troops began suddenly to retreat; and intirely left the Field, in spite of every effort that could be made to rally them."[22] "We ran from Victory," was Wayne's bitter comment.[23]

The flight left Greene isolated, but coolly he sought to extricate his division. Scott and McDougall kept open the line of retreat, while Muhlenberg fought his way back from his advanced position. Muhlenberg lost the prisoners he had taken, and Colonel Mathews's regiment as well, which was forced to surrender. But Greene saved most of his division and even his guns despite the efforts of Cornwallis, now on the scene, to capture them. In fact, Greene's disengagement and retreat for the five miles that Cornwallis pursued him were remarkable achievements.

Thus ended the Battle of Germantown after two and one-half hours of intense action. The Americans lost one hundred and fifty-two killed, five hundred and twenty-one wounded, and four hundred captured, while Howe reported five hundred and thirty-four casualties in all categories.[24] The loss of the near-victory was a bitter blow to Washington and his generals. Knox blamed the "unusual fog" in which "it was impossible to know how to support, or what part to push."[25] The defense of the Chew mansion also was blamed, as well as the lateness of Greene, the failure of the militia contingents, the panic, and the blunder of Stephen, who was court-martialed for his conduct. All these were factors, but the British army historian is probably correct in his judgment that Washington's plan was too complicated for the half-trained Americans to execute, while the fog proved an advantage to the British with their better discipline.[26]

The situation turned even more dismal in the Philadelphia area after Germantown. In order to secure a safer and more direct supply route, the British proceeded to clear the Delaware. Had Washington avoided such an engagement as Germantown, thrown heavy reinforcements into the river forts instead, and watched for Howe's weak points as the Briton strove to reduce the forts, Howe might have found Philadelphia untenable.[27] Even after Germantown, Howe let two valuable weeks pass before concentrating on the forts, but Washington neglected to take full advantage of the opportunity. Very possibly Brandywine and Germantown had exhausted his army as a striking unit.[28]

The defenses below Philadelphia were formidable. They consisted of chevaux-de-frise across the channel of the Delaware at Billingsport on the Jersey side and a fort at the same place; Fort Mifflin on Mud Island below the mouth of the Schuylkill; Fort Mercer at Red Bank on the Jersey shore; chevaux-de-frise in the river channel between Red Bank and Mud Island; and galleys and floating batteries under Hazlewood. The chevaux-de-frise were iron-pointed timbers embedded in stone-filled cassions and angled so as to rip the hull of an opposing vessel. Against the defenses at Billingsport Admiral Howe moved on October 6, his light vessels acting in collaboration with a regiment landed at Chester which seized the garrison at Billingsport. Fort Mercer received the next blow on October 22. A cousin of Nathanael Greene, Colonel Christopher Greene, who had been with Prescott at Bunker Hill and Arnold at Quebec, commanded the garrison, two very small Rhode Island regiments, not over four hundred men in all. Greene put up a truly Homeric defense against the assaulting column of sixteen hundred Hessians under Colonel von Donop, who crossed at Gloucester. Donop failed, lost between three and four hundred casualties, and suffered a mortal wound. The Americans lost fewer than forty men and had the satisfaction, the next day, of seeing the big man-of-war *Augusta*, 64, take fire and blow up and the grounded sloop *Merlin* set afire to prevent her capture.

The Howes now realized that they had a serious problem to solve. General Howe sent to Clinton for reinforcements and withdrew his troops from their camp at Germantown to Philadelphia in order to spare men for the reduction of the forts. With heavy guns sent him by Admiral Howe he mounted shore batteries on the Pennsylvania side and, on November 10, opened fire on Fort Mifflin, which was garrisoned by about four hundred and fifty men under Colonel Smith. The bombardment continued until, on the 15th, Black Dick Howe worked a half dozen men-of-war and several floating batteries within range. The fort held out until nightfall; then, more than half the garrison dead or wounded, the remaining men escaped by night across the river to Fort Mercer. Against this last defense Cornwallis was sent with over five thousand troops on the 20th. Faced with this overwhelming force, the garrison abandoned the fort, while the Pennsylvania navy burned its galleys at Gloucester Point. Greene, who had been sent to menace Cornwallis, engaged in a bit of futile maneuvering with the earl before both were recalled by their chiefs. On the 23d, the first British vessel came up the Delaware to Philadelphia. By combining their efforts the Howes had thus cleared the Delaware of the most effective river obstructions the Americans created during the war.[29]

After the forts were taken, Howe suddenly emerged from the capital during the first week of December. Sweeping up to Washington's entrenchments at Whitemarsh on December 4 and 5, he engaged in a lively skirmish with the Americans, but, because of their strong position, never developed a serious attack. Washington described the movement to Governor Livingston of New Jersey with almost a puckish sense of humor. "Genl. Howe," he wrote, "after making great preparations, and threatening to drive us beyond the Mountains, came out with his whole force last thursday Evening, and, after manoeuvering round us till the Monday following, decamped very hastily, and marched back to Philadelphia."[30] By December 20, Washington had moved his troops into winter quarters, twenty-five miles up the Schuylkill from Philadelphia, among the gloomy hills of Valley Forge.

XIV

Burgoyne's Invasion of the North

A singular fascination lingers about the campaign of the famous "Gentleman Johnny." For the Americans its success could have meant as crippling a blow to the young republic as the Union's seizure of the Mississippi was to the Confederacy in the Civil War, while its failure ensured for them the French aid that was eventually to prove so necessary. For the British the success of the campaign might have brought an end to a rebellion which Howe could have finished the year before, a rebellion which the kingdom of France was now watching carefully with a view to assisting in a very positive manner if a decisive American triumph appeared likely. Burgoyne's failure, on the other hand, meant for the British the involvement of England in an international conflict in which she lost her American colonies and was humiliated before Europe. The stakes, therefore, were of the highest when Burgoyne received his appointment and understood his objective to be a junction with Howe's forces at Albany.

But there is more to this fascination than even the stakes. There is the spectacular backdrop, the beautiful lake-river-and-mountain country in which the contest was fought. There is the confidence of the theatrical but lovable general and of his British and German troops, whose varicolored uniforms make a brilliant splash of color against the blue of the water and the green of the woods. There is the menace of the rum-loving Indians who accompany the expedition, eager for loot and scalps. On the other side, there is the struggle for command between the vainglorious Gates and the stubborn Schuyler, as well as the sharp differences between Gates and the impulsive, dashing Arnold. There are the half-disciplined militiamen and Continentals, always hungry, easily panicked, and quick to retreat. Finally they begin to stand, reinforcements appear, the scalping of a young woman rouses angry thousands fearful of their homes, and soon the confident Burgoyne goes no farther. Furious battles flame along the Hudson, and the incredible eventually happens: the surrender of an entire British army. The campaign is solid with color, blood-stirring action, tragedy, and possesses even the saving grace of humor.

Burgoyne returned to Canada on May 6, 1777, eager to get his campaign under way. Through an insulting letter from Germain, Carleton then learned that, while the king wished to retain him as governor of Canada, he preferred Burgoyne, "a more enterprising commander," as the leader of the invasion.[1] Carleton, however, had a generous nature and co-operated faithfully in preparing the expedition. Burgoyne's command consisted of three British brigades under Major General Phillips and Brigadier Generals Fraser and Hamilton, and three German brigades, largely Brunswickers, under Major General Baron von Riedesel. These regular troops numbered only seven thousand, two hundred and thirteen. Both Burgoyne and Carleton had hoped to raise a large body of Canadians and Indians, but they secured only two hundred and fifty Canadians and American Loyalists and but four hundred Indians. Artillery included a cumbersome train of one hundred and thirty-eight fieldpieces and siege artillery, most of which Burgoyne would have been wise to leave behind. For this artillery and the rest of his transportation, Burgoyne required fifteen hundred horses. While these forces gathered on June 20 at Cumberland Point on Lake Champlain, Colonel Barry St. Leger, one of Wolfe's veterans, set off for Oswego and his Mohawk Valley raid with a force of about seven hundred regulars and Loyalists and nearly a thousand braves under the Mohawk chief, Joseph Brant, who had been educated in Connecticut by the Reverend Eleazer Wheelock (afterward president of Dartmouth College) had been presented at the court of George III, and had had his portrait painted by the popular artist, George Romney. Though neither of these armies was as large as Burgoyne had hoped, the two, working with Howe, who was to clear the river to Albany, were considered of sufficient size for their task.

Against Burgoyne's army, which moved by boat triumphantly down Lake Champlain, the Americans had a divided command and scarcely more than two thousand effectives under General Arthur St. Clair at Ticonderoga when the British appeared. The year before, Gates had been given command of the field army in the north but could not act independently of Schuyler.[2] When Gates brought reinforcements to Washington just prior to Trenton, he declined a position which Washington entreated him to take in connection with the battle, reported himself on sick leave, and hastened to Congress in order to lobby in his own behalf, a not uncommon practice among generals of the Revolution. Neither Congress nor Washington could forget that Gates had served exceptionally well as adjutant general, and both wished him to take his old post. At this juncture, Schuyler, upset by sharp criticism in and out of Congress, especially from New Englanders,[3] decided at last to resign. Congress appointed Gates to the command of Ticonderoga, but, when Schuyler appeared in Philadelphia, Congress accepted the report of the Board of War and made him chief of the Northern Department. Rather than serve under him, Gates gave up his Ticonderoga command and, after another visit to Philadelphia, reported to Washington's headquarters.[4] It was a sorry mess and one that was to become worse rather than better as Burgoyne arrived at Crown Point on June 27 and moved cautiously toward Ticonderoga.

The American works at Ticonderoga appeared formidable, thanks in part to the advice of the Polish engineer Kosciusko, the previous year. The neck of land commanding the narrow channel of Champlain and the creek to Lake George was studded with entrenchments, as was Mount Independence over on the Vermont shore. A bridge, protected against enemy craft on the north side by a boom of chained logs, connected the two sites. Unfortunately St. Clair's troops were too few to garrison properly both sites, let alone the eminence to the northwest of Ticonderoga known as Mount Hope. The major error lay in leaving unfortified the steep hill to the southwest, Mount Defiance, or Sugar Loaf Hill. Though Colonel John Trumbull had suggested its fortification the year before, and had demonstrated that a cannon shot could reach from the fort to the summit of the hill, no attempt was made to place batteries there.[5]

Burgoyne now moved on June 30 to envelop the American garrisons on both sides of the lake. Fraser advanced up the west side toward Ticonderoga, Riedesel pushed toward Mount Independence on

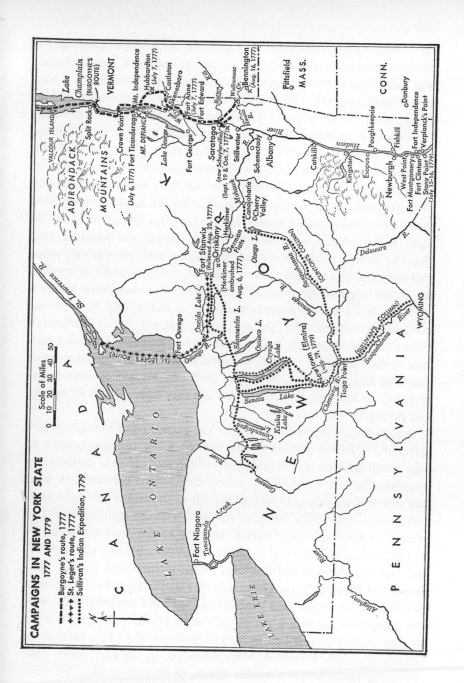

CAMPAIGNS IN NEW YORK STATE
1777 AND 1779

- - - Burgoyne's route, 1777
+ + + St. Leger's route, 1777
••••• Sullivan's Indian Expedition, 1779

Scale of Miles
0 10 20 30 40 50

CANADA

St. Lawrence R.

LAKE ONTARIO

Fort Niagara
Tonawanda Creek

LAKE ERIE

Genesee River

Canandaigua L.
Seneca Lake
Keuka Lake
Cayuga Lake
Owasco L.
Skaneateles L.
Otisco L.

Fort Oswego
(ST. LEGER'S ROUTE)
Oswego R.

Oneida Lake

Fort Stanwix
(Relieved Aug. 23, 1777)
Oriskany
(Herkimer ambushed Aug. 6, 1777)
Herkimer
German Flats

Otsego L.

NEW YORK

Newtown (Elmira)
(Aug. 29, 1779)
Tioga Point
Chemung R.
Chenango R.
Susquehanna R.
(CLINTON'S COLUMN)
(SULLIVAN'S COLUMN)

WYOMING

PENNSYLVANIA

Delaware R.

Allegheny River

Canajoharie
Cherry Valley
Mohawk River

Schenectady
Albany

Catskill

Hudson River

Kingston
Esopus
Newburgh
Poughkeepsie
Fishkill
West Point
Fort Montgomery
Fort Clinton
Stony Point
(July 15-16, 1779)
Fort Independence
Verplanck's Point

Saratoga
(now Schuylerville)
(Sept. 19 & Oct. 7, 1777)
Stillwater
Battenkill

Fort Edward
Fort Anne
(July 7, 1777)
Fort George
Lake George
MT. DEFIANCE
Fort Ticonderoga
(July 6, 1777)
Mt. Independence
(July 7, 1777)
Hubbardton
(July 7, 1777)
Castleton
Skenesboro
Wood Cr.

Hoosic R.
Walloomsac Cr.
Bennington
(Aug. 16, 1777)

Pittsfield

MASS.

Danbury

CONN.

ADIRONDACK MOUNTAINS

Crown Point
Split Rock
VALCOUR ISLAND

Lake Champlain
(BURGOYNE'S ROUTE)

VERMONT

the Vermont shore, while the fleet with the main army sailed up the channel keeping contact with both wings. By noon of July 2, Fraser was being shelled by the guns of Ticonderoga and Riedesel by a battery at Independence. Fraser soon seized the lightly defended Mount Hope, where cannon could easily command the creek connecting Champlain and George. Then the haughty but able General Phillips, who had moved to Fraser's right and taken possession of the sawmill, scanned Mount Defiance with the calculating eye of a skilled artillerist and consulted Lieutenant Twiss of the engineers about the possibility of getting cannon to the top. Reconnoitering the hill, Twiss reported it to be fourteen hundred yards from Ticonderoga and fifteen hundred from Independence, quite within cannon range. He reported, too, that the ground could be leveled for cannon and, by utilizing ropes and trees and clearing the ground in places, the guns could be brought up within twenty-four hours. Accordingly, after enormous labor, a way was hewn up the mountain on July 3 and 4, and Phillips had cannon in position by the 5th. As Thomas Anbury, one of Burgoyne's officers, wrote, "General Phillips has as expeditiously conveyed cannon to the summit of this hill, as he brought it up in that memorable battle at Minden, where, it is said, such was his anxiousness in expediting the artillery, that he split no less than fifteen canes in beating the horses."[6]

American reaction was swift, once the garrison at Ticonderoga discovered the British battery on the hill. St. Clair called a council of war which decided on an immediate withdrawal. Hence, in the early evening, Colonel Long with a strong detachment conveyed by boat the sick and wounded, as well as certain of the stores and light artillery, to Skenesborough. St. Clair followed with the main army at two o'clock in the morning of July 6, crossing to the Vermont shore by the bridge and heading for the same rendezvous by way of Hubbardton and Castleton. If the residence of the incompetent French commander at Independence, General Roche de Fermoy, had not caught fire, the retreat might have gone undetected until daylight. As it was, the Americans fell into a panic, the retreat became disorderly, while by four o'clock Fraser had hurried Grenadiers and Light Infantry in pursuit over the bridge of boats defended by cannon which four American artillerymen were too drunk to fire. Meanwhile Riedesel seized Independence at dawn and marched to support Fraser. Break-

ing the boom and bridge by nine o'clock, Burgoyne's navy flew up
the lake and destroyed a number of the retreating American galleys
and bateaux. Landing troops from Phillips's brigade near Skenesborough by midafternoon, Burgoyne started to envelop the stockade
there, only to see Long destroy the defenses and his boats and hasten
to Fort Anne. Although Long made a vigorous counterattack at Anne
on July 7 against the British 9th, which saved itself only by an equally
vigorous defense, he set fire to Anne and retreated quickly to Fort
Edward as the rest of Phillips's brigade moved up.[7]

Meanwhile Fraser ran into stiff resistance in his pursuit of St. Clair.
Though the latter got away to Castleton by evening, and eventually to
Fort Edward by way of Rutland, Seth Warner and Colonel Francis
fought a sharp rearguard action on the morning of the 7th at Hubbardton. Warner had tarried overlong at Hubbardton contrary to the
orders of St. Clair. It was his good fortune, however, to have twelve
hundred men available when Fraser, having rested his men from
darkness until three in the morning, drove in the American pickets at
five o'clock and attacked with eight hundred and fifty troops. Francis
and Warner, particularly the former, fought back with great skill,
while their men displayed fine courage and exceptional marksmanship.
Though Fraser's troops adjusted themselves to forest warfare with a
readiness and ability unusual in British troops, the American counter-
attacks on his left were so strong that he sent a messenger back to
Riedesel for help. The Brunswicker took a company of Jägers and an
advance guard of eighty men, including musicians, and hastened to
Fraser, leaving orders for Colonel Breymann to follow as rapidly as
possible with the main body of Brunswick troops. To give the impression that he had vast numbers with him, Riedesel had his sweating
bandsmen play his country's battle hymn. He arrived just in time and,
though heavily opposed, succeeded in swinging the battle to the British. Francis died on the field, while Warner, his retreat to Castleton
blocked, withdrew in great disorder through the mountains to the
east. He lost two hundred dead and probably about the same number
wounded.[8]

Burgoyne's campaign had thus got off to a flying start. He had taken
the forts, destroyed or captured over two hundred boats, seized more
than one hundred cannons and an enormous store of powder and
supplies at Ticonderoga, and given the American cause such a setback

that a cold wind of dismay swept through the colonies which was not
made more tolerable by Schuyler's alarming reports to Washington
throughout July and early August.[9] Conversely, the British were
elated, and George III rushed into his wife's boudoir shouting that
he had beaten all the Americans. American prospects appeared
gloomy beyond measure as Schuyler's men deserted rather than serve
under him, as Congress proposed to recall both Schuyler and St. Clair
to answer for the debacle, and as prominent New Englanders whis-
pered of treason and mentioned the possibility of shooting a general.[10]
Congress finally submitted to the obvious: if New England would not
support Schuyler and wanted Gates, then Gates should be given the
command since New England support was necessary. Accordingly,
Congress removed Schuyler, and, since Washington refused to appoint
a commander of the Northern army, designated Gates on August 4.[11]
Such action was regrettable, since it was grossly unfair to Schuyler.
It could be justified only because of the deteriorating military situation
at the time. The irony in the shift of command was that by August 19,
when Gates arrived in the north to take over the reins, the entire
military aspect was changing to the disadvantage of Burgoyne.

The change was effected by two thumping British defeats—one incurred by Burgoyne's forces near Bennington and the other by St.
Leger in the Mohawk Valley, the enormous transportation difficulties
encountered by Burgoyne, the skillful delaying tactics employed by
Schuyler, and the murder of the reputedly beautiful Jane McCrea.
After his victories, Burgoyne paused for an inexcusably long time to
catch his breath, his forces resting at Skenesborough except for a
strong Anglo-German garrison at Ticonderoga under Brigadier General Hamilton. Burgoyne had wanted Carleton to furnish the troops
for the garrison, but Carleton professed his inability. Hence Burgoyne
kept at the fort two regiments which he could well have used. Burgoyne's main task, however, in view of the route he chose, was to
hack a road through the woods and find transportation. Instead of
going south by way of Lake George, he selected the Skenesborough-
Wood Creek route for his men and the Lake George route for most of
his supplies, a colossal blunder which he explained on the ground
that he did not wish to make the retrograde movement to Ticonderoga
because of the effect it might have on the enemy. It is possible that his
Loyalist adviser, Major Skene, who would profit personally from the

road the army would have to construct, deliberately deceived Burgoyne into thinking the route easier and safer. On the other hand, Skene may have made an honest error.[12]

The army now had to advance through heavily wooded country intersected by many brooks that required bridges to be built, especially for such wagons and artillery as accompanied the army. Of the

Caricature of Burgoyne

guns, Burgoyne left most behind at Ticonderoga, though he took fifty-two to Fort George and forty-two thenceforth.[13] Meanwhile Schuyler complicated the British problem by sending a thousand axmen to fell trees so that they would interlock across the British path. Burgoyne took twenty days to move twenty miles to Fort Edward. He established a base of supplies at Fort George at the head of Lake George but the fifteen miles thence to the Hudson proved rugged, and his transportation facilities were so wretched that he was obliged to wait for supplies at Fort Edward,[14] which Schuyler evacuated, withdrawing to Stillwater, twenty-five miles to the south.

Burgoyne therefore decided to supply his army in part by using the enemy's resources. Intelligence reached him that at Bennington were large stores of food and ammunition, besides horses which the Brunswick dragoons could use and oxen for transport. He thus purposed to dispatch thence a mixed force consisting of about five hundred Brunswick, British, and Provincial troops, and Indians, under the command of Lieutenant Colonel Baum, with Skene as his adviser. Burgoyne hoped also to terrify those inhabitants who were hostile, encourage those who were loyal, and confuse the enemy by making him think the whole army might be swinging eastward to effect a junction with the forces in Rhode Island. This idea had been part of his original plan which Germain and the king had rejected. Accordingly Baum, who spoke no English, moved out on August 11 to the Battenkill, on the 12th to Cambridge, and on the 13th and 14th toward Bennington. To divert attention from Baum and to take advantage of the latter's success, Burgoyne sent troops southward to build a bridge across the Hudson near the mouth of the Battenkill.

Meanwhile, about a fortnight before, Jane McCrea had been shot and scalped. For some time the facts in the case were not completely clear as to her own political loyalties, those of her husband-to-be, or the identity of those who shot her, whether an Indian purposely or an American pursuit party accidentally. The generally accepted version now is that, living with her brother, a Patriot, she lingered near Fort Edward with a fat Mrs. McNeil, a cousin of General Fraser, with hopes of marrying her former neighbor and Loyalist lover, David Jones, who was returning in one of Burgoyne's units. On July 27, an Indian war party drove in an American patrol, invaded Mrs. McNeil's cabin, and seized her and Jane. Both were placed on horses and taken to the British camp. Because of Mrs. McNeil's obesity and the difficulty of getting her mounted, the Indians with her were slower in starting off than those with Jane. Yet Mrs. McNeil reached camp first, clad in her chemise. When the Indians left her with her cousin, she roundly scolded Fraser for sending Indians after her, while, red faced, he rushed to cover the huge woman with his greatcoat. Then Jane's captors appeared with a scalp of long hair which was quickly identified by Mrs. McNeil and the stricken Jones as belonging to Jane. The Indians had quarreled over her, and, as a result, they had shot, scalped, stripped, and mutilated her, besides crushing her skull with a tomahawk.[15]

Early in the campaign Burgoyne had addressed the Indians in a high-flown speech that excited great ridicule from the parliamentary opposition. In it, though he enlisted their help, he forbade them to kill indiscriminately or to scalp; and he enforced his injunction so rigidly that a number of Indians had already deserted in disgust. He was as

Cartoon: The Allies-Par Nobile Fratrum. The cartoon depicts George the Third and an Indian chief sharing a cannibal feast and indicates English aversion to the employment of Indians

shocked as anyone by the McCrea tragedy, and would have sentenced the offender to death had not his officers pointed out that this would alienate all the Indians. Furthermore, the damage was done: the tale flew all over New England and New York, and hundreds of men, seeing a possible similar fate for their own families from British Indians, rushed to join the "damned Dutchman," Schuyler.[16] Forgotten or ignored was that the Americans had already employed Indians as early as Bunker Hill.

The story of Jane McCrea was fresh in the minds of many of the militia from New Hampshire and Vermont as they gathered under Stark and Warner to resist the enemy attack. Stark had been ordered by General Lincoln to take his fifteen hundred men to Schuyler, but Stark refused, saying that he would decide the matter himself. Though Congress rebuked him for his attitude, one can only agree with the military historian who felt that this was one time when insubordination produced admirable results.[17] Stark was at the crucial point exactly when he was most urgently needed, and Warner, whom he sent for as soon as he heard of Baum's advance, was not far behind.

Baum, though not a bright man, foresaw difficulties as his advance guard ran into militia that hung like a cloud in front of him. He dispatched a messenger to Burgoyne for reinforcements, the man arriving on the night of the 14th. Riedesel, who had been against the expedition from the start, was greatly troubled by the news.[18] Burgoyne, however, remained confident that the original objective could be achieved, and sent the brutal Breymann with six hundred and forty-two men and two guns to support Baum. Meanwhile Baum started forward again on the morning of the 15th only to encounter a heavy body under Stark driving down from Bennington along the north bank of Walloomsac Creek. Baum at once sought high ground and entrenched himself, though the position was such as to disperse his troops too widely.[19]

Early on the 16th Stark decided to strike, and sent out columns of troops which surrounded Baum. These men approached in their shirtsleeves and in such a casual manner that Baum believed Major Skene, who told him they were probably Loyalists since they wore the Loyalist white paper badge on their hats. Baum thus let them get onto his flank and rear without resistance. When Stark launched a frontal attack, Baum was speedily disillusioned about the "Loyalists." The battle was exceedingly bitter, for, although the Indians and many of his Loyalists soon fled, the rest of Baum's troops fought until their ammunition was exhausted. Then Baum ordered them to rely on their swords. Twice the Brunswickers nearly cut a way through the enemy, but their numbers were too few. Stark himself was in the thick of the melee and is supposed to have uttered his famous remark, "Come on, my lads! We must get them beaten; or Molly Stark will be a widow tonight." By noon it was all over, Baum mortally wounded and what was left of his force captured, only nine of his three hundred and seventy-four Germans escaping to Burgoyne. Stark said it was the hottest action he had ever been in; evidently he had already forgotten Bunker Hill.

As Stark's men broke up, some to loot Baum's camp and others to chase the dragoons who got away, Breymann appeared, led by Skene, who had ridden off to hurry him along. Heavy rains on the 15th, ponderous equipment, and a military pedantry which slowed the movement by an insistence on parade-ground formation were responsible for Breymann's having marched at an over-all rate of barely more than one mile an hour.[20] Stark might have had trouble, for Breymann was a fighter, if Warner had not arrived at about the same time with nearly four hundred men, most of them veterans of Hubbardton. The combined forces then turned on Breymann and clawed him so ferociously that the Brunswicker left his guns and wagons behind and hurried back to Burgoyne. He lost twenty killed, sixty-nine wounded, and one hundred and forty-two missing; Stark's total casualties for both actions were thirty killed and forty wounded.[21] The Battle of Bennington was a blow from which Burgoyne never recovered.

XV

The Failure of Burgoyne's Campaign

Bennington was but the first blow that staggered Burgoyne; the second was struck in the Mohawk Valley. St. Leger arrived at Oswego in mid-July and was joined by two small battalions under Sir John Johnson and members from all the Iroquois except the Oneidas, who were friendly to the Americans. St. Leger now moved toward Fort Stanwix, which stood between the Mohawk River and Wood Creek, and which had been rebuilt by Colonel Peter Gansevoort. About the time that St. Leger reached Oswego, Lieutenant Colonel Marinus Willett arrived at the fort with reinforcements. Yet the garrison was only seven hundred and fifty strong when St. Leger invested the fort on August 3. Gansevoort was not discouraged, for word had reached him that General Nicholas Herkimer had raised eight hundred Tryon County militia to march to his relief. He did not know that Molly Brant, the Mohawk widow of Sir William Johnson and sister of Joseph Brant, also learned of the expedition and notified St. Leger, who dispatched a large force of Loyalists and Indians to halt Herkimer. Brant himself laid the ambush in a steep, wooded ravine near Oriskany about five miles from the fort. On August 6, Herkimer's militia walked squarely into the trap but, oddly enough, refused to panic as the Indians and Loyalists poured in a merciless fire. Taking to the trees and underbrush, the militia, possibly recognizing many of their former neighbors, fought back fiercely. Much of the affair was knife to knife and hatchet to hatchet, with no quarter shown. Herkimer, mortally wounded, had himself placed on his saddle with his back against a tree and his pipe in his mouth, and skillfully directed the stubborn defense. Meanwhile Willett made a sortie from the fort, capturing and sacking the British camp. When this information reached the woods, the Indians and Loyalists fled. Herkimer, however, retreated, one-third of his troops casualties, while St. Leger rallied his men and invested the fort again.[1]

The situation of the fort desperate, Colonel Willett and a companion ventured to crawl through the enemy camp during a violent storm at night to reach Schuyler. Schuyler called a council of war. Accused of wanting to weaken the army by helping Gansevoort, he crushed his pipestem between his teeth in anger, said he would assume that responsibility, and asked for a brigadier who would volunteer. When none was forthcoming, Arnold, now belatedly a major general, stepped forward, eager for the command and indignant at the treatment of Schuyler. Soon the drums were beating for volunteers, and Arnold moved to the relief of Fort Stanwix with a thousand men. He had expected that the militia of the countryside would rise, but they were now too terrified by St. Leger. Hesitating to commit his force against St. Leger's superior numbers, Arnold resorted to a clever ruse. A captive recently taken was a half-crazy Dutchman, Hon-Yost Schuyler, well-known to the Indians, who had a mysterious respect for one "touched" by the Great Spirit. When Arnold threatened to hang Hon-Yost, and the latter's mother came to plead for him, Arnold offered to spare his life if he would return to St. Leger and frighten his men with a report that the Americans were marching upon them with overwhelming numbers. With Arnold holding the half-wit's brother as hostage, Hon-Yost agreed. Arnold then had the fellow's coat riddled with holes and sent a friendly Oneida to corroborate Hon-Yost's tale.

Word reached the enemy of Arnold's approach, and already the Indians were uneasy. Then Hon-Yost appeared with his story of the enormous numbers of the Americans, said that he had escaped, and showed his bullet-torn coat as evidence. When the Indians asked how many men Arnold had with him, Hon-Yost pointed to the leaves of the trees. By this time the Oneida came in and said that Arnold was close at hand. This was enough for the Indians. Stealing the clothing and liquor of the British, they fled. The Loyalists threw away their own equipment and likewise scattered in terror. St. Leger, thus abandoned, withdrew so quickly toward Oswego that he left his tents standing. Soon Arnold marched up, and, on August 24, the siege ended.[2]

His ranks thinned by his losses at Bennington, and his prospects of success further darkened by St. Leger's defeat, Burgoyne was in a serious predicament. Gates, reinforced by Daniel Morgan's rifle regiment from Washington's command, and by Arnold, back from Stanwix, had more than six thousand men available, while the militia from New York and New England increased his number daily. In a gloomy

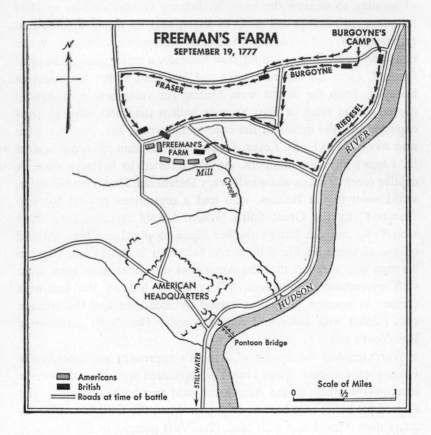

letter to Germain,[3] Burgoyne explained the situation, regretted that he had heard nothing from Howe, but felt that, since his orders were to force a junction with Howe, he had little choice but to cross the Hudson and proceed toward Albany. Hence, on September 13, having collected enough supplies from the north to subsist thirty days, and being reinforced by five hundred men, he crossed the Hudson on a pontoon bridge above the Battenkill and moved down toward

Gates. With him went many camp followers, the ladies of a number of officers, including the little blonde Baroness von Riedesel with her three little girls, the pregnant Lady Harriet Acland, and Burgoyne's mistress, the wife of a commissary official named Rousseau.[4]

Meanwhile the Americans prepared for the inevitable showdown. Arnold, who commanded the left wing, moved six miles north of

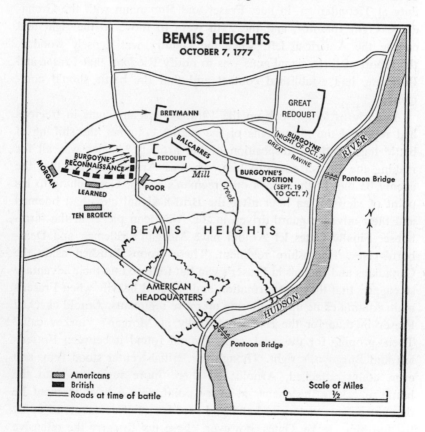

Gates's headquarters at Stillwater and, with Kosciusko's help, fortified the rolling ground known as Bemis Heights, the lines running along three sides of a rectangle two miles long and three-quarters of a mile wide, with the heavily wooded ravine of Mill Creek in front.[5] Behind these lines the Americans, now numbering between six and nine thousand, took position. But Burgoyne perceived an elevation on the American left which had been left unfortified. Possession of this site, even as possession of Mount Defiance at Ticonderoga, would give his guns command of the field. Hence he proposed to send out three columns on September 19. Riedesel, with Phillips in charge of the guns, was to march by the river road and assault the American right. Burgoyne himself was to cross the ravine with the center consisting of the 9th in reserve, and the 20th, 21st, and 62d, arrived from garrison duty at Ticonderoga, in line. Fraser and Breymann with the Grenadiers, Light Infantry, and the 24th were to move to the right and engage the American left. Since the country was densely wooded, the report of three signal guns was to notify Riedesel that Fraser and Burgoyne had established contact and that the battle should commence.

As early as ten o'clock on the 19th, American scouts in treetops had reported the movements of the scarlet columns, the shifting of battle flags, and the disposition of the artillery.[6] Gates was all for making the British come to him, whereas Arnold insisted that the enemy be met in the woods on Freeman's Farm. Gates clung to his point of view for an hour after the British signal guns had boomed and their advance guard driven in the American picket at the farmhouse. Finally Gates let Arnold have Morgan's riflemen and Dearborn's New Hampshire regiment. These troops brushed aside the Canadians and Indians in Fraser's van but followed up their advantage so eagerly that they lost formation and suffered heavily when Fraser's main column came up. Gathering up more regiments, Arnold checked Fraser in time for the riflemen to rally at Morgan's "turkey call." Then, groping for the weak spot, Arnold found it between Fraser's left and Burgoyne's right. Though the British center stood firm, and even counterattacked, Arnold fed three more regiments into the battle, checking the enemy at every point. For a brief moment he thought he saw victory at hand and sent for reinforcements to apply the finishing stroke. Gates, however, chose not to carry the offensive farther; and the moment passed as Phillips appeared with additional guns, followed by Riedesel, whose Germans quite clearly turned the day for the British. With nightfall Arnold withdrew. If the victory at Freeman's Farm remained technically with the British, it had been achieved at great cost, their losses being between five and six hundred. The Americans lost slightly over three hundred.[7]

While Burgoyne and Gates strengthened their respective lines, and wolves and Indians prowled among the dead, action burst out in other quarters. General Lincoln detached Colonel John Brown on a raid in Burgoyne's rear. Brown was supported by Colonel Seth Warner and Captain Ebenezer Allen. Pushing down the lake by way of Hubbardton, Brown and Warner carried Mount Independence, while Allen, marching by way of Skenesborough, took Mount Defiance. Ticonderoga itself proved too tough a nut for Brown to crack. Even so, he enjoyed a notable success, sweeping up two hundred and ninety-three prisoners from the 53d Regiment and scores of bateaux, and recovering one hundred American prisoners. He retreated up Lake George and rejoined Lincoln, who marched on September 27 with two thousand militia to join Gates.

It is possible that on learning of this assault on his communications Burgoyne might have retreated had not word arrived from Clinton on September 21, asking if Burgoyne wished him to "make a push" at Fort Montgomery above Peekskill.[8] Burgoyne's urgent affirmation placed upon Clinton the responsibility of trying something of an eleventh-hour nature to relieve Burgoyne. Though Howe had agreed in the summer that Clinton could not wisely leave New York with the forces at his disposal, he did suggest that a move up the Hudson might be useful. The arrival of reinforcements from England on September 24 made up Clinton's mind, though he did not act until October 3. He proposed to take three thousand men and, landing them at Verplanck's Point first in order to trick the American commander in the Highlands, Israel Putnam, into bringing his troops over to the east bank to meet him, he would make a swift crossing to the west bank and assault Fort Clinton and Fort Montgomery. When Clinton reached Verplanck's Point on October 5, Burgoyne's messenger was there with a letter dated the 27th in which Burgoyne first asked whether he should proceed to Albany or retreat to Canada, and then stated that he could not stay longer than October 12, if he had to retreat, or longer than the 16th, if he were to try to proceed.[9]

Clinton delayed replying until he had settled with the forts. His troops landing above Stony Point on the morning of the 6th, one column of nine hundred headed for Fort Montgomery, the other of eleven hundred under General Vaughan for Fort Clinton. Delivered almost simultaneously near the end of the day, both attacks were successful. Montgomery fell easily, though most of the defenders escaped. The Fort Clinton garrison, however, put up a bitter resistance, helped by the fact that the British had to advance over a narrow area protected with abattis and covered by cannon fire. Yet the British carried the fort with cool courage and skill. In both attacks they lost slightly under two hundred killed and wounded; the Americans, about three hundred, including prisoners. The crews of American gunboats set fire to their craft, while the British ships broke through the boom, sailed up to shell Fort Constitution on the east bank, across from West Point. Simultaneously Tryon attacked it by land and forced its abandonment.

It had been a vigorous and promising beginning, and Clinton wrote Burgoyne, "*Nous y voici* and nothing now between us but Gates; I sincerely hope this little success of ours may facilitate your operations."[10] At the same time, he said that he would not presume to order or even advise Burgoyne what to do. As luck would have it, the Americans captured his messenger and forced him to vomit up the silver bullet containing the message. Yet the next day, the 9th, a courier from Burgoyne reached Clinton further stressing the urgency of the situation. Clinton accordingly sent Vaughan up the river with the fleet toward Kingston, which Vaughan burned on the 16th, while Clinton himself returned to New York to collect more troops for the relief expedition. Though Clinton now received an order from Howe to send as reinforcements to Pennsylvania the very troops used on the Hudson, it seems by no means improbable that, had he immediately driven up to Albany after the fall of the forts, he might have taken the town, caught Gates between two fires, and saved Burgoyne. "Your movement was too late. . . ." General Phillips wrote him bitterly.[11] Clinton suffered from an overdose of caution about New York.

Meanwhile, except for work on the redoubts, a stalemate existed on Bemis Heights. Burgoyne put his men on half-rations on October 3, and became increasingly apprehensive as he heard nothing from Clinton and observed Gates's forces increasing constantly with the daily arrival of fresh militia detachments. Realizing that he had Burgoyne exactly where he wanted him, Gates hesitated to bring on another general engagement. He had, moreover, chosen not to mention either Arnold or the latter's division in his official report of the action on September 19. Hotly resentful, Arnold engaged in a sharp exchange with Gates during which Arnold asked for a pass to Washington. Gates was eager indeed to provide him with any means to get him out of camp. But when Arnold's officers, a number of whom had been close to Schuyler, begged him not to leave, he remained. Although Gates did not issue an order formally depriving him of command, he assumed charge of Arnold's division himself, placed Lincoln in command of the right wing, and ignored the impetuous little man.[12]

Arnold was not one to sulk forever in his tent when Burgoyne decided to try for the last time to turn the American left. Actually Burgoyne's was more a reconnaissance in force than a determined push and quite unnecessary, as well as imprudent. Taking fifteen hundred regular troops, British and German, ten guns, and one hundred and fifty Indians and Loyalists, Burgoyne, Riedesel, Fraser, and Phillips marched through the woods before noon and deployed in line. On the right were the Light Infantry under Lord Balcarres, a young fighter whose love for gambling won him a place at Burgoyne's own card table. Then came the 24th, followed by a few skeletonized German units, and finally the Grenadiers under the energetic, harddrinking Major John Acland who was killed after the war in a duel with a fellow officer in England whose derision of American courage impelled Acland to challenge him. Burgoyne's move failed to escape the keen eyes of American sentries, and Gates ordered Morgan to push against Burgoyne's right and Poor's brigade with two New York regiments and the Connecticut militia to assault the British left. Between two o'clock and half past two, the battle opened. The assault upon Acland was especially severe, and the hard-pressed Grenadiers gave ground rapidly after a German unit suddenly folded. Though Riedesel rallied the latter, the whole line was crumbling by this time as Morgan crashed against the British right. Fraser with the Light Infantry and the 24th sought to cover the retreat and support the Grenadiers at the same time, an impossible task. Yet the troops, at the sacrifice of many men and their guns, regained the fortified lines. Acland, shot in both legs, was captured. In the heat of the American onslaught Colonel Cilley of Poor's brigade had leaped upon a captured British fieldpiece, waving his sword exultantly before turning the cannon against the enemy, while an American surgeon, after dressing the wounds of one of Burgoyne's officers, held up gory hands in a frenzy of patriotism and shouted to Major Wilkinson, Gates's aid, that he had dipped them in British blood.

The battle (fought on Bemis Heights in the town of Stillwater, Saratoga County) now assumed a different guise from the holding action Gates favored. Early in the conflict, Arnold had dashed from his tent, leaped on his bay horse, and torn into the melee. Seeing him, the troops burst into cheers and eagerly followed. In a kind of frenzy he led part of Learned's brigade against the enemy's center. It was as a result of his second fierce assault that the Germans broke. Arnold saw that only Simon Fraser's gallantry and skill held the British line together, and it is said that regretfully Arnold asked Morgan to have his riflemen bring the Briton down.[13] Morgan assigned the task to Timothy Murphy, a happy-go-lucky Virginian whose skill with his double-barreled rifle and his tomahawk earned him a fabulous reputation among the Indians (he is alleged to have killed forty braves and scalped twenty of them during the war). Soon Fraser fell from his iron-grey horse, mortally and painfully wounded. General Ten Broeck now appeared with a large brigade of Albany County militia, and the British retired behind their lines. At once Arnold hurled himself with troops from Patterson and Glover's brigades against the British right center now held by Balcarres and the Light Infantry. Though Balcarres clawed off the furious assault, Arnold slid to the right, picked up Learned's brigade again, and fell upon the Canadians and Loyalists to Balcarres's right. These troops broke, thus uncovering Breymann's Germans at the extreme right of the British line. Riding to the left through a swarm of bullets from the Germans, Arnold encountered the regiments of Wesson and Livingston and the crack riflemen of Morgan moving up with long strides. At his order to assault the works, these troops, with fierce shouts, threw themselves at the redoubt, while Arnold, at the head of a portion of Brooks's regiment led the charge. Breymann fought desperately to hold off the masses of Americans, but his men, however brave, were too few. Finding the sallyport to the redoubt, Arnold spurred his way into the entrenchments. As a torrent of his troops poured through after him, his horse fell under him and a wounded German shot him in the same leg that had been pierced at Quebec. But the redoubt was carried, Breymann killed, and Burgoyne's entire position jeopardized. At this moment Major Armstrong from Gates's staff arrived with an order from Gates for Arnold to return to his quarters lest he do anything rash![14]

With his line shattered, and his loss at about six hundred as against one hundred and fifty for the Americans, Burgoyne at last recognized a defeat and gave the credit to Arnold: ". . . it was his doing, he wrote Clinton."[15] Even Gates unbent in his report to mention the "gallant General Arnold" and the fact that his leg was broken "as he was forcing the enemy's breastworks."[16] It was a pity, however, that the wounded German had not aimed at Arnold's fighting heart. As for Gates during the battle, the American commander quite properly remained at his headquarters, but he appeared less interested in the battle than in discussing the merits of the Revolution with a prisoner, Burgoyne's seriously wounded aide-de-camp, Sir Francis Clark. Finally, when Clark refused to admit the validity of Gates's arguments, Gates left the room, remarking angrily to an aide, "Did you ever hear so impudent a son of a bitch?" Sir Francis died of his wound.[17]

Burgoyne withdrew his tired army that night to previously prepared redoubts above the Hudson. Wisely Gates refused to accept the invited attack the next day but dispatched three columns past the enemy's right to his rear. Hence Burgoyne made up his mind to retreat. After Fraser was buried at sunset, while American cannon balls kicked dust over the funeral party until the cannoneers realized what was happen-. ing and then fired minute guns in solemn sympathy, Burgoyne left five hundred of his sick and wounded behind and drew back five miles to Saratoga. On the 9th he discovered American entrenchments springing up on the east bank of the Hudson. Though he ventured to construct new lines on the 9th and 10th, Gates had him surrounded by the 11th. After waiting a while longer for word from Clinton, which failed to come through, Burgoyne held four councils of war at which his officers decided the only recourse now was capitulation.[18]

In the negotiations with Gates, the latter initially held out for what was tantamount to unconditional surrender, but Burgoyne refused; and Gates relented as word reached him of Clinton's smashing victories on the Hudson. Anxious to expedite the surrender before Clinton should appear, he virtually permitted Burgoyne to impose his own terms. By this time, Burgoyne had also learned of Clinton's success and would have played for more time had not Gates threatened to renew hostilities without delay. The clause on which Burgoyne most prided himself was that his troops should march to Boston and embark at once for England on the condition that they serve no more during the war in America. With the signing of the famous "Convention" at Saratoga, the little army of less than five thousand effectives laid down their arms on October 17.[19]

Unhappily for both sides, a controversy soon broke out over the Convention which lasted for years because of a well-justified suspicion by Congress that the British might violate the terms. Congress especially feared that the British intended either to use the same troops again in America or, by stationing them in Britain, to release a similar number from the home country for service in America. As a result, the prisoners were shunted throughout the war from depot to depot in the States. Charges of perfidy since that time have been hurled now at Congress, now at the British. It may be true that Congress was guided largely by its suspicions rising from Burgoyne's indiscreet remarks and complaints while the troops were quartered in Boston, but research within the past quarter century has pretty well established the fact that the real perfidy was Sir William Howe's. In a letter of November 16 to Burgoyne, Howe revealed his intention of diverting to New York the homeward-bound transports and exchanging the Convention troops for American prisoners.[20]

The surrender of Burgoyne had the most momentous consequences. It placed the Americans in control of most of the Hudson, put Clinton on the defensive, and released troops to Washington. It sent a wave of confidence through the country. It shocked government supporters in England and pleased the Opposition. More than any other factor, the American victory at Saratoga was decisive in bringing France actively to the aid of the United States.

XVI

Valley Forge and the New American Army

Mention of Valley Forge still has power to stir one's sympathy. One pictures a ragged Continental sentry half freezing at his post in the driving snow, a shivering group huddled around a fire sharing their last scraps of food, a few pathetic figures dying in one of the dark, smoky huts for want of proper medicines and nourishment. Less well known is that the winter was mild and much of the suffering needless; that farmers preferred to sell to the British in Philadelphia for hard cash; that the grain surplus in the state of New York went to New England civilians and to New York and Long Island for the British; that Connecticut beef supplies to the army dried up because the state had imposed a price ceiling and farmers chose not to sell their cattle; that merchants in Boston would not move government clothing off their shelves except for cash and a colossal profit; that private contractors reaped a golden harvest by sending hundreds of government wagons north from Pennsylvania loaded with flour and iron while pork in Jersey awaiting shipment to the army spoiled for lack of transport.[1] It was an old tale, one of graft, speculation, meanness, selfishness, and gross mismanagement. But it should be remembered as well as the cold and anguish when one thinks of Valley Forge.

The condition of the American army was indeed wretched that winter. The location itself came in for sharp criticism, but it was near enough to Philadelphia for Washington to keep an eye on Howe and was easily defended. What made the winter so difficult to bear were the recurring problems of food and clothing. On three distinct occasions the army ran out of provisions, and once no meat was available for six days.[2] Though Pickering and Greene suggested such substitutes as soup thickened with bread and a cereal concoction of wheat and sugar, the men wanted meat. In the evening many a hungry soldier would stick his head out of his hut and shout, "No meat, no meat!" And the cry would be taken up all down the line of soldiers' huts.[3]

The lack of adequate clothing also produced hardship. Washington wrote Congress on December 23 that there were "no less than 2898 Men now in Camp unfit for duty because they are bare foot and otherwise naked."[4] Because of the scarcity of blankets men sat up all night rather than sleep and freeze. When the Pennsylvania legislature criticized his going into winter quarters, Washington scornfully wondered if the members thought the soldiers "were made of Stocks or Stones and equally insensible of frost and Snow"; obviously it was "a much easier and less distressing thing to draw remonstrance in a comfortable room by a good fire side than to occupy a cold bleak hill and sleep under frost and Snow without Cloaths or Blankets."[5] Six weeks later the number unfit for duty for want of shoes and clothing had increased by over a thousand. When Baron von Steuben arrived from Prussia to train the American army, he was shocked to see officers with nothing but a ragged blanket to serve as an outside garment. Quick to adapt himself, he gave a party to which no officer was invited who had a whole pair of breeches. Most of the soldiers had only one shirt, and so little soap was available that such clothing as they possessed was alive with lice. "The whole army is sick, and crawling with vermin," fumed Wayne.[6] Lafayette, who had joined the army in time to be wounded at Brandywine, wrote, "The unfortunate soldiers were in want of everything; they had neither coats, nor hats, nor shirts, nor shoes; their feet and legs froze till they grew black, and it was often necessary to amputate them."[7] In view of such conditions, it is not difficult to understand the bitterness that rankled one Continental: "poor food—hard lodging—Cold Weather—fatigue—Nasty Cloaths—nasty Cookery—Vomit half my time—smoak'd out of my senses—the Devil's in it—I can't Endure it—Why are we sent here to starve and freeze . . . a pox on my bad luck."[8] The situation was becoming a morale problem of the first magnitude.

The lack of food and clothing was due in large measure to poor management in the commissary and quartermaster departments. In May and June of 1777, Congress had attempted to regulate the business of the two departments.[9] Joseph Trumbull resigned as commissary general after Congress reorganized the department by establishing a commissary of purchases with four deputies and one of issues with three deputies. Since these deputies were appointed by Congress, and the commissary general therefore had trouble controlling them, Trumbull, who had done a good job, decided he would be well out of the mess. Under William Buchanan, who succeeded him, conditions deterioriated. Though Congress empowered Washington to commandeer supplies from farmers, and scolded him for not being tougher in this respect, the Virginian was reluctant to resort to such measures. He considered them inhumane, felt that people would resent such an exercise of military power, and deplored the probable effect upon discipline. When forced to such extremes by necessity in early 1778, he believed his fears confirmed by the results. Eventually, when the winter was about over, Congress reorganized the department again. It provided for purchasing commissaries who received two per cent of their cash disbursements, superintending deputy commissaries who were granted one-half of one per cent of theirs, and a commissary general who was to be paid on the same basis, and who could hire and fire all those in his department. In the person of Joseph Wadsworth of Connecticut, Congress found an efficient, honest commissary general whose work in keeping the army supplied with provisions Washington warmly praised.[10]

In the quartermaster department drastic changes were equally necessary. Thomas Mifflin served very satisfactorily as quartermaster general until his resignation early in 1776. Stephen Moylan took his place, but he, too, resigned. Congress then asked Mifflin to resume the position. Unfortunately, as Greene remarked, "General Mifflin, who ought to have been at the head of the business, has never been with the army since it came into the State."[11] Finally, on October 10, 1777, pleading ill-health, Mifflin again handed in his resignation, which was accepted on November 11. Congress, however, made no attempt to fill the vacancy. An inspection committee which went to Valley Forge pointed out to Congress the urgency of action in reorganizing the department and appointing as quartermaster general an experienced and capable man. The committee wished Greene to take over the duties, but Greene had a keen distaste for the job: "I hate the place," he wrote Knox.[12] Eventually, at the entreaties of Washington and his own friends, he reluctantly consented provided he be given as assistant quartermasters John Cox, a merchant of Philadelphia, and Charles Pettit, secretary of New Jersey. The committee and Congress quickly agreed, voted that the three men should be allowed one per cent of all funds issued in their department to be divided as they desired, and gave to Greene the appointive power over forage masters, wagonmasters, and all other departmental officers.[13] At the same time, the Board of War began to address itself so vigorously to procuring sufficient clothing and shoes throughout the states and getting the supplies to the army that, by late November, 1778, Washington was able to report the soldiers at last well clothed.[14] All these reforms were a trifle late, to say the least.

Another vital problem was that of recruiting. The army thinned out rapidly from disease, refusal to re-enlist, and desertion. Reinforcements sent by Gates from the Northern army were slow in arriving and were scarcely as many as expected; this was largely because, after Saratoga, so many of the militia returned to their homes. Appeals by Washington and Congress to the states to fill their quotas kept recruits trickling in but in discouraging numbers. Congress even attempted to get the states to fill up their battalions of Continentals "by drafts from their militia."[15] While this had some success, Congress felt impelled in May to offer $80 at the conclusion of the war to every enlisted man who had already signed up for "the duration" or who would consent to do so; by August, "a great spirit of inlisting" was being noted among the men drafted from the militia.[16]

The committee that considered army problems with Washington and his generals until the close of March returned to Congress just about as antagonized by the army as the army was antagonized by it. It may well have reflected some of the suspicion felt by Congress, for, during that crucial winter, Congress was extraordinarily critical of the army.[17] While suspicion of the military was to have been expected, what was particularly annoying and dangerous was that Congress should attempt to direct military operations in terms of strategy and even tactics, supervise discipline, arrogate to itself the role of military critic, appoint high-ranking foreign officers without consultation with the commander in chief as to their function or the effect such appointments might have upon native-born officers, and promote native-born officers without proper regard to either seniority or merit. Yet, as the executive, administrative, and legislative branches of the government all in one, Congress was bound to demonstrate extraordinary interest in military affairs. In fact, Congress might have interfered to an even greater degree if there had not been many members who were sympathetic with the army and its problems. But there were those who took a more jaundiced view, of which the most unfortunate manifestation occurred in the so-called Conway Cabal.

The Conway Cabal[18] was named after Thomas Conway, a sharp-tongued Irish colonel in the French army and one of those foreign

I *William Alexander Earl of Stirling major General in the armies of the United States* do acknowledge the **UNITED STATES of AME=RICA,** to be Free, Independent and Sovereign States, and declare that the people thereof owe no allegiance or obedience to George the Third, King of Great-Britain; and I renounce, refuse and abjure any allegiance or obedience to him; and I do *Swear* that I will to the utmost of my power, support, maintain and defend the said United States, against the said King George the Third, his heirs and successors and his or their abettors, assistants and adherents, and will serve the said United States in the office of *Major General* which I now hold, with fidelity, according to the best of my skill and understanding.

Sworn before at the Camp at Valley forge the 12th May 1778   *Stirling*

G Washington

Facsimile of the oath of allegiance required by Congress to be administered to the officers of the army before leaving Valley Forge

officers who hoped to improve their fortunes by joining the Americans. Appointed a brigadier in May, 1777, he proved himself an efficient officer and made his brigade the best drilled in the army. When Baron de Kalb received his major-generalship in September, Conway entreated Congress to give him equal status and cited promises made by Silas Deane in France. But when Congress proposed to promote him over the heads of men whom Washington considered equally deserving, the Virginian remonstrated. He contended that Conway's merit as an officer and his importance to the army existed "more in his own imagination, than in reality."[19] Members of Congress then considered giving to Conway the office of inspector general which Washington and his officers wished established.[20]

That same fall, Congress reconstituted the Board of War, appointing Gates as president, Mifflin, Pickering, Joseph Trumbull, and Richard Peters as secretary.[21] Trumbull's ill-health prevented him from serving. Washington and Gates had had difficulties over the question of reinforcements from Gates, but there is little evidence to suggest that the two were inimical. Yet as president of the Board of War Gates would be technically in a position of superiority to Washington.

Then Conway stepped onto the stage. Taking advantage of the quaint eighteenth-century custom of criticizing one's superiors with impunity, Conway had written to Congress on September 25 disparaging his commanding officer, Lord Stirling, as overly fond of drinking after dinner, and castigating other prominent officers as grossly lacking in military ability in battle. Though he got away with such criticism, which was not without truth, his real mistake occurred about a fortnight later when he addressed a laudatory letter to Gates. In this letter he expressed the wish to serve under Gates, and stated that the more he saw of the army the less he thought of its chiefs and discipline.[22] Wilkinson, Gates's young adjutant, brought the good news of Burgoyne's surrender to Congress, but stopped on the way to visit his sweetheart, and dropped in on old friends to celebrate the victory privately over a bottle of wine. He mentioned the Conway letter to Major McWilliams, Stirling's adjutant. McWilliams repeated the story to Stirling, who indignantly, and with considerable satisfaction at the chance to snipe at Conway, passed it on to Washington. Without waiting to sound out Gates, Washington sent Conway a brief stinging note on November 9.[23] Though Conway denied at once that he had attacked Washington, the latter ignored the reply. Meanwhile, hearing of what had happened from other sources, and growing angry or frightened, Gates dashed off a letter to Washington in which he professed ignorance and innocence and demanded to know who had been spying on his correspondence. He sent to Congress a copy of his letter, which was read on December 23, little more than a week after Congress, on the recommendation of the Board of War, had elected Conway to the office of inspector general.[24] This post, as delineated by the board, gave Conway an authority independent of that of the commander in chief.

The situation now became somewhat fantastic. Washington told Gates that Wilkinson had been the informer, whereupon Gates laid out his adjutant so roundly that Wilkinson challenged his commander to a duel; Gates hurriedly backed down. When Conway, late in December, reported at Valley Forge, he was accorded such a frigid

[138]

Inſtructions for the Captain.

A CAPTAIN cannot be too careful of the company the ſtate has committed to his charge. He muſt pay the greateſt attention to the health of his men, their diſcipline, arms, accoutrements, ammunition, clothes and ne-ceſſaries.

His firſt object ſhould be, to gain the love of his men, by treating them with every poſſible kindneſs and humanity, enquiring into their complaints, and when well founded, ſeeing them redreſſed. He ſhould know every man of his company by name and character. He ſhould often viſit thoſe who are ſick, ſpeak tenderly to them, ſee that the public proviſion, whether of medicine or diet, is duly admini-ſtered, and procure them beſides ſuch com-forts and conveniencies as are in his power. The attachment that ariſes from this kind of attention to the ſick and wounded, is almoſt in-conceivable; it will moreover be the means of preſerving the lives of many valuable men.

Instructions for the Captain from Steuben's *Regulations for the Order and Discipline of the Troops of the United States*

reception that he hastened back to York. Then, when Congress pur-posed to send to camp a committee composed in part of its own members and those of the Board of War, Gates, Mifflin, and Picker-ing declined to go. In the meantime, civilians like James Lovell and Benjamin Rush and those associated with them appear to have been very active in their criticism of Washington and their praise of the popular Gates.

Just how far the Board of War and the Congressional critics of Washington might have gone is conjectural, but Gates himself came up with the idea of an invasion of Canada which backfired disastrously. Without consulting Washington, the board proposed an "iruption" into Canada with Lafayette in command and Conway as his second.[25] The volatile marquis, having swung from admiration to detestation for Conway, told his friend Laurens, president of Congress, that if the board did not give him another second, he would return to France. He felt that Washington had been grossly insulted, and he refused to accept the command unless Washington appointed his second. This condition the board and Congress reluctantly assented to, whereupon Washington designated Baron de Kalb. Yet when Lafayette reached Albany in mid-February, he discovered Conway already there trying to organize the expedition. Even Conway, however, realized the invasion was hopeless because of the condition of the troops, while Lafayette bluntly stated that the Board of War had deceived him.[26] Congress then recalled Lafayette and Kalb and ordered Conway to join General McDougall at Peekskill. Conway spoke his mind to Congress and demanded a division from Washington. Eventually he tendered his resignation, which Congress accepted, to his surprise; Gates was placed in charge of the forts on the Hudson; and the Board of War lost greatly in prestige.

The cabal, if such it was, was mysterious and disturbing. Had Congress realized that Washington detested Conway, which it evidently discovered for the first time when Gates's letter was read on December 23, it is doubtful if Conway would have been made inspector general. Opposition to Washington by most members of Congress probably emanated from a desire to assert the supremacy of the civil government; the opposition of a number of members had a more personal animus. Gates's initial affront was something he could not help, namely, being the recipient of Conway's letter. On the other hand, supported by his personal friend Mifflin, he proceeded to embarrass Washington by directing the Board of War in such a way as to ignore or minimize the authority of the commander in chief. The officers at Valley Forge were outraged by the attitude of certain members of Congress and the board. In their minds there was little doubt that a conspiracy existed, though perhaps they were too sensitive, owing to the recent discouraging campaign. In later days,

Washington's erstwhile critics denied any malign intentions and avowed their respect and friendship for him. But the only man who ever apologized was Conway himself. Wounded during the summer of 1778 in a duel with General John Cadwalader, and believing himself near death, he sent a note to Washington expressing his "grief for having done, written, or said anything disagreeable."[27] Conway eventually recovered and returned to France.

While the army was being thus sorely tried by intrigue, maladministration, and climate, an individual arrived at camp who, perhaps more than anyone, was responsible for restoring morale and compelling the men to take pride in themselves as soldiers. This was Lieutenant General Baron von Steuben, aide-de-camp to the king of Prussia. Steuben had not been a baron for many years, had been an aide-de-camp to Frederick for but a short while, and had been only a captain when Frederick reduced his army after the Seven Years' War and dropped Steuben along with hundreds of officers. Out of a job again in 1777, he drifted to Paris where the Comte de Saint-Germain, minister of war, saw in him the answer to the American training problem and a way in which the American army could be made more effective. Steuben had been on Frederick's operations staff and was familiar with the European army systems. Yet as plain "Captain von Steuben" he would be just one of all too many foreign officers in America contending for preference. If, however, he were given a fictitiously exalted rank beforehand, there would be no hard feelings. Though Americans eventually discovered the truth, Steuben achieved such results that his prestige was in no way affected.

Steuben had not been long at camp before he demonstrated his ability. Accompanied by Alexander Hamilton and young John Laurens, both able to speak French with him, he consulted with division, brigade, and regimental commanders, went with company officers to examine the soldiers' huts and inspect their weapons, listened to the soldiers themselves, and reported to Washington that a European army could never have existed with such a lack of food, clothing, and shelter.[28] He proposed a training program which would give the army a uniformity it had never possessed. The states had their own systems of drill, some patterned after the English system, others the Prussian, and still others the French. The baron was not inflexible; recognizing the differences, he established his own system, which was essentially an adaptation of the Prussian. Time was too pressing for his drill regulations to be completed, printed, and then distributed; for that matter, there was no printing press in the army. Steuben had to proceed lesson by lesson, writing in French which was then rendered into English. But many copies had to be made of the original before every company officer and drillmaster possessed one. While the army practiced the first lesson, Steuben prepared the second, and so on.[29]

But Steuben was no desk soldier. However deep the snow or sloppy the mud, he spent hours on the drill grounds. American officers had followed the English tradition of letting sergeants drill the troops. Steuben would have none of this; the officers should assume this duty, and he intended to set the example by personally drilling a company. Starting on March 19 with a picked group, he soon had the whole army watching a lieutenant general instruct soldiers in the facings and the march steps. Crowds gathered on the succeeding days as the baron proceeded to the manual of the musket and the use of the bayonet, which, up to now, the Americans had chiefly employed to stick meat on for roasting over a fire.

The situation did not lack for comedy, because Steuben had trouble with his English and his temper. Once he gave a command that was unintelligible to a few men, who started marching in a different direction from the rest of the company. The baron's English giving out, he shouted to them in French, then in German, waved his arms, turned purple, and swore fervently. His assistants seemed unable to help him. Possibly they, like many of the watching troops, were convulsed with laughter. Then a young officer named Benjamin Walker came forward and, speaking in French, offered to assist. Accepting Walker with enormous relief, Steuben soon had the situation under control again. It is said that on one occasion after the choleric baron had blown up and sworn at a company slow to catch on, he turned to Walker and gasped, "Viens, Walker, mon ami, mon bon ami! sacré! Goddam de gaucheries of dese badauts. Je ne puis plus. I can curse dem no more."[30] The baron was not long in discovering that his "goddams" were popular with the soldiers, and, always something of a showman, he used them when he thought they would be particularly effective.

Steuben's work proved exceedingly valuable. Under his watchful eye the entire army started drilling on March 24. It learned how to load the musket quickly and how to employ the bayonet. It learned how to march in a column of fours instead of resorting to the Indian file of the previous campaign. It learned how to deploy from column to line and line to column. But the baron did not stop here. His infantry drill regulations were published as *The Blue Book* and were adopted throughout the army. He formulated plans of organization for the infantry, cavalry, artillery, and engineers, and Congress accepted them. He organized and trained the famous American Light Infantry. He established a system of accountability for public property. As a volunteer at Valley Forge and as inspector general from May 5, 1778, he rendered a service unique in the history of the Revolution.[31] Tested in the material and spiritual adversities of Valley Forge, and trained now by Steuben, Washington's army was no longer a force for the British to take lightly.

XVII

The British Withdrawal to New York

The dismal winter of 1778 brought the gratifying news of the French alliance. In the diplomatic maneuvers that preceded the treaty of February 6, the wily Franklin and his associates played now upon French hopes of a successful war of revenge which would smash the British Empire and now upon French fears that the Americans and the British might effect a reconciliation. Vergennes, the able foreign minister, dreaded what he thought might follow such a reconciliation: a combined British and American attack on the French West Indies. With the signing of the treaty, French ships and troops would presently be available to supplement the vast quantities of arms, munitions, clothing, and other supplies which France and Spain, acting through Caron de Beaumarchais, the playwright, and his "Hortalez and Company," had been shipping to America for nearly two years. Many of the muskets and cannons, and much of the powder and shot used in the campaigns of 1777 had been furnished by Beaumarchais.[1] Though Lord North had a plan for reconciliation which envisaged conceding about everything the Americans wanted except independence, the Earl of Carlisle, who headed the peace mission, discovered when he arrived in Philadelphia that Congress had just ratified the treaty with France and that the British army and navy, on orders from London, were on the point of evacuating the American capital. Small wonder, the commissioners might well conclude, that the mission was bound to fail.

The British evacuation was preceded by a change in the army command. In the fall of 1777, disappointed that the ministry would not send him more reinforcements, disturbed by the rumor of Burgoyne's surrender which he may have known to be true, and sick of

180

his role in a war that he did not like, Howe asked Germain to relieve him from "this very painful service."[2] The king accepted his resignation early in February, designated Sir Henry Clinton as his successor, but asked Howe to remain until Clinton should be able to take over.

Meanwhile the British had themselves a gala time in the American capital that winter. Weekly balls, theatrical performances, horse racing, cockfighting, and drinking bouts were popular. There was also a ceaseless round of parties for the officers at the mansions of prominent Loyalists, though it must have irked matrons with a sense of propriety that the British commander in chief spent most of his leisure hours with Mrs. Loring. Aside from such frivolities, the occupation started a wave of inflation throughout the city. Prices of commodities and of labor soared to such heights that Howe imposed ceilings. Even these, however, were sufficiently high to induce farmers to bring their grain and meat to Philadelphia where they could be sure of receiving cash rather than sell to the army at Valley Forge for a promissory note or paper issue of doubtful value.

Many Loyalists wondered why Howe with nearly twenty thousand men did not attack Washington and destroy his ragged, starving army; Patriots wondered the same, too, as did Britons at home. Yet, as Howe later indicated on his return to England, there was little point in trying to drive the Americans from Valley Forge during the winter when he could do it just as well and much more easily in the spring; then, when spring arrived, and he learned of Clinton's appointment, he had no wish to hazard the army of his successor. But how anxiously the Loyalists longed for Howe to sally forth and crush the rebels! As one Loyalist urged:

> Awake, arouse, Sir Billy,
> There's forage in the plain,
> Ah, leave your little Filly,
> And open the campaign.[3]

Howe had no intention of doing anything of the sort. Clinton arrived on May 8, but Howe lingered for a fortnight longer while a glorious celebration was accorded him by the officers of the army. The "Mischianza," as it was called, was organized by Captain John André, who spent a great deal of his time paying court to one Peggy Shippen. An extravagant occasion for parading, dancing, and dining, the

Mischianza celebrated Howe's victories and mourned his departure; Howe was popular with both the officers and the rank and file.

As the great affair broke up in the small hours of May 19, a messenger reached Howe with news that an American division under Lafayette was nearing the city. Washington had ordered Lafayette to make a reconnaissance in force to obtain intelligence of the enemy's "motions and designs."[4] Lafayette had accordingly advanced on the 18th to Barren Hill, two miles from the British at Chestnut Hill. Howe, in his last battle in America, moved rapidly with Clinton to catch "the Boy." He sent Grant with a force of five thousand to swing wide by way of Whitemarsh and take Lafayette in his left rear, ordered No-Flint Grey over the Schuylkill with two thousand to get at the Frenchman's right rear, and pushed forward with Clinton to divert Lafayette in front. These moves, effected on the night of the 19th, nearly caught Lafayette in a trap the following morning. Now Steuben's work began to tell. With his troops preserving strict discipline and marching swiftly, Lafayette feinted with his rearguard now at Grant and now at Clinton, while his advance elements similarly confused Grey long enough to enable the division to slide past No-Flint and cross the Schuylkill at Matson's Ford. Grant was blamed for the escape since he failed to carry out his part according to instructions, but it is entirely possible that he thought Lafayette's retreat feigned and that Washington, who was known to be on the march, might hit his flank, in which case he would be between two fires.[5] Losses did not exceed a dozen on either side.

Meanwhile, although the Franco-American alliance was not announced until March and the French declaration of war was deferred until July, the British were fully informed of what had happened and made their plans accordingly. Germain sent detailed instructions to Clinton on March 21 which called for a wide dispersion of the forces at his command. He was to send an expedition of five thousand to seize the island of St. Lucia in the French West Indies and another of three thousand to St. Augustine and Pensacola, the objectives being either the defense of Jamaica or an attack on New Orleans. In the meantime, he was to take the army by sea to New York. If Lord North's peace scheme collapsed, he was to leave garrisons at Rhode Island and Halifax and ship the rest to join Carleton's troops in Canada. The instructions were of the confused nature one might

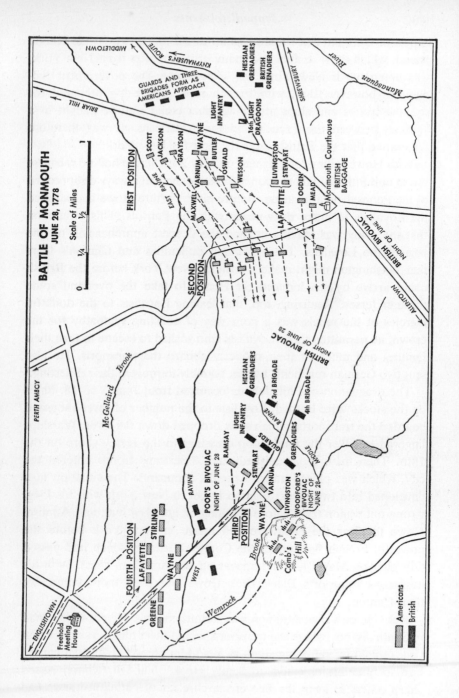

BATTLE OF MONMOUTH
JUNE 28, 1778

Scale of Miles
0   ¼   ½

FIRST POSITION

SECOND POSITION

THIRD POSITION

FOURTH POSITION

GUARDS AND THREE
BRIGADES FORM AS
AMERICANS APPROACH

KNYPHAUSEN'S ROUTE

MIDDLETOWN

BRIAR HILL

HESSIAN
GRENADIERS

BRITISH
GRENADIERS

16th LIGHT
DRAGOONS

LIGHT
INFANTRY

SCOTT

JACKSON

GRAYSON

BUTLER

OSWALD

WESSON

LIVINGSTON

STEWART

LAFAYETTE

OGDEN

MEAD

MAXWELL

VARNUM

WAYNE

EAST RAVINE

SHREWSBURY

Manasquan

Krager
River

Monmouth Courthouse

BRITISH
BAGGAGE

BRITISH BIVOUAC
NIGHT OF JUNE 27

ALLENTOWN

BRITISH BIVOUAC
NIGHT OF JUNE 28

HESSIAN
GRENADIERS

3rd BRIGADE

4th BRIGADE

MIDDLE

RAVINE

LIGHT
INFANTRY

GUARDS

GRENADIERS

RAMSAY

STEWART

VARNUM

LIVINGSTON

WOODFORD'S
BIVOUAC
NIGHT OF
JUNE 28

POOR'S BIVOUAC
NIGHT OF JUNE 28

McGellaird
Brook

PERTH AMBOY

RAVINE

WEST

WAYNE

Brook

Comb's
Hill

Wemrock

STIRLING

LAFAYETTE

WAYNE

GREENE

ENGLISHTOWN

Freehold
Meeting
House

Americans

British

expect of Germain since there was no threat to Canada, while Rhode Island, which drew its fuel and many of its supplies from New York, was untenable if New York was evacuated.[6] The government recognized, however, that, with French squadrons being prepared for sea, the troops and ships at Philadelphia could well be caught in a squeeze between the French and the Americans. It was therefore imperative that the British clear the port for New York.

With Howe sailing for England on May 24, Clinton had no recourse but to quit Philadelphia as soon as possible; he had always disapproved of the Pennsylvania invasion. Before his departure Howe had advised the Loyalists to make their peace with the Patriots. This intimation that the army was leaving created the deepest apprehension on the part of the Loyalists. Transportation difficulties and Clinton's fears that Washington might make a dash for New York before the British could arrive by sea induced Sir Henry to take the overland route through Jersey. Realizing, too, that leaving Loyalists to the doubtful mercies of the rebels was a poor way of enlisting sympathy for the crown, he permitted those Loyalists who wished to escape to take their families and much of their property aboard the transports. He also sent two German regiments by sea, possibly to prevent their deserting.[7]

The evacuation of Philadelphia occurred from June 8 to 18. Ships on the stocks were burned. Loyalists to the number of three thousand boarded the transports, which soon dropped down the river. Warships lingered to cover the final troop crossings to the Jersey shore on the 18th. Then they, too, vanished, and Americans troops entered the city, which was placed under Arnold's command. The situation now developed into two races: Clinton to get to New York with his long, strung-out wagon train before Washington attacked him, and Admiral Howe to clear the Delaware and arrive in New York before the powerful French fleet under the Comte d'Estiang, which had passed Gibraltar on May 16, could appear off the American coast. With his numerous transports Black Dick Howe was even more vulnerable than Clinton.

But Clinton's own situation was serious enough. He chose the road to South Amboy where the transports would meet him, but rumor that Gates might be marching south to head him off at the Raritan caused him to alter his objective to Sandy Hook.[8] Though Clinton issued sharp orders to keep the line of march clear of battalion horses and camp followers, his progress was so slow that at the end of six days he had covered only thirty miles. This rate was scarcely exceeded in ensuing days as the weather turned rainy and sultry. The road became heavy, and New Jersey militia units under General Philemon Dickinson destroyed bridges in front of him, felled trees, and stopped up the wells.[9] With his wagon train extending for twelve miles on the road to the Hook, Clinton was dangerously exposed to an American attack on his left flank.

The American attack was slow in developing. Washington moved out of Valley Forge on the 19th, crossed the Delaware at Coryell's Ferry north of Trenton, and on the 24th established contact with Clinton. It was now that Clinton changed his objective to Sandy Hook and sent Knyphausen ahead over the narrow, sandy road. Hitherto Clinton had proceeded by parallel roads; from this point he was greatly overextended. Washington, then as far as Hopewell, wanted to attack and called a council of war. With the exception of Wayne, the council vetoed an attack, a decision, raged Alexander Hamilton, "which would have done honor to the most honorable society of midwives, and to them only."[10] One of the most vocal members of the council was Charles Lee, who had returned that spring in a prisoner exchange. His enthusiasm for the American cause seriously shaken, and his respect for Steuben's training nonexistent, he thought it would be folly to pit American infantry against the disciplined Europeans in a general engagement. The result of the council's deliberations was a compromise. Fifteen hundred men were to be sent under Scott to harass the enemy's left rear and flank, these troops reinforcing Maxwell's brigade and Morgan's regiment, which were assisting the Jersey militia in impeding the enemy's progress.

But, on the 25th, when the army reached Kingston, Washington altered the plan. He detached Wayne, and placed all detached troops in an advanced corps under Lafayette. The Frenchman was to watch his chance to launch a full-scale attack upon the enemy's rear with the expectation that the main army would be ready to support him; Lee was offered the command but, disapproving of such an offensive move, declined.[11] On the morrow, when the British reached Monmouth and bivouacked on both sides of the courthouse, it was observed that Clinton with a strong body of the enemy constituted the rearguard. Accordingly, Washington ordered Lafayette, only five miles from Clinton's rear, to march north toward Englishtown, a half dozen miles west of Monmouth. As the gap between Washington and Lafayette closed, the former detached two additional brigades to the advanced corps. Lee, who had now changed his mind about the command of the advanced corps, was sent forward with the brigades, succeeding Lafayette as commander of the entire corps, now about five thousand men. But Washington stipulated that, if Lafayette had

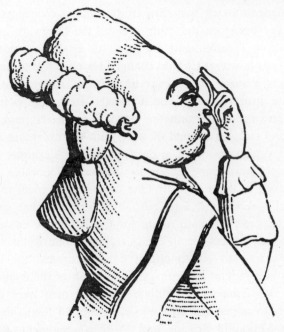

Caricature of Lord North (as Boreas) studying the Americans

already embarked on "some enterprise" that would not admit of "delay or alteration," Lee was to afford the marquis every assistance.[12]

If Washington expected Clinton to continue his retreat on Saturday, he was relieved to learn that the enemy still remained in the town of Freehold near Monmouth Courthouse. He himself lay with eight thousand men between Cranberry and Englishtown within easy support of Lee and his five thousand. The British were of about equal strength, and Clinton appears to have been agreeable to a fight at this juncture.[13] Lee, however, made no arrangements for reconnaissance even after Washington, at a council on Saturday noon, notified his officers that he would attack the enemy on Sunday. When Lafayette, Wayne, Maxwell, and, later, Scott met at five o'clock in the afternoon, Lee had no instructions for them. In a joint letter to Washington after the battle, both Wayne and Scott emphatically stated that "no plan of attack was ever communicated to us."[14] Lee was evidently quite indifferent about the battle, confident that he could meet any exigency as it arose, or possibly already convinced of defeat. Whatever the reason for his inaction, he was hardly the man to throw the advanced corps at a weak spot in the enemy's alignment and engage him until Washington came up. Perhaps he feared to attack Clinton on low ground broken by occasional ravines, swamps, and clumps of woods. Yet Washington wished to meet the British in this very area before they reached the low hills to the north, and particularly while the Americans had a line of hills in their own rear to which they could retreat if necessary.

On Sunday, June 28, a day which early turned hot and sultry and eventually reached 100°, Knyphausen moved out at daybreak, while, in order that he might not crowd the Hessian, Clinton waited until eight o'clock. Not until about ten o'clock did Lee, notified by Washington that morning that the main army was marching to support him, establish contact with the enemy north of the courthouse.[15] Such orders as he gave to Lafayette, Scott, and Wayne were confusing to those commanders, and the actions resulting were unco-ordinated. The 16th Light Dragoons chased a few American horsemen only to run into a heavy fire from American infantry which forced them to retreat. This check was not followed up by Lee. At one time, Lee had the extreme British rear flanked by the brigades of Varnum and Morgan, with Wayne across the dead rear position; these may have been the troops which the British Captain André conceded were "marching very rapidly and in good order."[16] At another time, Lee appears to have formed a ragged battle line with Scott on the left, Wayne in the center, and Lafayette on the right.[17] Then, as heavy columns of the enemy began to move up, Lee's advance elements fell back. Even as there had been no explicit orders to attack, so there were no explicit orders initially to retreat. Lafayette was moving to check a British column driving between himself and Wayne when

Lee, discovering that Scott appeared under extraordinary pressure, ordered a general withdrawal.[18]

The explanation was that Lee had been derelict in his duties. He had not reconnoitered the ground after having had all Saturday on which to do so. He had not worked out a co-ordinated plan of action with his commanders as he had been instructed to do. He had not maintained adequate liaison once his cannon opened on the enemy at ten o'clock. Especially disturbing to the morale of his troops was that he retreated when the battle had barely begun. Had he not withdrawn, it is possible that the British might not have had time to form the powerful line of battle which presently drove the Americans from two defensive positions on the high side of two ravines despite the stubborn resistance of isolated units, particularly the troops of Wayne's command. At first reluctant to press the issue, Clinton now resolved to bring on a general action.[19] Sending to Knyphausen for the 17th Light Dragoons and a British brigade, Clinton placed the Light Infantry on the right, the Guards in the center, and the Grenadiers to the left. The Hessian Grenadiers supported the Light Infantry, who moved to turn the American left, while the 3d and 4th Brigades supported the Guards and Grenadiers. Though the British losses were not light, the day was definitely theirs up to the point when Washington, who had early received encouraging news from Lee,[20] now learned from fugitives that Lee was in full retreat.

The situation soon changed after Washington, galloping up on his new white horse, encountered Lee. What exactly took place between the two generals is not clear, but it is evident that Washington used what Lee described as "very singular expressions," though Lee subsequently admitted that the manner in which his commander expressed himself was stronger and more severe than the actual words he employed.[21] Lee was at first too astonished to reply. When he finally started to explain heatedly about his part of the engagement, Washington cut him off, saying, "All this may be very true, Sir, but you ought not to have undertaken it unless you intended to go through with it."[22] But further altercation had to wait, for the scarlet host was near.

Washington met Colonels Stewart of Pennsylvania and Ramsay of Maryland with their regiments retiring in good order. When Washington asked them to support Oswald's battery until he could bring up the main army, they gallantly responded. In the severe fighting east of the ravine formed by Wemrock Brook, Stewart lost his life, while Ramsay was wounded and captured; but they held the line with help from Wayne. Lee, who was ordered to take charge of this defense, made his dispositions with skill and courage.

Washington quickly formed most of his battle line on the ridge west of the ravine. On the right were Greene and, beyond Greene, Knox with the artillery on Comb's Hill. On the left lay Lafayette and Stirling. Wayne held the center east of the ravine. When Lee asked if he could be of assistance, Washington permitted him to withdraw to Englishtown the tired troops of Stewart and Ramsay and there rest and re-form them, a disengagement action which Lee capably effected.[23] After that, with men dying of thirst and heat, general action broke out from one o'clock until nearly six o'clock as Clinton, his reinforcements from Knyphausen arriving, tested the American left, next the right, and finally the center, where Lieutenant Colonel Monckton hurled the Grenadiers at Wayne. The latter, deployed along an eminence in an orchard, drove Monckton back several times until the Englishman rallied and harangued his troops, dressed their lines, and led them in one last powerful thrust. Wayne's men held their fire until the sweating Grenadiers, their bayonets glittering in the late afternoon sun, came pushing up the ridge. Then, at Wayne's sharp command, the flintlocks blazed; and it was Bunker Hill all over again for the British, Monckton falling in the assault. But this time, thanks to Steuben's bayonet training, the Americans counterattacked with that weapon. Briefly Wayne's men and the Grenadiers locked in a fierce struggle over Monckton's body until the British sullenly gave way, leaving their dead leader in the hands of the Americans. Then Wayne himself retreated as heavy British supports arrived.[24]

But Clinton presently withdrew to the high ridge originally occupied by Lee before the latter's troops debouched to the plain where they had attacked the British in the morning. As Clinton explained, ". . . our men were so overpowered with fatigue, that I could press the affair no further."[25] Though both Clinton's flanks were securely anchored by thick woods and morasses and his center was approachable only by a narrow causeway through a swamp, Washington resolved to attack him, ordering General Poor with two brigades around to Clinton's right, General Woodford to his left, and the artillery to

open on the British front. The troops advanced spiritedly, but darkness set in. The army then lay on its arms, with Washington determined
to renew the engagement in the morning. Clinton, however, saw little
point in continuing the battle; he had saved his baggage train and
checked the Americans. Hence, late that night, he roused his tired
troops and stole away so silently that even Poor's men, who lay
between the main American army and the British, failed to detect the
enemy's departure.[26]

This battle had been extraordinarily hard fought, once Lee's retreat was halted. Today it is probably less well known for its importance or as the scene of Lee's singular behavior than as the occasion
on which Mary Hays, wife of an artillery sergeant, carried water to
her husband and his battery mates, thereby receiving the name "Molly
Pitcher"; when her husband was wounded, she took his place at his
gun and is said to have won the praise of both Greene and Washington for her performance. British casualties in the battle amounted to
three hundred and fifty-eight dead, wounded, and missing, with
Clinton reporting that about half his dead were killed by fatigue and
heat. Washington's own losses were almost precisely the same with
one exception: on the march to Sandy Hook at least six hundred
British and German soldiers deserted; of these, three-quarters were
German.[27] Washington, whose influence clearly saved the day,
counted the action as a victory, as did Congress, but if ever a battle
was a drawn struggle, Monmouth was it.[28]

For the battle's not being the decisive triumph on which he had
counted Washington held Lee directly responsible, and when Lee was
so indiscreet as to address two insulting letters to him following the
action, the commander in chief hastened to impanel the court-martial
that Lee desired. The court subsequently found Lee guilty on three
charges: disobedience in not attacking the enemy in accordance with
repeated instructions; misbehavior before the enemy by making an
unnecessary and, in certain instances, a disorderly retreat; and dis-
respect to Washington in his letters of June 28 and July 1.[29] Washington, however, must have thought the sentence of twelve months'
suspension from command rather lenient. But the British were of the
opinion that, if Lee had not retreated, he might have been destroyed.
If Lee was justified, the sentence was severe, but, since he was adjudged guilty, it was altogether unsatisfactory.[30] It is likely that Lee

had committed not an act of treachery or of cowardice but an error in judgment born of a failure in reconnaissance and a lack of faith in the ability of the American soldier to stand up to the British regular; after all, he had not seen Steuben's work at Valley Forge.[31] Congress upheld the verdict of the court-martial, never gave him another command, and dropped him in 1780 when Lee sent the politicians a supercilious letter.

Following Monmouth, Washington let Clinton go his way. He considered a pursuit impracticable in view of the heat, the sandy country with its scarcity of water, the men's fatigue, and the distance the enemy had gained by his night march.[32] Hence Clinton continued unmolested to Sandy Hook, where Howe's transports were waiting for him. Washington remained at Englishtown for a few days, then marched by way of New Brunswick and Paramus to the Hudson, crossed the river, and encamped at White Plains again. He considered the situation highly significant and wrote to a friend, "It is not a little pleasing, nor less wonderful to contemplate, that after two years Manoeuvring . . . both Armies are brought back to the very point they set out from and, that that, which was the offending party in the beginning is now reduced to the use of the spade and pick axe for defence."[33] In such a cycle with its shifts of strength the commander in chief saw the hand of Providence. But there were still to be five weary years before Providence was to call an end to the war and let everyone, including Washington, return to hearth and home.

XVIII

The Expansion of the War

The years 1778 and 1779 witnessed a vast expansion of what was now an international conflict. Fighting broke out in New England again, New York, the South, and the West; on the high seas off the American coast and in the West Indies; in European waters, especially near Gibraltar; in the great subcontinent of India and its adjacent seas. From the time France entered the war, to be followed eventually by Spain and Holland, with the Baltic nations aligned in the distinctly unneutral League of Armed Neutrality, Britain had her back to the wall and could no longer concentrate exclusively on the war in America. As for France, her policy was to be guided by considerations of where and how her paramount interests could be best served. Naturally Americans were certain that a French fleet operating off the American coast in concert with a powerful combination of French and American armies was the ideal way to defeat Britain; certainly this method was to the chief interest of the United States. But France, with world-wide commitments, was not always sure that her own best interests and those of the United States coincided. With such differing points of view, it is scarcely surprising if Franco-American relations were not infallibly harmonious.

A striking illustration of this difference is to be seen in the Rhode Island campaign of 1778. Estiang took so long crossing the Atlantic because of practice maneuvers en route that he failed to reach the Delaware capes until July 8, missing Admiral Howe's lumbering transports by ten days. Howe was so anxious that he even opened Clinton's dispatches to learn of Estiang's movements and those of a British squadron plowing heavy seas toward America under "Foul-Weather Jack" Byron, uncle of the poet.[1] But Howe caught a favoring wind to New York and arrived in time to ferry Clinton's troops to Manhattan. With only six 64-gun ships and three 50's he then evinced a remarkable degree of thought and energy in making his defensive dispositions against Estiang's twelve ships of the line and five frigates, which arrived off the Hook on July 11 and remained until the 22d. With several of the huge "liners" drawing twenty-three feet of water, the pilots refused to try to take them into the bay even when offered a fabulous sum of money. There was a chance on the 22d with a northeast wind and a high tide that raised thirty feet of water over the bar, but although Estiang approached the crossing, he dared not chance it and stood off to the south.[2]

While Estiang lay off Sandy Hook, French and American officials agreed that if the admiral failed to cross the bar, he should proceed to attack the British at Rhode Island with his fleet and his four thousand soldiers, and might expect the full co-operation of the American forces there under the command of General Sullivan. Washington urged Sullivan to ask Rhode Island, Massachusetts, and Connecticut to call out sufficient militia to make up a body of five thousand men, including the one thousand Continentals already with him. The response of these states was generous, for seven thousand eventually reported. Washington also sent Glover and Varnum's brigades under Lafayette and presently ordered Greene back to his home state, too. Sullivan, acting on Washington's orders, organized his army in two divisions under Greene and Lafayette, with himself in supreme command, and marched to a rendezvous with the French several miles north of Newport. Meanwhile General Pigot, in command of the three thousand British in Newport, strengthened his defenses.[3]

However promptly the militia swarmed, they swarmed too late. Although Estiang appeared off Newport on July 29, not until August 8 did Sullivan's forces arrive; on that same day, Estiang ran the British water batteries and started to disembark his troops. But the following day brought swift changes. Howe's intelligence of French movements, together with the arrival of several men-of-war as reinforcements, had made Clinton decide to defer the St. Lucia expedition and save Pigot.[4] First, however, the French fleet must be defeated. Hence, while Clinton prepared an expeditionary force of five thousand men, Howe, his fleet still only two-thirds as strong as the French, crowded on all sail for Newport. His arrival on August 9 prompted

Estiang, over Sullivan's protests, to re-embark his troops at once and sail out the next day to engage Howe. While the two fleets maneuvered, a violent storm rose on the night of the 11th, scattering both squadrons and causing such extensive damage that no decisive fighting occurred. Howe put back to New York for repairs, while Estiang entered Newport on the 20th and, on the morrow, sailed for Boston to refit.

Estiang's decision may have been wise from the French point of view, but it played hob with the Americans' hopes of taking Newport. In vain did Greene and Lafayette plead with him to leave his troops. Sullivan, however, exploded in anger, and, to the indignation of Lafayette, published an order condemning the French; Sullivan hoped "the event will prove America able to procure with her own arms that which her allies refused to assist her in obtaining."[5] So disgusted did the militia become with Estiang's decision that over five thousand went home. Sullivan retreated, pursued by Pigot, who, on the 29th, hurled his British and Hessians against Sullivan, particularly at Greene's wing. But the men of Glover and Varnum's brigades were veterans and refused to give ground. Though the armies remained quiet the next day, Sullivan learned that Howe and Clinton were closing in on the island. That night he ferried his men and guns over to Tiverton and Bristol. Casualties were very even, the Americans losing two hundred and forty-one in dead, wounded, and missing; the British, two hundred and sixty.[6]

The whole affair was hardly an auspicious beginning to the military aspect of the alliance. Riots broke out in Boston between French and American sailors and soldiers, and a French officer died of injuries. Responsible authorities on both sides, however, kept their heads and exchanged apologies. John Hancock, in particular, performed excellent service in smoothing the ruffled Gallic plumage. Nevertheless, Bostonians were not disappointed when Estiang sailed for Martinique on November 4.

For the rest of 1778 and 1779, while the Americans failed to develop an end-the-war offensive in the North, British strategy was moderately active. True, Lafayette proposed a Franco-American scheme for conquering Canada, and Congress, rarely able to resist the Canadian magnet, approved, until in November, 1778, Washington warned the political gentlemen not to be so naïve, since no nation, not even France, was to be trusted further than it was bound by its own interest.[7] But if such American grand strategy died aborning, thanks to Washington's objections and the disapproval of the French government, Lord George Germain was concerned about the debacle of the Carlisle peace commission. He strongly urged Clinton to force Washington to a general engagement. Failing that, Clinton was to drive Washington to seek safety in the Highlands or New Jersey. In any event, he was to contain the American commander while British troops, assisted by the navy, harried the coasts of New England and the South, and Indians, supported by troop detachments, attacked the frontier settlements.[8] Clinton's reply on May 14 rather pointedly reminded Germain that the object of every campaign since the war started had been to force a general and decisive action upon Washington, that Howe with a force far superior to Clinton's had not succeeded, that he, Clinton, would do his best to carry out the government's wishes but that he was not hopeful.[9]

A little more than a fortnight after he replied to Germain, Clinton acted. The American army had wintered in a rough semicircle about New York, troops being quartered at Middlebrook, Elizabeth, Ramapo, West Point, Fishkill, and Danbury. Washington's headquarters was at Middlebrook. Throughout the winter and spring, he built up the Hudson defenses, particularly the key to the system, West Point, at which he established his headquarters in midsummer. He also had a fort raised at Verplanck's Point on the east side of the river, while construction was started on the rocky promontory opposite, Stony Point. Suddenly Clinton moved up the river with six thousand men and, on May 31, seized both Stony Point and Verplanck's Point.

Clinton carefully explained his reasons. He sought not West Point as his objective but a general action. A sally up the Hudson would, he thought, fetch Washington at once; if Clinton could not force a general action there, he could still seize the American camp at Middlebrook, destroy the American supply depots at Trenton and Easton, draw Washington back into Jersey for their defense, and crush him. Much, of course, depended upon the reinforcements Germain had promised, reinforcements which never came in the strength Clinton expected. Then the return of Sir George Collier and General Matthews from raiding the Chesapeake area, particularly Norfolk and Portsmouth, inspired Clinton to try to draw Washington eastward out of the Highlands, to which he had gone as soon as he learned of the loss of the two Hudson forts. Hence, in early July, Clinton sent Collier and Governor Tryon on a destructive series of raids on New Haven, East Haven, Fairfield, Green's Farms, and Norwalk. But even Tryon's calculated frightfulness, which far exceeded Clinton's orders, failed to bring Washington to Connecticut's defense. Had the Virginian swallowed the bait, Clinton said he would have marched for Middlebrook.[10]

Clinton's strategy failed for reasons other than the lack of reinforcements. The principal reason was Washington's own countermove which envisaged a swift night attack upon Stony Point and Verplanck's Point. Washington decided to take Stony Point first since it was the more important and, if it fell, he could proceed with less secrecy and attendant difficulties against the other. He sent Major Harry Lee and his men through the area to learn all they could of the post through deserters and farmers, and dispatched Colonel Rufus Putnam to map the surrounding terrain.

For his assault troops he chose the elite corps of the army, the newly formed American Light Infantry. On his recommendation Congress had provided in 1778 that in all battalions there should be one company of Light Infantry but that, on campaign, the companies should be formed into a corps. Thanks to Steuben's reorganization of the infantry in 1779, battalions of equal strength were created. The principle carried over into the formation of the Light Infantry so that orders were issued on June 15 by which the sixteen companies of Light Infantry drawn from the three divisions with Washington were organized into four battalions, each battalion having four companies. Presently four complete regiments of two battalions each were formed. The men were all veterans between twenty and thirty years of age, five feet seven to five feet nine inches tall, lithe, active, rugged, and trustworthy. They were drawn from every state, and had been rigorously drilled in the use of the bayonet.[11] In February, General Wayne had asked for a command with the Light Infantry; in late June, he received the command and his orders: to storm Stony Point at midnight, July 15, 1779.

The assault was carried out with masterly efficiency, courage, and secrecy. With twelve hundred men under his command and three hundred under Muhlenberg as a reserve, Wayne marched south and west at noon. He passed under Torn Mountain and around Bear Mountain toward Queensboro, where he rested, then over the western end of Donderberg to the farm of Davis Springsteel, one and one-half miles west of Stony Point. Arriving there at half past eight, the troops were divided into two columns and, for the first time, were told of their objective. Muskets were unloaded except for Major Murfree's two companies, which were to make a feint in the center. On the right were the regiments of the Danish Colonel Febiger, Colonel Meigs of Quebec experience, and Lieutenant Colonel Hull; on the left was the regiment of Colonel Richard Butler, the most capable field officer of the Pennsylvania Line.[12] Ahead of each column were volunteers with axes to clear away obstructions, and ahead of them were two determined advance parties. To preserve secrecy, inhabitants within a considerable radius were taken into temporary custody and dogs on the line of march destroyed to prevent their barking.

At half past eleven the columns silently moved off. The tide still not down, they waded through two feet of water for twenty minutes before reaching solid ground where the heavy column with Wayne moved to the right, Butler's column to the left, and Murfree's companies directly ahead in front of the British lines.[13] British sentries spied the dark mass of Wayne's column while it was still plunging through the water, and at once the fort opened with roundshot, grape, and musketry. Undeterred by losses, the troops fanned out and drove uphill. Suddenly Wayne fell to the ground, stunned by a musket ball that grazed his skull. Almost immediately, however, he raised himself on one knee and shouted to his men to go forward.[14] Word of Wayne's fall electrified his men. With shouts of anger, they went bounding up the rocks, tore over the parapet, and burst into the fort just ten minutes before Butler's column poured in from the opposite side, driving a large number of redcoats before them. The memories of the "Paoli Massacre" still fresh, there was some bitter work with the bayonet before the British raised anguished cries of "Quarter!" and surrendered. Then Wayne, bleeding profusely, was borne into the fort in triumph.

The entire affair was executed with comparatively small loss to the Americans, fifteen killed and eighty-three wounded.[15] Of the enemy sixty-three were killed, over seventy wounded, and five hundred and forty-three captured. Only one man escaped, a lieutenant who swam to the sloop-of-war *Vulture*, which was soon driven down the river as the guns of Stony Point were turned against it. The project against Verplanck's Point, however, took longer than anticipated. By the time it got under way, days later, Clinton had recalled Collier and Tryon, who were about to sail for New London, and pushed up the river. Washington evacuated Stony Point, taking its guns and stores with him. Clinton admitted that Wayne's success, together with reports of the proximity of a French squadron, forced him to give up his idea of a campaign in Jersey.[16] Within a few months, needing the garrisons for the campaign to open in Georgia and the Carolinas, he evacuated both Stony Point and Verplanck's. Yet even before his evacuation, the Americans stung him again, Major Harry Lee making a spirited attack on Paulus Hook on August 19 after the manner of Stony Point. He lost only five men while killing and wounding fifty and taking more than three times that number prisoner. It was a clever little exploit.[17]

Another venture by the Americans in 1779 was made in July by Massachusetts, acting on its own, against a British force at Castine, Maine. This force consisted of about six hundred troops under General Francis Maclean who had been sent from Nova Scotia to build a fort as a protection for that province and for an anticipated settlement of Loyalists, though the Americans believed the British present for the purpose of getting masts and spars for their shipping. A body of nearly one thousand militia under Generals Solomon Lovell and Peleg Wadsworth was sent down east in transports convoyed by armed vessels under Commodore Saltonstall. Once the expedition was ashore on July 28, co-operation broke down between Marines and militia, while American attacks were frustrated by the defenders, of whom one young officer especially distinguished himself, Ensign Moore, later the great Sir John Moore of Peninsular War fame. The Americans proved so dilatory in their operations that finally the ubiquitous Sir George Collier appeared with a small but powerful squadron. Collier, who was just recovering from a fever, considered Maine a dreary country fit for nothing but wild beasts. The Americans lifted the siege, and their ships fled wildly up the Penobscot, where they were run ashore, burned, or otherwise destroyed by their crews. After the men painfully floundered back through the wilderness to their homes, the General Court of Massachusetts held an inquiry and censured Saltonstall. This "unfortunate expedition," as Washington described it, conducted without reference to the commander in chief, administratively and tactically mismanaged, reflected the lack of central control and co-ordination so prevalent during the Revolution.[18]

The third principal offensive in the North in 1779 was Sullivan's Indian expedition, which was prompted by frontier devastations of Loyalists and Indians. Colonel John Butler, his spectacular and even bloodier-minded son, Walter, Sir John Johnson, and the great Brant kept western New York in a frenzy of terror. In July, 1778, Sir John Butler struck at the Wyoming Valley in Pennsylvania, which was largely settled by people from Connecticut. Hundreds perished in a dreadful massacre and the subsequent flight. Shrieking in anguish, men were burned at the stake and others roasted over live coals and kept pinned down by pitchforks while their horrified families looked helplessly on. Still others were arranged in a circle while a ghastly half-breed squaw, Queen Esther, chanting a wild hymn of triumph, chopped off their heads.[19] With the frontier raw from such scenes, isolated families killed and scalped, and entire hamlets wiped out, Walter Butler and Brant struck at the settlement of Cherry Valley in New York on November 10, where a few troops were stationed. The houses were destroyed and more than fifty men, women, and children massacred after resistance ceased. Though Brant tried to restrain the prisoner killing, particularly of women and children, Butler was less squeamish. Such gory affairs as these finally led to the dispatch of a large American expedition to destroy once and for all this menace to the frontiers: Indian towns were to be razed and crops destroyed, while Fort Niagara, which served as the springboard for these raids, was to be taken.[20]

The command of the expedition was offered to Gates, who declined it as too strenuous for one of his years, whereupon it was given to the popular, garrulous, and never-very-successful Sullivan. It comprised nearly five thousand men starting in two columns. The left under Sullivan moved up the Susquehanna from Wyoming, destroying the town of Chemung, while the right under General James Clinton, burning fourteen villages, pushed up the Mohawk Valley to Canajoharie, then veered southwest to join Sullivan at Tioga Point on August 22. Leaving a strong body together with the sick, wounded, and heavy baggage at a fort erected near the forks of the Tioga and the Susquehanna, Sullivan broke camp on the 26th. Three days later at Newtown, near the present Elmira, the only pitched battle of the campaign was fought when Sir John Johnson, both the Butlers, and Brant sought to check the Americans with fifteen hundred Loyalists and Indians. Sullivan easily routed the enemy.[21]

After Newtown, the army struck the Long House a blow from which it never completely recovered. Standing crops of corn, squash, and beans were systematically ruined, granaries burned, and fruit trees cut down. During the campaign, forty towns were destroyed, some of them consisting of more than one hundred houses. Sullivan reported that, with one exception, not a single town remained in the Iroquois country.[22] In the succeeding winter, one so severe that New York harbor froze over, hundreds of Indian families starved to death. Throughout this destruction Indian resistance collapsed except when the savages saw a chance to cut off stragglers or ambush scouting parties.

But Sullivan failed to reach Fort Niagara. He had such difficulty with his commissariat that his army was on short rations for most of the time following Newtown. Some grain was obtained from Indian supplies, but, since most of their crops were in the growing stage, they were not edible. Hence, in view of the food shortage and the approaching autumn, Sullivan returned eastward. His expedition was thus not a complete success, and for two years longer Brant scourged the frontier. Indeed Sullivan's expedition might not have achieved all it did had not Colonel Daniel Brodhead with six hundred men moved from Pittsburgh up the Allegheny Valley during August and early September and devastated towns and crops belonging chiefly to the Senecas. This attack from the west[23] diverted the attention of many Indians who would otherwise have joined against Sullivan.

While the expedition into western New York was being organized, another venture was running its course farther west. This was the conquest of the Illinois country by that dashing young frontiersman who, years later, was to come to such a pathetic end in drink, debt, and disintegration of personality and mind, George Rogers Clark. Clark had been on the frontier even before the war began, while, since the war started, he had observed at first hand the hazards and hardships faced by the settlers at Boonsboro, Harrodsburg, Logan's

Station, and other settlements in the Kentucky and Ohio country. Even as New York and Pennsylvania suffered because of Fort Niagara, so the people of the west suffered because of Detroit, from which Colonel Henry Hamilton, the lieutenant governor, sent out Loyalists (including Simon Girty, a ruthless, corrupt white man who had been adopted by the Senecas when a boy), and war parties of Mingoes, Wyandots, and other western tribes against the Americans. Known as the "Hair-Buyer," Hamilton soon acquired an unenviable reputation among the settlers. Though it is by no means certain that he promised rewards for scalps, frontiersmen believed him guilty of it, the Council of Virginia accused him of it when he was captured, and it is pretty well established that he paid for scalps brought in. On the other hand, ruthless opponent though he was, he, like Johnson and the Butlers, was but another instrument for waging war against the frontier, an integral part of the total war policy of Lord George Germain.[24]

Clark, appointed leader of the militia at Harrodsburg, conceived of a way of eliminating the menace from Detroit: the conquest of the territory north of the Ohio. In that area were such British-held French villages as Kaskaskia and Vincennes. Hence, in the spring of 1777, after hearing favorable reports from two white spies concerning the defenses of Kaskaskia and the attitude of the French there,[25] Clark made the dangerous journey to the east in the fall of 1777 and laid his plans before Governor Patrick Henry. When men like Jefferson, George Mason, and George Wythe warmly supported the project, the council agreed to it in January, 1778. Since secrecy was paramount, the Assembly was not informed of the real objective. Clark was commissioned a lieutenant colonel and authorized, publicly, to enlist men for the defense of Kentucky, but, secretly, to take Kaskaskia; it is highly likely that the agricultural and mineral wealth of the region was a compelling reason in Virginia's decision.[26] Although Clark had difficulty raising troops because of the bad feeling between Virginia and Pennsylvania, he finally floated down the Ohio with one hundred and seventy-five men, hid his boats ten miles below the mouth of the Tennessee, and marched his men single file through the forest toward the northwest. On July 4, the Americans reached the Kaskaskia River at a point three miles from the town, and crossed the river that night. With one column surrounding the town, and a second driving through the open gate of the fort, Clark captured Kaskaskia without firing a shot. When the terrified people learned that France and America were allies, and that they would not be molested in their persons, property, or religion if they took the oath of allegiance, they eagerly accepted the Americans. The priest, Father Gebault, then expressed his belief that he could win over the French inhabitants of Vincennes. Clark let him go. When he returned on August 1, reporting complete success, Clark sent men to take possession, while other towns, including Cahokia, also submitted. The entire territory was now organized as the county of Illinois in the state of Virginia, and Clark dispatched a force to the east with news of the exploit.

But Hamilton was full of fight. While Clark worked to hold his gains with financial aid furnished by Oliver Pollock, a merchant in New Orleans and an agent of Virginia, Hamilton organized an expedition of about two hundred and fifty whites and Indians to recover the territory, build a fort at the junction of the Ohio and the Mississippi to regain the river trade, and, if possible, secure control of the mouth of the Missouri.[27] Setting off in October, with low water in the rivers, Hamilton made slow progress up the Maumee and across to the headwaters of the Wabash. He gathered almost three hundred more Indians and pushed into Vincennes on December 17, the French surrendering in panic.

Meanwhile Clark, on his way to Cahokia, raced back to Kaskaskia, where he first provided for the defense of the post. Then, by dint of entreaty, exhortation, and promises, he raised a force of one hundred and thirty men, half of them French, and marched for Vincennes on February 6, 1779. The heavy rains had caused the four rivers he must cross to overflow, with the result that the men were constantly soaked to the skin. At length, half drowned, Clark pushed into Vincennes on February 23 after marching his troops back and forth behind a slight elevation to give the impression of having at least a thousand men. The populace turned out with cheers, many of the British Indians fled, and Hamilton shut himself up in the fort, refusing Clark's demand for an unconditional surrender. But soon the British and Indians suffered so greatly from Clark's sharpshooters that Hamilton asked for a truce to discuss the situation. While the conference was going on, a war party was captured; to impress the savages, Clark had a half dozen Indian prisoners tomahawked in public and thrown into the river.

Shocked, Hamilton surrendered the next day, February 25, to a force hardly larger than his own, and was taken to Williamsburg, Virginia.[28]

Although the Vincennes campaign was a remarkable feat, it failed to bring peace, and Clark never realized his hope of seeing Detroit captured.[29] American occupation, moreover, brought distress to many of the French settlers who, in 1780, vainly sought aid against the Miami Indians from the Spanish commandant in St. Louis.[30] On the other hand, without expeditions like Clark's, Sullivan's, Brodhead's, and the stands made by James Robertson, "Nolichucky Jack" Sevier, and Evan Shelby in Tennessee, the British and Indians might have pushed the frontier appreciably eastward. They caused enough havoc in any event, while in the South, for a while, the redcoats enjoyed a series of sweeping victories.

XIX

The British Offensive in the South

The British decision to transfer major offensive operations to the South was made in early 1778.[1] Unsuccessful in the North, the government thought it might be easier to secure the South in view of the large numbers of Loyalists it expected to find there. If the South could be brought back into the fold, the other colonies could be distressed by cutting off their supplies and blockading their ports. As the year progressed, it became desirable, moreover, to obtain control of either Charleston or Savannah in order to supply the West Indies from South Carolina or Georgia. Georgia was recommended as the first step of conquest since its fall would greatly facilitate passage into South Carolina. To this end, in November, 1778, Clinton dispatched thirty-five hundred British, Hessians, and Tories from New York and New Jersey under Lieutenant Colonel Campbell. Commodore Hyde Parker landed the expedition two miles below Savannah on December 29. Campbell knew he could shortly expect help from General Augustine Provost, who was to push up through Florida with such troops as he could spare from St. Augustine.

Opposing Campbell was Major General Robert Howe with one thousand Georgia and South Carolina militia. He left part of his small force at Sunbury to check Prevost, and took the rest to Savannah, where he posted them to the east of the town, his right resting on a swamp and his left on rice paddies, though covered from the rear by a fort on the Savannah River bluff. Learning from captives how small Howe's force was, Campbell attacked energetically in the early afternoon of December 29. While he feinted against Howe's left with one column, another column, led by a Negro, picked its way through the swamp, brushed aside a covering force of Georgia militia, and drove

204

deeply into Howe's right. At this juncture, Campbell converted his feint into an assault, and, after a brief resistance, the Americans fled. Howe escaped with two Carolina regiments, but lost over five hundred dead, wounded, and captured and much valuable war matériel; the British loss was trifling.[2] Three weeks following the victory, Prevost, who had taken Sunbury with its garrison of two hundred, arrived in Savannah, and sent Campbell to seize Augusta and establish garrisons in the west of Georgia. By the middle of February, Georgia appeared to be thoroughly subdued.

The struggle now entered a seesaw stage. Urging Virginia and North Carolina to send troops southward, Congress had dispatched General Benjamin Lincoln to take command.[3] Lincoln had arrived in Charleston on December 19 and found only fifteen hundred troops available. With these subsequently increased to thirty-five hundred, he pushed toward Savannah, taking post on January 3 at Purysburg opposite Prevost, who was at Ebenezer on the Georgia side of the Savannah River. An able defense by Moultrie at Beaufort on February 3 and a smashing victory by Colonel Andrew Pickens over the Loyalist militia at Kettle Creek encouraged Lincoln to send General John Ashe with fifteen hundred troops to take Augusta.[4] Lincoln then ordered Ashe to follow Campbell to Briar Creek. At that point, Prevost's younger brother, Colonel Mark Prevost, took nine hundred men in a wide turning movement of fifty miles and fell upon Ashe's rear while other troops engaged him in front. The result on March 3 was disaster. The Americans lost nearly four hundred killed, wounded, and captured and the British a mere sixteen. Six hundred of Ashe's men fled to their homes, while only slightly over four hundred eventually reached Lincoln.

Though this was a severe blow, Lincoln had a fighter's heart as large as his massive stomach. Seven weeks later, on April 23, he marched up the river to cross near Augusta and prevent the enemy from receiving supplies from the west. At the same time, he left Moultrie with a thousand men at Purysburg and Black Swamp to guard against any passage of the Savannah. Discovering Moultrie to be weaker than he had supposed, Prevost crossed the river and drove toward Charleston. Despite delaying tactics by Moultrie, Prevost summoned the city, on May 12, to surrender. The South Carolinians, so redoubtable in 1776, now proposed that the city remain neutral for the duration of the war. Prevost scornfully refused to consider the proposition and insisted on an unconditional surrender.

But Prevost withdrew from his advanced position almost as quickly as he had appeared. He had only three thousand men, and an examination of the city's defenses convinced him that they were strong. He knew, moreover, that Count Pulaski had reached the city with a small body of cavalry and infantry and that Lincoln was now puffing up the road from Savannah with a force larger than his own.[5] Hence, on May 13, at night, he recrossed the Ashley, occupied John's Island, and established a strong bridgehead on the mainland at Stono Ferry. Meanwhile, as Prevost withdrew through the islands, Lincoln made a vigorous attack at Stono Ferry on June 19 against the British rearguard of nine hundred, including Hessians, under Lieutenant Colonel Maitland. The fighting was fierce, and, had a demonstration by Moultrie on James Island been made in time, Lincoln might have won. Unfortunately the arrival of British reinforcements compelled him to retreat after losing three hundred casualties as against the enemy's one hundred and thirty.[6] Prevost now completed his island hopping back to Savannah. With the seasonal temperature hovering around one hundred degrees, both sides ceased operations until September.[7]

Meanwhile, after a winter of inconclusive campaigning in the West Indies, Estiang assisted in capturing Grenada and St. Vincent in the summer of 1779, defeated Admiral Byron, and appeared off the Georgia coast in early September with a large fleet and over four thousand troops. His arrival was as unpleasant a surprise to the British as it was pleasant to the Americans. Though a brig got away to New York to warn Clinton and his new admiral, Arbuthnot, the French seized the frigate *Experiment* with the troops' pay chest aboard, the frigate *Ariel*, and two storeships.[8] Prevost, however, worked with furious haste to withstand a siege of Savannah. The four men-of-war in the harbor were run up the river and their crews and guns brought ashore. Transports were sunk to block the river passage below the port, and fire rafts were prepared. More than four thousand Negroes were set to work strengthening the network of defenses running for three-fifths of a mile from the swamp west of the town to the river. With over three thousand effectives, Prevost was prepared to give the Allies a warm reception.

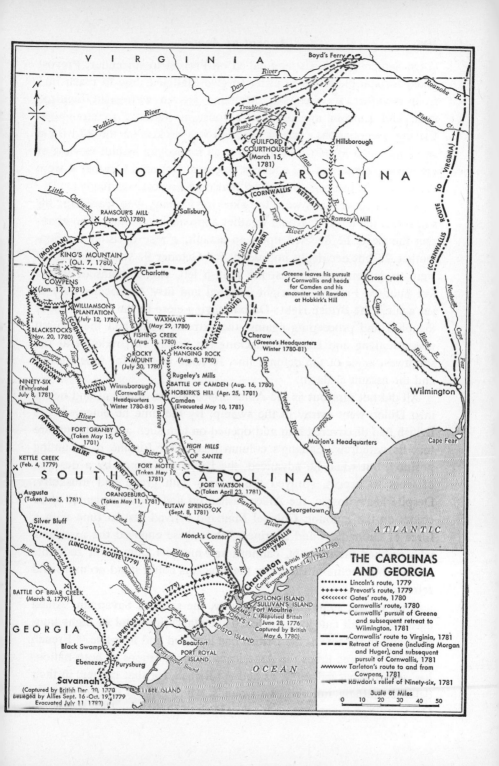

VIRGINIA

Boyd's Ferry

Roanoke R.

Dan River

Fishing Cr.

(CORNWALLIS ROUTE TO VIRGINIA)

Yadkin River

Troublesome Cr.

Ready Cr.

GUILFORD
COURTHOUSE
(March 15,
1781)

Hillsborough

NORTH CAROLINA

Little Catawba R.

Salisbury

(CORNWALLIS' RETREAT)

Deep River

Haw R.

Ramsay's Mill

RAMSOUR'S MILL
(June 20, 1780)

(MORGAN)

KING'S MOUNTAIN
(Oct. 7, 1780)

Charlotte

Little R. (HUGER)

Cross Creek

COWPENS
(Jan. 17, 1781)

WILLIAMSON'S
PLANTATION
(July 12, 1780)

Greene leaves his pursuit
of Cornwallis and heads
for Camden and his
encounter with Rawdon
at Hobkirk's Hill

Cape Fear River

Northeast Cape Fear R.

Black R.

BLACKSTOCKS
Nov. 20, 1780

FISHING CREEK
(Aug. 18, 1780)

WAXHAWS
(May 29, 1780)

Cheraw
(Greene's Headquarters
Winter 1780-81)

NINETY-SIX
(Evacuated
July 8, 1781)

(TARLETON'S

ROUTE)

ROCKY
MOUNT
(July 30, 1780)

HANGING ROCK
(Aug. 6, 1780)

Catawba R.

(CORNWALLIS 1781)

Enoree R.

Tiger R.

Broad R.

Winnsborough
(Cornwallis'
Headquarters
Winter 1780-81)

Rugeley's Mills

BATTLE OF CAMDEN (Aug. 16, 1780)

HOBKIRK'S HILL (Apr. 25, 1781)

Camden
(Evacuated May 10, 1781)

(GATES' ROUTE)

Great Pedee River

Little Pedee River

Wilmington

(RAWDON'S RELIEF OF NINETY-SIX)

FORT GRANBY
(Taken May 15,
1781)

Saluda River

Congaree River

Wateree R.

HIGH HILLS
OF SANTEE

Marion's Headquarters

Cape Fear

KETTLE CREEK
(Feb. 4, 1779)

FORT MOTTE
(Taken May 12,
1781)

FORT WATSON
(Taken April 23, 1781)

SOUTH CAROLINA

Augusta
(Taken June 5, 1781)

North Fork

South Fork

ORANGEBURG
(Taken May 11, 1781)

EUTAW SPRINGS
(Sept. 8, 1781)

Santee River

Georgetown

ATLANTIC

Silver Bluff

Edisto R.

Monck's Corner

Briar Creek

(LINCOLN'S ROUTE 1779)

Savannah R.

Little Edisto R.

Ashley R.

Cooper R.

(CORNWALLIS
1780)

BATTLE OF BRIAR CREEK
(March 3, 1779)

(PREVOST'S ROUTE)

Coosawhatchie R.

Saltcatcher R.

1779

Combahee R.

Charleston
(Captured by British May 12, 1780)
Evacuated Dec. 14, 1782)

GEORGIA

Black Swamp

Ebenezer

Purysburg

Beaufort

PORT ROYAL
ISLAND

Port Royal Sound

JOHN'S I.

EDISTO ISLAND

JAMES I.

LONG ISLAND
SULLIVAN'S ISLAND
Fort Moultrie
(Repulsed British
June 28, 1776
Captured by British
May 6, 1780)

OCEAN

Savannah
(Captured by British Dec. 29, 1779
Besieged by Allies Sept. 16-Oct. 19, 1779
Evacuated July 11, 1782)

TYBEE ISLAND

THE CAROLINAS
AND GEORGIA

••••••• Lincoln's route, 1779
+++++++ Prevost's route, 1779
<<<<<<< Gates' route, 1780
———— Cornwallis' route, 1780
⊢⊢⊢⊢⊢ Cornwallis' pursuit of Greene
and subsequent retreat to
Wilmington, 1781
· · · · · Cornwallis' route to Virginia, 1781
– – – – Retreat of Greene (including Morgan
and Huger), and subsequent
pursuit of Cornwallis, 1781
wwwww Tarleton's route to and from
Cowpens, 1781
⊢⊢⊢⊢⊢ Rawdon's relief of Ninety-six, 1781

Scale of Miles
0 10 20 30 40 50

On September 15, Estiang called on Prevost to surrender. Prevost asked for specific terms in order to give Maitland time to reach him from Beaufort. By the 17th, Maitland arrived with eight hundred men, and Lincoln appeared with fourteen hundred to strengthen Estiang. Negotiations ceasing,[9] ground was broken on the 23d for a siege, although Moultrie held out for an immediate assault in view of the incompleteness of the enemy's defenses. Not until October 4 were the siege guns in position, and by that time Prevost was ready.

But siege operations were too slow for Estiang, who feared for his ships with the heavy seasonal weather approaching. Rather than abandon the siege, he decided upon an assault, a wise decision for September 23 but decidedly imprudent for October 9. While the militia were to demonstrate against the British left, two columns of thirty-five hundred French and eight hundred and fifty Americans were to act against the British right: Dillon moving close to the swamp under the bluff and proceeding against the extreme right, and the column under Estiang and Lincoln attacking the Spring Hill redoubt at the southwest angle of the defense line. Reveille was set for four o'clock and the assault at dawn.

All did not turn out as the Allies hoped. In the dim light and heavy mist Dillon went astray in the swamp. By the time he emerged, the British had discovered him and opened on him such a devastating fire that he withdrew. Estiang's column had better fortune in assuming position, but when he advanced, the British, informed by a deserter of what to expect, sprayed the column with grape and musketry. Despite heavy losses, the Allies rushed on and actually planted their colors on the redoubt. Colonel Maitland arrived just in time with a force of Grenadiers and Marines. While these engaged the assailants who reached the redoubt, cannons and muskets from other redoubts enfiladed the column. Presently the attackers could stand no more and retreated.

Thus ended, somewhat ingloriously, the siege of Savannah. Allied casualties in all categories reached the staggering total of eight hundred and thirty-seven, the British one hundred and fifty-five.[10] French losses were three times the Americans', but the troops of both nations had shown great gallantry, as had the British, for that matter, in their defense. Estiang suffered two wounds, while Pulaski died of his. By October 28, Estiang was on his way back to France, and his departure necessitated Lincoln's withdrawal. Of Estiang's failure De Grasse wrote, "Great God! It would have been necessary to have seen it to believe it, and, in not saying the half, we would be thought to exaggerate and be partial."[11] Estiang's good intentions were hardly sufficient.

All this time, Clinton had been immobile since his recovery of Stony Point. He resented the drain on his forces with the dispatch of troops to Florida, Georgia, the West Indies, and Canada. In fact, Germain's facility for suggesting expeditions exasperated Clinton. "For God's sake, my lord," he remonstrated, "if you wish to do anything, leave me to myself, and let me adapt my efforts to the hourly change of circumstances."[12] Reinforcements arrived but in small numbers, while the troops sent to the West Indies remained there for want of a convoy. The British inferiority at sea so impressed both Clinton and Arbuthnot that they resolved on October 7 to evacuate Rhode Island, a decision which later incensed the redoubtable Admiral Rodney.[13] Reinforced by the Rhode Island garrison, Clinton felt sufficiently secure to sail for Charleston on December 26 with a force of seven thousand, six hundred troops. After bucking wild winter gales that scattered his fleet, he arrived off the Tybee on February 1, 1780.

Unlike his campaign in 1776, Clinton now had a base to work from and a less hazardous plan of operations. After arranging with General Patterson, now in command at Savannah, to assist him overland, Clinton moved by way of John's Island and James Island, seized the southern bank of the Ashley River opposite Charleston, and took Fort Johnson on March 6. Sending part of the fleet back to New York for reinforcements, he waited until the arrival of twelve hundred troops from Georgia, some of them mounted, before he pushed cautiously up the Ashley for twelve miles, crossed it without opposition, and extended his lines to the Cooper River. With most of the city clustered at the tip of land between the Cooper on the north and the Ashley on the south, Clinton now had to cut off the town by sea and sever land communications which were kept open by a small force of cavalry and militia under Huger thirty miles up the Cooper. The first task was achieved when British men-of-war crossed the bar, ran the batteries of Moultrie on April 9, and ranged up near the town. The second task was accomplished on April 12 when Clinton sent the huge dashing cavalryman, Colonel Banastre Tarleton, against Huger. Striking at night, Tarleton dispersed Huger's entire force. Meanwhile the British siege batteries opened fire on Charleston.

Lincoln was not the kind of man to give up easily. By means of Commodore Whipple's five ships stationed behind a barrier of sunken vessels at the mouth of the Cooper, Lincoln hoped to keep open his communications with the mainland. Fort Moultrie he knew to be reasonably potent, although its performance against Arbuthnot had been a bitter disappointment. On the other hand, Charleston had strong water batteries and on the land side powerful works mounting over sixty guns, a line of trenches in front flanked by strong redoubts, a canal in front of the trenches, and a network of abattis in front of the canal. Manning the works were more than five thousand Continentals, militia, and irregulars.

But Clinton, with his fourteen thousand troops, sailors, and Marines ashore, and his fleet in the harbor, had too much power and skill at his command. In the eighteenth-century tradition, he inched forward by digging saps (zigzag trenches directed toward an enemy's lines) and parallels (trenches parallel to an enemy's lines). Lord Rawdon, who arrived from New York with reinforcements on April 18, carried Haddrell's Point, and Fort Moultrie, assailed by land and sea, surrendered on May 6. When, on May 8, Lincoln again refused to submit, Clinton smashed the outer defense works to pieces and prepared to mount an assault. At that point Lincoln gave in, surrendering on May 12 his entire army of nearly fifty-five hundred, a mass surrender of United States forces exceeded only by General Julius White's submission to the Confederates at Harpers Ferry in 1862 and General Jonathan Wainwright's capitulation to the Japanese at Bataan in 1942. Lincoln had suffered ninety-two killed and one hundred and forty-six wounded; Clinton, seventy-six killed and one hundred and seventy-nine wounded.[14]

Lincoln was harshly criticized for letting himself be cooped up in the city. On the other hand, he could not very well have refused to defend it; public opinion was strong on this point. When he was deliberating a retreat to the mainland after Arbuthnot ran the batteries, a number of irate South Carolinians interrupted the council of war and threatened to destroy Lincoln's boats. Furthermore, Lincoln realized that most of the troops were Southerners and recognized the supremacy of state authority over that of Congress. Wounded at

Saratoga, Lincoln had no taste for the role of hero or martyr; nor was he an unintelligent man. He may have considered that if he failed to make a real effort to defend Charleston, the South Carolinians might throw in the sponge in disgust or despair and cease resisting the crown. It was Hobson's choice for Lincoln. Under the circumstances, he acquitted himself well.[15]

With Charleston in his possession, Clinton decided to return to New York with a third of the army and leave the 42-year-old Cornwallis in charge of mopping-up operations. After issuing a proclamation inviting the return of rebels to the king's allegiance, and threatening property confiscation for those who refused, Clinton sailed on June 5. Meanwhile Cornwallis had moved upstate with twenty-five hundred men on May 18. Learning on the 25th that Colonel Buford with the 3d Virginia had been marching to Charleston and was now withdrawing, Cornwallis sent Tarleton after him. His horses dying of exhaustion, Tarleton made one hundred and five miles in fifty-four hours and caught up with Buford at the Waxhaws. Though the Americans preserved excellent discipline, they held their fire too long; Tarleton's dragoons burst among them, sabering and shooting. Tarleton lost nine killed and twelve wounded; Buford, one hundred and thirteen killed, one hundred and fifty wounded, and fifty-three captured.[16] Organized resistance now appeared at an end in both Georgia and South Carolina.

But the British task of holding the two states was not simple. Lines of communication, largely along the rivers, were long, outposts few and scattered, and Patriot guerrillas becoming active. The main bases were on the seaboard: Savannah, Beaufort, Charleston, and Georgetown. Along the Savannah River control extended westward through Augusta to Ninety Six, where the Loyalists were especially strong. On the Santee, Camden was the most important center, with control reaching to Rocky Mount. Finally, along the muddy Pee Dee, control extended north and west to Cheraw. Communications between advanced posts were kept open by troop columns. To garrison his bases and his intermediate and advanced posts, as well as to furnish an invasion force for North Carolina at the end of the summer, Cornwallis had one Hessian, six British, and six Provincial regiments, slightly more than eight thousand men in all. Although Loyalist militia were presently available, many of those who took the oath deserted when they found it opportune. Consequently, Cornwallis was strongly opposed to the issuance of indiscriminate pardons and protections as a policy prejudicial to the crown.[17] This was one of the early points of difference between him and Clinton in the campaign in the South.

Cornwallis's troubles started early, especially after such partisan fighters as Thomas Sumter, Francis Marion, and Andrew Pickens became active. Though the earl discouraged a premature Loyalist rising in North Carolina, four hundred Loyalist militia tangled with an equal number of Patriot militia at Ramsour's Mill on June 20 in a bloody battle in which both sides lost heavily. On July 12, at Williamson's plantation in South Carolina, one of Sumter's lieutenants, Bratton, nearly wiped out a body of Loyalists and British dragoons. As Sumter himself crossed into South Carolina, Lord Rawdon evacuated Cheraw, sending his sick down the Pee Dee under an escort of Loyalist militia. Suddenly shifting their allegiance, the militia carried the sick men into North Carolina as prisoners and joined Sumter. With such reinforcements, Sumter smashed at Rocky Mount on July 30, but the garrison of New York Provincials withstood the assault. Foiled here, he struck, on August 8, at another outpost at Hanging Rock, where the British again repulsed him. More fortunate was the Georgia partisan, Colonel Clarke, who soundly trounced a detachment of dragoons at Green Spring on August 1. In all these contests, particularly where rival militia units were involved, the fighting often assumed the nature of a grudge feud, violent, bloody, and merciless. The skirmishes, moreover, signified that South Carolina was far from conquered. In fact, Cornwallis wrote Clinton on August 6 that the whole country between the Pee Dee and the Santee was in "an absolute state of rebellion, every friend of Government has been carried off, and his plantation destroyed."[18]

The nerve center of these activities, according to Cornwallis,[19] was the small force of Maryland and Delaware Continentals brought into the South from Washington's army by Baron de Kalb and led by General Gates since July 25. Thanks to Gates's friends in Congress, he had been given the Southern Department on June 13 without previous consultation with Washington. The arrival of militia from North Carolina and Virginia presently increased Gates's force to such an extent that he resolved to take the offensive against Rawdon at Camden. Though Kalb had worked out a plan of operations which involved a detour to the west where supplies were plentiful, Gates considered the direct road preferable, despite the shortage of supplies, in order to strike at Rawdon before the British consolidated their forces.[20] Starting on July 26 for Rugeley's Mills, twelve miles north of Camden, Gates took two weeks to march one hundred and twenty miles. Such slow progress may have been intentional to permit twelve hundred North Carolina militia to join him on the way. But his men, living on green apples, peaches, and half-ripe corn, nearly starved.

Alive to the danger, Rawdon called in his outposts and sent a courier to Charleston. Thus warned by Rawdon of Gates's approach, Cornwallis started for Camden on the night of August 10. Though the British had about three thousand men, the sick list numbered over eight hundred. Thinking that the Americans had seven thousand men, Cornwallis had to decide whether to leave his sick and make a hasty retreat to Charleston, which would have meant the loss of the province and, as he thought, of all Georgia except Savannah, or to make a vigorous attack.[21] As he was later to prove in India, Lord Cornwallis had real military ability. He chose to attack at daybreak of August 16, and, to that end, had his troops on the march at ten o'clock on the night of the 15th.

By an odd coincidence Gates also decided on a night march and a surprise attack. In British and American armies of that day rum formed an important part of the ration. Unfortunately Gates had no rum available. Instead, he issued a gill of molasses to each man along with a ration of half-cooked fresh meat and corn meal. The internal effect on his ravenous troops was nothing short of explosive. His adjutant general reported the next morning that the number of men present and fit for duty was only three thousand and fifty-two; of these many were debilitated. As if the gastronomical disturbances were not sufficiently inauspicious, Gates's advance under Colonel Armand stumbled upon the British advance guard at two o'clock in the morning, nine miles north of Camden, and retired in disorder.

But Cornwallis did not press his advantage. Learning that Gates's whole army was in front of him and that the pine forest through which he was marching was only a mile wide and flanked by marshes, a situation favorable to his small numbers, he decided not to risk his army in the dark. He made his dispositions in the following order: on the right under Lieutenant Colonel Webster were the Light Infantry, the 23d and 33d Regiments; on the left under Lord Rawdon were the Volunters of Ireland, the Legion infantry, part of the North

Carolina Regiment, and four guns; in reserve lay the 71st Regiment with two guns, and in the rear the cavalry of Tarleton's Legion. Gates also disposed his troops in the dark: on the right, under Baron de Kalb, the 2d Maryland Brigade and the Delaware Regiment; on the left, under Generals Caswell and Stevens, the militia from North Carolina and Virginia; in reserve, the 1st Maryland Brigade.

It was a calm morning, slightly hazy, when Cornwallis observed a movement on the American left. This was the American militia either forming to attack the British left, an incredible procedure considering the militia's lack of discipline and training, or changing position, an equally incredible performance since the armies were on the point of engaging. Cornwallis at once ordered Webster forward. Webster hit the militia with such power that they fled across the left flank of the 1st Maryland, sweeping away Armand's troops and carrying Gates along with them in their stampede. But, except for the initial disorder in the 1st Maryland, the men from Maryland and Delaware stood firm. The 1st Maryland coolly effected a change of front to oppose Webster, while Kalb, after holding back two assaults by Rawdon, counterattacked with the bayonet and backed him deep into the woods; there the baron, fighting like the giant he was, died of eleven wounds. Rawdon's line, though bent, refused to break, while Webster's pressure on the left flank of the Continentals soon became intolerable. Harassed now by both Webster and Rawdon, and confused by the heavy pall of smoke that refused to rise in the still air, the Continentals might still have preserved a semblance of order had not Tarleton's dragoons come crashing down upon their rear. The American regulars fled in all directions, and Tarleton pursued the flying troops for twenty miles to complete the rout.

While Cornwallis lost only three hundred and twenty-four casualties, Camden was a disaster for the Americans. Casualty reports were never compiled, but Cornwallis estimated between eight and nine hundred killed and wounded and a thousand captured. They lost all their guns, baggage, most of their wagons, and nearly all their muskets. Ten days after the battle, barely seven hundred of the Continentals assembled at Hillsborough, one hundred and sixty miles away, a place which Gates reached in about three days. Although this was about as swift a disengagement action as a general could make in those times, Gates denied that he had fled. He wanted, he explained, to reach a base which would be most advantageous for creating a new army from Virginia and North Carolina. It was certainly desirable that he organize a new army and by no means unlikely that he could have prevented his being swept from the field; Frederick the Great had suffered a similar and even more humiliating experience. Nathanael Greene, who stood up warmly for Gates, pointed out that the chief criticism to which Gates was liable was not what he did or did not do during or after the action but that he ever fought at all. A resolution to inquire into his conduct was defeated in Congress two years after the battle; by 1783, he again occupied a distinguished position in the army.[22]

Only one American force of consequence remained in the South, Sumter's partisans, whom Gates had reinforced with four hundred Maryland troops on August 15. Gates would have been wiser to have sent militia and kept his regulars. On the day of the battle, Sumter cut off a British convoy bound for Camden from Charleston, but he headed for the Catawba country in the northwest when he learned of the disaster at Camden. Cornwallis sent Tarleton in pursuit. His force melting away from sunstroke and fatigue, Tarleton, with one hundred dragoons and sixty infantry, finally caught up with Sumter and his eight hundred at Fishing Creek on the 18th when the Americans were lolling about camp at midday. Tarleton's men, fanning out, pounced upon the camp. Although small centers of resistance sprang up, Tarleton soon liquidated these, killing and wounding one hundred and fifty men; capturing three hundred prisoners, two cannons, all the wagons and supplies; and barely missing Sumter himself, who escaped minus hat, coat, and boots. In addition, one hundred British regulars and one hundred and fifty Loyalists were released from captivity. Tarleton lost one officer killed and fifteen men wounded.[23]

It was a brilliant stroke, which, linked with Camden, seemed convincing evidence that large-scale resistance operations had been smashed for some time to come. Cornwallis assured Germain that "the internal commotions and insurrections in the province will now subside."[24] Nothing now appeared to stand between the earl and a successful invasion of North Carolina and Virginia. The South was surely lost to the Americans, and Lord North's government became jubilant; the news of Cornwallis's victories helped the government weather a crisis in parliament. But for the Patriots in America the Revolution appeared to have entered upon its darkest days.

XX

The Critical Year, 1780-1781

Few periods during the Revolution were as discouraging as the months from the middle of 1780 to the spring of 1781. Hopes built upon the arrival of a French expeditionary force at Rhode Island in July, 1780, crumbled as superior British naval forces bottled up the French in Newport, where they remained for eleven months. The treason of Benedict Arnold shocked and dismayed thousands of his countrymen. Congressional and state finances were in a deplorable condition and led directly to the mutinies of January, 1781, when the troops of the Pennsylvania and New Jersey Lines took matters into their own hands to persuade the authorities to recognize and redress their grievances. In addition to the lack of money and the distress resulting from insufficient supplies of food, clothing, and medicines, the manpower problem became worse as fewer and fewer men enlisted. National feeling in America, particularly in the North, reached a lower point than at any time since Christmas, 1776.

The winter of 1780 surpassed the rigors of the Valley Forge season, and, as usual, the army at Morristown was fighting for survival. Occasionally the commissary was empty for two or three days. On December 16, 1779, Washington considered the supply situation indescribably alarming, was sure that the army had never experienced such an extremity during the war, and feared lest a breakup occur within a fortnight.[1] While this did not happen, the soldiers soon started to loot the local farmyards in order to keep from starving. Washington now resorted to the course he had been so hesitant to adopt at Valley Forge, the impressment of supplies. Although the starvation crisis passed, the army remained precariously close to the condition of Mother Hubbard's dog until late in the spring. The ironical feature of the situation was that food was plentiful in that part of the country. While several herds of cattle previously purchased by the army were overlooked by the commissary, the main difficulty was that the farmers of New Jersey were reluctant to sell their produce and livestock for the depreciated Continental currency.[2]

Anger over the lack of food and clothing mounted to a climax in May. On the night of the 25th, two Connecticut regiments, incensed

André's sketch of himself the day before his execution

at what they fancied to be prejudicial treatment by the commissary, and furious over the fact that they had received no pay for five months, assembled on the parade ground. In vain Colonel Meigs and his officers sought to get them back to their hutments. Someone struck Meigs, and the attitude of the men became so recalcitrant that a veteran Pennsylvania brigade was summoned. With the ringleaders arrested, most of the mutineers returned to their quarters.[3]

The increasing number of American deserters who reached the British lines, together with word of the defection in the Connecticut Line, prompted Knyphausen to launch an expedition into Jersey.

Crossing from Staten Island on the night of June 6 with five thousand troops under Generals Edward Matthews and Thomas Stirling, he pushed through Elizabeth toward Morristown. Almost at once, militia gathered on his flanks, and the Jersey brigade in front harassed his every step. Near Springfield he halted, while Washington pressed forward with the hope of making a night attack. Knyphausen, however, withdrew in a violent thunderstorm to Elizabethtown Point, leaving in his wake the smoking ruins of the village of Connecticut Farms and a legacy of bitterness born of the wanton killing of the local minister's wife.[4]

But the British were not through with New Jersey. By the 21st, Washington with the main portion of his army was on his way toward the Hudson forts as reports reached him of Clinton's return from the South and of British vessels in the river off Verplanck's Point. He left Greene in the vicinity of Springfield with about a thousand men consisting of Maxwell and Stark's brigades and the troops under Major Harry Lee. In addition, Greene had the Jersey militia, who soon became active again as, on June 23, Clinton sent Knyphausen crashing into Jersey from his bridgehead at Elizabethtown Point with over five thousand horse, foot, and artillery.

It was a strange day. Knyphausen swept rapidly toward Springfield. Three miles east of the town at the Elizabeth River he sent Matthews with one column directly toward Springfield, while with the other column he marched toward Greene's left along the Vauxhall road. Vigorous resistance along the way and at the bridges permitted Greene to disengage his troops gradually and in good order and form a strong defense behind the town at the junction of the two roads, where the pass through Short Hills began. Although it was late afternoon by this time, there was enough daylight remaining for Knyphausen to test Greene's defenses, and it is doubtful if Greene could have withstood an assault. But, to the American's surprise, the British did not attack. Instead, they set fire to the town and retreated in a manner which the amazed Greene described as "precipitate."[5] A futile expedition if there ever was one, it might have become fruitful had it not been suddenly withdrawn by Clinton, possibly on the basis of information reaching him from Benedict Arnold that French forces were presently expected in Rhode Island.[6]

A French fleet and army were indeed nearing American shores. In

France since early in 1779, Lafayette had worked with unflagging enthusiasm to obtain support for the United States. The shelving, in October, 1779, of a plan for the invasion of England as impracticable led directly to serious consideration of a scheme submitted in July by Lafayette which envisaged the dispatch to America of a fleet and army which should co-operate closely with Washington.[7] Vergennes's own enthusiasm for the Americans had cooled, particularly in view of the slackening of the American war effort, the extent of America's appeals for aid, and the factionalism in Congress.[8] On the other hand, with the demise of the invasion plan, it was essential to strike somewhere soon, and effectively too. In the discussions that ensued during the fall and winter, Lafayette took an eager interest, sending to the Comte de Maurepas a letter in which he again pointed out the urgency of dispatching an expedition.[9] Finally, in February, the government decided to do so, and provided that the expedition should be placed under Washington's command. The choice of a French commander was a happy one, the judicious Comte de Rochambeau, a veteran of the Seven Years' War. Rochambeau cleared Brest on May 2 with about fifty-five hundred troops, his transports convoyed by Admiral de Ternay with seven ships of the line and five frigates. Rochambeau expected that a second detachment would soon sail which would raise his numbers to the eight thousand designated, but tardiness on the part of the Ministry of Marine in supplying transports, together with the appearance of a British blockading squadron, kept this detachment permanently in port.

Meanwhile Lafayette had sailed for America in March to bring the good news to Washington. Especially well received was the provision that Washington should be responsible for drawing up the plan of campaign in which the French troops could be most effectively employed.[10] Of all the projects that Washington proposed during the war, the one nearest his heart was the seizure of New York. At once he set to work on a plan to take the port, the operation to start in August. After Ternay arrived at Newport on July 11, Lafayette was sent at once to Rhode Island with Washington's instructions. If the Virginian ever rubbed his hands in gleeful anticipation, this must have been one of those times.

Fortune, however, turned coy. When Admiral Thomas Graves's squadron arrived in New York a few days after the French disembark-

ation, the British were ready to challenge the French. Within a few
days, Admiral Arbuthnot sailed for Newport with his and Graves's
ships. Ternay at once placed his squadron in a defensive position,
while Rochambeau, strengthened by General Heath and heavy contingents of militia, threw up shore batteries. But this was to be no
exclusive ship-and-shore action, for Clinton loaded six thousand
troops aboard his ponderous transports and sailed for Point Judith
on the 27th. Rochambeau might have found his situation dubious
indeed had not Washington countered Clinton's move by crossing
the river at Dobbs Ferry and marching swiftly toward Kingsbridge
as if to attack New York. Hastily Clinton turned back. Though much
of the pressure was now off Rochambeau, the naval blockade of
Newport tightened, and after that aging, dissolute, but superb fighter,
Admiral Sir George Rodney, arrived in mid-September with a powerful squadron, there was no immediate chance of shaking the British
supremacy despite the enfeebling of British fighting strength through
the acrimonious disagreements between Rodney and Arbuthnot.[11]

Washington now resolved to reach an understanding with Rochambeau. To this end he and his staff rode over the Connecticut hills to
Hartford, where he arrived on September 21. Hartford gave him a
hero's welcome and then almost immediately accorded another to
Rochambeau, whose approach was announced by the Swedish aristocrat, Count Ferson, the beloved friend of Marie Antoinette. In
the conference that ensued at Colonel Wadsworth's home that evening, the commanders agreed that any move by the French army,
particularly one to effect an Allied attack on New York, which Rochambeau was never enthusiastic about, must be contingent upon
French naval superiority. Despite the presence of a French fleet in
the West Indies, the necessary superiority was not attained until
well into the following year. Hence, while Rochambeau and his staff
returned to Newport to enjoy the somewhat decorous pleasures of
the town, Washington rode back over the hills to face a winter in
which his army stood in danger of dissolving. But even before this
hazard rose to haunt him, he confronted personal and national tragedy in the guise of Arnold's treason.

Arnold's defection was an event which, in its relation and evalua-
tion, properly requires a psychiatrist as well as a historian. Certainly
his would make an interesting mental case study. But, disordered or

not, he was judged by his contemporaries as responsible for his acts and was condemned as few traitors have ever been. On the other hand, the man's nature, impulsive, violent, morbidly sensitive to slights, made his life a veritable hell of suspicion. That Congress discriminated against him can hardly be doubted, but he was the aggressive, ruthless, impetuous type that raised a vast crop of enemies. Some men envied his ability as a leader, others feared his sharp tongue, while still others smelled something unpleasant in his inability to keep his public accounts straight. When he shifted his allegiance, even his friends could defend him no longer. "Analysis," as Carl Van Doren has neatly pointed out, "cannot do justice to Arnold's story. It must be narrated. . . ."[12] Although the narration thereby required would be too extensive for this study, the enormity of the offense and its military significance compel at least a summary.

Unable to take the field because of his wounded leg, Arnold was given the military command of Philadelphia. He soon fell in love with the reputedly charming Peggy Shippen, the youngest of three daughters of the wealthy and distinguished Judge Edward Shippen, whose residence had been frequented by British officers during the occupation. Arnold married Peggy in 1779, against, it is said, the initial opposition of Judge Shippen.[13] Having purchased a beautiful estate overlooking the Schuylkill, Arnold threw lavish parties to which members of Congress, officers of the command, and important citizens were invited.[14] All this was quite beyond his means, as indeed, for that matter, was his whole manner of living after he took command of Philadelphia.

But Arnold was not the man to let the lack of money stand in the way of the kind of life to which he thought he was entitled. He speculated in real estate, fought to secure property left behind by Loyalists, and made at least one venture into privateering. Other officers and even congressmen had been guilty of similar activities, but Arnold occupied an eminent position of trust and power which left him especially vulnerable. After he employed government wagons to secure his own property from possible capture at Egg Harbor, property which had been conveyed in a ship to which he had given a permit to sail from Philadelphia despite an express prohibition by Congress, his enemies attacked him. It scarcely mattered that he intended to pay for the use of the wagons; the exasperated Arnold and the touchy Council of Pennsylvania, a difficult body for any soldier to get along with, had become mutually incompatible. The council preferred charges, Arnold on Washington's advice demanded a court-martial, and while the trial, beginning in June, 1779, dragged on for months, Arnold resigned his command. Eventually the court found him guilty on two charges and sentenced him to receive a reprimand from Washington. After Congress confirmed the sentence in February, 1780, Washington, in April, complied in cool, straightforward language, stating that "a sense of duty and a regard to candor oblige him to declare, that he considers his [Arnold's] conduct in the instance of the permit as peculiarly reprehensible, both in a civil and military view, and in the affair of the waggons as 'Imprudent and improper.' "[15]

Between June, 1778, when he entered Philadelphia after the British evacuation, and May, 1779, Arnold decided to change the color of his coat from blue to scarlet. He was desperately in need of money, and deeply antagonized by the action of both Congress and the Pennsylvania politicians. Possibly, too, the more vexed he became at Americans the more he began to question the wisdom of the colonies in breaking away from the empire and allying with France, which he mistrusted. Yet it is likely that any high-level political thinking was largely a rationalization for what was primarily a venal motive. Back in 1776, Major John Brown had remarked that money was Arnold's god and that he would sell even his country to get enough of it.[16]

Without waiting for his court-martial to start, Arnold opened negotiations in May, 1779. From the first, moreover, the charming Peggy was evidently aware of her husband's negotiations.[17] Determined to set as high a price as possible upon his betrayal, Arnold induced General Schuyler to try to persuade Washington to secure command of West Point for him. Innocent of Arnold's intent, Schuyler complied, and Arnold received the assignment in August. His price for the surrender of the fortress was £10,000.

With Washington away in Connecticut conferring with Rochambeau, and West Point almost denuded of troops, Arnold and Clinton worked swiftly. In order to expedite the plans for the surrender, Clinton sent to Arnold the only man who had any affection for the British commander, his young adjutant general, Major John André. André sailed upriver on the sloop-of-war *Vulture* and met Arnold on the night of September 21 on the west shore below Haverstraw. An American battery at Teller's Point opened fire in the morning, forcing the *Vulture* downstream and thus obliging André to return by land. In disregard of Clinton's instructions, he submitted to Arnold's insistence that he assume civilian guise and carry documents back to New York; the documents he placed between his stockings and his feet. While Arnold then returned to his headquarters at the Robinson house opposite West Point, André made his way back through the woods. He was captured on the 23rd near Tarrytown. When this intelligence reached Arnold, he left his wife and child, and rode at breakneck speed to his barge, which met the *Vulture* below Verplanck's Point. Washington arrived at Arnold's headquarters a bare hour after Arnold's departure. Stricken with sorrow and anger at the information contained in the incriminating papers and in a letter from André, he ordered Arnold pursued, a hopeless task. The gallant André was subsequently tried and hanged as a spy on October 2 at high noon, to the anguish of Sir Henry Clinton, who moved heaven and earth to save him but failed with the implacable American commander in chief.[18]

Arnold's treason horrified Americans, burying memories of the good he had accomplished, while the involvement of André won him few friends among the British. Though Arnold proved especially unpopular with many of the younger British officers, and though he had failed to bring off the surrender of West Point, the British authorities kept their word. He was made a brigadier general with all the perquisites, including a pension upon retirement; given a command; awarded £6,315, a yearly pension of £500 for his wife, £100 for each of his children; and, in 1798, granted more than thirteen thousand acres of land in Upper Canada for meritorious service in the current war with France.[19] Quite literally Arnold had made crime pay on a rather handsome scale. On the other side of the ledger, however, were the indignities he suffered for the rest of his life, the humiliating duel he fought with the Earl of Lauderdale in defense of his honor, the bitter disappointment and unhappiness in his closing years at finding his offers of service bluntly refused. He lost a great deal of his money through unwise investments and died in considerable financial distress. According to tradition, Arnold, when on his deathbed, asked his wife, to whom he ever remained devoted, for the old uniform in which he had fled to the *Vulture*, and entreated Providence to forgive him for ever putting on another. Evidently the price of honor was higher than even Benedict Arnold had calculated.[20]

The year 1780 continued gloomy for the American army. Conditions which had incited the rebellious spirit among the Connecticut troops in the spring failed to show improvement. Much of the difficulty was caused by excessive delay and administrative detail in the government departments, the lack of central direction in Philadelphia, and the slackness of the states, with the politicians reportedly caring more for the rhetoric and punctuation of their resolutions than for their effectiveness.[21] Congress, however, strove to cut down some of the expense by eliminating many offices and throwing more responsibility upon the individual states. Greene, who was very unhappy in the office of quartermaster general and had sought to resign in 1779, opposed the new system as containing all the evils of the old, and handed in his resignation on July 26. Harassed by the intricacies of the department and by Congressional criticism, he expressed his opinion so bluntly that Congress demanded his dismissal from service.[22] Fortunately, the intervention of both Washington and its own investigating committee induced Congress to change its mind. Yet its new appointee, Timothy Pickering, who took over in September, could do little better at first. The troops entered the winter on half-rations and with scant clothing. Not until the summer of 1781 were many of the unsatisfactory conditions finally removed. By that time, greater centralization was effected, a superintendent of finance replacing the Board of Treasury, and a clothier general, who acted upon the financier's approval, relieving the states of their responsibility for clothing the troops. The system of specific supplies was eliminated, and necessary financial arrangements to provide the army with food were established.[23]

All this was too late to prevent the difficulties that arose in the winter of 1781. By that time, the nearly half-billion dollars in paper money issued by Congress and the states had little value. A hat cost $400; a suit of clothes, $1,600; and a pair of shoes, a captain's pay for an entire year.[24] Of all the soldiers affected by the hardships those of the Pennsylvania Line considered themselves the most aggrieved. Many of them claimed that they had signed up for three years only and were being held for the duration now that the three years were up.

They were reduced almost to nakedness, were poorly fed, and had not been paid for a year. While the officers recognized the insufficiency of clothing, food, and pay, they insisted that most of the men had signed for the duration. The regimental papers, however, were not available at Morristown where the line was quartered. The Pennsylvanians, who were probably superior to any other line because of their long service, were not made happier by rumors of lush living in Philadelphia, of high bounties being offered by other states, and of inmates of the Philadelphia jails being pardoned and promised substantial bounties if they would enlist.[25]

The veterans finally resolved to take matters into their own hands. Acting under the command of their sergeants, and stimulated by a New Year's Day issue of rum, they suddenly paraded that night to the accompaniment of a wild firing of muskets. Officers who sought to control the affair were roughly handled, one losing his life. General Wayne and members of his staff quickly left off their own New Year's celebration and rode to the scene, but the men would not listen to Wayne's commands and entreaties. They said their business was with Congress, which alone had the power to right their wrongs. When Wayne persisted, shots were fired over his head. At once he opened his coat and challenged them to shoot him, but they retorted that, with a few exceptions, they had no desire to hurt any officer of the Line. Then they moved off with baggage and cannon toward Princeton, preserving the strictest behavior, while Wayne and his officers followed futilely at some distance. Further attempts to conciliate the men were made at Princeton but to no avail, and the mutineers marched on to Trenton.

It was an extraordinary performance, but the mutineers were not Arnolds; discovering two of Clinton's spies in their midst, they handed them over to the authorities for trial and execution. In the meantime, while Joseph Reed, now president of the Pennsylvania Council, met the mutineers at Trenton and discussed the situation with the committee of sergeants elected by the men, Washington experienced acute embarrassment and perturbation lest the mutinous spirit prove contagious. Though anxious for the states to redress the grievances of their men, he would have employed force rather than permit the Pennsylvanians to ruin his army. On the other hand, sympathy for the mutineers was prevalent among a number of units, while the

Pennsylvanians, well over a thousand strong, would have taken considerable subduing.

Notwithstanding their own sympathies, New Englanders were ready to march against the rebellious troops. Possibly the one unit which showed real satisfaction at the prospect of helping scotch the mutiny was a detachment belonging to a Connecticut brigade whose own uprising, the previous spring, had been kept under control by the Pennsylvania Line. Troops and guns were assembled under General St. Clair on the west bank of the Delaware to bar a crossing should the negotiations fail. Thanks to cool heads in Trenton and a disposition to right at least a portion of the soldiers' wrongs, nothing serious occurred. Part of the back pay and articles of clothing were assured, while, until the regimental papers arrived, discharges were given on the basis of a man's word as to the terms of his enlistment. By January 29, Wayne could report that the settlement was finished. But so was half of the Pennsylvania Line.[26]

Encouraged by the action of the Pennsylvanians, the smaller New Jersey Line at Pompton also mutinied on January 20 while the New Jersey legislature was trying to meet their demands. This time Washington would have nothing to do with negotiation. As he wrote Congress, "Unless this dangerous spirit can be suppressed by force there is an end to all subordination in the Army, and indeed to the Army itself."[27] He sent General Robert Howe of South Carolina with a strong body of New Englanders to use summary measures in dealing with the mutineers. Howe marched at night from Ringwood and, by the morning of the 28th, surrounded the huts of the mutineers. The latter were at once paraded without arms and the chief ringleader of each of the three regiments was singled out. Twelve of the most guilty mutineers were then chosen as a firing squad and compelled to shoot two of their leaders, the third being spared on the recommendation of his officer.[28] Amid such distressing scenes the mutiny of the New Jersey Line collapsed.

Those were dark days in the military history of the Revolution. It was no insignificant measure to execute American soldiers without adequate trial. Naturally mutiny could never be legally justified, but, granted the presence of some radicals and perjurers among the mutineers in both rebellious lines, many of the soldiers sincerely believed themselves justly aggrieved in regard to the terms of their enlistment, while all had suffered from the lack of food and clothing, not to mention the arrears of pay. Possibly their offense, however serious, was second to that of the public at large, which, in the words of the distinguished historian of the mutinies, "had broken its contract with the soldiers of all the Continental Lines by failing to supply and pay them, while they were kept in the service by military discipline."[29]

In view of the scarcity of recruits, Congress reduced the army in 1780. The one hundred and four battalions authorized in 1776 had been reduced to eighty in 1779 and were now further consolidated in October, 1780, into fifty regiments of infantry, four each of cavalry and artillery, and one of artificers.[30] Had these units been filled, there would have been slightly more than forty thousand men enrolled, but the regiments were far below strength. In fact, in 1781, before the Yorktown campaign, the total number of troops definitely known to be under arms, Continentals and militia, did not exceed twenty-one thousand.[31] Washington firmly believed that the war had been protracted because of the inability of the country to maintain adequate forces on a permanent basis; he felt that Gates's defeat at Camden confirmed him.[32]

The prospects for 1781 were hardly encouraging. Though John Laurens left for France in February to seek a loan and to state the situation as Washington saw it, that, without more aggressive assistance, the war could not be much longer sustained, months would pass before such aid could materialize. Meanwhile, in this period of exhaustion and discouragement in the South and appalling apathy in the North, whatever happened was not likely to be good news. Even at sea, despite the presence of French squadrons in the West Indies, Rodney captured the great depot of St. Eustatius in February, and in the spirit of the freebooters of an age gone by confiscated all private as well as public wealth. Both the French in the West Indies and the Americans on the mainland had used the Dutch island as a receiving and shipping point. Britain might be facing heavy odds, but the Allies had certainly not succeeded in making the most effective use of their superiority. Unless they did so soon, the United States might collapse. Washington feared the prospect keenly and wrote to Laurens in April that "we are at the end of our tether, and now or never our deliverance must come."[33]

XXI

American Retaliation in the South

If the situation in the North appeared critical early in 1781, conditions in the South had begun to show evidence of improving. The main reason lay in the appointment of Nathanael Greene as commander of the Southern Department in October, 1780. Chagrined by the failure of its favorite, Gates, Congress turned to Washington for his choice in the emergency. He selected Greene with alacrity, and Congress confirmed with relief and even pleasure the appointment of the very man whom it had wanted to dismiss from the service but a few weeks before.

While the chunky, neatly dressed Greene was en route to the South with Steuben and "Light Horse Harry" Lee, the former being left in Virginia to watch General Leslie, who threatened the state via the James River, Cornwallis was having trouble in the Carolinas. His troops were so sickly after Camden that he resolved to push northward toward a healthy country notwithstanding his need of an immediate vigorous diversion by Clinton in Virginia. Though Clinton subsequently sent Leslie to Virginia, Cornwallis had suffered a severe check before Leslie arrived. On September 7, he started his army in two columns up the Wateree toward Charlotte. Meanwhile a third column, largely Loyalists, under the crack rifleman of the British army, Major Patrick Ferguson, moved along the foothills of the Alleghenies, covering Cornwallis's left flank and endeavoring to scotch guerrilla activities along the British lines of communication. It was while pursuing a guerrilla band that Ferguson learned of the approach of a large force of backwoodsmen superior to his own under such leaders as McDowell, Campbell, Shelby, Sevier, and other capable fighters. Hurrying messengers to Cornwallis for reinforcements, Ferguson at first retreated;

then, on October 6, against Cornwallis's positive orders to continue
to retire,[1] he decided to make a stand on King's Mountain, a narrow,
forested hill on the border of South Carolina and thirty miles west of
Charlotte. As soon as the mountain men, now bivouacked at Cowpens,
learned of his retreat, about one thousand left off eating cattle
belonging to a Loyalist, mounted their horses, and, after a rainy night
ride, caught up with Ferguson the next day. Unbeknownst to the
major his messengers were intercepted and shot.

King's Mountain was an unusual battle. The British were in a
strong position, and against a force of regulars they would likely have
staved off what actually happened. It was their misfortune at midafternoon of October 7 to be facing men who were forest-wise and
handy with the long rifles of the frontier. In three divisions, the
Americans worked their way skillfully up the hill. When Ferguson
drove off the center with the bayonet, a second division opened on
his flank. Turning furiously upon this body, Ferguson received a deadly
blast in the rear from the third division. But the British were game
and held off their cagey foe until Ferguson was killed. Then they soon
surrendered. They lost nearly four hundred killed and wounded, while
more than seven hundred were captured. American casualties were
eighty-eight killed and wounded. Less glorious was the sequel: scores
of prisoners shot after they surrendered, a dozen hanged as a reprisal
for the British having strung up several deserters taken in arms
against them, and the survivors marched for two days without food.
After this rough treatment of the Loyalists, most of the mountain men
went back to their homes.[2]

The disaster was fatal to Cornwallis's plans. It intimidated the
Loyalists and painfully exposed Cornwallis's small force, many of
whom were on the sick list, including the earl himself. Hence he retreated to Winnsborough, South Carolina, on October 14. Lord
Rawdon, who succeeded to the command during Cornwallis's illness,
wrote to Clinton of the difficulties of relying on the North Carolina
Loyalists. When Clinton informed him that Leslie had sailed for the
Chesapeake, Rawdon persuaded Leslie to come to the Cape Fear
River. Subsequent orders directed Leslie to disembark at Charleston
and march to Camden, which he reached on January 4, 1781. Meanwhile, with Cornwallis inactive, Tarleton was withdrawn from his
energetic ripostes with Francis Marion along the Pee Dee and sent

against Sumter, who was raiding northwest of Winnsborough. In a sharp action at Blackstocks on November 20, Sumter, though wounded, repulsed the dragoon leader, who lost over one hundred casualties. Thus even before Greene was ready to move with the main American force, the British had suffered considerably in prestige and position compared with the high tide of their successes during the past summer.

Clinton, meanwhile, strove to take some of the pressure off his Southern army by dispatching Benedict Arnold to Virginia on a December raiding expedition with about fifteen hundred British Provincials. Instructed to make Portsmouth his base, Arnold swept up the river to Jamestown, marched to Richmond with half his force, and destroyed the town and a great quantity of military stores. Further activities were curtailed as Steuben with the Virginia militia compelled him to retreat to Portsmouth. Washington then sent Lafayette with twelve hundred men to reinforce Steuben. At the same time, he tried to get the French at Newport to move by sea and nip off Arnold. The successor of Ternay, Admiral Destouches, sent only a tiny squadron, which returned in February with scant success. Washington then hurried to Newport and personally induced the French commanders to make a serious effort. Destouches sailed on March 8 with a small but powerful squadron and twelve hundred troops. Knowing full well that Arnold's safety depended upon their retaining command of the sea, Clinton and Arbuthnot kept anxious eyes on Newport. As soon as they learned that the French were at sea, Arbuthnot sailed. Off Cape Henry, on March 16, he engaged Destouches. Although the Frenchman showed the greater skill and had the better of the action, he failed to follow up his advantage and withdrew, leaving the sea lanes open to Arnold. Washington was bitterly disappointed, nor was his disposition improved by intelligence that Clinton soon dispatched General Phillips with two thousand men to reinforce Arnold. Phillips was to create a diversion in Cornwallis's favor and establish a post which should command the Chesapeake.[3]

During the preliminaries to the ultimate struggle in Virginia, the conflict farther south, to which these preliminaries were related, was sharpening. With only two thousand men against Cornwallis's thirty-two hundred, Greene decided to concentrate on guerrilla tactics. To that end he divided his force, detaching Morgan with more than five

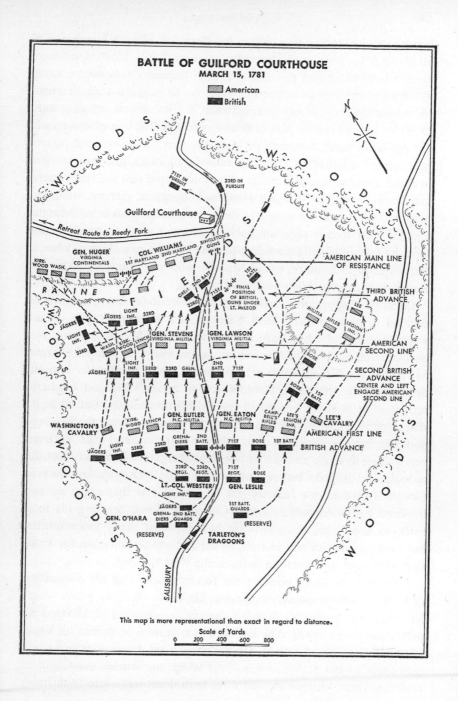

BATTLE OF GUILFORD COURTHOUSE
MARCH 15, 1781

American
British

This map is more representational than exact in regard to distance.

Scale of Yards

0   200   400   600   800

hundred men. Morgan was to ford the Catawba, effect a junction with Sumter to the west, and watch his chances for a move southward against Ninety Six and possibly Augusta. Greene established a camp at Cheraw, or the falls of the Pee Dee. As he explained his decision, "It makes the most of my inferior force, for it compels my adversary to divide his, and holds him in doubt as to his own line of conduct."[4] On the other hand, Greene's dividing his own forces exposed him to possible annihilation if Cornwallis resolved to attack him and Morgan in detail. Nearly one hundred and fifty miles separated the two American forces, with the "English Hannibal" between. Greene, however, prepared for a possible attack in detail by arranging to bring Morgan and his own troops together back in North Carolina. At the same time, he felt sufficiently confident to send Harry Lee's Legion, when it arrived early in January, to aid Marion, who was operating along the Santee between the High Hills and the sea.

Greene's dispositions made Cornwallis hesitate, but presently he decided to push toward North Carolina and destroy Morgan on the way. Tarleton, who had been hurried to the relief of Ninety Six, was now ordered to strike at Morgan or, in any event, to compel Morgan to recross the Broad River where, presumably, Cornwallis himself, driving up the left bank, would force an action.[5] Morgan began to retreat as soon as he learned of the British movements, but when he suspected that Cornwallis was waiting for Leslie to cross the Wateree and join him at Turkey Creek before advancing, and that Tarleton was itching to strike as soon as possible, Morgan resolved to meet the redoubtable dragoon before Cornwallis should arrive. Falling back to Cowpens at dusk on January 15, he was joined that night by two hundred additional militia under Colonel Pickens, bringing his total force to about one thousand. He had expected many more militia, but Cornwallis's activity in rallying the Indians to fall upon the frontier posts kept many militia units in the west.[6]

Morgan's choice of position the following day and his disposition of his troops were scarcely orthodox. He chose an open wood, which left room for Tarleton's dreaded cavalry to operate and afforded no protection to his flanks. The Broad River, moreover, was at his back, effectually cutting off retreat. On the other hand, there were two slight eminences in the 500-yard area over which the British must fight to reach the river. Morgan formed three lines. First was a strong skirmish line of one hundred and fifty riflemen from Georgia and North Carolina. Second, about three hundred militia from Georgia and both Carolinas under Andrew Pickens extended for three hundred yards on a line one hundred and fifty yards in front of the main line of resistance. This main line was established near the crest of the long slope of the first hill. The center, and fighting core, consisted of two hundred and eighty Maryland regulars flanked on the left by reliable militia from Virginia and more militia from Georgia—the total line numbering about four hundred. On the short second hill, approximately one hundred and fifty yards back, were eighty cavalry and forty volunteer horsemen under the fat but able cavalryman, Colonel William Washington, who had been wounded at Trenton.

Morgan had no illusions about his militia. When criticized for not finding a swamp on which to anchor his line, he said that he would not have had a swamp in the view of the militia "on any consideration; they would have made for it, and nothing could have detained them from it." Criticism that he should have covered his wings Morgan countered by retorting that he knew Tarleton and was perfectly sure that he would have nothing but "downright fighting." As for retreat, "it was the very thing I wished to cut off all hope of . . . When men are forced to fight, they will sell their lives dearly . . . Had I crossed the river, one half of the militia would immediately have abandoned me."[7] The old wagoner, however, knew that if not required to stand up to the British for long, they would acquit themselves well. Hence he told the militia to give the enemy two blasts "at killing distance" and then retire to the left behind the main line, while he warned the Continentals and their supporting militia not to worry about this retreat since it was all a part of his plan.

Tarleton drew up before the American battle line at eight o'clock on the morning of January 17 after a five-hour approach march. He placed the Legion infantry and the Light Infantry on the right, the 7th Infantry on the left, the 71st in reserve behind the left of the 7th, his Legion cavalry as his second line of battle, and dragoons on either flank. As Cornwallis reported to Clinton, "Everything now bore the most promising aspect."[8] But when the advance started, the aspect changed. The American skirmish line fell back before a troop of cavalry but sent fifteen horses off the field riderless. The line of militia opened a damaging fire at one hundred yards and sustained it until the enemy was upon them. At that point they broke and scurried to the left. Although shaken by the loss of many officers, the British experienced such a feeling of triumph as the militia fled that they cheered and pushed forward so rapidly as to fall into disorder. The sturdy resistance of the main American line brought them up short. Tarleton threw in his reserve and would have given much to have had his cavalry available. Unfortunately for him, William Washington had broken the British horse as it rushed forward to harass the flying militia. Even so, the advance of the 71st overlapped the American right, and the latter, as it received a command to change front, misunderstood and started to retreat. Momentarily startled, Morgan was in the process of re-forming when a courier from Washington reported that the enemy was coming on like a mob and if the infantry would give them another shot, he would charge them. Instantly the line faced about, staggered the British with a deadly fire, and charged with the bayonet. Pickens's militia, who had swept clear to the rear of the American line and formed ranks again, completed the circuit and struck Tarleton's left, while Washington's cavalry dashed against his right. It was a double envelopment, beautifully executed.

The effect was disastrous for the British. Their rigid discipline collapsed, many of them running for their lives, others surrendering. Tarleton lost one hundred killed, two hundred and twenty-nine wounded, and six hundred captured out of a total of about eleven hundred engaged. He himself barely escaped after a sharp personal encounter with Washington. Rallying a few officers and twoscore of cavalry, he covered the flight of his hard-pressed fugitives. Morgan lost only twelve killed and sixty-one wounded in this astonishingly successful conflict which lasted not even one hour. Tactically no more brilliant action was fought during the war.[9]

As soon as Cornwallis learned of the battle, he pushed rapidly toward Morgan, who left the wounded of both sides behind, crossed the Broad River, and retreated with his prisoners and train overland and across the Catawba. Cornwallis reached Ramsour's Mill on the 24th, angered to discover that Morgan was still twenty miles ahead of him. Yet the earl had only himself to blame. If he had been less apprehensive of Greene and had pushed on more rapidly before the battle at Cowpens occurred, he would probably have intercepted Morgan. Now the bird had flown, but Cornwallis resolved to catch him. Destroying his heavy baggage, tents, spare clothing, and supplies, including his rum, he mounted infantry on his wagon horses and started after Morgan on January 27, only to be delayed in crossing the river by two days of heavy rain that caused the Catawba to rise.

Meanwhile Greene dispatched his jubilant troops toward Salisbury under Major General Huger, and with a corporal's guard of followers raced one hundred and fifty miles over country heavy with rain and swarming with Loyalists to take command of Morgan's force. The latter was now partially depleted; the time of the Virginia militia had expired, and they, as well as numbers of the militia from Georgia and South Carolina, had gone home. Morgan himself suffered from rheumatism, found it difficult to agree completely with Greene, and left the army to recuperate. Greene rightfully considered his own proper place to be in front of Cornwallis, but neither he nor high water, let alone the militia guard under General Davidson, could prevent the earl from crossing the Catawba.[10] As Morgan made for the Yadkin, Cornwallis just a day behind him, Greene changed the rendezvous with Huger from Salisbury to Guilford Courthouse. Reaching the Yadkin, Morgan's infantry and artillery crossed on boats provided by Greene's foresight and reached the other shore on February 3 just as Cornwallis's advance guard stormed into view. Lacking boats, the earl had to march twenty-five miles upstream and ford the river. Then, certain that Greene could not cross the lower Dan River, he headed for the fords at the upper Dan. His entire army together at Guilford on February 9, Greene played with the idea of making a stand there, but, since the militia simply were not available in the numbers expected, his officers advised against it. Greene then resolved to push on to the Dan.

The march was rugged. The season was blustery, and the roads were a quagmire by day and sharp broken ruts at night which cut the bare feet of many of the shoeless troops. Though the British were better clothed and shod, neither army had tents, and both were hungry. For that matter, American troops were often half famished during the campaigns in the South because of the inadequate system of supply and the rapid movements of the armies.[11] The Americans now suffered particularly at night since there was only one blanket for three men. Heading toward Boyd's Ferry, Greene detached seven hundred picked men under Otho Williams to hold off Cornwallis, while he pushed on toward the river, where boats were being collected by Carrington, his quartermaster, and where Kosciusko was erecting breastworks on the north bank. His main body was considerably reduced as all but eighty of the North Carolina militia quit the war. Yet Williams's column effectually screened the movement toward Boyd's Ferry, Cornwallis still unaware that Greene did not need to cross at the upper Dan. He pressed his pursuit of Williams so closely that for a time men in the latter's force wondered if they might have to sacrifice themselves to save the main column. Finally, as the weary troops slogged through the muddy slime on the 15th after four days of marching with little sleep, word arrived toward evening that Greene was over the Dan and his boats were waiting for them. With hearty cheers the men drove for the Dan and crossed over. Lee's cavalry, which had done extraordinary work holding off the energetic Tarleton, swam the river.

Cornwallis must have looked longingly toward the American bivouac fires across the Dan that evening. Bitterly he acknowledged to Rawdon his failure to catch Greene.[12] The American commander might be dead tired, but he had the satisfaction of having saved his army after a grueling retreat of constant maneuvering for two hundred miles. Tarleton, who may have been influenced by the differences that eventually arose between himself and Cornwallis, admitted that "Every measure of the Americans, during their march from the Catawba to Virginia, was judiciously designed and vigorously executed."[13] Cornwallis had now driven Greene out of North Carolina, but the triumph was illusory. He had no boats, suffered from lack of supplies, was dangerously far from his base, and faced a hornets' nest if he tried to invade Virginia at this time and Steuben should reinforce Greene. Hence he reluctantly fell back on Hillsborough and tried to rally the North Carolina Loyalists.

The earl's withdrawal was the signal for Greene to recross the Dan. On February 25, Lee slaughtered a force of three hundred Loyalist militia who thought at first that his cavalry was Tarleton's. News of this disaster reaching Cornwallis, the earl at once moved to bring Greene into action. The Quaker general was as eager as the English Hannibal for a meeting but not until the promised reinforcements and supplies from Virginia arrived. For ten days, both armies maneuvered and skirmished until Greene finally was ready to accept a trial of strength on ground of his own choosing at Guilford Courthouse, the very place where he had wanted to engage Cornwallis on his retreat to the Dan. Heavily reinforced, he had approximately forty-five hundred men available for battle on March 15, while Cornwallis had slightly over nineteen hundred in the line.[14]

Greene wrote Lee that he dreaded only two things, "a heavy rain and a night attack";[15] to his relief the 15th was clear and cool, and the enemy did not attack until after midday. The broken, hilly country was studded with clearings and woods. Greene formed astride the Salisbury road on a slope that crested in front of Guilford Courthouse. His plan was generally similar to Morgan's at Cowpens. In front were the North Carolina militia under Generals Butler and Eaton. Three hundred yards back stood the Virginia militia under Generals Stevens and Lawson. Four hundred yards to the rear of the Virginians and on the right of the highway were the Continentals under Huger and Williams. These consisted of two Virginia regiments and the 1st and 2d Maryland Regiments, the 1st being one of the finest regiments raised during the war. Stationed in the woods as flankers for the first line were Washington on the right and Lee on the left. These dispositions had one serious fault: the distance between lines was so great as to prevent adequate support and would permit an enemy to re-form should his ranks be shaken in driving through any one line. It is doubtful, knowing militia as he did, that Morgan would have made Greene's mistake.

Shortly after noon, Cornwallis came in sight of the American lines following a skirmish between Tarleton and Lee. After a brisk cannonade from three 3-pounders, Cornwallis moved to the attack at half past one o'clock. On his right, under Major General Leslie, he stationed Bose's regiment of Hessians and Fraser's Highlanders, with a battalion of Guards in support. On his left were the 23d and 33d under Colonel Webster, with Brigadier General O'Hara and the Grenadiers and a second battalion of Guards in support. He placed his three guns across the road, Jägers and Light Infantry to the left of the guns, and Tarleton in the rear of the entire line. The North Carolina militia, about fourteen hundred strong, gave the redcoats only two of the three rounds Greene is alleged to have asked for,[16] then fled completely from the battle. The cavalry and infantry under Washington and Lee fell back in an orderly manner as Bose's regiment

swung out of line against the latter and the 33d with the Light Infantry and the Jägers moved against the former. The gaps in the
British lines were filled by the 1st and 2d Battalions of Guards, respectively. The Virginians at first showed no such apprehension as
had unnerved the Carolinians. Their rifles did terrible execution
among the enemy. But Cornwallis's line came on and thrust aside the
American right under Lawson, though Stevens's men stubbornly
sought to hold their ground against Bose's regiment. Webster now
smashed against that part of the third American line held by the 1st
Maryland. This regiment thinned the tired British line with a wither-
ing fire, then broke it with a bayonet charge, and inflicted a mortal
wound upon Webster. If Greene had dared follow up this attack, the
day might have been his, but he considered the risk too great.

The British now rallied for another assault. Receiving from Leslie
the 23d and the Highlanders as support, O'Hara led these and the
2d Guards Battalion against the 2d Maryland. This regiment, newly
recruited, collapsed. But as the Guards poured exultantly through the
gap, the 1st Maryland swung coolly to the left and caught them in
the flank, while Washington's cavalry folded them up with a smashing charge. Horse and foot swirled in wild confusion as the Guards
fled and Washington pursued. Again Greene decided against the
hazard of a finishing stroke by his Continentals. Even so, it was
touch and go for the British until Cornwallis, whose horse was shot
from under him, personally intervened by ordering his artillery to
open with grapeshot on the mass of men and horses. These guns,
which had taken a new position in a clearing near the woods on a
hill commanding the field, killed both British and American soldiers
but effectually halted Washington. Cornwallis soon regrouped with
the aid of the now badly wounded O'Hara, sent Bose's regiment and
Tarleton against the American left flank, and with his other regiments
moved grimly forward to end the conflict.

By this time Greene had had enough. A glimpse at the scarlet forms
lying still or writhing on the field told him he had ruined Cornwallis's
little army. At the same time, he was haunted by the realization that
if he lost his own army he could not raise another. Hence he abandoned his four guns and ordered a retreat which placed him ten miles
from the courthouse at the ironworks across the Haw River by day-

break; Cornwallis did not pursue beyond that point. The earl had lost ninety-three killed, four hundred and thirteen wounded, and twenty-six missing, such a crippling proportion of his small force that, on March 18, he left behind his sick and wounded, many of whom had perished in the cold, driving rain that fell on the night after the battle, and headed for Cross Creek. Greene's losses had amounted to seventy-eight killed and one hundred and eighty-three wounded, a total which he described to Jefferson as "very trifling."[17] More serious in his estimation was the defection of the North Carolina militia. He felt that if they had come up to expectations, the British would have been defeated, and he regretted his dependence on a militia army that destroyed the resources of a country more speedily than three times their number of regular troops.[18] On the other hand, the Virginia militia had fought heroically, far better indeed than the regulars comprising the 2d Maryland, the explanation being that many of the Virginians were veterans of campaigns in the North.

Though Greene had lost the field, Cornwallis's stalwart little army was so reduced that the earl may be said to have forfeited the campaign. Greene followed him as far as Ramsay's Mill on Deep River, but, choosing not to beard the wounded lion, let Cornwallis continue to Wilmington. From here, as we shall see in a consideration of the Yorktown campaign, the earl decided to march to Virginia, join his force to Phillips's, and create a new theater of action. Greene let him go and turned to the conquest of South Carolina.

The campaign that subsequently developed was bitterly fought. Lord Rawdon, the British commander, was a young man, not in good health, but a veteran of the American war since Bunker Hill and possessed of a judicious turn of mind. He had slightly over eight thousand men in South Carolina and Georgia but only about fifteen hundred as a striking force. The latter was stationed at Camden. The rest of the troops garrisoned the system of forts by which the British maintained their control over the area. The two great ports were Savannah and Charleston. Up the Savannah River lay Augusta. Running to the northwest along the Santee and its tributaries lay Fort Watson, Fort Motte, Fort Granby, and Ninety Six. Between Motte and Granby and to the south on a tributary of the Edisto was Orangeburg, while at the mouth of the Great Pee Dee was Georgetown. Most important in South Carolina were Georgetown, Camden on the

Catawba, and Ninety Six near the Saluda. To master these posts, Greene could count on a core of fifteen hundred Continentals. The militia might turn out on occasion, but they were an uncertain quantity. More reliable, though disposed to follow their own whims, were such guerrilla leaders as Pickens in the west, Marion in the swamps of the Pee Dee, and Sumter on the Broad River. Without these leaders Greene knew he could not clear the state; he therefore supported them wherever possible and endeavored to co-ordinate their activities. Greene proposed to march to Camden and to contain Rawdon with Sumter's assistance, while he gave Lee freedom of movement to join Marion against Fort Watson and urged Pickens to move against Ninety Six.

As Greene started his slow two-week march toward Camden on April 5, Lee kept a wary eye on Cornwallis in the event the earl should decide to re-enter South Carolina; then, satisfied that the earl would sit tight, he hastened to join Marion on the 14th. The following day, Lee and Marion invested Fort Watson. Built on an old Indian mound rising above the surrounding lowland, the fort offered a real problem to besiegers armed only with rifles. Happily one of Marion's officers thought of building a wooden tower higher than the walls of the fort. Working under cover of darkness, the men cut and shaped the timbers. Finally, late on the night of the 22d, they assembled the beams and raised the structure. The next morning, protected by a deadly fire from rifles aloft, the troops breached the walls and compelled the garrison to surrender. Lee and Marion then tried to cut off Colonel Watson, whom Rawdon had sent against Marion with five hundred men, but Watson slipped safely away.

By the time Watson returned, Rawdon had inflicted a defeat on Greene that was the American leader's own fault. An attempt to take Camden by surprise on April 19 was foiled by prior intelligence reaching Rawdon. When Greene retired to Hobkirk's Hill, two miles from the town, Rawdon decided to attack him before Lee and Marion appeared. Without Watson's men, Rawdon had but nine hundred available; against him Greene mustered fourteen hundred and twenty-two men, nearly four-fifths of them Continentals. Greene's mistake occurred in trying to do too much. When Rawdon advanced on a narrow front, Greene waited until his opponent was within grapeshot range; then his two center regiments drew aside, uncovering his guns.

Surprised at the deadly blast, the British momentarily drew back. In accordance with Greene's instructions, the center regiments, the 1st Maryland and the 2d Virginia, charged with the bayonet, while the flank regiments, the 2d Maryland and the 1st Virginia, tried to effect a double envelopment, with Washington dashing against the British rear.[19]

But the 26-year-old Rawdon was no novice. He quickly extended his line to overlap the American front. Previously Greene had complained of the unsteadiness of militia, but now it was his choicest regiment that was guilty. When one of the companies of the 1st Maryland lost its captain, it fell back, along with another company, thus breaking up the regimental line. In the attempts to re-form, the regiment lost all order and retired from the field. Soon it was joined by the jittery 2d Maryland, while the 1st Virginia also was shaken. Only the 2d Virginia held its ground, but as Rawdon moved briskly forward to strike its flank, Greene ordered a retreat. In his anxiety to save his guns he laid hold on a rope himself and was not far from being captured when Washington, who had made too wide a circuit of the British rear to have been of use in carrying out Greene's attack order, appeared on the scene. Washington dispersed the British cavalry, saved the guns, and, with the steady 2d Virginia, prevented effective pursuit. Greene lost one hundred and thirty-four killed and wounded, and more than one hundred captured. Rawdon's losses in all categories amounted to two hundred and seventy.[20]

While Greene nursed his disappointment, news of the fall of Fort Watson and of the guerrilla activities against his lines of communication made Rawdon decide to evacuate Camden on May 10 and withdraw cautiously to within thirty miles of Charleston. With his retirement, the guerrillas sprang to life. On the 11th, Sumter captured Orangeburg and its garrison, while, on the 12th, Marion took Fort Motte by shooting flaming arrows into the main structure and setting it afire. Fort Granby fell to Lee on the 15th, an occurrence which caused bad feeling until Greene intervened; Sumter had previously marked out Granby as his special prey. Lee and Pickens, with Colonel Clarke and the Georgia militia, now moved rapidly to the Savannah and invested Augusta on May 22. This post was manned by a garrison of over six hundred and commanded by a Lieutenant Colonel Thomas Browne whose feet had been roasted by members of the Patriot party early in the war, and who had since been industrious hanging Patriots in reprisal. A brave soldier, Browne put up a gallant defense in a siege notable for its lack of mercy on both sides. Only after the besiegers resorted to the type of tower used at Fort Watson and mounted a 6-pounder on top did the garrison surrender.

Meanwhile Greene, joined subsequently by Lee and Pickens, had marched to Ninety Six, starting its siege on May 22. The little fort, taking its name from its distance from Keowee, the principal village of the powerful Cherokees,[21] was the center of a region usually fertile but now devastated by the bloody, ruthless struggle between the Georgia Whigs and Tories, a struggle singularized, as in the Carolinas, by destruction of property, torture, rape, and assassination. The fort's commander was Lieutenant Colonel John Harris Cruger of New York, and most of his five hundred and fifty men were in two fine Loyalist regiments, one from New York and one from New Jersey. Rawdon's withdrawal and the fall of posts along the Congaree and Wateree had cut off Cruger. Though orders had been sent him to retire, they never reached him. But Cruger put up a vigorous and skillful defense[22] against Kosciusko's parallels, the famous wooden tower device, fire arrows, and a heavy assault on June 18 upon his star-shaped main fort. Suffering horribly from thirst after his water supply was captured, Cruger held on and repulsed the attack. Greene would still have won if Rawdon, after a punishing march from Charleston, had not arrived to save the garrison. Had Sumter got in front of him, as Greene had wanted, Rawdon might have been too late. Unfortunately, Sumter was not so co-operative or so farsighted as the other partisan leaders. The siege cost the Americans one hundred and forty-seven casualties to the enemy's eighty-five, and Greene was greatly cast down at its failure. But as Greene withdrew, good news soon arrived of the fall of Georgetown to Marion on June 20 and the evacuation of Ninety Six on July 3. Again, though tactically defeated, Greene had won his strategic objective. Rawdon now fell back to Orangeburg. He left Lieutenant Colonel Stewart of the 3d Regiment in command, retired to Charleston, and soon sailed for home broken in health, only to have his ship overtaken by Admiral de Grasse's fleet, which was bound for the Chesapeake.

During that sweltering summer, Greene took his little army to the High Hills of Santee, those long, 200-foot-high masses of sand, clay, and gravel where the air was comparatively pure. From that location, ninety miles from Charleston, Greene trained his army, raised recruits, and kept a careful eye on Stewart, who was encamped only sixteen miles away, a short distance but one almost completely flooded over. Finally, on August 28, knowing he could count eventually on a total force of twenty-three hundred men, of whom one thousand were militia, Greene started for his enemy by a necessarily circuitous route, crossing the Wateree at Camden and the Congaree at Howell's Ferry. While Stewart slowly fell back on his supply depot at Eutaw Springs, Greene was joined by Marion.

Stewart appears to have been so unaware of the proximity of the American army that he permitted one hundred unarmed men under a small escort of cavalry to go digging for sweet potatoes, since his own army was short of bread. When Lee suddenly captured half this force, and horsemen galloped back with the alarm, the British commander quickly formed a line of battle with his three guns in the road. He had six veteran regiments, the 3d, 63d, 64th, the Grenadiers, the New York Volunteers, and the New Jersey Volunteers, about eighteen hundred men in all, deployed in a clearing astride the main road with a brick house and a fenced garden in his rear. At an obtuse angle to his own line was a force of three hundred under a very able major with the delightful name of Marjoribanks, while in echelon to his left rear was his cavalry. Against this formation Greene deployed a first line of North Carolina militia with detachments under Marion on the right and Pickens on the left, and two guns in the road. His second line found two North Carolina regiments of regulars on the right—the militia fugitives from Guilford Courthouse who had been condemned to serve twelve months as Continentals, the two Virginia regiments in the center, and the two Maryland regiments on the left, with two guns in the road. Lee's Legion flanked on the right, Sumter's men now under Henderson on the left, while Washington's cavalry and the Delaware battalion brought up the rear.

Although the numbers engaged were not large, the Battle of Eutaw Springs on that warm September 8 was a singularly desperate affair that witnessed a double-back action, the British being at first soundly beaten and then rallying to drive the Americans from the field. After a heavy artillery duel, the militia slowly fell back. Although they halted presently and, fighting with unusual stubbornness for militia, regained some of the ground lost, the British left pushed them back again. Greene then hurled his Marylanders and Virginians forward with the bayonet and ordered Lee and Washington against the flanks. The British staggered under the impact, and, though the 63d and 64th fought tenaciously, the entire scarlet line finally drew back in confusion. True, Washington was routed and the dashing leader himself captured, but the British were pushed clear through their own camp with the exception of a detachment thrown into the brick house and the force under Marjoribanks, which drew back to the fenced garden.

The Americans now proceeded to lose the battle they had almost won. It was high noon, and, on their way through the British camp, the Americans discovered quantities of food and rum. Soon a large proportion of the army, including many of the regulars from Virginia and Maryland, was roaring drunk. Meanwhile the brick house and garden came to have a value to the British similar to that of the Chew House at Germantown. In vain did the men of Lee's Legion and the Delaware battalion, supported closely by the four guns, try to take the house and garden. The fire from the defense was too severe to be borne, and the fieldpieces were too light to be effective against the house. As the British cavalry charged the plunderers of their camp, the hard-fighting Wade Hampton countered with such American cavalry as he could collect and drove them back. Unfortunately, this brought him under fire from Marjoribanks' infantry, and he retired, his force shattered. Marjoribanks now made a vigorous sortie and seized two of the American cannons. Though the gallant major suffered a mortal wound in this attack, Stewart, who had reformed, came up with the main British force to take over.

True to his policy of preserving his army, Greene slowly withdrew from the field, neither routed nor even badly beaten as Stewart vaingloriously claimed in a report to Clinton.[23] Greene lost one hundred and twenty killed, three hundred and seventy-five wounded, and eight missing, while Stewart suffered eighty-five killed, three hundred and fifty-one wounded, and four hundred and eighty missing, most of the latter being captured. Heavy as were Greene's losses, those of Stewart were too calamitous for him to maintain his position. While Greene retired seven miles on the night of the 8th, Stewart turned back to Charleston the following day, destroying his stores and leaving his more seriously wounded behind. Greene pursued for a few miles, but, as reinforcements moved up from Charleston to support Stewart, he retired again to the High Hills.

Although a considerable number of guerrilla skirmishes persisted in the Carolinas and Georgia, and Wayne, sent to assist Greene, subsequently drove the British forces southward out of Georgia except for Savannah, serious fighting in terms of comparatively large forces ended with Eutaw Springs. Greene's accomplishments had been truly remarkable. Tactically he committed serious errors in every one of his battles, but his strategy was excellent, and since a number of his tactical mistakes occurred as a result of his determination to preserve his field army, and thereby ensure the success of his strategy, the over-all assessment is decidedly in his favor. With an army poorly provisioned, wretchedly clothed and equipped, undermanned, and lacking adequate artillery, he had completely reversed the gloomy situation that prevailed after Gates's collapse at Camden. It had taken a year, but the task was about done. So far as the South below Virginia was concerned, the British were largely confined to the ports and Florida.

For the British defeat there were many obvious factors responsible: the skill and tenacity of Greene, the ability of his troops occasionally to fight well, the existence of a small but effective cavalry, the deadliness of the guerrillas, the failure of the Loyalists to turn out in the numbers expected, the extraordinary hatred between the native factions, the problems of distance and terrain with their endless military complications, and the miscalculations of the British field leaders. But one should not forget, either, the mistakes made in London initially to sanction the campaign in the South with its necessary dispersion of the British forces in America and secondly to neglect to support the campaign in sufficient strength. The harvest from those mistakes had been reaped in the Carolinas and Georgia and was about to be reaped in Virginia. But the yield was totally different from what the British had anticipated. On the day following the action at Eutaw Springs, Admiral de Grasse sailed into the Chesapeake, cutting off any real hope of escape for Lord Cornwallis and his army of seven thousand men.

XXII

The Yorktown Campaign

Sometimes remote villages, important mainly for their location astride a crossroads or abutting a watercourse, have a way during wars of being thrust into a prominence from which they are never permitted to recover. Such a place was Gettysburg in 1863. Such a place was Yorktown in 1781. Prior to the Revolution, Yorktown was a port from which Virginians had shipped tobacco, but during the war its activity had been so curtailed and its unimportance made so obvious that the British had given it little trouble in their raids up and down the peninsula. Then Cornwallis moved into the village in 1781, and it has since become the focus of intense attention because of his surrender. Oddly enough, Cornwallis returned to England to receive a hero's welcome, and subsequently made such a name for himself in India as administrator and general that Yorktown became to him and his admirers merely a disconcerting recollection. But without taking anything from Washington and the French, and without relieving Germain, Clinton, or the British admirals of their share of the responsibility, one can say that the amiable but ambitious earl with his insubordination, his blindness to sea power, and his flair for taking long chances was the chief architect of his own defeat.

Clinton and Cornwallis differed greatly in their strategy. Clinton wished Cornwallis to use Charleston as his main base, which he considered strong enough for Cornwallis to defend against almost anyone. Meanwhile Clinton hoped to operate in the Chesapeake region, securing a base near Norfolk and gradually developing a two-pronged offensive against Pennsylvania in which he would employ the British forces stationed in New York. He also hoped the Virginia Loyalists would rally to the crown. Clinton was cautious. He was apprehensive

246

of losing command of the sea and dubious about any extravagant project which might extend his lines of communication and use up his slender forces such as a pincers movement against North Carolina from South Carolina and Virginia. Above all, he intended to hold onto New York as the principal base in America.[1]

But Cornwallis had his own ideas. He would have nothing to do with making short, safe raids from the comfortable security of Charleston. As we have seen, he struck inland. His smashing victory at Camden appeared convincing proof to himself and to Germain that his was sound and successful strategy. King's Mountain and Greene's ability to absorb defeats and remain in the field shook the earl's confidence in some measure, while Arnold's diversion in Virginia failed to take much of the pressure off him. The attempted squeeze on Arnold by land and sea prompted Clinton to send to Virginia General William Phillips, one of Burgoyne's veterans, and a large body of troops with instructions to establish a base, raid the peninsula, and co-operate with Cornwallis. While Phillips and Clinton waited for increasingly anxious weeks to learn something definite, Cornwallis won the ruinous victory at Guilford Courthouse, retreated toward the coast, and finally wrote to Clinton of his plight. He urged that, since the conquest of the Carolinas depended upon the reduction of Virginia, the commander in chief should make Virginia the major theater of action even if this entailed the evacuation of New York. Then, on April 25, without waiting for instructions from Clinton, Cornwallis started from Wilmington on his long march northward, thus exposing Rawdon, Charleston, and the British interior posts to great danger, and the Cross Creek Loyalists, whom he had pledged not to abandon, to merciless reprisal.[2]

Cornwallis's decision was his own and changed Clinton's policy in regard to Virginia. As Clinton later wrote in one of his numerous contributions to the controversy he waged against his aristocratic opponent, "Lord Cornwallis's march into Virginia, without consulting his Commander in Chief, forced us into solid operation in that province."[3] The first move was on the part of the ailing Phillips to march his force to Petersburg, where Cornwallis took command on May 20. By that time, Phillips had been dead a week. Clinton bitterly condemned Cornwallis's decision and hoped up to the time the earl reached Petersburg that he would return to the Carolinas.[4] Cornwallis, of course, had no such intention. With his army of fifteen hundred, Phillips's reinforcements in equal number which arrived on May 24, and Phillips's own force, Cornwallis had available approximately seventy-two hundred troops. Against these were Lafayette at Richmond with about forty dragoons, one thousand Light Infantry, and two thousand militia; Steuben at Point of Fork, southeast of Charlottesville, recruiting and training about five hundred Continentals for Greene; and Wayne still at York, Pennsylvania, with the Pennsylvania regiments. Cornwallis could have destroyed each of these detachments in detail, but he frittered away the weeks and the opportunity.

On the other hand, he could not let the forces nearest to him escape with complete impunity. Phillips had originally been instructed to seize either Yorktown or Old Point Comfort as a base if Portsmouth would not suffice; and he felt that the latter certainly would not do. Hence, while Cornwallis sent a force to occupy Portsmouth, he intended also to move toward Richmond, then to Yorktown. As he crossed the James and lunged at Lafayette, the alert Frenchman withdrew rapidly to the northwest. After Cornwallis reached the North Anna, he dispatched two divisions of cavalry, Tarleton against Charlottesville and Simcoe against Point of Fork, toward which Cornwallis himself presently marched. Those were exciting days that early June. Steuben raced southward to the Staunton River with his raw recruits to escape Simcoe and Cornwallis. On June 4, the Virginia legislature in Charlottesville fled to the mountains. Governor Jefferson, who was warned by a tavernkeeper's son, eluded by a margin of minutes Tarleton's dragoons as they rode swiftly up the hill on which Monticello is situated. Meanwhile Wayne had come to life and, after brisk marching, joined Lafayette. Cornwallis, his cavalry leaders having destroyed quantities of tobacco and munitions, now retired, according to his previously announced intention, through Richmond toward Williamsburg.[5] As he withdrew, Lafayette and Wayne followed him closely.

Soon after arriving at Williamsburg on June 25, Cornwallis opened a letter from Clinton informing him of a projected attack on New York, requesting him to send about two thousand troops to New York, and suggesting that he march the balance of his force to Baltimore or Delaware.[6] The request for troops was based on several

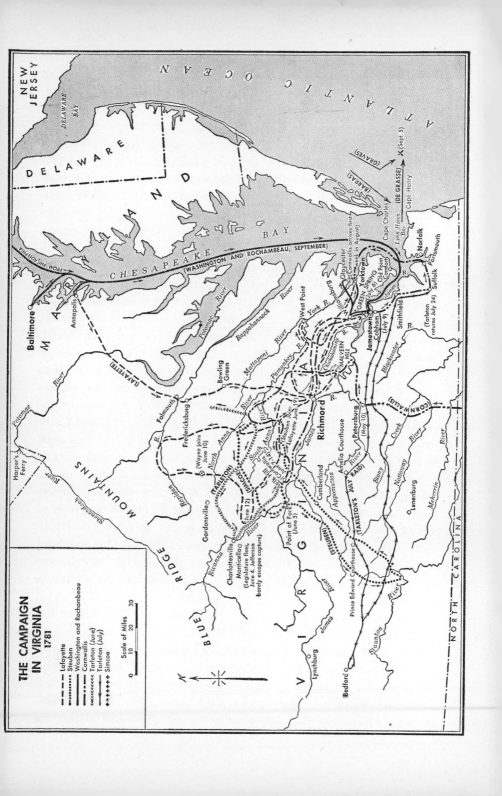

THE CAMPAIGN
IN VIRGINIA
1781

Lafayette
Steuben
Washington and Rochambeau
Cornwallis
Tarleton (June)
Tarleton (July)
Simcoe

Scale of Miles
0   10   20   30

ATLANTIC OCEAN

NEW JERSEY

DELAWARE BAY

DELAWARE

MARYLAND

CHESAPEAKE BAY

(WASHINGTON AND ROCHAMBEAU, SEPTEMBER)

FROM PHILADELPHIA

Baltimore

Annapolis

(LAFAYETTE)

Potomac River

Harper's Ferry

Shenandoah River

BLUE RIDGE MOUNTAINS

Potomac River

Rapidan River

Rappahannock River

Mattaponi River

Pamunkey River

West Point

York R.

Bowling Green

Fredericksburg

Falmouth

North Anna River

South Anna River

(Wayne joins June 10)

(TARLETON June 12)

(SIMCOE)

Gordonsville

Charlottesville
Monticello
(Legislature flees,
June 4. Jefferson
barely escapes capture)

Rivanna River

Point of Fork
(June 5)

James River

(STEUBEN)

Cumberland

Appomattox

Amelia Courthouse

(TARLETON'S JULY RAID)

Prince Edward Courthouse

Staunton River

Lynchburg

Bedford

VIRGINIA

NORTH CAROLINA

Meherrin River

Nottoway River

Lunenburg

Stony Creek

Petersburg
(May 10)

Richmond

(Steuben June 19)
Lafayette June 19

MALVERN HILL

Chickahominy R.

James R.

Jamestown
(July 9)

Cobham

GREEN SPRING
(July 6) Old Point
Comfort

Yorktown

Gloucester

(Cornwallis arrives, first
week in August)

York R.

Smithfield

Blackwater River

(Tarleton
returns July 24)

Suffolk

Norfolk

Portsmouth

(CORNWALLIS)

Cape Charles

DE GRASSE

(BARRAS)

(GRAVES)

X (Sept. 5)

Cape Henry

Lynn Haven Bay

mysterious dispatches intercepted by a British patrol outside New York on the night of June 5. The dispatches consisted of a number of letters from Washington to officers and civilians and letters from Rochambeau and Barras to Luzerne, the French minister in Philadelphia. Clinton learned that Washington and Rochambeau had met at Wethersfield, Connecticut. They had discussed the possibility of a joint move against Cornwallis but discarded it since they lacked command of the sea, and decided instead to move against New York. Subsequently, in view of what eventually happened in Virginia, there were not lacking Englishmen who contended that Washington deliberately contrived to have these dispatches captured. At any rate, Clinton believed New York in great danger and sorely wanted back some of the troops he had sent to Virginia.[7]

While Clinton began to get alarmed about New York, Cornwallis was becoming increasingly confused and disgruntled. He decided to march to Jamestown, cross the river, and head for Portsmouth as the most likely place from which to ship his troops to New York. On the way to Jamestown he collided with Lafayette at Green Spring in a sharp action on July 6, which resulted in one hundred and thirty-seven casualties for the Americans and about half that number for the British. Had Cornwallis followed up his little victory, he might have destroyed the Frenchman, but, instead, he continued to Portsmouth, though he dispatched Tarleton on a second raiding expedition across the state. Meanwhile Clinton bombarded Cornwallis with letters and instructions: at first the troops were not to be sent to New York but to Philadelphia; then Clinton directed them to be hurried to New York; Cornwallis was to return to Yorktown; he was to make his main base at Old Point Comfort, but if necessary also to fortify Yorktown; he was instructed to keep his entire force if he could not spare any troops but was requested to ship to New York such troops as he did not need![8]

It was a sad commentary on British conduct of the war that these three men, Germain, Clinton, and Cornwallis, worked at such cross-purposes. Germain's intervention at long distance was habitual and his favoritism to Cornwallis ill-advised. Cornwallis's procedure in reporting directly to him and often acting independently of Clinton was grossly insubordinate. Clinton might have been more peremptory with the earl had he not realized that now he was virtually sharing the command in America with Cornwallis. And the latter continued to regard Clinton's orders as of the widest discretionary nature. On the advice of his engineers, and after a personal reconnaissance, he decided against Old Point Comfort in favor of Yorktown and Gloucester on the opposite shore of the York River. Militarily Yorktown might be more defensible, but its security depended less upon a garrison than upon control of the sea. Without that control a garrison faced great danger in being easily blockaded by sea and nipped off by a hostile force astride the narrow neck of the peninsula.[9]

In the meantime, the British downfall was being methodically plotted. Washington and Rochambeau arranged at Wethersfield to move against New York, a decision facilitated by information that Admiral de Grasse, commander of the West Indian fleet, was sailing from France with instructions to be off the American coast in July and August and break the British blockade of the French squadron at Newport now under Barras. Thus effectually had Laurens and Franklin represented to Vergennes the dire need of assistance. The march of the French troops from Newport to New York was accomplished with a minimum of inconvenience to the inhabitants. That the French could pay in hard cash for their supplies was an ingratiating factor. The army broke camp at Newport on June 10 and spent a week in Providence; then the Bourbonnais Regiment led off on the 18th, while on successive days marched the Royal Deux-Ponts, Soissonnais, and Saintonge. Cheers greeted them as they left Providence and as they entered Hartford, an experience also shared by the Duc de Lauzun's Legion moving on the left via Middletown, Wallingford, and North Stratford. By July 5, Rochambeau and Washington clasped hands at White Plains, and the Frenchman wrote Barras, "Our junction was made with great acclamation on the part of the Americans."[10]

But the junction of the two armies failed to bring about the object for which Washington wanted them together, an attack on New York. He tested Clinton's outposts and found them strong. He was troubled by the failure of the New England militia to come forward in sufficient numbers in answer to their governors' calls, and by the possibility of British reinforcements from Cornwallis. The arrival of three thousand German troops in New York from Bremen on August 11 further complicated his problem. He was therefore in a doubting mood when an announcement reached him on the 14th that De Grasse was sailing for the Chesapeake on the 13th with three thousand French troops from the San Domingo garrison, the regiments Agenois, Gatinais, and Touraine. Little did Washington realize that, in writing of the Wethersfield conference, Rochambeau, who never liked the idea of a New York offensive, had given De Grasse the option of bringing his fleet to the Chesapeake. Whatever was done now would have to be brief since De Grasse intended to return on October 15 because of commitments to the Spaniards. "Employ me promptly and usefully that time may be turned to profit," the count wrote Rochambeau.[11]

However disappointed he may have been at having to leave New York, Washington was wise enough to fall in immediately with the new project. Orders were dashed off to Lafayette to prevent Cornwallis from escaping, while preparations were pushed to ready both armies. At the same time, in order to deceive the enemy into thinking a southward movement of troops might mean an attempt to possess Staten Island as a preliminary to an attack on New York, roads were improved, and a small body of the French at Chatham, close to Staten Island, started to construct bake ovens as if for a siege. Then suddenly, on the 19th, the armies broke camp for King's Ferry. Leaving about three thousand men under General Heath in the Highlands, Washington sent his expeditionary force of two thousand across the river on the 20th and 21st, while the French were on the Jersey shore by the 26th. The two armies now slowly converged in three columns toward Chatham, none except the staffs knowing what the ultimate objective was. Pausing to rest on the 28th, the troops cleared for the Morristown-New Brunswick area on the 29th, then, on the morrow, broke away for Princeton, Trenton, and points south. The march to the Chesapeake had begun in earnest.

In the meantime, Sir Henry Clinton was passing the uneasiest summer of his life. Rochambeau's junction with Washington seemed convincing evidence that New York was the Allied objective. Though it was agreed that old Admiral Arbuthnot should remain in close touch with New York in the event De Grasse should appear, Barras' small squadron, which was to transport the heaviest of Rochambeau's siege guns, greatly tempted Clinton. But Arbuthnot would have nothing to do with the project since the menace of De Grasse was so imminent. Admiral Thomas Graves, Arbuthnot's successor, was a courteous,

Sketch of Rochambeau, probably by Count Ferson, friend of
Marie Antoinette

kindly gentleman by no means lacking in courage, but he was a slow-thinking, wretched tactician. It was to assist him that, before leaving the West Indies for England, Admiral Sir George Rodney directed his able subordinate, Sir Samuel Hood, to sail for American waters; a less happy circumstance was Rodney's decision to take several of his most powerful ships back to England with him. Had he believed, as he most certainly did not, that De Grasse would refuse to detach a portion of his fleet to escort a large convoy from San Domingo to France, the Yorktown campaign might have ended quite differently. De Grasse showed remarkable initiative for a French admiral of his era. Though explicitly directed by his government to send ten ships to escort the convoy, he resolved, after hearing from Washington and Rochambeau, to sail to the Chesapeake with his entire fleet. Arriving on August 30, he landed the troops he had brought with him and blockaded the mouths of both the James and the York River. Unless effective naval aid arrived soon from New York, Cornwallis was caught.

Back in New York the British were confused, to say the least. On his way from the West Indies, Hood with his fourteen men-of-war had looked in at the Chesapeake but saw no sign of De Grasse. When he arrived off New York on August 28, he found Graves making leisurely preparations for a combined assault with Clinton on Barras and Newport. Hood pointed out the need of haste, and intelligence received that evening indicated that Barras had put to sea three days before. De Grasse, however, might still be caught, so, on September 1, Graves and Hood cleared Sandy Hook with nineteen ships of the line to look for him. That same day, the British became aware of the southward movement of American army units.[12]

If it appeared that Clinton had been successfully duped by the Allied commanders into thinking New York the objective and therefore had done nothing, the appearance was by no means the entire truth. Though he may have been duped, and though evidently overwork produced temporary spells of blindness which impaired his judgment and his capacity to act, he had served a long apprenticeship to sea power, as he once admitted, and he knew that as long as the British held control of the sea, both New York and Yorktown were safe. He was sure the fleet promised him would be sufficient to take care of De Grasse, which would probably have been true had Rodney not taken part of the fleet to England, and had De Grasse not decided to sail with his own fleet intact to the Chesapeake. Moreover, Clinton also knew that, with command of the sea, he could always supply or even relieve Cornwallis but that, if he left New York to chase Washington, he forfeited the advantage of sea power which could move him swiftly to either Rhode Island or Yorktown as necessary.[13]

Clinton's inaction was scarcely more reprehensible than the clumsy tactics employed by Graves when he discovered De Grasse anchored in the Chesapeake on September 5. With his own fleet running in formation before the wind, and the French straggling out to find sea room, he let one superb opportunity pass to smash their van as it cleared the harbor and another opportunity as the French van became separated beyond supporting distance from De Grasse's center and rear. Furthermore, signals were misunderstood, and a number of British captains showed a grave want of initiative. After a severe but indecisive action, the fleets maneuvered. Hood advised Graves to make for the Chesapeake, but Graves delayed. When he finally moved toward the Chesapeake on the 11th, he discovered that De Grasse was already back in the bay with Barras and the Newport squadron. With thirty-six ships of the line the French were far too strong, and Graves returned to New York. Sea power had been decisive in making the surrender of Cornwallis to the Allied armies virtually inevitable.

Meanwhile, as Lafayette's troops and De Grasse's French contingent under Saint-Simon assumed positions on the peninsula to prevent Cornwallis from escaping, Washington and Rochambeau were sweeping toward Virginia. The Continentals moved through Philadelphia on the warm afternoon of September 2, striding rather slowly and solemnly to the drum and fife, and receiving the cheers of the crowds that lined the streets and filled every window. Two days later, the white-coated French, their military bands briskly thumping out marches, quickstepped through the streets, and the usually dignified town went wild. After a review before Congress, the armies pressed on. When Rochambeau caught up with Washington at Chester, the Virginian waved his hat and joyfully announced that De Grasse had arrived.[14] The spirits of the troops mounted as the news spread, and probably soared even higher in the next few days when De Grasse, a veritable Santa Claus by this time, sent frigates and transports into the upper Chesapeake to convey most of the armies by water, thus sparing the infantry many a weary march. Between September 14 and 24, the troops arrived in Williamsburg by sea and land, and, on September 28, took up siege positions before Yorktown. Meanwhile, at the meeting of Washington and De Grasse aboard the French flagship, it is said that the admiral, a big man himself, embraced the tall American, kissed him on both cheeks, and cried out, "My dear little General!" At the salutation the polite French managed to keep reasonably straight faces, but fat General Knox doubled up with laughter.

The disparity of forces at Yorktown was considerable. Aside from the huge French fleet, there were seven thousand, eight hundred French troops and eight thousand, eight hundred and forty-five Americans, of whom thirty-two hundred were militia under Governor Nelson of Virginia, the most vigorous contribution made during the war by that state, which had been notorious for its military supineness. Cornwallis's total force was over seven thousand, but, not having envisaged withstanding a siege or making Yorktown other than a naval station, he considered his army inadequate to defend the post. "Nothing," he later informed Clinton, "but the hopes of relief would have induced me to attempt its defence. . . ."[15] He mounted sixty-five guns, but these were mostly light fieldpieces except for the 18-pounders from the frigate *Charon*, which, with the sloop-of-war *Guadeloupe* and several transports, had fled up the river to escape De Grasse. His inner defense line with its ten redoubts and fourteen batteries was fairly strong, and, to secure this line, he established an outer defense line a half mile beyond. Although the extension spread his forces rather thinly, he initially believed the ground between his two lines so favorable to the enemy that it must be occupied and held.

The siege opened with the Americans moving into camp on the right and the French on the left in a semicircle from Wormley Creek to the York above Gloucester Point, while the Duc de Lauzun on the Gloucester shore contained Tarleton in the Gloucester defenses. The morning of September 30 revealed that Cornwallis had evacuated his outer line of defenses. Though this move was criticized by both Allied and British officers, the earl had his reasons. He had just received word from Clinton that relief would be on the way from New York about October 5, and he believed that by contracting his lines he could prolong the siege; certainly he could prevent his left from being turned at Wormley Creek.[16] Yet his action greatly facilitated the task

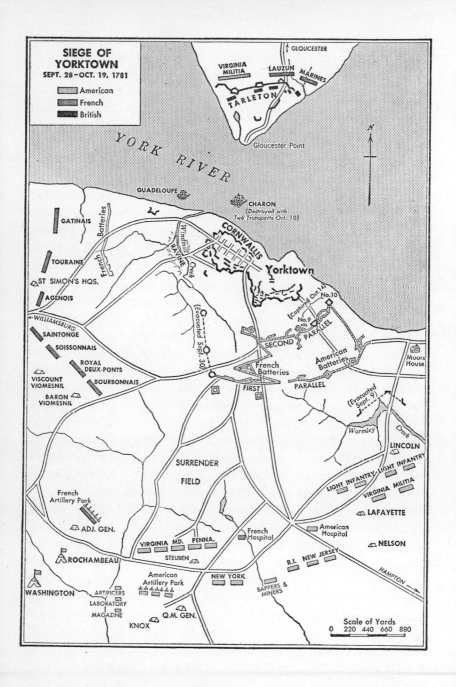

SIEGE OF YORKTOWN
SEPT. 28–OCT. 19, 1781

American
French
British

GLOUCESTER

VIRGINIA
MILITIA
LAUZUN
MARINES
TARLETON

Gloucester Point

YORK RIVER

GUADELOUPE

CHARON
(Destroyed with
Two Transports Oct. 10)

GATINAIS

French Batteries

Windmill
CORNWALLIS
RAVINE
Yorktown

TOURAINE

ST SIMON'S HQS.

AGENOIS

No. 10
(Captured Oct. 14)

WILLIAMSBURG

No. 9

SAINTONGE

(Evacuated Sept. 30)

SECOND PARALLEL

SOISSONNAIS

American
Batteries

ROYAL
DEUX-PONTS

French
Batteries

Moore
House

VISCOUNT
VIOMESNIL

BOURBONNAIS

FIRST

PARALLEL

BARON
VIOMESNIL

(Evacuated
Sept. 9)

Wormley

LINCOLN

Creek

SURRENDER

LIGHT INFANTRY LIGHT INFANTRY

FIELD

VIRGINIA MILITIA

French
Artillery Park

LAFAYETTE

ADJ. GEN.

French
Hospital

American
Hospital

NELSON

VIRGINIA MD. PENNA.

STEUBEN

R.I. NEW JERSEY

ROCHAMBEAU

HAMPTON

American
Artillery Park

NEW YORK

WASHINGTON

ARTIFICERS

LABORATORY

SAPPERS &
MINERS

MAGAZINE

Q.M. GEN.

KNOX

Scale of Yards
0 220 440 660 880

of the besiegers, and was indeed rather a surprising decision to reach before the Allies had scarcely completed deploying their forces.

The Allies now moved rapidly. Occupying the enemy's works, they broke ground on the night of the 30th. On the night of October 6, the first parallel was opened at about six hundred yards. The next three days, the digging continued with only feeble efforts from the enemy's artillery to interrupt the work. Siege guns were dragged up and several quickly emplaced. At three o'clock on the 9th, a French battery on the left opened fire, forcing the *Guadeloupe* over to Gloucester. At five o'clock, Washington touched off the first cannon shot from an American battery on the right, the missile crashing into a house and killing one British officer and wounding three others.[17] From then on, the firing was incessant. A French hot shot set the frigate *Charon* and two smaller vessels afire on the night of the 10th; the flames leaping furiously up the masts and rigging, the ships burned to the water's edge while the siege guns continued to crash and the mortar shells traced fiery arcs over the doomed army.

The second parallel was opened by Steuben's division at three hundred yards on the night of the 11th under a very heavy fire. In extending the parallel on the right, it was found necessary to take two British redoubts near the river, Numbers 9 and 10. For the first a French storming party of four hundred picked troops was selected with Colonel Deux Ponts in command. For Number 10, a smaller redoubt close to the river, an equivalent number of American Light Infantry was chosen with Alexander Hamilton, at his own energetic solicitation, in command. The attack took place on the night of the 14th. After fierce resistance that cost them fifteen killed and seventy-seven wounded, the French carried Number 9 in less than a half hour. The Americans took Number 10 with the bayonet in ten minutes, losing nine killed and twenty-five wounded. These were brilliant little feats, and the parallel was quickly run forward during the night to include both works. The British, however, counterattacked spiritedly at three o'clock in the morning of October 16 with four hundred Grenadiers and Light Infantry. Eleven guns were spiked and about one hundred of the French troops were killed or wounded. Yet, by Cornwallis's own admission, the spiked guns were soon made fit for service again, and by nightfall the parallel was completed.[18] So critical was the earl's plight that but for a sudden storm of rain and wind which made the passage impracticable, he would have attempted to transport his troops to the Gloucester shore that very night. Early on the 17th, with the ground trembling under the incessant roar of "not less than one hundred" heavy guns, the British artillery virtually silenced, and their works going to ruin, a red-coated drummer boy climbed to a parapet on the British left and beat a parley, while a brilliantly clad officer stood by his side waving a white handkerchief.[19] Lord Cornwallis was ready to consider terms of capitulation.

Meanwhile, in New York, British military and naval officers discussed the earl's appeals for help, which were brought by small craft that slipped past the French fleet at night. On September 17, he wrote that, unless he was relieved soon, Clinton should be prepared to hear "the worst."[20] At councils held on the 23d and 24th it was agreed by both services, and Cornwallis was notified, that the fleet would sail by October 5 with over five thousand men.[21] Then Clinton began to think that the earl could contrive a retreat, and he doubted in a council meeting on the 26th that "the worst" meant anything more serious than a retreat. Other members saw little that was obscure about the expression.[22]

With Clinton turning this problem over in his head, the navy began belatedly to consider how it could complete refitting by October 5, in view of the dockyard limitations, and how it could break through the French cordon and land the relief force. Both Hood and Rear Admiral Digby, who had arrived with three powerful ships, envisaged more difficulties than had first been apparent,[23] though Hood was ready to take a chance. Eventually it was resolved to push relief preparations as rapidly as possible, but repairs proceeded so slowly that the departure date was set back to October 8 and then to the 12th.[24] Clinton wrote prophetically to the Duke of Newcastle, "If Lord Cornwallis's Army falls, I shall have little hopes of seeing Brittish Dominion Reestablished in America."[25] When the 12th passed and the fleet lingered, Clinton grew frantic. Lack of adequate dockyard space and workers, scarcities in powder, other military stores, and lumber, as well as time spent in celebrating the arrival of Prince William, had all contributed to delay the sailing. Even after seven thousand troops embarked on the 17th and the ships dropped down to the Hook, the expedition was forced to wait for a favorable wind and tide before putting to sea on the 19th. Off Cape Charles, five days later, Clinton and Graves learned from a schooner bearing refugees from Yorktown precisely what Cornwallis had meant by "the worst." As confirmation was subsequently received, and the ships came about and headed back for New York, the heartsick, bitter Clinton must even then have been preparing in his mind the denunciations and apologies that were to poison the rest of his days.

Negotiations for the surrender of Cornwallis were worked out at the Moore house with a meticulous eye for detail and, generally speaking, a fine, old-fashioned regard for the feelings of one's defeated opponents. Military and naval personnel were to be surrendered as prisoners of war, the navy to become prisoners of France, the troops prisoners of the United States. Officers were permitted to go on parole to New York or Europe or any American post in British possession. A sloop-of-war was even provided to carry Cornwallis's dispatches to New York. The surrender itself was to take place on the 19th, the garrison at Yorktown marching out ·with shouldered arms and cased colors at two o'clock, the garrison at Gloucester at three o'clock. Hence, on the 19th, the British, in brilliant new scarlet uniforms, marched to the surrender field between a long line of white-coated French regulars and an opposite rank of war-weary Continentals who had cleaned and mended their ragged uniforms as well as possible, while the bands of the vanquished played a quaint old British march, "The World Turned Upside Down."[26]

But however considerate the Allies were, even to dining the British staff lavishly for days and Rochambeau going so far as to make a personal loan to Cornwallis,[27] the surrender came hard. Cornwallis could not face it and, pleading illness, turned the unpleasant duty over to General O'Hara. When the latter presented the earl's sword to Washington, the Virginian directed General Lincoln to receive it, and the corpulent New Englander must have felt that this was satisfaction indeed for having had to submit at Charleston. The British rank and file were affected too. They kept their eyes on the French rather than on the Americans. Some showed their anger by throwing down their muskets violently. Others wept without restraint.

In terms of casualties the siege had been as easy for the Allies as it was severe for the British.[28] The Americans lost only twenty killed and fifty-six wounded; the French, fifty-two killed and one hundred and thirty-four wounded. The British lost one hundred and fifty-six killed and three hundred and twenty-six wounded, and surrendered seven thousand, one hundred and fifty-seven soldiers, eight hundred and forty seamen, and eighty camp followers. At the time of his surrender, Cornwallis had over two thousand sick in his hospitals. Even thus handicapped, the earl, with ample supplies of food and ammunition remaining,[29] might have held on for ten days longer. He knew Clinton was about to sail. Though the British had twenty-seven as against the French thirty-six ships of the line, the British had won battles before with as great disparity. And if the navy had been able to land Clinton and his seven thousand redcoats, the result of Yorktown might have been quite different. But Cornwallis refused to wait. He felt that the powerful artillery of the besiegers could not be resisted, and that a continuation of the siege would have meant that the blood of the bravest men would be shed in vain.[30] A number of his opponents expressed their surprise at the speediness of his submission, a Virginia colonel remarking, "His surrender was eight or ten days sooner than the most sanguine expected."[31]

The surrender shook people everywhere. A Te Deum was sung in Paris amid unrestrained exultation. In London, Lord North is said to have thrown up his hands and exclaimed that it was all over, though, a few days later, he went down to Parliament and vigorously defended his government. George III maintained his composure when informed of the disaster but neglected to enter the hour and minute of what he was then writing, a significant omission for a precise, determined man. In America, the Loyalist center of New York was plunged into gloomy despair. North and South, however, people rejoiced wherever the Patriot party was strong. Connecticut took a particularly grim satisfaction in the news, for feelings were still raw from Arnold's diversionary raid on New London on September 7, a raid that failed to draw Washington from his Yorktown mission, but one which saw the stoutly resisting American garrison, including its commander, Colonel Ledyard, massacred and the town burned.

Nowhere were greater demonstrations of joy manifested than in sedate Philadelphia, that prize of contending armies. When Tench Tilghman galloped into the slumbering city with Washington's communication, an old German watchman conducted him to the residence of the president of Congress, then continued his nightly rounds, calling out lustily as he passed through the streets with his lantern, "Basht dree o'glock, und Gorn-val-lis isht da-ken!"[32] Candles were lighted and windows flew open as men and women sought to know more. The streets quickly filled with cheering throngs. Congress attended divine service in the early afternoon and offered prayers of thanks and gratitude. Salutes were fired, banquets held, and many toasts pledged. The city was then illuminated, and people danced in the homes and the streets despite Congressional admonitions to preserve decorum. The surrender was exhilarating news. For the second time, a British army had laid down its arms in this long, tedious war. Few people doubted that this was truly the end, and they thought rightly, as did Lord North. Except for isolated skirmishes, largely in the South, it was all over.

XXIII

The End of the War

Bringing a war to an end is never an easy or speedy procedure. In the War of the American Revolution, the peace treaty was not signed in its definitive form until early 1783, and the British evacuation of New York did not occur until November of that year. The details of the diplomatic negotiations and the ebb and flow of the political tides in England are not for consideration here, but it is important to note that, however humble England's military status had become in October, 1781, she had retrieved her prestige to an astonishing degree within a year, with the result that peace terms in 1783 were quite different from what they might have been immediately after Yorktown.

At first British strength appeared on the point of collapse throughout the world. True to his commitments to the Spaniards, De Grasse returned promptly to the West Indies despite the pleas of Washington for a joint campaign against Charleston. De Grasse conquered several islands and prepared a Franco-Spanish attack on Jamaica. Although, in India, Warren Hastings had the French on the run by 1779, a French fleet under the great Suffren eventually secured naval superiority, and the massive revolt by Hyder Ali threatened British control of the subcontinent. In Europe, Dutch and French men-of-war still posed a threat for the Channel and the North Sea, while the Spanish with French assistance recovered Minorca in February, 1782. The two nations then vigorously pressed their siege of Gibraltar in the spring and summer.

But presently came the amazing turn in fortune: Rodney's smashing victory over De Grasse in April, 1782, in the Battle of the Saints in the West Indies; Admiral Hughes's stalwart resistance in the series of dingdong battles with Suffren in Indian waters; Sir Eyre Coote's

263

decisive defeat of Hyder Ali; General Elliot's redoubtable "last ditch" stand at Gibraltar, and Lord Howe's skillful and effective relief of that fortress despite the superior fleet opposed to him. With such an improvement of the military situation, the new British government, even under such friends of America as Rockingham, Shelburne, and Fox, was hardly disposed to concede more than the minumum, least of all Canada, which Franklin dearly hoped he might procure as the price of Anglo-American friendship. Nor is the evidence amassed convincing that George Rogers Clark's victories were responsible for Britain's cession of the old Northwest, particularly since Britain still held Oswego, Niagara, Detroit, and Michilimackinac. Shelburne appears to have hoped that by getting the United States to agree to a preliminary treaty, he could maneuver her out of the war and turn his full attention to Britain's other enemies.[1] Amid a welter of conniving and conspiring which found the British endeavoring, not altogether unsuccessfully, to split the French and Americans, a preliminary Anglo-American peace treaty, generally favorable to the Americans, was signed in November, 1782, but did not go into effect until the final treaty of peace was signed with the Bourbon powers early in 1783.

Meanwhile military dispositions in America were made by the British with a view to holding the ports and by the Americans largely with the object of containing them there. Washington took his Continentals back to the Hudson, where he preserved a vigilant watch over the unhappy Clinton, who was relieved in the spring by the able and gracious Sir Guy Carleton; this appointment delighted the New York Loyalists.[2] Wayne marched the Pennsylvania Line southward to join Greene, who sent him into Georgia while keeping his own eye on Leslie at Charleston.[3] With spring, Carleton proceeded with the task of evacuating the Southern ports. As he wrote Leslie with a realistic pen, "All other operations are suspended till these evacuations have taken place. The evacuation is not a matter of choice but of deplorable necessity in consequence of an unsuccessful war."[4] At his urging, Savannah was first evacuated, then Charleston, the former on July 11, 1782, the latter on December 14.

Most of this time, the French remained inactive. The three regiments comprising the San Domingo garrison returned at once with De Grasse to the West Indies. The four regiments and auxiliary troops of Rochambeau spent the winter in Williamsburg, where the officers passed many a pleasant hour over their punch in the Raleigh Tavern. In late June, the army started its hot, dusty march for the north. After remaining several weeks near Compound on the left of the Continentals, the troops took the road again in the fall over the Connecticut hills and valleys bright with the yellow of the birch and the scarlet of the swamp maple. In their old quarters in Rhode Island they received a warm welcome but lingered only until enough shipping was assembled in Boston, from which they sailed the day before Christmas. Of these gay veterans, a number were to be heard from again, divided as to loyalties, during the enthusiasm, violence, and bloodshed of the French Revolution and the brief, flashy grandeur of the Napoleonic Empire.[5]

The winter following the sailing of the French was marked by considerable dissatisfaction in the Continental army, principally among the officers. A commission placed an officer under a financial strain which became heavier as Continental money depreciated in value. Washington deplored that an officer usually had to rely on his own private resources for support. He had strongly urged Congress to assure half pay for seven years with a gratuity of $80 for noncommissioned officers and soldiers. Even so, by the end of 1778, many officers were leaving the service for want of funds, while those who remained were becoming impoverished. Finally Congress, in the latter part of 1779, recommended that the states grant half pay for life to duration officers, an acceptable award to enlisted men, and pensions to widows of officers and soldiers killed in service. But this provision failed to take care of the immediate needs, and, in December, 1782, the officers sent a distinguished committee to Congress to press for payment of their arrears of pay, assurance for the rest, and half pay for life. In the discussions with Congress, the committee proposed a commutation of the half-pay provision. A motion that half pay for life be commuted to six years full pay was lost, and when the officers back in Washington's camp at Newburgh learned of the failure of their proposals, the kettle began to boil.

While the officers bitterly attacked their government, two papers, the *Newburgh Addresses*, began to circulate. These brilliant, anonymous papers set forth the situation in powerful language, called upon representatives from all branches of the army to meet on March 11 to consider how redress of grievances could best be obtained, and suggested that, until redress was granted, the army should resist being disbanded. The author was probably Major (later General) John Armstrong, aide-de-camp of General Gates. His scheme was not without support, and certainly not without sympathy, from men in and out of Congress. Yet the whole proceeding was so extraordinary and alarming in its implications that Washington called a meeting of officers for March 15 to hear the report of the officers' committee to Congress. Gates, now back in service and the senior officer present, was to chair the assembly.

It was an exciting moment. The officers were fully aware that they had been unjustly treated by Congress, though it is likely that they realized neither the degree of insolvency of Congress nor the difficulty that Congress experienced in securing the co-operation of the states in matters of finance. But in their indignation the officers were not of a mind to be tolerant. Despite his sympathies, Washington realized the danger in letting this outburst of anger go too far. Few could miss the implications in one of the *Newburgh Addresses* which urged the officers to tell Congress "that the slightest mark of indignity from Congress now must operate like the grave, and part you forever; that, in any political event, the army has its alternative." Moreover, should peaceful measures fail, the author went on, the army could move to the west, and defy Congress to destroy it. This was close to mutiny, and Washington met the challenge with consummate tact and skill.

His appearance in the hall, used for assembly and divine worship, was a surprise. A hush fell over the audience as he spoke. Praising the powerful composition of the addresses, he deplored the character of their content as unmilitary and unreasonable. He announced his belief in the justice of Congress and his intention of assisting the officers in any honorable way possible. He then appealed to their patriotism and read a private letter from a congressman who explained certain of the difficulties faced by Congress. Probably more effective than anything else he said or did was a little human detail. In the course of his reading, he drew out a pair of spectacles, an act which surprised many who did not know that his sight had become impaired. Half apologizing, he said, "Gentlemen, you will permit me to put on my spectacles, for I have not only grown gray, but almost blind, in the service of my country." The statement evoked genuine emotion. When he withdrew, the officers voted to leave their problem with him. Thanks in good part to his intercession, Congress agreed to full pay for officers for five years to be settled at its own option as a cash payment or in securities at six per cent, while enlisted men were granted full pay for four months. This arrangement proving generally acceptable to the army, the dangerous excitement died down.[6]

Meanwhile, informed by General Carleton and Admiral Digby that Britain had announced an end to hostilities, Congress proclaimed a cessation on April 11 and ratified the provisional peace treaty on April 15. After Washington published the intelligence three days later, and congratulated the army, the soldiers started a rush back to the farm, the shop, and the profession. At the same time, they wanted their money, and Washington advised Congress that three months' pay should be available before the army disbanded. As eager to see the army disband as the men themselves were to leave, Congress clamored for the states to send in their tax collections, and sought a loan from France. Then, realizing that the definitive treaty of peace was still to be signed, Congress decided to furlough the troops with a note in their pockets and an assurance of a discharge pending the signing of the treaty.

But the end had not been reached. On June 7, a group of officers petitioned for financial relief before being sent home, but Congress could only forward their memorial, together with Washington's letter in their behalf, to the states with the plea that the states honor the notes issued. A week later, several sergeants from one of the furloughed units in Philadelphia sent a sharp notice to Congress demanding payment. Fortunately the secretary of war and General St. Clair were able to calm them.

More serious was the mutinous action of eighty recruits at Lancaster, who, on June 17, marched on Philadelphia, where they were joined by several hundred troops quartered in the city. They barricaded Congress and the executive council of Pennsylvania and demanded from the latter redress of their grievances in twenty minutes. The time limit passed without violence, but neither body dared withdraw through the line of troops, who, as the afternoon wore along, began to get noisy from the liquor passing around and pointed their muskets at the windows. Since Pennsylvania obviously had no control over its own soldiers, Congress sent urgent appeals to Washington, who called on his old mutiny scotcher, General Robert Howe. Meanwhile, in a rather laudable display of courage, Congress left the building at three o'clock. Happily the mutineers offered nothing other than verbal insults as the politicians passed through their cordon. But Congress had had enough of Philadelphia as the permanent national capital and met next in Princeton. Before Howe and his fifteen hundred regulars arrived, the mutineers dispersed; several of their number were court-martialed. Though Washington bitterly condemned the mutiny, part of the fault properly belonged to Congress; by its neglect, shilly-shallying, empty promises, and general spinelessness it had made itself thoroughly hateful and contemptible in the eyes of both officers and enlisted men.[7]

While the soldiers of the American army were disappearing that summer with only a pittance of money to pay their debts and to support themselves and their families long enough to find jobs again, the British in New York were engaged in the painful task of evacuating Loyalists and troops. Sir Guy Carleton tried to find shipping space for as many Loyalists as cared to leave this country. This had been their native land, and in it they left homes, possessions, and memories —sweet and excruciating. Thousands sailed to exile in the wilderness of Nova Scotia, others to the West Indies, many to England. Not even the generosity of the British Parliament in granting pensions and financial compensation for losses could assuage the bitterness of their departure or ease greatly the hardships to be faced. Carleton spared neither time nor energy to make the Loyalist leave-taking as mercifully short as possible. At the same time, he proceeded with the embarkation of troops and arranged to evacuate Brooklyn and New York on November 25.

A clear, bracing day, November 25 started auspiciously with the embarrassment of the brutal provost marshal, William Cunningham. Seeing an American flag flying from Day's Tavern on Murray Street, he emitted a volley of oaths and dashed toward the tavern to tear down the offending banner. To his discomfiture, the formidable Mrs. Day blocked the entrance and clouted him so vigorously on his neatly powdered head with her by no means feeble hand that he retired in some confusion as the onlookers burst into raucous laughter.[8] Presently crowds gathered to watch the few picked units under General Knox move down to the Bowery, where they broke ranks until the

British rearguard retired. At one o'clock, the British marched to their boats at the East River wharves, and the Americans wasted little time in occupying the lower part of the town. At Fort St. George, some delay occurred in raising the flag because the pole had been greased and the cleats and halyards removed. Sawing a board into cleats which he nailed to the pole, a sailor mounted to the top, strung the halyards, and hoisted the flag, while the crowd cheered wildly and cannon roared in salute. Then Washington with Governor Clinton entered the city. It was a far cry indeed from the disastrous days of the late summer and fall of 1776 when Washington was last there. Now the long war was over, men felt they had reaffirmed the principle of liberty, the country was independent with powerful friends abroad, and a glorious if unknown future beckoned. Such thoughts animated the toasts of the distinguished company of officers and civilians who gathered that evening as the guests of Governor Clinton at the tavern on the corner of Pearl and Broad Streets converted from a warehouse to a famous eating establishment by Samuel Fraunces, a West Indian of French and Negro extraction (it still enjoys a high culinary reputation, thanks to the Sons of the American Revolution, who own the building).

The denouement followed swiftly. On December 4, also at Fraunces's Tavern, Washington said farewell to his officers. But this gathering was one of sadness, and none was more deeply affected than the great Virginian himself. Filling his glass with wine, he wished that their days to come would be as "prosperous and happy" as their former ones had been "glorious and honorable." Then he drank his toast, and, beginning with Knox, who, like many present, was struggling with his feelings, he shook hands with every officer in a silence too meaningful for words.[9] Something of the same emotion gripped him and others, too, on December 23 at Annapolis when, in the presence of Congress and the legislature of Maryland, he laid down his commission. Tears came to his auditors' eyes, and the general's hand shook as he read his address.[10]

While Washington returned to his neglected Mount Vernon, Congress finished with his army. By the new year, there were but a few companies of artillery and one infantry regiment remaining. Then, on June 2, 1784, Congress declared that "standing armies in time of peace, are inconsistent with the principles of republican Governments, dangerous to the liberties of a free people, and generally converted into destructive engines for establishing despotism."[11] Congress therefore disbanded the army completely except for a handful of officers and eighty enlisted men who were retained to guard military property at West Point and Fort Pitt. Thus did Congress signalize not only the conclusion of the war and the demise of the Continental army but the end of an era as well. The future belonged to the republic, and the republic, as Napoleon III said of his empire, clearly meant peace.

In conclusion, what can one say of the military significance of the American Revolution apart from the obvious fact that without military action the colonies could not at that time have achieved their independence? Actually a number of interesting lessons were revealed, whether or not they were regarded of value. Important in the list was that the American Revolution was a civil war until 1778 and merged thereafter with the international conflict known in Europe as the War for American Independence. Without French military and financial assistance, moreover, the United States would doubtless have ceased to exist. That dependence has occasionally been forgotten or slighted in our self-adulation.

The Revolution, furthermore, could not have been won without a preponderance of French sea power at the right time and in the right place. By the same token, the British were able to co-ordinate their activities, in so far as that co-ordination existed, simply because they controlled the sea throughout the war except for forty-one days in 1779 and sixty-four fateful days in 1781.[12] Washington, like Clinton, but quite unlike Cornwallis, acquired a strong respect for sea power. Unhappily Congress lacked the money to build an effective navy, and when it got around to outfitting the semblance of a fleet, it was dependent largely on the states whose seagoing citizens found privateering much more alluring and profitable than service in the regular navy. Furthermore, the British held such enormous superiority that, after a dismal attempt by Esek Hopkins of Rhode Island early in the war to operate a half dozen converted merchantmen on a squadron basis, such American ships as were sent to sea became commerce destroyers. John Paul Jones's gallant efforts were valuable chiefly for their effect on national prestige and morale. Operations of more concrete value were those of Arnold at Valcour Island and the Pennsylvania gondolas in the Delaware. But the delivery of the coup de grâce at Yorktown required a formidable battlefleet, and Admiral de Grasse possessed exactly that.

Another outstanding, and at times lamentable, feature of the war was the American reliance on militia and short-term enlistments. The militia had its place, but it was unreliable in long-sustained campaigns. Washington's opinion of the use of militia was frequently and tartly expressed on many occasions throughout the war. Ill disciplined, poorly trained, rarely available in sufficient strength when needed, unsteady in battle, here today and gone after the first rainy night or repulse, they were a broken staff on which to rest, and the Virginian considered that dependence on them, together with short-term enlistments in their ranks and in the Continental army, to be the origin of both American military misfortunes and the great accumulation of debt. Enough men were enlisted during the war to overwhelm the British, in short, 395,858, of which total the number of militia was 164,087; the British at no time had more than forty-two thousand men available.[13] Yet without French military and naval aid Yorktown would have been impossible to accomplish. Nor need much be said of the enormous expense in terms of pay, bounties, and pensions! Still, the same mistakes were repeated in 1812 and 1861.

But if we made mistakes, so did the British. Among their costliest were the division of their army into forces too small to accomplish their missions, the dispatch of these forces too far from sea bases, and the almost fantastic reliance on the Loyalists to rise in behalf of the crown. Possibly the most acute comment on the Loyalist policy by a contemporary was made by that splendid, self-effacing Englishman, Lieutenant Mackenzie, when he said in early August, 1781, ". . . we cannot with reason expect those that are Loyal will declare their sentiments until they find us so strong in any one place as to protect them after having joined. Our taking post at different places, inviting the Loyalists to join us, and then Evacuating those posts, and abandoning the people to the fury of their bitterest Enemies, has deterred them from declaring themselves until affairs take a decisive turn in our favor; we shall then find the people eager to shew their loyalty; while the issue remains doubtful we should not expect it."[14] These wise words might apply equally as well to situations much nearer our own lives.

The war also brought out very clearly the necessity for a unity of command and, conversely, the folly of a division of authority. Until Congress ceased its interference in matters of strategy and acting without consultation with its own field commander, the American war effort resembled the late Stephen Leacock's rider who jumped on his horse and rode off in all directions. Furthermore, until unity of command between the Allies was attained, and a harmonious relationship among the commanders achieved through a common objective and satisfactory personal relations, the war could not be concluded. It was the Allies' good fortune, and that of the United States in particular, that while this felicitous arrangement was being effected, Clinton and Cornwallis were disputing the British command, and Germain was supporting Cornwallis against the latter's nominal superior in New York. Likewise, the British generals and admirals demonstrated during those crucial autumn days of 1781 very little of the co-operation occasionally evinced by the Howes when heads of their respective services in America.

Even as the war demonstrated the need for a unity of command, so, too, it revealed that conventional tactics would not suffice. The Revolution was largely a war of movement waged over great distances, on all types of terrain, and in a variety of climates. Americans, with their tradition of frontier fighting, tended to emphasize the loose skirmish line and individual marksmanship; the British, the heavy European linear formation and the smashing volley. On the other hand, as the conflict wore along, the Americans leaned toward a compromise in the guise of "formed bodies" supporting skirmishers. Similarly the British gave up the three ranks in linear formation in favor of two, effected a wider lateral interval between their men, developed the skirmisher, and emphasized marksmanship. As one authority has pointed out, both combatants were approaching the same idea of flexibility from opposite directions.[15] Particularly impressed by the lessons of American war was the genial, capable Sir John Moore, plain Ensign Moore during the Penobscot campaign. In charge of infantry training during the early years of the great struggle with Napoleon, Moore used both American and Prussian experience in training a division of Light Infantry, one of the most effective corps ever developed by the British army.[16]

The Americans saw their answer in the Light Infantry, and French experiments with Light Infantry from the middle of the century received fresh inspiration from their American experience prior to and during the wars of the French Revolution. Leaders in those struggles included both nobles and enlisted men who had served at Yorktown: such men as Lafayette, Rochambeau, Berthier, who became Napoleon's chief of staff, Dumas, intendant general of Napoleon's Grand Army, Lauzun, Custine, Jourdan, who had been a sergeant of infantry at Yorktown, and Pichegru, who had served as a private of artillery during the siege. It was scarcely a coincidence that there was much in common between the French Revolution armies and the American Light Infantry.[17]

The military paladin of the age was Frederick the Great of Prussia, who had early used Jägers with his heavy formations. It is likely that he kept abreast of the revolution in tactics produced by the American Revolution. But Cornwallis, present at Frederick's last review in 1785, and with his own American experience fresh in mind, wrote of the Prussians, "Their manoeuvres were such as the worst General in England would be hooted at for practising; two lines coming up within six yards of one another, and firing in one another's faces till they had no ammunition left: nothing could be more ridiculous."[18] Perhaps it was just as well that Frederick did not live to see his army, the finest in Europe in the middle of the century, defeated and destroyed by the new tactics and formations of the French.

The military events of the Revolution also bore witness to the need for vigilance and flexibility of mind in regard to the future. One of the great misapprehensions of the war was that in an emergency a large mass of men with only militia training at best would spring to arms and show itself capable of defending this country. Advocates of this theory pointed to Bunker Hill as the supreme example, and minimized or ignored the arguments of critics who ventured to explain that Bunker Hill was decidedly an exception. For years, the obsession persisted in American thinking and has finally disappeared only in this century under the shock of two World Wars. To Congress, however, given the exhaustion of the treasury, an adequate regular establishment seemed an extraordinary and unnecessary expense. Congress, moreover, evinced the traditional English distrust of a standing army, which was the product of England's unhappy experience with Cromwell and the Stuarts in the seventeenth century. But adherence to tradition and faith in the deceptively easy expedient of employing militia demonstrated a strange failure to comprehend such hard realities as the reluctance of the British to evacuate the western posts and the ever-present menace of the Indians in the South and across the Alleghenies. For that matter, many Americans have always displayed a markedly naïve hesitation to accept adequate military preparations as an indispensable method of ensuring a reasonably secure future.

The American Revolution, in comparison with subsequent conflicts in which this country has been involved, may appear almost trivial, and certainly its military significance has by no means warranted the glorification by early American historians or the fantastic romanticization by most historical novelists. On the other hand, quite apart from its tremendous import as an economic and social upheaval, a conflict which wrought the downfall of the British military establishment and secured the political independence of this country was no inconsequential struggle. The forces of the combatants might be small, and the tactics might resolve at times into mere bushfighting, but it was these little armies and their maneuvers which helped settle the great issues of the war. Viewed in such perspective, Bunker Hill, Saratoga, Guilford Courthouse, and Yorktown are of enormous historical importance. Furthermore, if there was more than ample evidence of an astonishing amount of American incompetence, maladministration, corruption, villainy, desertion, mutiny, and civilian apathy, the achievements stand forth bright and shining by contrast. Americans of that day were just learning to make a nation out of many diverse elements and had to fight a war at the same time. Perhaps it is the more remarkable that they succeeded at all. Thanks, however, to the ability of a number of outstanding leaders, to the devotion for a certain conception of liberty on the part of both leaders and an enduring few of the rank and file, to the mistakes of the British, and to the assistance of the French, the war was won, the new nation sustained, and the foundation established for that structure of democratic government and society which was to become the envy and admiration of the world.

Notes

The Military Background of the Revolution

1) L. C. Hatch, *The Administration of the American Revolutionary Army* (New York, 1903), 1-2.
2) *Ibid.*, 2; *The Lee Papers* (4 vols. New York, 1872-75), *New York Historical Society Collections*, II, 247; *Records of the Colony of Rhode Island and Providence Plantations, in New England* (Edited by J. R. Bartlett. 10 vols. Providence, 1856-65), VII, 269-70; *Documents and Records Relating to the Province of New Hampshire, from the Earliest Period of Its Settlement; 1623-1776* (Edited by N. Boulton. 7 vols. Concord, N. H., 1867-73), VII, 267; *The Memorial History of the City of New York* (Edited by J. G. Wilson. 5 vols. New York, 1892-96), II, 420-21; A. French, *The First Year of the American Revolution* (Boston, 1934), 44-45.
3) A fine account of the action of the Provincial Congress and the existence of these earlier emergency organizations may be found in C. K. Bolton, *The Private Soldier under Washington* (New York, 1902), 6-9. See also *The Journals of Each Provincial Congress of Massachusetts* (Boston, 1838), 33; French, *The First Year of the American Revolution*, 41-43; A. French, "The Arms and Military Training of Our Colonizing Ancestors," in *Proceedings of the Massachusetts Historical Society*, LXVII (1945).
4) Percy to H. Reveley, Aug. 8, 1774, and Percy to his father, Sept. 12, 1774, quoted from MSS at Alnwick by Bolton, *The Private Soldier under Washington*, 14, 9.
5) *Massachusetts Historical Society Collections*, 5th series (10 vols.) IX, 288; *Writings of Benjamin Franklin* (Edited by A. H. Smyth. 10 vols. New York, 1905-07), V, 259.
6) *Principles and Acts of the Revolution* (Edited by H. Niles. Baltimore, 1822), 12, 20.
7) See S. Pargellis, *Lord Loudoun in North America* (New Haven, 1933), 1 ff.
8) The whole problem of command is discussed by C. E. Carter, "The Office of Commander in Chief: A Phase of Imperial Unity on the Eve of the Revolution," in *The Era of the American Revolution* (Edited by R. B. Morris. New York, 1939), 170-213.
9) A recent first-rate study is that by J. R. Alden, *General Gage in America* (Baton Rouge, 1948).
10) See *Correspondence of General Thomas Gage* (Edited by C. E. Carter. 2 vols. New Haven, 1931; 1933), *passim*. The *Gage Papers* in the William L. Clements Library (Ann Arbor, Mich.) are a mine of information.

11) The following information on the British army is derived chiefly from E. E. Curtis, *The Organization of the British Army in the American Revolution* (New Haven, 1926), 1-80, but also from H. Belcher, *The First American Civil War* (2 vols. London, 1911), II, 242-349; French, *First Year of the American Revolution*, 88-109; C. M. Clode, *Military Forces of the Crown* (2 vols. London, 1869), *passim;* R. Lamb, *Memoir* (Dublin, 1811), 66-238; J. Burgoyne, *Orderly Book* (Edited by E. B. O'Callaghan. Albany, 1860), 74; J. W. Fortescue, *History of the British Army* (13 vols. London, 1899-1930), III, *passim;* G. O. Trevelyan, *The American Revolution* (New Edition. 4 vols. New York, 1917), II, 32-34, 93, III, 271.

CHAPTER II

The Guns of Lexington and Concord

1) See J. R. Alden, "Why the March to Concord?", in *American Historical Review,* LXIX (1944), 446-54, and his *General Gage in America,* 240-44.

2) Gage to Barrington, Feb. 10, 1775. *Gage Corr.*, II, 669.

3) *Ibid.*, II, 179-83. The letter is analyzed in detail in Alden, "Why the March to Concord?," in *A.H.R.,* XLIX, 446-54, and Alden, *General Gage in America*, 238-42.

4) H. Murdock, *The Nineteenth of April, 1775* (Boston, 1923), 47; A. French, *The Day of Concord and Lexington* (Boston, 1925), 73.

5) The route is carefully followed in F. W. Coburn, *Battle of April 19, 1775* (Lexington, 1912).

6) E. Forbes, *Paul Revere and the World He Lived In* (Boston, 1942), 238, 460, no. 27. See also the two letters by J. L. Watson in *Massachusetts Historical Society Proceedings,* 1st series, XV, 163 ff.; W. Wheildon, *The Paul Revere Signal Lanterns* (Concord, 1876).

7) For the incident see C. Stedman, *History of the American War* (2 vols. Dublin, 1794), I, 134. See also W. Gordon, *History of the Rise, Progress, and Establishment of the Independence of the United States of America* (3 vols. New York, 1794), I, 139, for his remark that a so-called daughter of liberty, "unequally yoked in the point of politics," had warned Adams. J. R. Alden disposes pretty successfully of the legend in his *General Gage in America,* 247-50.

8) French, *The Day of Concord and Lexington,* 95.

9) *Ibid.*, 104-5.

10) See Parker's deposition in P. Force, *American Archives* (9 vols. Washington, 1837-53), 4th series, II, 491.

11) The most reliable British account is Gage's "Circumstantial Account," in *ibid.*, II, 435. The most dispassionate contemporary American version is the Reverend Ezra Stiles' analysis in his *Literary Diary* (Edited by F. B. Dexter, 3 vols. New York, 1901), I, 604-5.

12) See French, *The Day of Concord and Lexington,* and Murdock, *The Nineteenth of April, 1775*. It is all very well for the American historian, J. T. Adams, and the British army historian, J. W. Fortescue, to dismiss the question of which side fired first as now having little importance his-

torically (Adams, *Revolutionary New England, 1691-1776* [Boston, 1923], 419; Fortescue, *History of the British Army*, III, 152). At the time, however, the question was of paramount importance and helped inflame feeling on both sides.

13) Private Amos Barrett's account in French, *The Day of Concord and Lexington*, 157-58.

14) E. Ripley, *A History of the Fight at Concord, on the 19th of April, 1775* (Concord, 1827), 14; L. Shattuck, *A History of the Town of Concord* (Boston, 1835), 109.

15) *Ibid.*, 113; French, *The Day of Concord and Lexington*, 168-69.

16) Gage to Barrington, April 22, 1775. *Gage Papers* (Clements Library).

17) C. K. Bolton, *Letters of Hugh, Earl Percy from Boston and New York, 1774-1776* (Boston, 1902), 51.

18) Fortescue, *History of the British Army*, III, 154.

19) *Diary of Frederick Mackenzie* (2 vols. Cambridge, 1930), I, 27.

CHAPTER III

The Costly Victory at Bunker Hill

1) R. Frothingham, *History of the Siege of Boston and of the Battles of Lexington, Concord, and Bunker Hill* (4th Edition. Boston, 1873), 92.

2) Gage to Carleton, April 19, 1775. *Gage Papers* (Clements Library).

3) E. Allen, *Narrative* (Burlington, 1849), 98. An interesting account of the capture of Ticonderoga is by A. French, *The Taking of Ticonderoga in 1775: the British Story* (Cambridge, 1928). See also French, *First Year of the American Revolution*, 143-159; J. H. Smith, *Our Struggle for the Fourteenth Colony* (2 vols. New York, 1907), I, 110-40; J. Pell, *Ethan Allen* (London, 1929), 80-86.

4) French, *First Year of the American Revolution*, 168-69.

5) E. B. de Fonblanque, *Political and Military Episodes . . . Derived from the Life and Correspondence of the Right Hon. John Burgoyne* (London, 1876), 119.

6) Frothingham, *Siege of Boston*, 114.

7) Force, *Amer. Archives*, 4th ser., II, 968-70.

8) Frothingham, *Siege of Boston*, 116.

9) *Ibid.*, 116-17.

10) Alden, *General Gage in America*, 265-66; French, *First Year of the American Revolution*, 20.

11) The chief points of the Bunker Hill-Breed's Hill controversy are discussed in detail in Frothingham, *Siege of Boston*, 123-24.

12) *Clinton Papers. Private Notes to the History* (Clements Library).

13) See *Massachusetts Historical Society Proceedings*, XLIV (1910), 96-103.

14) French, *First Year of the American Revolution*, 222; C. F. Adams, *Studies Military and Diplomatic, 1775-1865* (New York, 1911), 9.

15) William Howe to Richard Howe, June 22, 1775. Historical Manuscripts Commission, *Stopford-Sackville MSS*, II, 4.

16) Gage to Dartmouth, June 25, 1775. *Gage Papers* (Clements Library).

17) Frothingham, *Siege of Boston,* 134.

18) Lt. John de Bernière made the charge. See *ibid.,* 134.

19) Stedman, *The American War,* I, 127; C. H. Van Tyne, *The War of Independence* (Boston, 1929), 46, n. 26.

20) Frothingham, *Siege of Boston,* 140, n. 4.

21) J. Codman, *Arnold's Expedition to Quebec* (New York, 1901), 241; T. Jones, *New York During the Revolutionary War* (2 vols. New York, 1879), I, 610; S. G. Fisher, *The True History of the American Revolution* (Philadelphia, 1902), 253.

22) Burgoyne's letter of June 25, 1775. Quoted in B. Partridge, *Sir Billy Howe* (New York, 1932), 19-20.

23) Clinton's account of Bunker Hill. *Clinton Papers* (Clements Library).

24) Howe to Gage, June 21, 1775. From the *Firle Papers,* printed in Belcher, *First American Civil War,* I, 198.

25) Frothingham, *Siege of Boston,* 142; Fortescue, *History of the British Army,* III, 161.

26) J. W. Fortescue, *George III, King of England, Correspondence from 1760 to December 1783* (6 vols. London, 1927-28), III, 220-24; Historical Manuscripts Commission, *Hastings MSS,* III, 157, Fortescue, *History of the British Army,* III, 162.

27) See French, *First Year of the American Revolution,* 241; H. Murdock, *Bunker Hill, Notes and Queries on a Famous Battle* (Boston, 1927), 122; Howe to Gage, June 21, 1775. From the *Firle Papers,* printed in Belcher, *First American Civil War,* I, 198.

28) *Corr. of George III,* III, 225.

29) Frothingham, *Siege of Boston,* 152.

30) Howe to Gage, June 21, 1775. From the *Firle Papers,* printed in Belcher, *First American Civil War,* I, 197. See also French, *First Year of the American Revolution,* Appendix 23.

31) For casualties, see Force, *Amer. Archives,* 4th ser., II, 1098-99; French, *First Year of the American Revolution,* 252; Murdock, *Bunker Hill,* 32-33; Frothingham, *Siege of Boston,* 193.

32) Adams, *Studies Military and Diplomatic,* 5.

33) *Ibid.,* 11-13.

CHAPTER IV

The Trials of Organizing an Army

1) Force, *Amer. Archives,* 4th ser., II, 621.

2) *Works of John Adams* (Edited by C. F. Adams. 10 vols. Boston, 1856), II, 415-18. See also the discussion in French, *First Year of the American Revolution,* 284-87.

3) *The Writings of George Washington from the Original Manuscript Sources* (Edited by J. C. Fitzpatrick, 26 vols. Washington, D.C., 1931-38), III, 293, 296.

4) *Lee Papers,* IV, 177-78

5) For an analysis, see F. V. Greene, *The Revolutionary War and the Military Policy of the United States* (New York, 1911), 14-15.
6) Fitzpatrick, *Writings of Washington*, III, 299.
7) *Secret Journals of the Acts and Proceedings of Congress* (4 vols. Boston, 1820), I, 18.
8) Fitzpatrick, *Writings of Washington*, III, 320-29.
9) *The Writings of George Washington* (Edited by J. Sparks. 12 vols. Boston, 1834-37), III, 492.
10) *Journals of the Continental Congress, 1774-1789* (Edited by W. C. Ford, G. Hunt, J. C. Fitzpatrick, and R. R. Hill. 34 vols. Washington, D.C., 1904-37), III, 323.
11) Hatch, *Administration of the Amer. Rev. Army*, 14; Fitzpatrick, *Writings of Washington*, III, 383, 429-30, 472-73.
12) W. B. Reed, *Life and Correspondence of Joseph Reed* (2 vols. Philadelphia, 1847), I, 243; R. Hughes, *George Washington* (3 vols. New York, 1926-30), II, 283-84.
13) Bolton, *The Private Soldier under Washington*, 127.
14) Fitzpatrick, *Writings of Washington*, III, 357, 339, 362.
15) B. Knollenberg, *Washington and the Revolution, a Reappraisal* (New York, 1941), 216-19; *Journals of the Continental Congress*, XX, 658. See also Bolton, *The Private Soldier under Washington*, 169-76.
16) Fitzpatrick, *Writings of Washington*, IV, 37, 57, 95, 97, 85, 86.
17) *Ibid.*, IV, 194, 195; *Journals of the Continental Congress*, IV, 60. See also Bolton, *The Private Soldier under Washington*, 22.
18) *Ibid.*, 24-25; *Writings of James Madison* (Edited by G. Hunt. 9 vols. New York, 1900-10), I, 106.
19) Fitzpatrick, *Writings of Washington*, III, 433.
20) *Ibid.*, IV, 137, 124, 122, 138.
21) *Ibid.*, IV, 124.
22) Bolton, *The Private Soldier under Washington*, 41.
23) Fitzpatrick, *Writings of Washington*, IV, 130, 132; Frothingham, *Siege of Boston*, 270. *The Diary of David How* (Edited by W. Chase and H. B. Dawson. Morrisania, N. Y., 1865), 8, bears the following entry for March 4, 1776: "Last Night there was Afireing all Night with Cannan and morters on both Sides; our people Splet *The Congress* the Third Time they fireed it."
24) Hatch, *Administration of the Amer. Rev. Army*, 88; G. W. Greene, *The Life of Nathanael Greene* (3 vols. New York, 1867), I, 97-99; Fitzpatrick, *Writings of Washington*, IV, 180; V. L. Johnson, *The Administration of the American Commissariat During the Revolutionary War* (Philadelphia, 1941), 27-49.

CHAPTER V

The Siege and Evacuation of Boston

1) Fonblanque, *Burgoyne*, 143; F. J. Hudleston, *Gentleman Johnny Burgoyne* (Indianapolis, 1927), 71; Historical Manuscripts Commission, *Dartmouth*

MSS, II, 315; Frothingham, *Siege of Boston*, 277; F. Moore, *Diary of the American Revolution from Newspapers and Original Documents* (2 vols. New York, 1865), I, 176; Alden, *General Gage in America*, 272-86.

2) Historical Manuscripts Commission, *Dartmouth MSS*, II, 357; Trevelyan, *The American Revolution*, I, 340-43; Fonblanque, *Burgoyne*, 180-81, 197, 198; S. Curwen, *Journals and Letters, 1775-1784* (Edited by S. A. Ward. New York, 1842), entry for Oct. 18, 1776.

3) *Correspondence of George III with Lord North* (Edited by W. B. Donne. 2 vols. London, 1867), II, 7, 51, 52; Curtis, *Organization of the British Army in the Amer. Rev.*, 81, 88, 92-95; Van Tyne, *War of Independence*, 80-81; "The History of Europe," chap. ii, in *Annual Register*, XIX (1776).

4) Historical Manuscripts Commission, *Hastings MSS*, III, 159, 161.

5) Frothingham, *Siege of Boston*, 280.

6) See *Howe's Orderly Book* (Edited by B. F. Stevens. London, 1890), entry for Dec. 5, 1775.

7) Fonblanque, *Burgoyne*, 17-18; Trevelyan, *The American Revolution*, I, 334.

8) For Howe's relationship with the Lorings, see Frothingham, *Siege of Boston*, 247; Jones, *History of New York during the Revolutionary War*, I, 171, 189, 253, 351, II, 57, 89, 423; Belcher, *First American Civil War*, I, 120, 195, II, 101, 145; Partridge, *Sir Billy Howe*, 33, 218, 219, 220, 227, 253, 254, 255; Hughes, *George Washington*, II, 316-18; French, *First Year of the American Revolution*, 546; T. J. Wertenbaker, *Father Knickerbocker Rebels* (New York, 1948), 125, 149.

9) Clinton to Gage, Aug. 7, 1775. *Clinton Papers* (Clements Library).

10) Fonblanque, *Burgoyne*, 190.

11) Howe to Dartmouth, Jan. 16, 1776. Force, *Amer. Archives*, 4th ser., IV, 701; Van Tyne, *War of Independence*, 88; Fortescue, *History of the British Army*, III, 179; Frothingham, *Siege of Boston*, 293; Alden, *General Gage in America*, 274-75.

12) Fitzpatrick, *Writings of Washington*, IV, 211.

13) *Ibid.*, IV, 211; Greene, *Nathanael Greene*, I, 138-39.

14) Frothingham, *Siege of Boston*, 295.

15) For reports of the council meetings, see *Calendar of the Correspondence of George Washington . . . with the Continental Congress. Prepared from the Original Manuscripts in the Library of Congress by John C. Fitzpatrick* (Washington, 1906). *Washington Papers*, I. See also Fitzpatrick, *Writings of Washington*, III, 483-85, IV, 260, 335, 336, 338-39, 348; C. Martyn, *The Life of Artemas Ward, the First Commander-in-Chief of the American Revolution* (New York, 1921), 194; French, *First Year of the American Revolution*, 653-54.

16) Martyn, *Artemas Ward*, 195.

17) Fitzpatrick, *Writings of Washington*, IV, 297. See also P. Davidson, *Propaganda and the American Revolution* (Chapel Hill, 1941), 131-33, 152, 215; A. Bowman, *The Morale of the American Revolutionary Army* (Washington, 1943), 97.

18) Force, *Amer. Archives*, 4th ser., III, 1672; Martyn, *Artemas Ward*, 193.

19) J. Almon, *The Remembrancer* (17 vols. London, 1775-84), III, 106; Howe

to Dartmouth, March 21, 1776. Force, *Amer. Archives*, 4th ser., V, 458-59; Howe to Clinton, March 21, 1776. *Clinton Papers* (Clements Library).

20) Howe to Dartmouth, March 21, 1776. Force, *Amer. Archives*, 4th ser., V, 459; *Orderly Book*, 225; Martyn, *Artemas Ward*, 206-7; Frothingham, *Siege of Boston*, 298-99; French, *First Year of the American Revolution*, 660-61; *The Kemble Papers* (2 vols. New York, 1883-84), *New York Historical Society Collections*, I, 71.

21) J. Winsor, *Memorial History of Boston* (4 vols. Boston, 1880), III, 164.

22) Force, *Amer. Archives*, 4th ser., V, 459-60.

23) See Stedman, *The American War*, I, 167; Fitzpatrick, *Writings of Washington*, IV, 405, 407.

24) N. W. Stephenson and W. H. Dunn, *George Washington* (2 vols. New York, 1940), I, 343.

25) Quoted in Frothingham, *Siege of Boston*, 322. See also W. Cobbett, *Parliamentary History of England from the Norman Conquest in 1066 to the Year 1803* (36 vols. London, 1806-20), XVIII (1774-1777), 1345-48.

CHAPTER VI

The Canadian Magnet

1) See *Journals of the Continental Congress*, II, 74, 109; *Letters of Members of the Continental Congress* (Edited by E. C. Burnett. 8 vols. Washington, D.C., 1921-36), I, 35; E. C. Burnett, *The Continental Congress* (New York, 1941), 68-69, 108-9.

2) Smith, *Fourteenth Colony*, I, 240-41. Arnold's letter is in the *Continental Congress Papers* (Library of Congress), No. 162, I, 12.

3) See Smith, *Fourteenth Colony*, I, 244-50; B. J. Lossing, *Life and Times of Philip Schuyler* (2d Edition. 2 vols. New York, 1872); Force, *Amer. Archives*, 4th ser., II, 1536, 1668, 1702, III, 242; French *First Year of the American Revolution*, 378-79.

4) Force, *Amer. Archives*, 4th ser., III, 1097; G. M. Wrong, *Canada and the American Revolution* (New York, 1935), 290; French, *First Year of the American Revolution*, 383-92.

5) See the excellent study by R. Coupland, *The Quebec Act* (Oxford, 1925), 91-107.

6) Force, *Amer. Archives*, 4th ser., III, 952; Fitzpatrick, *Writings of Washington*, IV, 46. See also Smith, *Fourteenth Colony*, I, 373, 394; French, *First Year of the American Revolution*, 422-24.

7) Force, *Amer. Archives*, 4th ser., III, 1133.

8) *Ibid.*, III, 1602.

9) C. Carroll, *Journal* (Maryland Historical Society, 1876), 97; Smith, *Fourteenth Colony*, I, 489, 614-15.

10) *Ibid.*, I, 614-15; Wrong, *Canada and the American Revolution*, 292.

11) Quoted in Smith, *Fourteenth Colony*, I, 490. See also Force, *Amer. Archives*, 4th ser., III, 1692; French, *First Year of the American Revolution*, 599.

12) Carleton's escape is well described in Smith, *Fourteenth Colony*, I, 490,

and in Wrong, *Canada and the American Revolution*, 292-93. See also Force, *Amer. Archives*, 4th ser., IV, 290.

13) I. N. Arnold, in his *Life of Benedict Arnold* (3d Edition. Chicago, 1897), 50-51, accepts the view that the invasion of Canada through Maine was Arnold's idea, as do Hughes, *George Washington*, II, 341, and Stephenson and Dunn, *Washington*, I, 341-42. Codman, in his *Arnold's Expedition to Quebec*, 20, implies a doubt that the project originated with Arnold, while Justin Smith, in his study, *Our Struggle for the Fourteenth Colony*, I, 498-99, 616, considers such evidence as exists to be in Washington's favor rather than Arnold's.

14) Fitzpatrick, *Writings of Washington*, III, 438.

15) Force, *Amer. Archives*, 4th ser., III, 442.

16) For estimates, see Codman, *Arnold's Expedition to Quebec*, 29; J. H. Smith, *Arnold's March from Cambridge to Quebec* (New York, 1903), 57; Historical Manuscripts Commission, *Stopford-Sackville MSS*, II, 15; French, *First Year of the American Revolution*, 432.

17) E. Squier, "Diary of Arnold's Expedition to Quebec," in K. Roberts, *March to Quebec* (New York, 1938), 619.

18) "Fobes' Narrative," in *ibid.*, 581.

19) Force, *Amer. Archives*, 4th ser., III, 960.

20) Smith, *Fourteenth Colony*, I, 525.

21) Smith, *Arnold's March to Quebec*, 80-81, 305; Codman, *Arnold's Expedition to Quebec*, 43-44.

CHAPTER VII

Death, Defeat, and Disaster in the North

1) Smith, *Arnold's March to Quebec*, 108.

2) "Col. Arnold's Journal of His Expedition to Canada," in Roberts, *March to Quebec*, 54.

3) Force, *Amer. Archives*, 4th ser., IV, 226.

4) For the Enos case, see Smith, *Fourteenth Colony*, I, 563-67; Smith, *Arnold's March to Quebec*, 161-63; Codman, *Arnold's Expedition to Quebec*, 79-87; French, *First Year of the American Revolution*, 438; Roberts, *March to Quebec*, 137, 210-13, 256-57, 516, 552, 624-28, 631-48.

5) "Dearborn's Journal," in *ibid.*, 137.

6) Particularly 7-Mile Stream, Rush Lake, and Spider Lake. The swamps at the mouth of 7-Mile Stream proved especially treacherous.

7) "Meig's Journal," in *ibid.*, 181.

8) Force, *Amer. Archives*, 4th ser., III, 1617. For a complete discussion of the enlistment situation, see Smith, *Fourteenth Colony*, II, 39-75.

9) *Ibid.*, II, 122-23.

10) Interesting accounts may be found in the journals in Roberts, *March to Quebec*; Arnold's letters of Dec. 31, 1775 and Jan. 2, 1776, in *ibid.*, 102-6; Arnold's letters of Jan. 6, 1776 and Jan. 14, 1776, in Force, *Amer. Archives*, 4th ser., IV, 589, 674; *Journals of the Continental Congress*, IV, 82-84; Smith, *Fourteenth Colony*, II, 111-47; Arnold, *Benedict Arnold,*

80-85; Codman, *Arnold's Expedition to Canada*, 212-49; French, *First Year of the American Revolution*, 614-20.

11) J. Graham, *Life of Daniel Morgan* (New York, 1856), 103.

12) For an analysis of the returns, see Smith, *Fourteenth Colony*, II, 581-82.

13) Carleton to Gage, May 31, 1775. *Gage Papers* (Clements Library).

14) Roberts, *March to Quebec*, 153-54, 192, 392, 486, 538, 566; French, *First Year of the American Revolution*, 627, 697.

15) Force, *Amer. Archives*, 4th ser., IV, 666; Fitzpatrick, *Writings of Washington*, IV, 255-56, 260; *Journals of the Continental Congress*, IV, 152, 156, 158, 159, 177. See also C. H. Jones, *History of the Campaign for the Conquest of Canada* (Philadelphia, 1882), 18-29, for the march of the 1st Pennsylvania Regiment to Quebec.

16) Force, *Amer. Archives*, 4th ser., VI, 451, 453, 454; French, *First Year of the American Revolution*, 694-95.

17) *Sullivan Papers* (3 vols. 1930-1939), *New Hampshire Historical Society Collections*, I, 237, 250-54.

CHAPTER VIII

The Awakening of the South

1) *Corr. of George III*, III, 266, 270-71; French, *First Year of the American Revolution*, 622; Fortescue, *History of the British Army*, III, 170; Van Tyne, *War of Independence*, 191.

2) H. J. Eckenrode, *The Revolution in Virginia* (Boston, 1916), 66.

3) *Ibid.*, 66-69; I. S. Harrell, *Loyalism in Virginia* (Durham, 1926), 38-42; Force, *Amer. Archives*, 4th ser., IV, 223-28.

4) *Ibid.*, 4th ser., IV, 981, 1488; W. L. Saunders, *The Colonial Records of North Carolina, 1662-1776* (10 vols. Raleigh, 1886-90), X, 441-45, 465-93.

5) *Ibid.*, X, 652-53.

6) See Clinton's letter of Jan. 11, 1776. *Clinton Papers* (Clements Library).

7) *Journals of the Continental Congress*, II, 107, 325, 463, IV, 15, 235; Burnett, *Letters of Congress*, I, 370; E. H. Tatum, *The American Journal of Ambrose Serle* (San Marino, 1940), 61.

8) W. Moultrie, *Memoirs of the American Revolution* (2 vols. New York, 1802), I, 140.

9) Parker to Clinton, June 23, 1776. *Clinton Papers* (Clements Library).

10) Clinton to Germain, July 8, 1776. *Ibid.*

11) See Clinton to Parker, June 26, 1776, July 12, 1776; Parker to Clinton, June 20, 1776, Dec. 21, 1776; Clinton to Germain, July 8, 1776; Parker to Stephens, Secretary of the Admiralty, July 9, 1776. *Ibid.*

12) *Lee Papers*, II, 100.

13) Parker to Stephens, July 9, 1776. *Clinton Papers* (Clements Library); *Lee Papers*, II, 111-13.

14) *Ibid.*, II, 93. See also J. Drayton, *Memoirs of the American Revolution* (2 vols. Charleston, 1821), II, 306.

15) *Lee Papers*, II, 93, 101.

16) Clinton to Germain, July 8, 1776. *Clinton Papers* (Clements Library).

17) Historical Manuscripts Commission, *Hastings MSS*, III, 176.
18) Germain to Clinton, August 24, 1776. *Clinton Papers* (Clements Library).

CHAPTER IX

The Gathering of the Armies before New York

1) *Journals of the Continental Congress*, IV, 180.
2) *Ibid.*, IV, 412. In the middle of May, he had 10,552 officers and men. Of this number only 7,952 were fit for duty as of May 12.
3) Force, *Amer. Archives*, 5th ser., I, 762, 766, 790, 886, 935; H. P. Johnston, *The Battle of Harlem Heights* (New York, 1897), 11-15; Fitzpatrick, *Writings of Washington*, V, 129, 134, 242 n., 372, 412, 452, 482, 493; E. M. Ruttenber, *Obstructions to the Navigation of Hudson's River* (Albany, 1860), 19 ff.; C. R. Harte, *The River Obstructions of the Revolutionary War* (Hartford, 1946), 6-15.
4) Treaties with Brunswick, Hesse, and Hanau may be found in Force, *Amer. Archives*, 4th ser., VI, 271-77.
5) The total number of Germans acquired as mercenaries amounted to 29,875. Only 17,317 returned to Germany at the end of the war, or about 58 per cent. Of the remainder, 1,200 were battle casualties, 6,354 perished in other ways, chiefly disease; and 5,000 deserted, many of them lured into the rich farming country of the Middle Colonies. For details, see E. J. Lowell, *The Hessians and the Other German Auxiliaries of Great Britain in the Revolutionary War* (New York, 1884), chaps. II, XXIV, and Appendix D.
6) Fitzpatrick, *Writings of Washington*, V, 219.
7) Harvey to Howe, June 30, 1775; Harvey to Smith, July 8, 1775. Fortescue, *History of the British Army*, III, 171.
8) Wertenbaker, *Father Knickerbocker Rebels*, 90.
9) Fitzpatrick, *Writings of Washington*, V, 213.
10) *Ibid.*, V, 214.
11) Lowell, *The Hessians in the Revolutionary War*, 56.
12) Greene, *The Revolutionary War*, 33.
13) Quoted in Wertenbaker, *Father Knickerbocker Rebels*, 88. See also Serle, *American Journal*, 62.
14) T. S. Anderson, *The Command of the Howe Brothers During the American Revolution* (New York, 1935), 51-60.
15) Reed, *Joseph Reed*, I, 197; Hughes, *George Washington*, II, 421-22.
16) Reed, *Joseph Reed*, I, 204; Serle, *American Journal*, 32-33.
17) Fitzpatrick, *Writings of Washington*, V, 274.
18) *Ibid.*, V, 321 n., 449; Doc. 230, *Carleton Papers* (Colonial Williamsburg); Reed, *Joseph Reed*, I, 205; *Pennsylvania Gazette*, July 31, 1776; Wertenbaker, *Father Knickerbocker Rebels*, 90-91; Stephenson and Dunn, *Washington*, I, 358; Anderson, *The Command of the Howe Brothers*, 154-56.
19) Serle, *American Journal*, 31, 33.
20) Fitzpatrick, *Writings of Washington*, V, 469.
21) Washington's force on August 7 was 17,225. By August 26, his total

strength in and around New York, including those unfit for duty, had been increased to approximately 27,000, the largest American force brought together under single command during the war.

CHAPTER X

Long Island: the Battle and the Retreat

1) Fortescue, *History of the British Army*, III, 184.
2) Lowell, *The Hessians in the Revolutionary War*, 61.
3) Fitzpatrick, *Writings of Washington*, V, 486-89.
4) Howe's estimate was 10,000; Cornwallis', 6,000-8,000, which was about right, though the exact number is a matter of speculation.
5) H. P. Johnston, *The Campaign of 1776 Around New York and Brooklyn* (*Memoirs of the Long Island Historical Society*, III. Brooklyn, 1878), 159, 176-78.
6) Fortescue, *History of the British Army*, III, 186.
7) Hughes, *George Washington*, II, 440; T. W. Field, *The Battle of Long Island* (*Memoirs of the Long Island Historical Society*, II. Brooklyn, 1869), 173.
8) Lowell, *The Hessians in the Revolutionary War*, 65; Field, *Battle of Long Island*, 187-93.
9) Fitzpatrick, *Writings of Washington*, V, 228-29, 234-35, 236-37, 240, 242, 249, 251-52, 260, 286, 295; Burnett, *Letters of Members of the Continental Congress*, I, 314, 443, 448. Charles Francis Adams has an interesting discussion of Washington's failure to appreciate the value of cavalry. Congress, however, had strongly urged him to pare expenses, and cavalry maintenance can be dear. On the other hand, forage at that time of year must have been plentiful, and these troops, though a ludicrous assortment in terms of training and disparity of age, could have been useful as patrols. Adams, *Studies Military and Diplomatic*, 50-113; A. Graydon, *Memoirs of a Life Chiefly Passed in Pennsylvania* (Harrisburg, 1811), 136; *Sullivan Papers*, I, 551-52, 575.
10) H. B. Carrington, *Battles of the American Revolution* (New York, 1876), 210; Field, *Battle of Long Island*, 202; Serle, *American Journal*, 78-79.
11) Adams, *Studies Military and Diplomatic*, 34.
12) According to Howe's report, the British and Hessians took 1,097 prisoners, of whom 91 were officers. Washington estimated 700 to 1,000 killed and captured. See Field, *Battle of Long Island*, 415-19; Johnston, *The Campaign of 1776*, 202-206; Moore, *Diary of the American Revolution*, I, 300-304; Force, *Amer. Archives*, 5th ser., I, 1256; Fitzpatrick, *Writings of Washington*, V, 507; *Kemble Papers*, I, 85-86.
13) W. C. Abbott, *New York in the American Revolution* (New York, 1929), 193.
14) Moore, *Diary of the American Revolution*, I, 302.
15) This was Clinton's opinion as stated in his comments on Stedman's *American War*, I, 196. Clinton's notes may be found in the Carter-Brown Library, Providence, R. I. On the other hand, Clinton admitted that, on

military grounds, Howe may have been correct. See Anderson, *The Command of the Howe Brothers,* 133-42.

16) Johnston, *The Campaign of 1776,* 218-19; Adams, *Studies Military and Diplomatic,* 42.

17) Johnston, *The Campaign of 1776.* Page 31 of "Original Documents."

18) Moore, *Diary of the American Revolution,* I, 297 n.

19) Graydon, *Memoirs of A Life,* 147-48.

20) Field, *Battle of Long Island,* 280-82. The account was given by Colonel Hand.

21) *Ibid.,* 276-78.

22) For an examination of the weather reports of various authorities and for his own interesting analysis, see Adams, *Studies Military and Diplomatic,* 46-47.

23) W. M. James, *The British Navy in Adversity* (London, 1926), 46-47. For a defense of Lord Howe, see Anderson, *The Command of the Howe Brothers,* 143-44.

24) Clinton to Harvey, Sept. 3 and 4, 1776. *Clinton Papers* (Clements Library).

CHAPTER XI

The Loss of New York and the Retreat across Jersey

1) Quoted in Wertenbaker, *Father Knickerbocker Rebels,* 94.

2) Fitzpatrick, *Writings of Washington,* VI, 5.

3) Quoted in Johnston, *The Campaign of 1776,* 233.

4) Fitzpatrick, *Writings of Washington,* VI, 58; Anderson, *The Command of the Howe Brothers,* 176-77.

5) J. Thacher, *Military Journal of the American Revolution* (Hartford, 1862), 58-59; Johnston, *The Campaign of 1776,* 238-40. But see Anderson, *The Command of the Howe Brothers,* 177-79.

6) Johnston, *Battle of Harlem Heights,* 135.

7) *Ibid.,* 56-91; Johnston, *The Campaign of 1776,* 246-62; Serle, *American Journal,* 107-108; *Diary of Frederick Mackenzie,* I, 51-52.

8) Serle, *American Journal,* 104.

9) Wertenbaker, *Father Knickerbocker Rebels,* 102; Doc. 9388, *Carleton Papers* (Colonial Williamsburg).

10) *The Narrative of Lieut. General Sir William Howe* (London, 1780), 6. See the criticism by his deputy adjutant general in *Kemble Papers,* I, 104-105.

11) Hughes, *George Washington,* II, 515.

12) Quoted in Wertenbaker, *Father Knickerbocker Rebels,* 111.

13) See Fortescue, *History of the British Army,* III, 191.

14) *Ibid.,* III, 191-92; Heads of Speech, April 2, 1779. *Germain Papers* (Clements Library). For an analysis of Howe's reasons, see Anderson, *The Command of the Howe Brothers,* 190-97.

15) Fitzpatrick, *Writings of Washington,* VI, 258.

16) *Journals of the Continental Congress,* VI, 866; Force, *Amer. Archives,* 5th ser., II, 1117, III, 619.

17) See Knollenberg, *Washington and the Revolution*, 129-39; Greene, *Nathanael Greene*, I, 273-75; Johnston, *The Campaign of 1776*, 281-86.

18) Fortescue, *History of the British Army*, III, 195; Lowell, *The Hessians in the Revolutionary War*, 82-83.

19) *Diary of Frederick Mackenzie*, I, 111.

20) Force, *Amer. Archives*, 5th ser., III, 1058, 1059.

21) Fitzpatrick, *Writings of Washington*, VI, 289-91; *Lee Papers*, II, 293-309 *passim*.

22) L. Lundin, *Cockpit of the Revolution* (Princeton, 1940), 143-46.

23) Fitzpatrick, *Writings of Washington*, VI, 347.

CHAPTER XII

The American Counterattack at Trenton and Princeton

1) A. T. Mahan, *The Major Operations of the Navies in the War of American Independence* (Boston, 1913), 3-26; Force, *Amer. Archives*, 4th ser., VI, 1107-8, 5th ser., I, 1186-87; C. O. Paullin, *The Navy of the American Revolution* (Cleveland, 1906), 75-78; Fonblanque, *Burgoyne*, 218-20. One of the most reliable accounts (and certainly the liveliest) of the battle in terms of chronology of events, background, and detail of action is to be found in the novel by Kenneth Roberts, *Rabble in Arms*.

2) *Lee Papers*, II, 348.

3) Howe to Germain, Nov. 30, 1776. *Germain Papers* (Clements Library); Lundin, *Cockpit of the Revolution*, 170-78.

4) See *ibid.*, 153-56; Anderson, *The Command of the Howe Brothers*, 183-84, 204-6, 208-9; Partridge, *Sir Billy Howe*, 101-2.

5) Howe to Germain, Dec. 20, 1776. *Germain Papers* (Clements Library).

6) Fitzpatrick, *Writings of Washington*, VI, 366.

7) W. S. Stryker, *The Battles of Trenton and Princeton* (Boston, 1898), 40.

8) Quoted in *ibid.*, 108.

9) Force, *Amer. Archives*, 5th ser., III, 1401. But see Stryker, *Trenton and Princeton*, 85-86.

10) *Ibid.*, 113; Fitzpatrick, *Writings of Washington*, VI, 438, n. 86.

11) *Ibid.*, VI, 443-44; Stryker, *Trenton and Princeton*, 194-96, 207-8, 427-28; Lowell, *The Hessians in the Revolutionary War*, 92-96.

12) *Ibid.*, 185.

13) *Ibid.*, 193.

14) Quoted in A. H. Bill, *The Campaign of Princeton, 1776-1777* (Princeton, 1948), 88.

15) *Ibid.*, 84-89; T. J. Wertenbaker, "The Battle of Princeton," in *The Princeton Battle Monument* (Princeton, 1922), 59-63; Stryker, *Trenton and Princeton*, 248, 256-65.

16) *Ibid.*, 270-73; Bill, *The Campaign of Princeton*, 90-93.

17) Fortescue, *History of the British Army*, III, 203.

18) Quoted in Bill, *The Campaign of Princeton*, 110.

19) *Ibid.*, 100-113; Wertenbaker, "The Battle of Princeton," in *The Princeton*

Battle Monument, 65-118; Stryker, *Trenton and Princeton,* 274-90; Lundin, *Cockpit of the Revolution,* 208-11.
20) Quoted in J. C. Miller, *Triumph of Freedom* (Boston, 1948), 160. For a British criticism of Howe's garrison policy, see *Kemble Papers,* I, 105.

CHAPTER XIII

Howe's Invasion of Pennsylvania

1) Burgoyne to Clinton, Nov. 7, 1776. *Clinton Papers* (Clements Library).
2) "Thoughts for conducting the War from the Side of Canada," Feb. 28, 1777. *Germain Papers* (Clements Library).
3) Howe to Germain, Nov. 30, 1776, Dec. 20, 1776, April 2, 1777; Germain to Howe, Jan. 14, 1777, March 3, 1777, May 18, 1777. *Ibid.; Howe's Narrative,* 9-13. For an analysis of the instructions to Howe which were never sent, see Anderson, *The Command of the Howe Brothers,* 255-57; G. H. Guttridge, "Lord George Germain in Office, 1775-1782," in *A.H.R.,* XXXIII (1928), 29.
4) Anderson, *The Command of the Howe Brothers,* 269-73.
5) Clinton's minutes of conversation with Howe, July 6, 8, 13, 1777. *Clinton Papers* (Clements Library).
6) Anderson, *The Command of the Howe Brothers,* 224-26; G. H. Moore, *The Treason of Charles Lee* (New York, 1860), 93 ff.
7) Fitzpatrick, *Writings of Washington,* VII, 288.
8) Serle, *American Journal,* 240.
9) For a more extensive criticism of Washington's policy, see Adams, *Studies Military and Diplomatic,* 132-49.
10) Germain to General Irwin, Aug. 23, 1777. Historical Manuscripts Commission, *Stopford-Sackville MSS,* I, 139.
11) Fitzpatrick, *Writings of Washington,* IX, 207; T. C. Amory, *The Military Services and Public Life of Major-General John Sullivan* (Boston, 1868), 43-53.
12) Fortescue, *History of the British Army,* III, 217; *Sullivan Papers,* I, 454-78.
13) Greene, *Nathanael Greene,* I, 449.
14) Howe's report, in H. B. Dawson, *Battles of the United States* (2 vols. New York, 1858), I, 278; Greene, *The Revolutionary War,* 87.
15) Howe's report, in Dawson, *Battles of the U. S.,* I, 317; Moore, *Diary of the American Revolution,* I, 498-99.
16) *Journals of the Continental Congress,* VIII, 752.
17) For Washington's arrangements, see Fitzpatrick, *Writings of Washington,* IX, 307-8; Hughes, *George Washington,* III, 185-90.
18) Quoted in Trevelyan, *The American Revolution,* IV, 242. See also Hughes, *George Washington,* III, 195-96.
19) Greene, *Nathanael Greene,* I, 475.
20) *Major André's Journal* (Tarrytown, 1930), 57.
21) B. J. Lossing, *The Pictorial Field-Book of the Revolution* (2 vols. New York, 1855), II, 111.
22) Fitzpatrick, *Writings of Washington,* IX, 310.

23) Quoted in Miller, *Triumph of Freedom*, 206.

24) *Kemble Papers*, I, 137; Dawson, *Battles of the U. S.*, I, 324; Fitzpatrick, *Writings of Washington*, IX, 398.

25) Knox to Ward, Oct. 7, 1777. N. Brooks, *Henry Knox* (New York, 1900), 110.

26) Fortescue, *History of the British Army*, III, 223.

27) Adams, *Studies Military and Diplomatic*, 157.

28) *Ibid.*, 158.

29) Harte, *The River Obstructions of the Revolutionary War*, 6.

30) Fitzpatrick, *Writings of Washington*, X, 149; *André's Journal*, 70; Anderson, *The Command of the Howe Brothers*, 298-99; B. A. Uhlendorf and E. Vosper, *Letters from Major Bauermeister to Colonel von Jungkenn Written during the Philadelphia Campaign, 1777-1778* (Philadelphia, 1937), 35-39.

CHAPTER XIV

Burgoyne's Invasion of the North

1) Germain to Carleton, March 26, 1777. Historical Manuscripts Commission, *Stopford-Sackville MSS*, II, 60-63; George III to North, Dec. 13, 1776. Fonblanque, *Burgoyne*, 225.

2) *Journals of the Continental Congress*, V, 448, 526.

3) *Ibid.*, VII, 180-81; Knollenberg, *Washington and the Revolution*, 12-15.

4) *Journals of the Continental Congress*, VII, 202, 336, 364, VIII, 375, 540.

5) W. L. Stone, *The Campaign of Lieut. Gen. John Burgoyne* (Albany, 1877), 16; H. Nickerson, *The Turning Point of the Revolution* (Boston, 1928), 131-32.

6) Quoted in Stone, *Burgoyne's Campaign*, 17 n.

7) *Ibid.*, 24-27; J. Burgoyne, *State of the Expedition from Canada* (London, 1780), App. XXX; W. L. Stone, *Memoirs of Major General Riedesel* (2 vols. Albany, 1868), I, 117-18; Nickerson, *The Turning Point of the Revolution*, 155-57.

8) *Ibid.*, 148-53; Stone, *Riedesel's Memoirs*, I, 114-16; Burgoyne, *State of the Expedition*, App. XXX, XXXIII; Gordon, *History of the Independence of the United States*, II, 484; Fortescue, *History of the British Army*, III, 226-27.

9) Knollenberg, *Washington and the Revolution*, 15-17.

10) *Ibid.*, 16; Van Tyne, *War of Independence*, 391-92.

11) *Journals of the Continental Congress*, VIII, 603-4.

12) Nickerson, *The Turning Point of the Revolution*, 168; Fonblanque, *Burgoyne*, 269.

13) Nickerson, *The Turning Point of the Revolution*, 163-65.

14) *Ibid.*, 188; Burgoyne, *State of the Expedition*, 16-19; Fonblanque, *Burgoyne*, 268-69.

15) For able discussions of the case, see Stone, *Burgoyne's Campaign*, 302-13; Nickerson, *The Turning Point of the Revolution*, 183-86, App. X.

16) Davidson, *Propaganda and the American Revolution*, 371-72.

17) Greene, *The Revolutionary War*, 112.
18) Stone, *Riedesel's Memoirs*, I, 127, 130.
19) Nickerson, *The Turning Point of the Revolution*, 243.
20) *Ibid.*, 246, 260; Stone, *Riedesel's Memoirs*, I, 130; Fortescue, *History of the British Army*, III, 230.
21) *Ibid.*, III, 231; Stone, *Riedesel's Memoirs*, I, 132; Burgoyne, *State of the Expedition*, App. XLIII; Nickerson, *The Turning Point of the Revolution*, 262.

CHAPTER XV

The Failure of Burgoyne's Campaign

1) Greene, *The Revolutionary War*, 106-7; Arnold, *Benedict Arnold*, 149-52; Lossing, *Pictorial Field-Book of the Revolution*, I, 243-47; Nickerson, *The Turning Point of the Revolution*, 201-11.
2) Arnold, *Benedict Arnold*, 152-62; Lossing, *Pictorial Field-Book of the Revolution*, I, 243-52; Stone, *Burgoyne's Campaign*, 210-19; Burgoyne, *State of the Expedition*, App. XLVI; Nickerson, *The Turning Point of the Revolution*, 273-75.
3) Fonblanque, *Burgoyne*, 274-77.
4) K. Roberts, *I Wanted to Write* (New York, 1949), 414-16.
5) Greene, *The Revolutionary War*, 115-16; Arnold, *Benedict Arnold*, 166-67, 169.
6) *Ibid.*, 171.
7) The best secondary account of the battle may be found in Nickerson, *The Turning Point of the Revolution*, 304-19. See also Burgoyne, *State of the Expedition*, App. XIV; Stone, *Riedesel's Memoirs*, I, 144-50; Arnold, *Benedict Arnold*, 170-90.
8) Written on September 10, this letter must be read with the hourglass mask to ascertain its true meaning. *Clinton Papers* (Clements Library).
9) Burgoyne to Clinton, Sept. 27, 1777. *Ibid.*
10) Clinton to Burgoyne, Oct. 8, 1777. *Ibid.*
11) Phillips to Clinton, Oct. 25, 1777. *Ibid.*
12) Arnold, *Benedict Arnold*, 194-95; J. Wilkinson, *Memoirs of My Own Times* (3 vols. Philadelphia, 1816), I, 254-60.
13) Lossing, *Pictorial Field-Book of the Revolution*, I, 61-62; Stone, *Burgoyne's Campaign*, 61-62, 249-50; Arnold, *Benedict Arnold*, 200-1.
14) *Ibid.*, 196-209; Nickerson, *The Turning Point of the Revolution*, 356-68; Fortescue, *History of the British Army*, III, 239-40; Burgoyne, *State of the Expedition*, App. XC-XCII; Stone, *Riedesel's Memoirs*, I, 198-99.
15) Burgoyne to Clinton, Oct. 25, 1777. *Clinton Papers* (Clements Library).
16) Report of Oct. 12, 1777. *Gates Letters*, II. Force Transcripts (Library of Congress).
17) Wilkinson, *Memoirs*, I, 269-70.
18) See Minutes of the Councils, Oct. 12, 13, 14, 15. *Clinton Papers* (Clements Library); Stone, *Riedesel's Memoirs*, I, 175-84; Stedman, *The American War*, I, 385-92.

19) For numbers of troops and losses, see Returns in *Clinton Papers* (Clements Library); Wilkinson's returns in *Gates Letters*, II. Force Transcripts (Library of Congress); Nickerson, *The Turning Point of the Revolution*, App. II. For the "Convention," see Stone, *Riedesel's Memoirs*, I, 184-86; J. Winsor, *Narrative and Critical History of America* (8 vols. Boston, 1884-89), VI, 317-18.

20) Howe to Burgoyne, Nov. 16, 1777. *Clinton Papers* (Clements Library); J. Clark, "The Convention Troops and the Perfidy of Sir William Howe," in *A.H.R.*, XXXVII (1932), 721-23; Knollenberg, *Washington and the Revolution*, 140-50.

CHAPTER XVI

Valley Forge and the New American Army

1) On this paragraph, see Miller, *Triumph of Liberty*, 222-23.

2) Fitzpatrick, *Writings of Washington*, XI, 117.

3) Bolton, *The Private Soldier under Washington*, 87; Greene, *Nathanael Greene*, I, 554. For the food situation in detail, see Johnson, *The Administration of the American Commissariat*, 77-108.

4) Fitzpatrick, *Writings of Washington*, X, 195.

5) *Ibid.*, X, 196.

6) Quoted in Trevelyan, *The American Revolution*, IV, 296.

7) Quoted in C. Tower, *The Marquis de La Fayette in the American Revolution* (2 vols. Philadelphia, 1895), I, 255.

8) Quoted in Miller, *Triumph of Freedom*, 224.

9) Burnett, *The Continental Congress*, 274; *Journals of the Continental Congress*, VII, 355-59, VIII, 433-48.

10) *Ibid.*, VII, 266-67, VIII, 477, 598, 607-10, 751-52, IX, 1013-15, X, 248-52, 327-28; Hatch, *Administration of the Amer. Rev. Army*, 89-98 *passim*; Fitzpatrick, *Writings of Washington*, X, 159-60, 183-84, 192-94, 267-68, XII, 277; Johnson, *The Administration of the American Commissariat*, 108-10.

11) Greene, *Nathanael Greene*, I, 543.

12) *Ibid.*, II, 47.

13) *Journals of the Continental Congress*, X, 210.

14) Fitzpatrick, *Writings of Washington*, XIII, 352.

15) *Journals of the Continental Congress*, X, 200.

16) *Ibid.*, XI, 502; Bolton, *The Private Soldier under Washington*, 59.

17) Burnett, *The Continental Congress*, 299.

18) In the extensive literature on the Conway Cabal two works are outstanding for their fairness and clarity: Burnett, *The Continental Congress*, 279-97, and Knollenberg, *Washington and the Revolution*, 37-92. The latter is especially valuable for its consideration of the many authorities and points of view. See also L. Gottschalk, *Lafayette Joins the American Army* (Chicago, 1937), 60-166 *passim*.

19) For Washington's full opinion, see Fitzpatrick, *Writings of Washington*, IX, 387-88.

20) *Ibid.*, IX, 441-42.

21) *Journals of the Continental Congress*, IX, 818, 874, 971.

22) Sparks, *Writings of Washington*, V, 511.

23) Fitzpatrick, *Writings of Washington*, X, 29.

24) *Journals of the Continental Congress*, IX, 1023-26.

25) *Ibid.*, X, 84-85, 87.

26) Burnett, *The Continental Congress*, 294; Gottschalk, *Lafayette Joins the American Army*, 152-65.

27) Quoted in Burnett, *The Continental Congress*, 297.

28) J. M. Palmer, *General von Steuben* (New Haven, 1937), 137.

29) *Ibid.*, 140-41.

30) Quoted in *ibid.*, 148. See also F. Kapp, *Life of Frederick William von Steuben* (New York, 1859), 615.

31) *Journals of the Continental Congress*, XI, 465; Greene, *The Revolutionary War*, 137.

CHAPTER XVII

The British Withdrawal to New York

1) J. B. Perkins, *France in the American Revolution* (Boston, 1911), 232; Van Tyne, *War of Independence*, 491; C. H. Van Tyne, "French Aid Before the Alliance of 1778," in *A.H.R.*, XXXI (1926), 37-40.

2) Howe to Germain, Oct. 22, 1777. Historical Manuscripts Commission, *Stopford-Sackville MSS*, II, 80.

3) Quoted in Partridge, *Sir Billy Howe*, 215.

4) Fitzpatrick, *Writings of Washington*, XI, 419.

5) See Gottschalk, *Lafayette Joins the American Army*, 186-93; *Baurmeister's Letters*, 63.

6) See Fortescue, *History of the British Army*, III, 252.

7) Lowell, *The Hessians in the Revolutionary War*, 212-13.

8) Clinton to Germain, July 5, 1778. *Clinton Papers* (Clements Library).

9) *André's Journal*, 78; W. S. Stryker, *The Battle of Monmouth* (Princeton, 1927), 55-56.

10) *Lee Papers*, II, 468; Stryker, *Battle of Monmouth*, 75-78; Gottschalk, *Lafayette Joins the American Army*, 207-10.

11) *Ibid.*, 210-11.

12) *Ibid.*, 216-17; Fitzpatrick, *Writings of Washington*, XIII, 120.

13) Stryker, *Battle of Monmouth*, 94-96.

14) *Lee Papers*, II, 440.

15) *Ibid.*, III, 180; Fitzpatrick, *Writings of Washington*, XII, 142.

16) *Lee Papers*, III, 180; *André's Journal*, 79.

17) *Lee Papers*, III, 182.

18) *Ibid.*, III, 183-84; Stryker, *Battle of Monmouth*, 150-62.

19) Clinton to Germain, July 5, 1778. *Clinton Papers* (Clements Library). The clearest secondary account of the action up to this point is in Gottschalk, *Lafayette Joins the American Army*, 218-26.

20) Stryker, *Battle of Monmouth*, 134, 141-42.

21) *Lee Papers*, II, 435, III, 191.

22) *Ibid.*, III, 192.

23) *Ibid.*, III, 189-90; Stephenson and Dunn, *Washington*, II, 90; Lossing, *Pictorial Field-Book of the Revolution*, II, 153-54.

24) *Ibid.*, II, 156; Stryker, *Battle of Monmouth*, 214-18; Hughes, *George Washington*, III, 375-76.

25) Clinton to Germain, July 5, 1778. *Clinton Papers* (Clements Library).

26) *Ibid.; André's Journal*, 81; Fitzpatrick, *Writings of Washington*, XII, 144; Stryker, *Battle of Monmouth*, 227-28.

27) *Ibid.*, 258-62, 288-95; Fortescue, *History of the British Army*, III, 256; Fitzpatrick, *Writings of Washington*, XII, 129.

28) *Ibid.*, XII, 130; Bowman, *Morale of the American Revolutionary Army*, 102; *Journals of the Continental Congress*, XI, 672-73.

29) *Lee Papers*, II, 435-38, III, 208.

30) Stryker, *Battle of Monmouth*, 246.

31) *Ibid.*, 246; O. L. Spaulding, *The United States Army in War and Peace* (New York, 1937), 90; H. Lee, *Memoirs of the War in the Southern Department* (Philadelphia, 1812), 38; Gottschalk, *Lafayette Joins the American Army*, 230; Hughes, *George Washington*, III, 382-401.

32) Fitzpatrick, *Writings of Washington*, XII, 145.

33) *Ibid.*, XII, 343.

CHAPTER XVIII

The Expansion of the War

1) Lord Howe to Clinton, July 1, 1778. *Clinton Papers* (Clements Library).

2) A. T. Mahan, *The Influence of Sea Power Upon History, 1660-1783* (Boston, 1897), 360-61.

3) Fitzpatrick, *Writings of Washington*, XII, 174, 184-85, 201-3, 211, 237-38; Pigot to Clinton, July 20, 1778. *Clinton Papers* (Clements Library).

4) Clinton to Germain, July 27, 1778; Lord Howe to Clinton, July 28, 1778. *Ibid.*

5) Amory, *John Sullivan*, 77; Greene, *Nathanael Greene*, II, 127; *Sullivan Papers*, II, 237-38, 240-46, 266-67, III, 644-45; Gottschalk, *Lafayette Joins the American Army*, 250-56.

6) *Ibid.*, 256; *Sullivan Papers*, II, 273-76; Pigot to Clinton, Aug. 31, 1778; British Return, Aug. 29, 1778. *Clinton Papers* (Clements Library).

7) *Journals of the Continental Congress*, XII, 1042-48, 1052-53; Fitzpatrick, *Writings of Washington*, XIII, 256.

8) Germain to Clinton, Jan. 23, 1779. H. P. Johnston, *The Storming of Stony Point* (New York, 1900), 28-29.

9) Clinton to Germain, May 14, 1779. *Ibid.*, 31.

10) Clinton to Haldimand, Sept. 9, 1779. *Ibid.*, 143.

11) Fitzpatrick, *Writings of Washington*, XV, 283; J. W. Wright, "The Corps of Light Infantry in the Continental Army," in *A.H.R.*, XXXI (1926), 455.

12) Johnston, *The Storming of Stony Point*, 70, 73-74.

13) *Ibid.,* 78; H. B. Dawson, *The Assault on Stony Point* (Morrisania, N. Y., 1863), 47-48.

14) *Ibid.,* 50-51.

15) Johnson to Clinton, July 24, 1779; Clinton to Germain, July 25, 1779. *Clinton Papers* (Clements Library); Johnston, *The Storming of Stony Point,* 87.

16) Clinton to Haldimand, Sept. 9, 1779. *Ibid.,* 143-44.

17) Clinton to Germain, Aug. 21, 1779. *Clinton Papers* (Clements Library).

18) Fortescue, *History of the British Army,* III, 288; Fitzpatrick, *Writings of Washington,* XVI, 268; Lossing, *Pictorial Field-Book of the Revolution,* I, 594; Thacher, *Military Journal,* 173-74; Greene, *The Revolutionary War,* 161-62; McLean to Clinton, Aug. 23, 1779, and Collier to Clinton, Aug. 24, 1779. Docs. 2214 and 2218, *Carleton Papers* (Colonial Williamsburg).

19) C. Miner, *History of Wyoming* (Philadelphia, 1845), 225-28.

20) Fitzpatrick, *Writings of Washington,* XV, 189-93.

21) Amory, *John Sullivan,* 121-24; A. H. Wright, *The Sullivan Expedition of 1779* (Ithaca, 1943), Part III, 1-2.

22) Amory, *John Sullivan,* 138; *Sullivan Papers,* III, 123-37.

23) See Brodhead's report in Wright, *Sullivan's Expedition,* Part II, 16-18.

24) J. A. James, *George Rogers Clark Papers, 1771-1781, Collections of the Illinois State Historical Library,* VIII (Springfield, 1912), xxxvii, 338. For a favorable estimate of Hamilton, see N. V. Russell, "The Indian Policy of Henry Hamilton, a Revaluation," in *Canadian Historical Review,* XI (1930). For Germain's encouraging the use of Indians in the war, see Historical Manuscripts Commission, *Stopford-Sackville MSS,* II, 40, 60, 62, 223.

25) James, *Clark Papers,* lvii, 218; C. W. Alvord, *Kaskaskia Records, 1778-1790, Collections of Illinois State Historical Library,* V (Springfield, 1909), xvi-xxv.

26) T. Bodley, *George Rogers Clark* (Boston, 1926), 44.

27) James, *Clark Papers,* lxx.

28) See Clark's "Memoir" in *ibid.,* 288.

29) R. A. Billington, *Westward Expansion* (New York, 1949), 185-91.

30) *Annual Report of the American Historical Association for 1945,* II, Part I, 406-7, 411-12.

CHAPTER XIX

The British Offensive in the South

1) Germain to Clinton, March 8, 1778. Historical Manuscripts Commission, *Stopford-Sackville MSS,* II, 94-99.

2) Stedman, *The American War,* II, 71.

3) *Journals of the Continental Congress,* XII, 950-51, 1021.

4) Fortescue, *History of the British Army,* III, 281.

5) Stedman, *The American War,* II, 112-15.

6) *Ibid.*, II, 115-19; Lowell; *The Hessians in The Revolutionary War,* 241; Lee, *Memoirs of the War,* 130-31.

7) Prevost to Clinton, July 14, 1779. *Clinton Papers* (Clements Library).

8) James, *The British Navy in Adversity,* 160.

9) The correspondence between Estiang and Prevost is published in C. C. Jones, *The History of Georgia* (2 vols. Boston, 1883), II, 379-83.

10) Stedman, *The American War,* II, 125-33; Gordon, *History of the Independence of the United States,* III, 328-32; Lee, *Memoirs of the War,* 55-60.

11) Quoted in C. L. Lewis, *Admiral De Grasse And American Independence* Annapolis, 1945), 80-81.

12) Quoted in Fortescue, *History of the British Army,* III, 286.

13) Clinton to Prescott, Oct. 7, 1779; Clinton to Germain, Oct. 9, 26, 1779. *Clinton Papers* (Clements Library); Rodney to Germain, Dec. 12, 1780. Historical Manuscripts Commission, *Stopford-Sackville MSS,* II, 193.

14) For the attack on Moultrie, see Arbuthnot to Germain, May 15, 1780, in *ibid.*, II, 162-65. For the Clinton-Lincoln correspondence and Articles of Capitulation, see *Clinton Papers* (Clements Library). Lieutenant Colonel Banastre Tarleton, *History of the Campaigns of 1780 and 1781 in the Southern Provinces of North America* (London, 1787), 1-84 *passim,* gives the best British account of the siege; the best contemporary American account is found in Moultrie, *Memoirs,* II, 65-106. See also Stedman, *The American War,* II, 176-95.

15) Moultrie, *Memoirs,* II, 97. See the excellent discussion in Greene, *The Revolutionary War,* 211-12.

16) Return of Casualties at Waxhaw Creek, May 29, 1780. *Clinton Papers* (Clements Library); Tarleton, *The Campaigns of 1780 and 1781,* 30-31; Stedman, *The American War,* II, 193.

17) C. Ross, *Correspondence of Charles, First Marquis Cornwallis* (3 vols., London, 1859), I, 46-48.

18) *Ibid.*, I, 54.

19) *Ibid.*, I, 53.

20) F. Kapp, *Life of John Kalb* (New York, 1884), 206-9.

21) Cornwallis to Germain, Aug. 21, 1780. Historical Manuscripts Commission, *Stopford-Sackville MSS,* II, 179.

22) For Camden, see *ibid.*, II, 178-81; Return (of casualties), Aug. 16, 1780. *Clinton Papers* (Clements Library); Gates to Congress, Aug. 20, 1780. *Papers of the Continental Congress,* No. 154, II, 234-37 (Library of Congress); Tarleton, *The Campaigns of 1780 and 1781,* 104-10; Stedman, *The American War,* II, 204-18; Kapp, *Kalb,* 220-38; Fortescue, *History of the British Army,* III, 323-25; Greene, *Nathanael Greene,* II, 216-19; O. Williams' account in W. Johnson, *Nathanael Greene* (2 vols. Charleston, 1822), I, Appendix B; Knollenberg, *Washington and the Revolution,* 10-11, 169-71.

23) Tarleton, *The Campaigns of 1780 and 1781,* 110-16; Cornwallis to Germain, Aug. 21, 1780. Historical Manuscripts Commission, *Stopford-Sackville MSS,* II, 181-82.

24) *Ibid.*, II, 182.

CHAPTER XX

The Critical Year, 1780-1781

1) Fitzpatrick *Writings of Washington,* XVII, 273-74.
2) Lundin, *Cockpit of the Revolution,* 420; Thacher, *Military Journal,* 181, 184-86; Johnson, *Administration of the American Commissariat,* 159-61.
3) C. Van Doren, *Mutiny in January* (New York, 1943), 22-23; Thacher, *Military Journal,* 197-98.
4) Lundin, *Cockpit of the Revolution,* 428-29; Stedman, *The American War,* II, 240-41; Greene, *Nathanael Greene,* II, 190-94.
5) *Ibid.,* II, 200.
6) Clinton to Germain, July 4, 1780. *Clinton Papers* (Clements Library); Van Doren, *Mutiny in January,* 25-26.
7) L. Gottschalk, *Lafayette and the Close of the American Revolution* (Chicago, 1942), 33-38; Tower, *La Fayette in the American Revolution,* II, 487-99.
8) Perkins, *France in the American Revolution,* 289-90.
9) Tower, *La Fayette in the American Revolution,* 499-504.
10) For instructions, see H. Doniol, *Histoire de la participation de la France à l'établissement des Etats-Unis d'Amérique* (5 vols. Paris, 1886-92), IV, 314-20.
11) James, *The British Navy in Adversity,* 233-34.
12) C. Van Doren, *Secret History of the American Revolution* (New York, 1941), 145.
13) Arnold, *Benedict Arnold,* 230.
14) *Ibid.,* 232.
15) Fitzpatrick, *Writings of Washington,* XVIII, 225.
16) Van Doren, *Secret History,* 159. For a possible religious motive, Arnold's New England Protestant conscience indignant at the alliance with Catholic France, see Hughes, *George Washington,* III, 538-39.
17) *Ibid.,* III, 539, 554-56; Van Doren, *Secret History,* 200-2.
18) Clinton to Germain, Oct. 12, 1780. *Clinton Papers* (Clements Library).
19) Van Doren, *Secret History,* 384-88; Arnold, *Benedict Arnold,* 363, 389.
20) See *ibid.,* 395.
21) Greene, *Nathanael Greene,* II, 300; Hatch, *Administration of the Amer. Rev. Army,* 106-7.
22) Greene, *Nathanael Greene,* II, 314-16; *Journals of the Continental Congress,* XVII, 615-35, 690-91, 697.
23) *Ibid.,* XIX, 126-28, 176-78, XX, 597-98, 663-67; Hatch, *Administration of the Amer. Rev. Army,* 113; Johnson, *The Administration of the American Commissariat,* 191-206.
24) E. Upton, *Military Policy of the United States* (Washington, D. C., 1904), 51.
25) Van Doren, *Mutiny in January,* 34-35.
26) *Ibid.,* 232.
27) Fitzpatrick, *Writings of Washington,* XXI, 136.
28) Thacher, *Military Journal,* 251-53; Van Doren, *Mutiny in January,* 220-24.

29) *Ibid.*, 237. For Lafayette's views as a soldier and a humanitarian, see Gottschalk, *Lafayette and the Close of the American Revolution*, 171-72, 174.
30) *Journals of the Continental Congress*, XVIII, 893-97.
31) Upton, *Military Policy of the U. S.*, 57.
32) Fitzpatrick, *Writings of Washington*, XIX, 407-11, XX, 137-38.
33) *Ibid.*, XXI, 439.

CHAPTER XXI

American Retaliation in the South

1) *Cornwallis Corr.*, I, 316.
2) For the battle, see L. C. Draper, *King's Mountain and Its Heroes* (Cincinnati, 1881), 236-328; W. de Peyster, "The Affair at King's Mountain," in *Magazine of American History*, V, 401-23; Billington, *Westward Expansion*, 188-89.
3) James, *The British Navy in Adversity*, 269-75; Fortescue, *History of the British Army*, III, 359-61.
4) Greene, *Nathanael Greene*, III, 131.
5) *Ibid.*, III, 137; Tarleton, *The Campaigns of 1780 and 1781*, 211-13, 218-20; *Cornwallis Corr.*, I, 82-83.
6) *Ibid.*, I, 76-77; Greene, *Nathanael Greene*, III, 134-35.
7) Quoted in Graham, *Daniel Morgan*, 316.
8) *Cornwallis Corr.*, I, 83.
9) For the battle, see *ibid.*, I, 82-83; Tarleton, *The Campaigns of 1780 and 1781*, 214-18, 220-22; Graham, *Daniel Morgan*, 289-312; Greene, *Nathanael Greene*, III, 144-47.
10) *Ibid.*, III, 155-57; Cornwallis to Rawdon, Feb. 4, 1781. *Clinton Papers* (Clements Library).
11) Johnson, *Administration of the American Commissariat*, 187-88; S. G. Fisher, *The Struggle for American Independence* (2 vols. Philadelphia, 1908), II, 375, 412, 445.
12) *Cornwallis Corr.*, I, 85.
13) Tarleton, *The Campaigns of 1780 and 1781*, 229.
14) Fortescue, *History of the British Army*, III, 374 n.; Field Return, March 15, 1781. *Clinton Papers* (Clements Library); Gordon, *History of the Independence of the United States*, IV, 54; Greene, *Nathanael Greene*, III, 190.
15) Greene to Lee, March 14, 1781. Photostat. *Greene Papers* (Clements Library).
16) Greene, *Nathanael Greene*, III, 196.
17) Greene to Jefferson, March 16, 1781. *Greene Papers* (Clements Library); Greene, *Nathanael Greene*, III, 189-202; Tarleton, *The Campaigns of 1780 and 1781*, 269-79, 303-12; Lee, *Memoirs of the War*, 170-80.
18) Greene to Sumter, March 18, 1781; Greene to John Mathews, March 16, 1781. *Greene Papers* (Clements Library).
19) Greene, *Nathanael Greene*, III, 246.

20) *Ibid.*, III, 242-52; Fortescue, *History of the British Army*, III, 385-87; Stedman, *The American War*, II, 356-62.
21) Greene, *Nathanael Greene*, III, 302.
22) *Ibid.*, III, 301-17; Fortescue, *History of the British Army*, III, 387-89; Stedman, *The American War*, II, 364-73; Tarleton, *The Campaigns of 1780 and 1781*, 479-503 *passim;* Dawson, *Battles of the U. S.*, I, 692-97. For an unusually vivid account based on fact, see the novel by Kenneth Roberts, *Oliver Wiswell.*
23) Doc. 3882, *Carleton Papers* (Colonial Williamsburg). For the battle, see Stedman, *The American War,* II, 377-81; Gordon, *History of the Independence of the United States*, IV, 168-71; Tarleton, *The Campaigns of 1780 and 1781*, 508-18; Greene, *Nathanael Greene*, III, 391-405; Greene, *The Revolutionary War*, 254-57; Fortescue, *History of the British Army*, III, 389-92.

CHAPTER XXII

The Yorktown Campaign

1) Clinton to Eden (probably), May 30, 1780; Clinton to Cornwallis, June 8, 1780; Clinton to Germain, July 4 and Aug. 25, 1780. *Clinton Papers* (Clements Library); B. F. Stevens, *The Clinton-Cornwallis Controversy* (2 vols. London, 1888), I, 213-14, 399, 433-35. See the analysis by W. B. Willcox, "The British Road to Yorktown," in *A.H.R.*, LII (1946), 5-7.
2) *Ibid.,* LII, 10-12; Stevens, *C.-C. Controversy,* I, 347-50, 356, 395-99, 410-13, 424; *Cornwallis Corr.*, I, 88-89; Clinton's comment on Cornwallis' letter of April 10, 1781. *Clinton Papers* (Clements Library); Fortescue, *History of the British Army*, III, 382-84.
3) *Narrative of . . . Sir Henry Clinton Relative to His Conduct . . . in North America* (London, 1783. Reprinted in Philadelphia, 1865), 28.
4) Clinton to Germain, May 13, 1781. *Clinton Papers* (Clements Library); Stevens, *C.-C. Controversy*, I, 395-99, 424-25, 441-45, 476-77, II, 110-12.
5) *Ibid.*, I, 488; Tarleton, *The Campaigns of 1780 and 1781*, 294-302; Gottschalk, *Lafayette and the Close of the American Revolution*, 238-59.
6) Clinton to Cornwallis, June 8, 1781. *Clinton Papers* (Clements Library).
7) See R. G. Adams, "A View of Cornwallis's Surrender at Yorktown," in *A.H.R.*, XXXVII (1931-32), 26-28.
8) Willcox, "The British Road to Yorktown," in *A.H.R.*, LII, 19; Stevens, *C.-C. Controversy*, I, 467, II, 19-78; Clinton, *Narrative*, 6-11; Fortescue, *History of the British Army*, III, 396-97.
9) A. H. Miles, "Sea Power and the Yorktown Campaign," in *United States Naval Institute Proceedings*, LIII (1927), 1173.
10) Quoted in S. Bonsal, *When the French Were Here* (New York, 1945), 99.
11) Quoted in Perkins, *France in the American Revolution*, 362.
12) *Mackenzie Diary*, II, 610. See also W. B. Willcox, "Rhode Island in British Strategy, 1780-1781," in *Journal of Modern History*, XVII (1945), 324-30.
13) For this paragraph, see Willcox, "The British Road to Yorktown," in *A.H.R.*, LII, 23-24; Adams, "A View of Cornwallis's Surrender," in *ibid.*, XXXVII, 36-43; James, *The British Navy in Adversity*, 282-88.

14) Quoted in Bonsal, *When the French Were Here.* See also Hughes, *George Washington,* III, 649.
15) *Cornwallis Corr.,* I, 127. Tarleton contended that Cornwallis should have broken out of Yorktown when only Lafayette and Saint-Simon were in front of him. See Tarleton, *The Campaigns of 1780 and 1781,* 368-70.
16) *Cornwallis Corr.,* I, 127; H. P. Johnston, *The Yorktown Campaign and the Surrender of Cornwallis, 1781* (New York, 1881), 106-8, 120-21; Fitzpatrick, *Writings of Washington,* XXIII, 158. See also J. W. Wright, "Notes on the Siege of Yorktown in 1781 with Special Reference to the Conduct of A Siege in the Eighteenth Century," in *William and Mary Quarterly,* XII (1932), 228-49.
17) Johnston, *The Yorktown Campaign,* 138; Thacher, *Military Journal,* 283.
18) *Cornwallis Corr.,* I, 128.
19) *Ibid.,* I, 129; Johnston, *The Yorktown Campaign,* 151; Thacher, *Military Journal,* 286.
20) Stevens, *C.-C. Controversy,* II, 158.
21) Minutes, in *Clinton Papers* (Clements Library). See also Stevens, *C.-C. Controversy,* II, 160.
22) Minutes for Sept. 26, 1781. *Clinton Papers* (Clements Library).
23) Minutes for Sept. 28, 1781. *Ibid.*
24) Graves to Clinton, Sept. 28, 1781; Minutes of Council, Sept. 29, 1781. *Ibid.*; Stevens, *C.-C. Controversy,* II, 172.
25) Clinton to Newcastle, Oct. 3-16, 1781. *Clinton Papers* (Clements Library).
26) Stevens, *C.-C. Controversy,* II, 199-203; Johnston, *The Yorktown Campaign,* 155-57, 187-89; Hughes, *George Washington,* III, 674-79.
27) *Docs.* 3943, 4003, 4061. *Carleton Papers* (Colonial Williamsburg).
28) Johnston, *The Yorktown Campaign,* 164-65, 168-69, 195; Return of Casualties by Despard, Sept. 28 to Oct. 19, 1781. *Clinton Papers* (Clements Library); Lewis, *De Grasse,* 189.
29) For returns of ammunition, food, and stores, see Tarleton, *The Campaigns of 1780 and 1781,* 451-57.
30) *Orderly Book of Lord Cornwallis.* Entry for Oct. 19, 1781 (Colonial Williamsburg). See also *Cornwallis Corr.,* I, 129-30. Tarleton's criticism of Cornwallis in the entire Yorktown campaign is singularly penetrating. See Tarleton, *The Campaigns of 1780 and 1781,* 392-93.
31) Johnston, *The Yorktown Campaign,* 178.
32) Moore, *Diary of the American Revolution,* II, 518; Hughes, *George Washington,* III, 680.

CHAPTER XXIII

The End of the War

1) S. F. Bemis, *A Diplomatic History of the United States* (New York, 1936), 60; Billington, *Westward Expansion,* 191.
2) Doc. 4650. *Carleton Papers* (Colonial Williamsburg).
3) Docs. 4088, 5104. *Ibid.*
4) Doc. 5071. *Ibid.*
5) See the delightful pages in Bonsal, *When the French Were Here,* 217-34.

6) For the officers' troubles, see Hatch, *Administration of the Amer. Rev. Army*, 142-78; Burnett, *The Continental Congress*, 551-74, Upton, *Military Policy of the U. S.*, 36-43, 62-63; Stephenson and Dunn, *Washington*, II, 184-86; Sparks, *Writings of Washington*, VIII, 551-66, for the "Addresses."

7) Burnett, *The Continental Congress*, 575-80; Upton, *Military Policy of the U. S.*, 64; *Journals of the Continental Congress*, XXIV, 410-21; Fitzpatrick, *Writings of Washington*, XXVII, 32-36, 42.

8) Wertenbaker, *Father Knickerbocker Rebels*, 267.

9) Stephenson and Dunn, *Washington*, II, 188-89.

10) Quoted in Burnett, *The Continental Congress*, 591.

11) *Journals of the Continental Congress*, XXVII, 518. See also J. R. Jacobs, *The Beginning of the U. S. Army* (Princeton, 1947), 14.

12) Greene, *The Revolutionary War*, 279.

13) Upton, *Military Policy of the U. S.*, 58-59.

14) *Mackenzie Diary*, II, 581-82.

15) Spaulding, *The United States Army*, 112. See also Fortescue, *History of the British Army*, III, 536-37.

16) *Ibid.*, III, 540.

17) Spaulding, *The United States Army*, 113.

18) *Cornwallis Corr.*, I, 212.

Index

Acland, Major John, 165
Adams, John, 48, 139
Adams, Samuel, 4, 14, 15, 16, 20, 32
Albany, 99, 102, 134, 136, 176
Alexander, General William (*see* Stirling, Lord)
Allen, Ethan, 28-30, 68, 70, 71, 104
American Light Infantry, 196-98, 258; organization and training of, 179, 196; influence on French, 272-73
American Revolution, 1, 126, 133, 270-74
André, Major John, 71, 182, 187, 222, 223
Annapolis, 269
Arbuthnot, Admiral, 206, 209, 210, 220, 230, 252
Armand, Colonel, 213, 214
Armstrong, Major John, 140, 266
Army, British, 7-11, 42, 43, 59, 100, 102, 106, 126-27, 166, 189, 190, 238-39, 258, 269, 271-72; caliber of generals, 11, 32, 46; supply problems of, 58; use of cavalry, 211, 214, 215; inferiority of numbers, 168, 237, 256, 271
Army, Continental (*see also* American Light Infantry, Discipline, Mutiny, Recruiting, and Training), generals appointed to, 48-50; pay scale, 52-53; organization of, 52-55; difficulty with officers of, 51-52, 54, 265-67; use of cavalry, 110, 233, 234, 236, 238; desertions from, 115, 123, 217, 236; reduction of, 227; numbers, 271; disbanded, 269-70
Army, French, 208, 218, 219, 251, 255-61 *passim*, 264-65
Arnold, Benedict, 28, 29, 30, 67, 73, 74, 75, 77, 78, 86, 87, 126, 132, 135, 146, 159, 160, 161, 164-65, 184, 216, 218, 230, 247, 261, 270; besieges Quebec, 79-84; at Valcour Island and Split Rock, 125; at Free-

man's Farm, 162; at Bemis Heights, 165-67; treason of, 220-24
Atlee, Colonel, 108, 110, 111
Augusta, 205, 211, 232, 239, 241

Balcarres, Lord, 165, 166
Baltimore, 124, 248
Barras, Admiral, 251, 255
Barren Hill, skirmish at, 182
Barrett, Colonel, 20, 22
Baum, Colonel, 154, 156, 157
Beaufort, 205, 211
de Beaumarchais, Caron, 180
Bemis Heights, 161, 164; battle of, 165-67
Bennington, 152, 158, 160; battle of, 156-57
Blackstocks, battle of, 230
Blue Book, The, 179
Board of War, 172, 174, 175, 176
Bordentown, 127, 128, 129, 131
Boston, 4, 7, 13, 34, 48, 56, 62, 74, 90, 93, 97, 98, 134; siege of, 30-66
Brandywine, battle of, 136-39
Brant, Chief Joseph, 85, 147, 158, 199, 200
Brant, Molly, 158
Breed's Hill (for battle, *see* Bunker Hill), 33, 34, 35, 36, 37, 38, 44, 45
Breymann, Colonel, 151, 156, 157, 162, 166
Briar Creek, battle of, 205
Brodhead, Colonel Daniel, 200, 203
Brooklyn, 98, 105, 106, 107, 108, 111, 112, 268
Brown, Captain Jacob, 81, 82
Brown, Colonel John, 70, 71-72, 163, 222
Browne, Colonel Thomas, 241-42
Brunswick, 99, 147, 154
Bunker Hill, 25, 31, 33, 35, 48, 52, 53, 57, 58, 61, 100, 105, 106, 111, 117, 239, 273; battle of, 36 47
Burgoyne, Sir John, 9, 31, 32, 33, 41-42, 45, 57, 59, 60, 125, 134, 136,

301

146, 147, 148, 151, 153, 154, 156, 158, 160, 161, 163, 164, 168, 174; Indian policy of, 155; at Freeman's Farm, 162; at Bemis Heights, 165; surrender of, 167-68
Burr, Aaron, 74, 82, 116
Butler, Colonel John, 199, 200, 201
Butler, Colonel Richard, 197
Butler, Walter, 199, 200, 201

Cadwalader, General John, 128, 129, 131, 132, 177
Cambridge, 45, 46, 61, 66, 74, 77
Camden, 211, 212, 215, 228, 229, 239, 240, 241, 245, 247; battle of, 213-14
Campbell, Colonel, 204, 205
Canada, 84, 97, 125, 134, 176, 182, 184, 194, 209, 264; invasion of, 67-86
Carleton, Sir Guy, 28, 68, 69, 71, 72, 80, 82, 84, 85, 86, 87, 89, 99, 134, 147, 152, 182, 267, 268; invades New York State, 124-25; succeeds Clinton, 264; evacuates New York, 268-69
Carlisle, Earl of, 180, 195
Carroll, Charles, 72, 85
Carroll, John, 85
Castine, expedition to, 198-99
Caswell, General Richard, 90, 214
Chambly, Fort, 69, 70, 85, 86
Charleston, 91-92, 204, 205, 209, 215, 239, 242, 243, 244, 245, 247, 260, 263, 264; repulses British, 92-96; surrender of, 210-211
Charlestown, 14, 15, 24, 25, 33, 34, 35, 36, 37, 41
Cheraw, 211, 212, 232
Cherry Valley Massacre, 199
Chesapeake Bay, 135, 195, 229, 230, 242, 245, 254, 255
Civilians, profit at expense of army, 169
Clark, George Rogers, 198-203, 264
Clinton, Fort, 163, 164
Clinton, Governor George, 118, 269
Clinton, Sir Henry, 31, 32, 35, 36, 42, 44, 45, 47, 60, 89, 100, 113, 114, 116, 124, 135, 144, 163, 164, 167, 182, 184, 193, 194, 198, 204, 206, 209, 218, 220, 228, 229, 233, 244, 252, 254, 256, 259, 260, 270, 272; attacks Charleston, 91, 93, 95, 96;

at Long Island, 108, 111, 114; succeeds Howe, 181; evacuates Philadelphia, 184-85; at Monmouth, 188, 190; strategy of, 195-96; besieges Charleston, 209-11; sends André to Arnold, 222-23; differs with Cornwallis, 246, 247, 248, 250-51; resigns, 264
Clinton, General James, 199
Clothing (*see also* Quartermaster Department), 51, 169, 170, 172, 216
Colburn, Reuben, 73, 74, 75, 76
Collier, Sir George, 195, 196, 198
Commissary Department (*see also* Food), 50, 170, 171, 216
Concord, 13-15, 20-21, 22-23, 25-26, 47; battle of, 21-22
Congress, Continental, 5, 27, 29, 48, 51, 52, 53-54, 67, 84, 91-92, 97, 103, 115, 121, 124, 138, 152, 156, 168, 170, 180, 190, 191, 194, 205, 212, 224, 225, 226, 261, 262, 267, 268, 269, 274; raises troops, 52, 105, 135, 172; reorganizes departments, 171-72, 179; critical of army, 172-73; factionalism in, 219; opposition to Arnold, 221-222; reduces army, 227; sends Greene to South, 228; difficulties with officers, 265-67; disbands army, 269-70
Congress, Provincial, 4, 5, 12, 27, 48, 53, 73
Connecticut, 3-4, 27, 30, 49, 50, 51, 54, 56, 60, 65, 68, 84, 97, 110, 116, 135, 165, 169, 193, 199, 222, 250, 261; mutiny of Line, 217, 224
Conway Cabal, 173-77
Conway, General Thomas, 141, 173-77 *passim*
Cornwallis, Lord, 2, 89, 100, 107, 108, 111, 118, 120, 122, 124, 126, 127, 131, 132, 133, 139, 142, 143, 144, 211, 212, 215, 228, 229, 230, 232, 233, 234-36, 239, 240, 245, 250, 252, 254, 255, 270, 272, 273; pursues Washington, 123; at Brandywine, 137; defeats Gates at Camden, 213-14; checks Greene at Guilford Courthouse, 237-39; invades Virginia, 247; differs with Clinton, 246, 247, 248, 250, 251; defense of Yorktown, 256-61
Cowpens, 229, 237; battle of, 232-34
Crown Point, 30, 86, 125, 148

Danbury, 135
Dartmouth, Earl of, 13, 64, 89
Dawes, William, 15, 16
Deane, Silas, 173
Delaware, 97, 110, 111, 120, 123, 212, 214, 243, 244, 248, 270
Delaware River, 130, 140, 143-45, 226
Destouches, Admiral, 230
Detroit, 201, 203, 264
Digby, Admiral, 259, 267
Discipline (*see also* Mutiny and Training), 51, 52, 150, 216, 244
von Donop, Colonel Carl, 106, 107, 144
Dorchester, Lord (*see* Carleton, Sir Guy)
Douglas, Colonel William, 116, 118
Dunmore, Lord, 53, 88, 89, 90

Eaton, General, 237
Enos, Colonel Roger, 74, 75, 77, 87
d'Estiang, Comte, 184, 192, 193, 194, 206-9
Ewing, General James, 129, 130

Falmouth, (Portland), 62
Ferguson, Major Patrick, 228-29
Finance, 28, 48, 53, 216, 217, 224, 265-67, 271
Fishing Creek, battle of, 215
Florida, 209, 245
Food (*see also* Commissary Department), 56, 77-78, 169, 170, 171, 213, 216, 225
France, 1, 146, 184, 192, 194, 195, 202, 219, 230, 251, 254, 270, 271, 272-73, 274; alliance with United States, 168, 180, 182
Francis, Colonel, 151
Franklin, Benjamin, 5, 85, 140, 180, 251, 264
Fraser, General, 147, 148, 150, 151, 154, 162, 165, 166, 167
Freeman's Farm, battle of, 161-64

Gage, General Thomas, 6, 7, 9, 12-13, 14, 15, 22, 23, 28, 32-33, 35, 36, 39, 42, 45, 57
Gansevoort, Colonel Peter, 158
Gates, General Horatio, 50, 61, 73, 126, 136, 146, 160, 161, 165, 167, 184, 199, 212, 228, 245, 266; difficulties with Schuyler, 148; at Free-

man's Farm, 162; favors holding action at Bemis Heights, 166; involved in Conway Cabal, 174-76; crushed at Camden, 213-15
George III, 2, 11, 103, 126, 134, 147, 152, 154, 181, 261
Georgetown, 211, 239
Georgia, 198, 204, 205, 206, 209, 213, 233, 239, 242, 245, 264
Germain, Lord George, 11, 89, 134-35, 154, 160, 182-83, 195, 201, 209, 215, 246, 247, 272
Germantown, battle of, 140-43
Gloucester, 251, 256, 259, 260
Glover, Colonel John, 112, 113, 119, 130, 166, 193, 194
Granby, Fort, 239, 241
Grant, General Sir James, 108-10, 128, 131, 142, 182
de Grasse, Admiral, 242, 245, 251, 252, 254, 255, 256, 263, 264, 271
Graves, Admiral Samuel, 25, 30-31, 34, 35, 36, 57, 58
Graves, Admiral Thomas, 219, 220, 252-53, 254, 255, 259
Great Bridge, battle of, 90
Great Britain, 5, 7-8, 60, 146, 180, 192, 263, 264, 267, 268
Greene, Colonel Christopher, 74, 75, 77, 144
Greene, General Nathanael, 27, 49, 50, 60, 61, 62, 105, 115, 118, 123, 129, 130, 135, 144-45, 169, 189, 190, 194, 215, 218, 224, 230, 232, 235-36, 236-37, 239, 241, 242, 243-45, 247, 248, 264; saves army at Brandywine, 138; at Germantown, 140-43; quartermaster, 171-72; sent to South, 228; at Guilford Courthouse, 237-39; skill of, 245
Green Spring, battle of, 250
Grey, General, 139, 142, 182
Gridley, Colonel Richard, 27, 28, 35, 45, 63
Guerrillas, 211, 212, 215, 229-30, 233, 240-42, 245
Guilford Courthouse, 247; battle of, 237-39

Hale, Nathan, 118
Halifax, 64, 65, 99, 182
Hamilton, Alexander, 120, 139, 177, 185, 258
Hamilton, General, 147, 152

Hamilton, Colonel Henry, 201, 202, 203
Hancock, John, 14, 15, 16, 33, 48, 80, 194
Hanging Rock, action at, 212
Harlem, 116; battle of, 117-18
Hartford, 220, 251
Haslett, Colonel, 110, 120
Heath, General William, 5, 24, 49, 54, 61, 105, 112, 121, 126, 220, 252
de Heister, General Philip, 106, 107, 108, 110, 111
Henry, Governor Patrick, 201
Herkimer, General Nicholas, 158-59
Hessians, 99, 100, 102, 106, 107, 110, 111, 126, 251; at Trenton, 127; desertion of, 184, 190
Hobkirk's Hill, battle of, 240-42
Holland, 192
Hood, Sir Samuel, 254, 255, 259
Hotham, Commodore, 100, 102, 116
Howe, Lord Richard, 100, 103, 104, 106, 114, 115, 144-45, 192, 193, 194, 264, 272
Howe, General Robert, 204, 205, 226, 268
Howe, Sir William, 8, 9, 31, 32, 35, 38, 42, 43, 44, 45, 46, 57, 58, 59, 60, 62, 77, 89, 97, 99, 100, 101, 102, 103-6, 107, 118, 119, 120, 122, 124, 126, 127, 133, 134, 136, 140, 144, 145, 146, 147, 160, 164, 168, 182, 184, 195, 272; at Bunker Hill, 39, 40, 41; evacuates Boston, 64-65; at Long Island, 108, 110, 111-12, 114; captures Fort Washington, 123; at Brandywine, 137-38; captures Philadelphia, 139; at Germantown, 141; resigns, 181
Hubbardton, 150; battle of, 151
Hudson River, 67, 98, 99, 100, 102, 135, 160, 164, 167, 168, 176, 191
Huger, General, 209, 210, 235, 237

Illinois, 202
Indians, 94, 95, 147, 155, 158, 159, 162, 163, 199, 200, 201, 202, 203, 242
Inspector General, 174, 179
Isle-aux-Noix, 86

Jamaica, 182, 263
James Island, 206, 209

Jamestown, 230, 250
Jasper, Sergeant William, 95
Jay, John, 115
Jefferson, Thomas, 88, 201, 248
John's Island, 206, 209
Johnson, Sir John, 158, 199, 200, 201
Johnson, Sir William, 49
Jones, John Paul, 270

de Kalb, Baron, 173, 176, 212, 214
Kaskaskia, 201-2
Kentucky, 201
Kettle Creek, battle of, 205
King's Mountain, battle of, 2, 228-29, 247
Kip's Bay, 115-16
Knowlton, Colonel Thomas, 34, 38, 117
Knox, General Henry, 61, 116, 130, 133, 141, 143, 171, 189, 268
von Knyphausen, General William, 121, 122, 137, 138, 185, 188, 189, 217, 218
Kosciusko, Thaddeus, 148, 161, 236, 242

de Lafayette, Marquis, 170, 176, 182, 185, 186, 187, 189, 193, 194, 219, 230, 248, 250, 252, 255, 273
Lake Champlain, 29, 67, 125, 134, 147
Lake George, 148, 152, 153
Laurens, John, 177, 227, 251
de Lauzun, Duc, 251, 256, 273
Lawson, General, 237, 238
Lee, General Charles, 49, 61, 91, 93, 94, 95, 97, 98, 121, 123, 126, 135, 191; behavior at Monmouth, 185-89; court-martial of, 190
Lee, Fort, 98, 119, 120, 121; capture of, 123
Lee, Major Harry, 196, 198, 218, 228, 232, 236, 237, 242, 243, 244
Leslie, General, 117, 228, 229, 232, 237, 238, 264
Lexington, 25-26, 47, 61; battle of, 17-20
Lincoln, General Benjamin, 135, 156, 163, 165, 205, 206, 208, 209, 210-11, 260
Livingston, Colonel James, 69-70, 81, 82
Long, Colonel, 150, 151

Loring, Joshua, 59, 159
Loring, Mrs. Joshua, 59-60, 181
Lovell, General Solomon, 198
Loyalists, 10, 60, 88, 89, 90, 91, 96, 100, 115, 118, 131, 135, 147, 152, 156, 158, 159, 166, 181, 198, 199, 200, 201, 204, 205, 211, 212, 221, 228, 229, 236, 242, 245, 246, 247, 261, 264, 271; evacuated from Boston, 64, 65; leave Philadelphia, 184; wretched plight of, 268

McCrea, Jane, 152, 154-55
McDougall, General, 120, 142, 143, 176
McDowell, Colonel, 228
McGowan's Pass, 116, 117, 119
Mackenzie, Lieutenant, 271
Maclean, Allan, 78-79, 80
Magaw, Colonel Robert, 121, 122
Maine, 62, 73-78, 198
Maitland, Colonel, 206, 208
Marion, General Francis, 94, 212, 229, 232, 240, 241, 242, 243
Marjoribanks, Major, 243, 244
Martin, Governor, 88, 89, 90, 91
Maryland, 3, 52, 97, 110, 111, 122, 188, 212, 214, 233, 243, 269
Massachusetts, 4, 6, 27, 29, 30, 38, 48, 49, 51, 54, 56, 60, 66, 84, 116, 126, 193, 198, 199
Matthews, General Edward, 195, 218
Maxwell, General, 185, 187, 218
Meigs, Colonel, 75, 197, 217
Mercer, Fort, 144
Mercer, General, 121, 132, 133
Middlebrook, 136, 195
Mifflin, Fort, 144
Mifflin, General Thomas, 50, 56, 113, 132, 171, 174, 175, 176
Militia, 4, 5, 16-26 *passim*, 28, 37-47 *passim*, 51-52, 54, 56, 97, 123, 140, 142, 204, 233, 235, 236, 237, 251; help crush Burgoyne, 160; Greene regrets dependence on, 239; Washington's opinion of, 115, 271
Mitchel, Major, 16, 17, 18
Monckton, Colonel, 189
Monmouth, battle of, 185-90
Monroe, Lieutenant James, 131
Montgomery, Fort, 163
Montgomery, General Richard, 49, 50, 70, 71, 72, 76, 79, 80, 81-83, 84, 87

Montreal, 67, 69, 70, 71, 72, 79, 80, 104
Montressor, Captain John, 75, 77
Moore, Sir John, 198, 272
Moore's Bridge, battle of, 90
Morale, 112, 114, 170, 177-79
Morgan, General Daniel, 74, 75, 82, 83, 84, 160, 162, 165, 166, 185, 230, 232-34, 235, 237
Morristown, 133, 135, 136, 216, 218, 225, 252
Motte, Fort, 239, 241
Moultrie, Fort, 92-96, 102, 209, 210
Moultrie, Colonel William, 92-96, 205, 208
Moylan, Stephen, 171
Muhlenberg, General, 138, 142, 143, 197
Munitions, 28, 30, 55, 56, 60-61, 94, 95, 123, 124, 151, 180, 198
Mutiny, of Connecticut Line, 217, 224; of Pennsylvania Line, 216, 224-26, 227; of New Jersey Line, 216, 226-27; of Lancaster recruits, 267-68

Navy, American, 30, 125-26, 129, 144, 270
Navy, British, 35-36, 37-38, 45, 71-72, 93-96, 102, 125-26, 144, 192-94, 219, 230, 255, 259-60, 261, 270
Navy, French, 184, 192-94, 198, 218, 219, 220, 230, 255, 261, 270, 271
Negroes, 53, 113, 204, 206; American policy toward, 53-54
Nelson, Governor Thomas, 256
New Brunswick, 123, 127, 128, 132, 133, 191, 252
Newburgh Addresses, 265, 266
New England, 2, 3, 27-28, 49, 51-52, 66, 99, 126, 132, 133, 134, 136, 160, 225
New Hampshire, 3, 27, 30, 49, 54, 56, 60, 68, 70, 155, 162
New Haven, 196
New Jersey, 97, 112, 123, 124, 126, 130, 169, 185, 195, 198, 204, 217, 218, 242; mutiny of Line, 216, 226-27
New London, 198, 261
New Orleans, 182, 202
Newport, 193, 194, 209, 216, 219, 220, 230, 251, 255
Newtown, battle of, 200

New York, 3, 49, 60, 64, 65, 68, 70, 97-98, 106, 115, 118, 124, 136, 160, 165, 184, 195, 201, 204, 206, 223, 242, 248, 250, 251, 254, 256, 259, 260, 261, 264; Howe arrives at, 99, 100; evacuation of, 263, 268-69
Niagara, Fort, 199, 200, 201, 264
Ninety Six, 211, 232, 239, 240; siege of, 242
Norfolk, 62, 88, 90, 195, 246
North Carolina, 88, 90, 91, 92, 198, 205, 212, 213, 214, 215, 229, 232, 233, 247
North, Lord, 2, 4, 88, 103, 180, 182, 215, 261, 262
North River (*see* Hudson River)

O'Hara, General, 237, 238, 260
Orangeburg, 239, 241
Oriskany, battle of, 158
Oswego, 134, 147, 158, 264
Otis, James, 4

Paine, Tom, 62, 130
"Paoli Massacre," 139, 197
Parker, Captain John, 16, 17-18
Parker, Sir Peter, 89, 91-92, 93, 94-96, 102
Parliament, 99, 110, 120, 268
Patriots, 1, 12, 90, 97, 215, 242, 261
Paulus Hook, storming of, 198
Peace, treaty of, 263, 264, 267
Pee Dee River, 211, 212, 229, 232, 239, 240
Pennsylvania, 52, 74, 97, 108, 123, 129, 131, 136, 140, 142, 143, 144, 169, 199, 201, 222, 225, 264, 267; mutiny of Line, 216, 224-26, 227
Percy, Lord, 5, 14, 23, 24, 25, 26, 64, 119, 121, 122
Perth Amboy, 127, 131, 133
Philadelphia, 50, 123, 124, 129, 134, 135, 140, 144, 145, 169, 221, 225, 250, 255, 262, 268; capture of, 139; evacuation of, 184
Phillips, General William, 147, 150, 151, 162, 164, 165, 230, 247, 248
Pickens, Colonel Andrew, 205, 212, 232, 233, 234, 240, 242, 243
Pickering, Timothy, 3, 24, 169, 174, 175, 224
Pigot, General, 39, 40, 41, 42, 43, 44, 193, 194

Pitcairn, Major John, 13, 17, 18, 20, 21, 39, 44
"Pitcher, Molly" (Mary Hays), 190
Pomeroy, General Seth, 4, 45, 49, 54
Poor, General, 165, 189
Portsmouth, 195-96, 230
Prescott, Dr. Samuel, 16
Prescott, Colonel "Savage," 70, 72, 104, 126
Prescott, Colonel William, 33, 34, 35, 37, 38, 40, 41, 44, 46, 53
Prevost, General Augustine, 204, 205, 206, 208
Princeton, 127, 225, 252, 268; battle of, 132-33
Pulaski, Count, 206, 208
Putnam, General Israel, 27, 30, 33, 37, 38, 40, 41, 44, 45, 49, 54, 56, 60, 61, 62, 64, 98, 105, 118, 121, 163
Putnam, Colonel Rufus, 63, 196

Quartermaster Department, 50, 170, 171-72, 224
Quebec, 67, 69, 71, 72, 73, 78, 80; battle and siege of, 81-85

Rall, Colonel Johann, 120, 122, 127, 128, 130, 131
Ramsour's Mill, battle of, 212
Rawdon, Lord, 58, 96, 210, 212, 213, 214, 229, 239, 240-41, 242, 247
Recruiting, 56, 172, 216, 225, 227; inducements for, 52-53, 124; tardiness of, 135; short-term enlistments, 52, 54, 60, 80, 81, 271
Reed, Joseph, 55, 103, 117, 132, 225, 226
Revere, Paul, 12, 14, 15, 16
Rhode Island, 3, 27, 49, 50, 51, 60, 117, 124, 144, 154, 182, 184, 192, 209, 216, 217, 265, 270; battle of, 193-94
von Riedesel, General Baron, 147, 148, 150, 151, 156, 162, 165
Robertson, James, 203, 251
de Rochambeau, Comte, 219, 220, 222, 250, 251, 252, 254, 255, 260, 265, 273
Rocky Mount, 211, 212
Rodney, Sir George, 209, 220, 227, 254, 263
Roxbury, 34, 61, 62
Rugeley's Mills, 213

St. Augustine, 90, 182, 204
St. Clair, General Arthur, 132, 148, 150, 151, 226
St. Johns, 30, 69, 80, 86, 125; capture of, 71
St. Lawrence River, 67, 69, 73, 78, 87, 106
St. Leger, Colonel Barry, 147, 152, 158-59
de Saint-Simon, Comte, 255
Saltonstall, Commodore, 198, 199
San Domingo, 252, 254, 264
Saratoga (for battles of, see Freeman's Farm and Bemis Heights), 68, 168, 211
Savannah, 211, 213, 239, 245; capture of, 204-5; British defense of, 206-9; evacuation of, 264
Schuyler, General Philip, 49, 67, 68, 69, 73, 80, 84, 125, 126, 136, 148, 152, 153, 155, 156, 159, 165, 222
Schuylkill River, 139, 140, 182, 221
Scott, General, 142, 143, 185, 186, 187
Sea Power, 7-8, 36, 102, 114, 254, 255, 270
Sevier, John, 203, 228
Shelburne, Lord, 264
Shelby, Colonel, 203, 228
Shippen, Margaret ("Peggy"), 181, 221, 222
Shuldham, Admiral, 57-58, 64
Skene, Major Philip, 30, 152-53, 154, 156, 157
Smith, Colonel Francis, 5, 14, 17, 20, 21, 22, 23, 25
Society, agrarian type, influence on war, 2
South Carolina, 88, 89, 92, 93, 198, 204, 211, 212, 229, 239, 240, 247
Spain, 180, 192
Spencer, General Joseph, 27, 49, 54, 61, 105, 120
Split Rock, naval action off, 125
Springfield, battle of, 218
Stanwix, Fort, siege of, 158-59
Stark, General John, 27, 37, 38, 44, 155, 156, 157, 218
Staten Island, 100, 106, 218, 252
Stephen, General Adam, 135, 137, 140-41, 143
von Steuben, General Baron, 177-79, 185, 191, 228, 230, 248, 258
Stevens, General, 214, 237, 238

Stewart, Colonel, 242, 243-45
Stirling, Lord, 65, 108, 110, 111, 112, 135, 136, 137, 140, 174, 189
Stirling, General Thomas, 218
Stono Ferry, 206
Stony Point, 195, 209; storming of, 196-98
Strategy, of Americans, 67, 194, 195; of British, 99, 134-35, 194, 195, 198, 204, 245-51, 271-72; of French, 251-52, 255
Sullivan, General John, 49, 61, 62, 85-86, 107, 111, 126, 129, 130, 135, 137-38, 140-42, 193, 194, 203; defeat at Long Island, 105, 108, 110; Indian expedition of, 199-200
Sumter, Thomas, 212, 215, 230, 232, 240, 242

Tarleton, Colonel Banastre, 209, 210, 214, 215, 229, 232-34, 236, 237, 238, 250, 256
de Ternay, Admiral, 219, 220, 230
Thomas, General John, 5, 27, 50, 54, 61, 62, 85
Three Rivers, battle of, 85-86
Ticonderoga, Fort, 28-30, 61, 67, 68, 69, 71, 86, 98, 102, 148-49, 152, 153, 162, 163
Tories (see Loyalists)
Tory Ministry or Party, 1, 4, 27, 32, 103
Training, American, 2, 3, 4, 50-53, 56, 68, 177-79, 185, 191, 196, 272; British, 10-11, 58-59, 272
Trenton, 123, 127, 132, 140, 185, 195, 225, 226, 233, 252; battle of, 129-31
Trumbull, Colonel Joseph, 50, 174
Tryon, Governor, 100, 116, 135, 164, 196, 198

United States, 67, 87, 270

Valcour Island, battle of, 125, 270
Valley Forge, 145, 169, 170, 175, 176, 179, 216
Varnum, General, 187, 193, 194
Vaughan, General, 163, 164
de Vergennes, Comte, 180, 219, 251
Vermont, 28, 29, 74, 148, 150, 155
Verplanck's Point, 163, 195, 196, 198, 218

Vincennes, campaign to take, 201-3
Virginia, 3, 48, 50, 52, 53, 74, 88, 90, 92, 117, 134, 201, 202, 205, 212, 214, 215, 228, 230, 233, 236, 237, 238, 239, 245, 247, 250, 255, 256

Wadsworth, Joseph, 171
Wadsworth, General Peleg, 198
Ward, General Artemas, 4, 27, 28, 33, 37, 45, 46, 49, 61
Warner, Seth, 30, 68, 151, 155, 157, 163
Warren, Dr. Joseph, 14, 15, 24, 28, 33, 38, 45
Warren Tavern, Americans stand at, 139
Washington, Fort, 98, 119, 120; capture of, 121-22
Washington, George, 11, 50, 51, 52, 54, 61, 62, 64, 65, 70, 73, 77, 78, 84, 97, 98, 102, 103, 104-5, 107, 110, 115, 119, 120, 121, 126, 136, 148, 152, 160, 170, 172, 181, 182, 185-86, 188, 190, 193, 194, 196, 198, 212, 216, 219, 220, 223, 227, 230, 246, 250, 251, 261, 264, 268, 270, 271; accepts command of army, 48; character and abilities of, 66; at Long Island, 112, 114; at Harlem, 117-18; Jersey retreat of, 123; given dictatorial powers, 124, 139; plans to take Trenton, 128-29; at Princeton, 133; relation to Conway Cabal, 173-77; at Monmouth, 188-89, 191; besieges Yorktown, 252-60 *passim*; calms officers, 266-67; resigns, 269
Washington, Lund, 54, 123
Washington, Colonel William, 131, 233, 234, 237, 238, 241, 243, 244
Watson, Fort, 239, 240, 241, 242
Wayne, General Anthony, 138, 139, 140, 141-42, 143, 170, 185, 187, 188, 189, 196-98, 225-26, 245, 248, 264
Webster, Colonel, 213, 214, 237, 238
West Indies, 58, 180, 182, 204, 206, 209, 227, 254, 263, 264, 268
West Point, 164, 195, 222, 223, 270
Wethersfield Conference, 250, 251
Whigs, 1, 5, 27, 32, 102, 120, 242
White Plains, 191, 251; battle of, 120
Wilkinson, James, 130, 131, 174, 175
Willet, Colonel Marinus, 158
Williams, Colonel Otho, 235, 236, 237
Williamsburg, 203, 248, 255, 265
Wilmington, 90, 239
Woodford, General William, 90, 189
Wooster, General David, 49, 68, 84, 135
Wyoming Valley Massacre, 199

York, 175
Yorktown, 227, 239, 246, 248, 250, 251, 254, 271, 273; siege of, 256-61